GW00670516

YOU
CAN'T TELL
THE
PEOPLE

YOU CAN'T TELL THE PEOPLE

THE COVER-UP OF BRITAIN'S ROSWELL

Georgina Bruni

with a foreword by
Nick Pope

SIDGWICK & JACKSON

First published 2000 by Sidgwick & Jackson
an imprint of Macmillan Publishers Ltd
25 Eccleston Place, London SW1W 9NF
Basingstoke and Oxford
Associated companies throughout the world
www.macmillan.co.uk

ISBN 0 283 06358 0

5 7 9 8 6 4

A CIP catalogue record for this book is available from
the British Library.

Typeset by SX Composing DTP, Rayleigh, Essex
Printed and bound in Great Britain by
Mackays of Chatham plc, Chatham, Kent

DEDICATION

This book is dedicated to all those who were reluctantly caught up in the Rendlesham Forest incident, and all the men and women in the military who have been involved in similar encounters and are still searching for the truth.

CONTENTS

LIST OF ILLUSTRATIONS

ACKNOWLEDGEMENTS

This book has only been made possible thanks to a great many people. I am deeply indebted to my agent, Andrew Lownie, for his encouragement, support and efforts. My thanks also to my editor Gordon Scott Wise, Editorial Director at Sidgwick and Jackson, for his enthusiasm and patience and for helping me to turn this extraordinary, complex case into a valuable casebook. To Nick Pope for contributing the foreword, for advising me on the best way to obtain government documents and for his precious contributions. To my parents, family and friends for their understanding of my isolation whilst working on this investigation.

This story could not have been told without the generous assistance of the witnesses and many people who have played an important role in these strange events. I am especially grateful to Major General Gordon E. Williams USAF (ret.) for his patience and contributions and allowing me to interview him in person. To former Special Agent Wayne Persinger, Deputy Commander, Air Force Office of Special Investigations (Bentwaters), USAF (ret.), for his contributions. To Colonel Sam P. Morgan USAF (ret.), for providing me with the first copy of the 'Halt Tape'. To Ray Gulyas USAF (ret.) and his wife Maryann, for their contributions and for leading me to the original photographs of the initial landing site. I am grateful to all these men and women for allowing me to interview them and for assisting me with my enquires: Rick Bobo USAF (ret.), Lieutenant Colonel Fred 'Skip' Buran USAF (ret.), Adrian Bustinza USAF (ret.), Tony Brisciano USAF, Edward N. Cabansag USAF (ret.), Gary Collins, Lieutenant Colonel Bernard E.

Donahue USAF (ret.), Major Edward Drury USAF (ret.), Timothy Egercic USAF (ret.), Betty Garfield, Colonel Charles I. Halt USAF (ret.), Gerry Harris, James Hudnall USAF (ret.), Anthony Johnson USAF (ret.), Nigel Kerr RAF (ret.), Dave King, William Kirk USAF (ret.), Steven La Plume USAF (ret.), Squadron Leader Donald Moreland RAF (ret.), Richard Nunn, Diana Persinger, Maisie Pettit, James W. Penniston USAF (ret.), Lori Rehfeldt USAF (ret.), Steve Roberts USAF (ret.), Lieutenant Colonel Park Simms USAF (ret.), William Sone USAF (ret.), Harry Thompson RAF (ret.), Jerry Valdes-Sanchez USAF (ret.), Lindy 'Cookie' Vaughn USAF (ret.), Larry Warren USAF (ret.), Roy Webb, Lieutenant Colonel Malcolm Zickler USAF (ret.) and to all those who wish to remain anonymous.

Special thanks to Baroness Margaret Thatcher. To Michael Portillo for taking my questions. To Admiral of the Fleet, The Lord Hill-Norton GCB for allowing me to use his exchange of correspondence with Lord Gilbert. To historian Gordon Kinsey for his knowledgeable help with understanding the history of Orfordness and Bawdsey. To Brenda Butler for showing me the landing sites, allowing me to interview her and for sharing her important files. To Dot Street for her humour, valuable assistance and for allowing me access to her files. To Ray Boeche, Antonio Huneeus, Mark Birdsall and Nicholas Redfern for opening their old files on the case for me to study. Many thanks also to the following people who have given much of their time and assistance, thus making a valuable contribution to my research. David Bonner BSc CCQSW DHP (NC) MNRHP for his expert help on hypnotherapy. Chuck de Caro for his humour and contributions, and Barry Greenwood for his valuable assistance. Budd Hopkins for taking my questions and Bill Kemball for helping with local information. Captain Mike Martin USAF (ret.) for his contacts, Chris Pennington for sharing his knowledge of the early years. Dave Piggot for his scientific evaluations and George Plume for his professional advice. To Peter Robbins for his friendship, patience and understanding, and for his precious contributions. Many thanks to Max Shortley, Ronnie Spaine, Mike Topliss, Vincent

Thurkettle, George Wild and Marjorie Wright for sharing their stories.

I would also like to thank the following people for their assistance and patience: James Anderson, Derek Barnes, Linn Barringer, Keith Beabey, Graham William Birdsall, Mrs David Boast, James Buckles USAF (ret.), John Lawrence Briggs, Lieutenant Colonel Al Brown USAF (ret.), Robin D. Cole, Paul Crowther, Jacquieline Davis, Vernon Drane, Sean Emerson USAF (ret.), Jackie Errington, Mary Everest, Lucius Farish, Halan E. Girard, Walter F. Hern USAF (ret.), Tony McEvoy, Fred Nunn, Lieutenant Colonel Pevsky USAF (ret.), Peter Phillips, Jeff Rense, Ian Ridpath, Nick Ryan ARRS, USAF (ret.), Malcolm Scurrah, Andrew Sheepshanks, Simon Smith, Steve Smith USAF (ret.), Gaynor South, Lee Speigel and Robert Todd.

And last but by no means least: Alan Akeroyd, Dennis Bardens, Ron Burrell USAF (ret.), Sally Brown, Charles Chow, Neil Cunningham, Brian Creswell, Jonathon Dillon, Ann Drury, Mrs Drury SRN, Timothy Good, Dr Jane Grundy BSc (Hons) PhD DSc FRCPath, Ron Harlan, Bob Higgins, Kane, Michele Kaczynski, Dr Gerhard Knecht, Dr Helmut F. Lammer, Rowena Naylor, William John Naylor, Dan Sherman USAF (ret.), Martin Stout, Bruce Taylor, Bernard Thouanel, Glenmore Trenear-Harvey RAF (ret.), Jenny Randles, Sonia White, Martin Wood, Anglia International Airpark, CAUS, CompuServe, Colchester Barracks, Kodak, Ministry of Defence for Air, Ministry of Defence Police, Ministry of Defence Library, *Sightings Magazine*, Suffolk Constabulary, Suffolk Record Office, *UFO Magazine* (UK), *Unopened Files*. To friends Penelope Bouchot-Humbert, Lady Anna Brocklebank, Robert A. Bell and Lord Anthony Leitrim, for you know what, Walter F. Hern USAF (ret.), CUFON, East Anglian Press, Quest, United States Air Force. To everyone I might have failed to mention, my apologies, and of course not forgetting Alan, because you always knew.

FOREWORD

BY NICK POPE

I work at the Ministry of Defence, where between 1991 and 1994 I did what must be one of the most bizarre jobs in the department. Essentially, my task was to evaluate the several hundred UFO sightings reported to the MOD each year and to determine whether there was evidence of any threat to the defence of the United Kingdom. Each sighting was carefully investigated and I was able to determine that somewhere between ninety and ninety-five per cent could be attributed to the misidentification of ordinary objects or phenomena. There remained, however, a hard core of sightings that defied conventional explanation and involved what appeared to be structured craft of unknown origin, capable of manoeuvres and speeds beyond the abilities of anything in our inventory – prototype craft included. The best such cases were ones involving trained observers, such as police officers, airline pilots and military personnel, or ones where the sightings could be correlated by photographs, videos or radar tapes.

The MOD's public position on the UFO phenomenon is that it is of 'no defence significance'. But my official research and investigation turned up numerous cases that seemed to contradict such a conclusion: RAF jets had been scrambled to intercept mystery craft tracked on radar; civil and military pilots were having close encounters with UFOs; unidentified craft the size of jumbo jets were flying over military bases. Such incidents led me to speak out publicly about the UFO phenomenon and warn that there were serious defence and national-security issues at stake, given that our sophisticated air-defence network was being routinely penetrated by these unidentified craft.

Although there have been attempts to portray me as a maverick, I'm certainly not the only person within the establishment to think along these lines. There have, for example, been several dozen UFO-related questions tabled in parliament over the last few years and there are plenty in the RAF and at the MOD who share my concerns. Despite this, there is a curious and infuriating tendency in certain quarters to ignore the best evidence. There are a number of possible reasons for such an attitude: ufology certainly attracts more than its fair share of cultists and crackpots and this may have led some people to dismiss the entire phenomenon, thereby throwing out the baby with the bathwater. It's also possible that narrow-mindedness is to blame, as certain individuals refuse to contemplate possibilities that would challenge deeply held belief systems. Others would doubtless suggest a more sinister explanation: the idea that some within government are involved in a conspiracy to keep the truth about UFOs from the public is widely held among ufologists.

While investigating UFO sightings for the government I had access to a massive archive of over two hundred relevant files, dating from the early forties. These contained accounts of previous UFO sightings and the subsequent official investigations, together with public correspondence and more general policy work. Until Britain gets its eagerly anticipated Freedom of Information Act, the public is denied access to all but a handful of these files. Yet even those that are currently available at the Public Record Office in Kew contain more than enough to challenge the idea that UFOs are of 'no defence significance': many of the documents are stamped 'Secret' and show just how seriously the subject is taken by those charged with the defence of the realm.

One file that is certainly *not* available to the public attracted my attention more than the others. It seemed to offer the most tanta-lizing clues yet that some UFO sightings really did involve some-thing truly exotic and not entirely benign. This was the file on the Rendlesham Forest incident and this book tells the story of this fascinating case.

Even the most basic information about this incident is

extraordinary; a series of UFO encounters took place in Rendlesham Forest in Suffolk, between the twin bases of RAF Bentwaters and RAF Woodbridge. Though nominally RAF bases, they were actually United States Air Force facilities and most of the witnesses to these events were USAF personnel. The official report on these incidents was submitted to the MOD by Lieutenant Colonel Charles Halt, the deputy base commander, who was himself a witness to some of the events. His memorandum described a glowing object, triangular in shape and metallic in appearance, which was seen manoeuvring through the forest and at one point even appeared to land. Nearby farm animals were sent into a frenzy. Subsequent investigation revealed three strange indentations on the forest floor in the clearing where the craft was seen to land and to damage the trees at the edge of the clearing. Radiation readings were taken from the area and peaked in the indentations. This initial incident, together with later UFO sightings involving spectacular displays of light, was witnessed by numerous military witnesses and correlated by radar evidence.

These events alone, one might assume, would contradict any idea that UFOs are of 'no defence significance', yet this is precisely the position that the MOD takes on this incident. On several occasions when members of the public have written to the MOD or when questions have been tabled in parliament, the department's response has been to describe the event as involving the sighting of 'unusual lights in the sky' or 'unexplained lights'. This has prompted some to argue that there is an official policy to downplay the events, because even Halt's memorandum – which has been in the public domain for some years – makes it *abundantly* clear that there was much more to this incident than just lights in the sky. One person who has confirmed that, contrary to the official line, these events were of great defence significance is Admiral of the Fleet, The Lord Hill-Norton. Lord Hill-Norton is a former chief of the defence staff and chairman of the NATO military committee, so there can be few people better qualified to offer an informed view on this case.

Extraordinary though these events are, much of the story remained untold until now, despite diligent research from ufologists, coupled with considerable pressure from various MPs and peers. This book changes everything and tells as full a story as currently possible of the incidents themselves and the no less extraordinary aftermath of these events. Georgina Bruni has uncovered a wealth of new material which finally blows the lid off an event that might, in time, come to be regarded as a turning point in human history. This is certainly a book that will challenge people's worldview and dent the reputations of certain institutions and individuals. Parts of it will leave an unpleasant taste in the mouth and will lead to some awkward questions for certain people. I have no doubt that many of those caught up in these events will regard this as long overdue, because some of these people have undeniably suffered as a result of what happened, and if some of this suffering could have been prevented, it is only right that there should be a reckoning. This book, as well as setting the record straight about what actually happened at Rendlesham Forest, might help bring about such a reckoning.

Georgina Bruni, it has to be said, does not fit the public image of a ufologist – indeed, she would not classify herself as such. Trained as a private detective she has been a freelance investigative writer who specializes in exposing the activities of cults. But she is also a successful businesswoman who organizes social functions, promotes celebrity clients and runs an Internet magazine. She is well connected and mixes freely with politicians, diplomats and other key movers and shakers. It is this that has enabled her to access information, track down witnesses and elicit informed comments that have eluded other researchers. Few aside from Georgina would have been able to obtain comments on the UFO phenomenon from former Prime Minister Baroness Thatcher, or arrange a face-to-face meeting with Gordon Williams, the retired USAF major general who commanded RAF Bentwaters/Woodbridge at the time of the incident. This unprecedented access, together with the fact that the MOD gave Georgina a guided tour of the Woodbridge base during her research, will doubtless cause some to wonder whether this book has been written with official blessing, as a way of finally releasing the full story of this incident. While this goes too far, it would certainly be true to say that Georgina has persuaded most of those involved in the events to speak out about what happened in a way that will bring this information into the public domain. While this certainly doesn't make the book an official venture, it does mean that it contains much of the information that would be contained in any official history of the incident that were to be written.

I believe this interesting, disturbing and well-researched book will come to be regarded as the definitive account of the Rendlesham Forest incident. But aside from appealing to the general public, it is my hope that it will be widely read by politicians, civil servants and the military and that it will serve as a briefing document for the establishment in the continued absence of any detailed and definitive official comment on these events.

Nick Pope is a civil servant at the Ministry of Defence, where he is a higher executive officer – a rank broadly equivalent to that of a major in the army. Best known for his official research and investigation of UFOs, alien abductions, crop circles and other paranormal phenomena, he is recognized as a leading authority on such matters. He is the author of Open Skies, Closed Minds; The Uninvited; Operation Thunder Child *and* Operation Lightning Strike.

THE MAJOR PLAYERS

Military RAF Bentwaters/Woodbridge

Colonel (later Major General) Gordon E. Williams (ret.)
ROLE: Colonel Williams was the wing commander of the 81st Tactical Fighter Wing at RAF Bentwaters/Woodbridge. The Rendlesham Forest incident occurred under his leadership. In 1983 former Airman First Class Larry Warren told *The News of the World* newspaper that Gordon Williams was involved in the Rendlesham Forest incident and that the commander had communicated with alien entities. CONTACT: Major General Gordon Williams has never gone on record until now. He contacted the author in January 1998.

Colonel Theodore J. Conrad (ret.)
ROLE: Colonel Ted Conrad was the base commander at RAF Bentwaters/Woodbridge. He was in charge of the overall running of the airbases. CONTACT: In 1983 Ted Conrad was interviewed for *OMNI* magazine and admitted that the Rendlesham Forest incident did take place.

Colonel Sam P. Morgan (ret.)
ROLE: Colonel Sam Morgan was the base commander at RAF Bentwaters/Woodbridge in 1983. He was responsible for stewarding copies of Halt's tape recording of the events to interested parties. CONTACT: He was first interviewed in 1983 by researcher Dot Street. The author contacted him in 1998.

Lieutenant Colonel (later Colonel) Charles I. Halt (ret.)
ROLE: Lieutenant Colonel Charles Halt was the deputy base commander of RAF Bentwaters/Woodbridge and an important witness to the Rendlesham Forest incident. Halt took a patrol of men into the forest where they witnessed several objects under intelligent control. In January 1981 he composed an official Air Force memorandum listing details of the events. The memo was then dispatched to the Ministry of Defence. Halt also made an audio tape recording of the incident. CONTACT: In 1991 he made his first public appearance in a television documentary where he confirmed the authenticity of the Rendlesham Forest incident. The author first talked to him in 1997.

Wayne Persinger Deputy Commander of AFOSI Bentwaters (ret.)
ROLE: Special agent, Air Force Office of Special Investigations and deputy commander of AFOSI Bentwaters/Woodbridge during the incident. CONTACT: He gave his first interview to the author in 1999.

Major (later Lieutenant Colonel) Malcolm F. Zickler (ret.)
ROLE: Major Malcolm Zickler was the major in command of the 81st Security Police and Law Enforcement Squadrons at Bentwaters/ Woodbridge. Larry Warren claims he was involved in the incident. CONTACT: He gave his first interview to the author in 1998.

Major Edward Drury (ret.)
ROLE: Major Ed Drury was deputy to Major Zickler. He ordered the first investigation of the landing site. CONTACT: CNN journalist Chuck de Caro contacted him in 1984 but he refused to talk because he was still in the USAF. He gave his first interview to the author in 1998.

Captain Mike Verrano (present status unknown)
ROLE: The on-duty day shift commander. He interviewed Jim Penniston and John Burroughs the morning after the incident. He

also investigated the landing site. CONTACT: Has not gone on record.

First Lieutenant (later Lieutenant Colonel) Fred Buran (ret.)
ROLE: First Lieutenant Buran was the on-duty shift commander at Central Security Control. He was in charge of the bases and the Security and Law Enforcement Squadrons on the night of the initial incident. He claims he sent Staff Sergeant Penniston's patrol out to the forest to investigate the UFO. CONTACT: He gave his first interview to the author in 2000.

Second Lieutenant (later Major) Bruce Englund (ret.)
ROLE: Second Lieutenant Englund was the on-duty shift commander and a primary witness. He was also with Lieutenant Colonel Halt's patrol. CONTACT: Chuck de Caro contacted him in 1985 but he refused to discuss the incident. The author was given his location and acquired his telephone number but when she tried to call the number it was unobtainable. She was told by an operator that he did not want to take her call.

Master Sergeant Ray Gulyas (ret.)
ROLE: Day flight chief for the Security and Law Enforcement Squadrons. He was briefed about the incident daily by witness Master Sergeant Ball. He also investigated the landing site with Captain Verrano. CONTACT: Chuck de Caro first interviewed him in 1984. The author contacted him in 1998.

Master Sergeant J. D. Chandler (present status unknown)
ROLE: On-duty flight chief on 25/26 December. He followed Staff Sergeant Penniston's patrol out to the forest and relayed the transmission to Central Security Control. Alleged to have witnessed the incident. CONTACT: He has not gone on record.

Master Sergeant Robert Ball (ret.)
ROLE: On-duty flight chief during 26/27–28/29 December. He

witnessed the UFOs for three nights and was one of the witnesses with Lieutenant Colonel Halt's patrol. CONTACT: First interviewed by Chuck de Caro in 1984.

Technical Sergeant William Kirk (ret.)
ROLE: Communications operator during the incident and had to deal with an overloading of Flash calls. CONTACT: He gave his first interview to the author in 1998.

Staff Sergeant (later Master Sergeant) James Penniston (ret.)
ROLE: On-duty flight chief. He was a primary witness and the only known person to have actually touched the UFO. He waited fourteen years to tell his story. CONTACT: He was interviewed for a British television documentary in 1994. The author contacted him in 1998.

Staff Sergeant Bud Steffens (present status unknown)
ROLE: Law enforcement supervisor and the first person along with John Burroughs to report the UFO incident. CONTACT: Has not gone on record.

Staff Sergeant Munroe Nevilles (present status unknown)
ROLE: Disaster preparedness. He was the Geiger counter operator with Lieutenant Colonel Halt's patrol. He took the radiation readings. CONTACT: Has not gone on record.

Sergeant Adrian Bustinza (ret.)
ROLE: Security police supervisor and primary witness to a landed UFO which was under intelligent control. CONTACT: Ray Boeche and Larry Fawcett first interviewed him in 1984. The author contacted him in 1998.

Sergeant Rick Bobo (ret.)
ROLE: Security police. He was in the Bentwaters Control Tower and was instructed to keep an eye on the UFO whilst it hovered over

the base for almost five hours. CONTACT: He gave his first interview to the author in 1998.

Staff Sergeant John Coffey (present status unknown)
ROLE: Security controller on duty at Central Security Control during initial incident. Relayed transmissions from Penniston's patrol. CONTACT: Has not gone on record.

Airman First Class (later Sergeant) John F. Burroughs (ret.)
ROLE: Law enforcement. Then airman first class, he was the only known witness to have been involved in two events. He was the first person to report the UFO. He was with Staff Sergeant Penniston's patrol when he witnessed a landed UFO. CONTACT: First contacted in 1984 by Ray Boeche but could not discuss incident because he was still in the service. First interviewed by Jim Speiser in 1989. First published interview with Antonio Huneeus 1990. First appeared publicly on a British documentary in 1994.

Airman First Class (later Sergeant) Jerry Valdes-Sanchez (ret.)
ROLE: Law enforcement. Then airman first class, witnessed UFO over the Woodbridge base during the incident. Heard the radio traffic. CONTACT: First went public on *Sightings* radio in 1999. The author interviewed him that same year.

Airman First Class Edward N. Cabansag (ret.)
ROLE: Security police. First-hand witness to the initial incident. Went out with Staff Sergeant Penniston's patrol. CONTACT: He gave his first interview to the author in 1999.

Airman First Class Steve Roberts (pseudonym) (ret.)
ROLE: Security Police. First known person to discuss the incident with civilians. A few days after the incident he told Chris Pennington and Brenda Butler he had witnessed a landed UFO with an alien crew. CONTACT: The author interviewed him in 1999.

Airman First Class Greg Battram (ret.)
ROLE: Security police. He claims he witnessed a landed UFO.
CONTACT: Interviewed in 1984 by Larry Fawcett. The author
spoke to his wife in 1999.

Airman First Class Timothy Egercic (ret.)
ROLE: Security police. On duty in the weapons storage area,
Bentwaters. Took over the airwaves from Central Security Control
and heard the radio transmissions. CONTACT: First contacted
Peter Robbins in 1997. The author interviewed him in 1998.

Airman First Class Larry Warren (ret.)
ROLE: Security police. He claims he witnessed a landed UFO with
an alien crew. He was the first witness to go public in 1983.
CONTACT: First interviewed by Larry Fawcett in 1983. First
contact with the author was in 1997.

Tony Brisciano (present rank withheld)
ROLE: Maintenance. Was responsible for filling the jeeps and light-
alls during the incident. CONTACT: First interviewed by the
author in 1998.

Wayne (present status unknown)
ROLE: Security police. He was a dog handler who claimed to have
witnessed a landed UFO with its alien crew. CONTACT: Has not
gone on record.

RAF

Squadron Leader Donald Moreland (ret.)
ROLE: Squadron Leader Donald Moreland was the British liaison
officer and was responsible for insisting that Lieutenant Colonel
Halt make a report to the Ministry of Defence. CONTACT: In
1983 he was interviewed for *OMNI* magazine. The author interviewed him in 1998.

Harry Thompson (pseudonym) Police Dog Handler (ret.)
ROLE: Security police. Witnessed strange encounter at RAF Watton during the same week as the Rendlesham Forest incident. CONTACT: He gave his first interview to the author in 1998.

Nigel Kerr Radar Operator
ROLE: Radar operator at RAF Watton. Witnessed the radar. Was on duty during the incident when RAF Bentwaters made the report. CONTACT: He gave his first interview to the author in 1999.

Suffolk Constabulary

Superintendent George Plume (ret.)
ROLE: Woodbridge police: He was in charge of the Woodbridge civil police during the incident. CONTACT: He gave his first interview to the author in 1999.

PC Dave King (ret.)
ROLE: Woodbridge police constable. He was sent out to investigate the first incident. CONTACT: First interviewed for British TV Documentary in 1994. The author interviewed him in 1998.

PC Martin Brophy (ret.)
ROLE: Woodbridge police constable. He was sent out to investigate the first incident along with Dave King. CONTACT: Has not gone on record.

PC Brian Creswell (ret.)
ROLE: Woodbridge police constable. He was sent out to investigate the landing marks the morning after the first incident. CONTACT: The author traced and contacted him in 1999.

Civilian Witnesses

Gary Collins: Primary witness to UFO (gave first interview to the author in 1999).

Diana Persinger: Primary witness to UFO (gave first interview to the author in 1999).

Gordon Levitt: Primary witness to UFO (author contacted him in 2000).

Gerry Harris: Primary witness to UFO (author contacted him in 1998).

Roy Webb: Primary witness to UFO (author contacted him in 1998).

Marjorie Wright: Her father, Bertie Coleman (deceased), witnessed the UFO (author contacted her in 1998).

Masie Pettit: Witnessed the stampede of cattle (gave first interview to the author in 1999).

Betty Garfield, Ministry of Defence secretary at RAF Bentwaters: Witnessed the goings-on during incident (gave first interview to the author in 1999).

Richard Nunn: Developed the photographs of the landing site (gave first interview to the author in 1999).

Mrs Sawyer: Alleged to have witnessed the incident.

SOME NEW USAF WITNESSES TO OTHER ENCOUNTERS AT WOODBRIDGE

Anthony Johnson (ret.) (gave first interview to the author)

William Sone (ret.) (gave first interview to the author)

Steven La Plume (ret.) (interviewed by the author)

Lindy Vaughn (ret.) (gave first interview to the author)

Lori Rehfeldt (ret.) (gave first interview to the author)

James Hudnall (ret.) (gave first interview to the author)

THE MEMORANDUM

Were it not for a memorandum, signed by Lieutenant Colonel Charles I. Halt (later Colonel), the Rendlesham Forest case would probably have remained buried in a dusty filing cabinet, along with other, as yet unknown, similar cases. The official memorandum which documented these unusual events was a researcher's dream and a nightmare for the United States Air Force. The document may never have come to light but for the enthusiasm of a group called Citizens Against UFO Secrecy (CAUS). The case had attracted their attention in early 1983 when a witness, using the pseudonym Art Wallace (real name Larry Warren), contacted them. At the time, CAUS investigators Larry Fawcett and Barry Greenwood were busy compiling a book entitled *Clear Intent*. The publication aimed to present new evidence to prove that the United States Air Force were still continuing enquiries into UFO reports, even though they claimed to have ceased interest in the late 1960s. To back up their case the investigators had obtained several files released through the United States Freedom of Information Act. The Rendlesham Forest incident no doubt intrigued them, but they were primarily paper-trail investigators and at that stage all they had to go on was Warren's word and a few rumours circulating from rural England. Nevertheless, they were convinced enough to begin enquiries and during the ensuing months Fawcett kept in regular telephone contact with British researcher Dot Street, who provided him with everything she had on the case. After several denials from the Bentwaters public affairs office, CAUS investigator Robert Todd was surprised to receive what became known as the famous 'Halt Memo'. This turned out to be a fascinating document, typed on official Air Force letterhead, titled 'Unexplained Lights'. Colonel Peter Bent of the 513th Combat Support Group had forwarded the memorandum to CAUS.

DEPARTMENT OF THE AIR FORCE
HEADQUARTERS 81st COMBAT SUPPORT GROUP (USAFE)
APO NEW YORK 09755

REPLY TO   13 Jan 81
ATTN OF: CD
SUBJECT: Unexplained Lights

TO: RAF/CC

1. Early in the morning of 27 Dec 1980 (approximately 0300L), two USAF security police patrolmen saw unusual lights outside the back gate at RAF Woodbridge.

Thinking an aircraft might have crashed or been forced down, they called for permission to investigate. The on-duty flight chief responded and allowed three patrolmen to proceed on foot. The individuals reported seeing a strange glowing object in the forest. The object was described as being metallic in appearance and triangular in shape, approximately two to three metres across the base and approximately two metres high. It illuminated the entire forest with a white light. The object itself had a pulsing red light on top and a bank(s) of blue lights underneath. The object was hovering or on legs. As the patrolmen approached the object, it manoeuvred through the trees and disappeared. At this time the animals on a nearby farm went into a frenzy. The object was briefly sighted approximately an hour later near the back gate.

2. The next day, three depressions 1 1/2' deep and 7' in diameter were found where the object had been sighted on the ground. The following night (29 Dec 80) the area was checked for radiation. Beta/gamma readings of 0.1 milliroentgens were recorded with peak readings in the three depressions and near the centre of the triangle formed by the depressions. A nearby

tree had moderate (.05–.07) readings on the side of the tree toward the depressions.

    3. Later in the night a red sun-like light was seen through the trees. It moved about and pulsed. At one point it appeared to throw off glowing particles and then broke into five separate white objects and then disappeared. Immediately thereafter, three star-like objects were noticed in the sky, two objects to the north and one to the south, all of which were about 10° off the horizon. The objects moved rapidly in sharp angular movements and displayed red, green and blue lights. The objects to the north appeared to be elliptical through an 8–12 power lens. They then turned full circles. The objects to the north remained in the sky for an hour or more. The object to the south was visible for two or three hours and beamed down a stream of light from time to time. Numerous individuals, including the undersigned, witnessed the activities in paragraphs 2 and 3.

[Signed]
CHARLES I. Halt, Lt Col, USAF
Deputy Base Commander

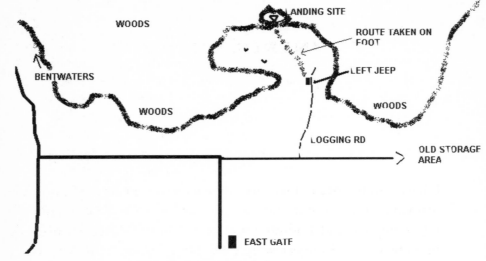

Jim Penniston's rough map

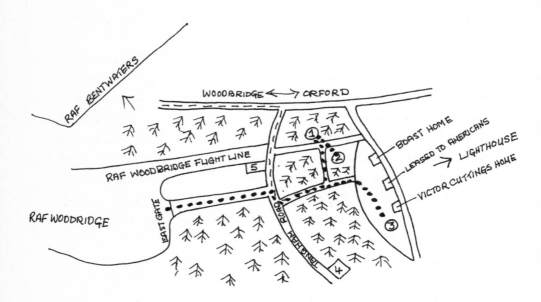

1. Initial landing site 25/6
2. Landing site pointed out by Brenda Butler and confirmed to Adrian Bustiza
3. Landing site. Larry Warren

4. Forestry offices
5. Foley cottages
• • • • depicts the route taken to landing sites

Georgina Bruni's rough map, taking into account witness statements

INTRODUCTION

I have always been interested in anything categorized as 'unexplained', but it was not until ten years ago that I stumbled upon the UFO enigma, and I admit I was very sceptical. I had erroneously thought that the subject verged on the fringe of crankiness, but I soon discovered that there are some very responsible people who claim to have been witnesses to these events. These include politicians, police officers, military personnel and civilian pilots. It was this conclusion that prompted me to learn more about these people and their encounters, but I was especially drawn to military witnesses. I was sure that these men and women would know the difference between a UFO and one of their own aircraft, and if they were claiming these were 'unknowns' then there must be some truth to it. Of course, 'unidentified flying objects' do not necessarily need to be extraterrestrial in origin. They could be any number of things, from balloons to secret aircraft being tested. According to the Ministry of Defence 90 per cent of UFO cases are eventually solved but that still leaves 10 per cent that are not, and it is that 10 per cent which interests me.

However, the Ministry of Defence claim that UFOs are of 'no defence significance' and on the surface other government departments appear to take a similar stand. I wondered if any of our political leaders had been briefed on the subject, if so then one would expect it to have been the Iron Lady herself, Margaret Thatcher. Thatcher was not your average leader: she had more than a passionate love affair with her country. If Britain was under threat, be it from her own citizens, a foreign power, terrorists or even extraterrestrials, Thatcher would want to know all the intricate details. Given the opportunity, I wanted to know if she was aware of the UFO enigma, which many people believe is a major threat to our national security.

That opportunity came unexpectedly in the spring of 1997. I had been invited to a charity dinner by a prominent lawyer friend from the City of London. We would be sharing a table with several other lawyers and it promised to be an entertaining evening. Like most private functions attended by political guests, there was a strict security code to guard against possible terrorist threat. The names of the guests attending these functions are usually forwarded in advance and often one never knows where the function will take place until the actual day. On this occasion Baroness Thatcher was to be the guest of honour.

We British are never more polite than when we attend these social gatherings, but pushing politeness aside, and realizing that the evening was quickly drawing to a close, I decided to introduce myself to the former prime minister. She was very pleasant, considering that just hours earlier she had returned from a visit to Washington DC and the tiredness and strain of a long hard day was beginning to show. For about ten minutes we exchanged polite conversation about the nicer side of politics, technological advancements and how Britain would keep abreast of it. I explained that I had launched one of the first British Internet magazines, and like most political minds Thatcher seemed nervous of the Internet but obviously realized its potential. I could see she was not averse to new technology though. It was then that I decided to tell her of my recent interviews with certain retired military men. I thought, what the hell, what have I got to lose; at the very worst she might think I had drunk too much champagne. Knowing of her close relationship with the United States, I asked her if she was aware that in the last few years several former US military officers had come forward with claims of a most unusual nature. I recounted my own personal interviews with scientists and military men, some of whom claimed they were actually working with alien technology. She listened in silence as if grasping every word I said, and I waited in anticipation whilst she quickly glanced around, as if looking to see if anyone was eavesdropping on the conversation. I could see her husband Dennis bending his ear. Not expecting much of a reply, but curious just the same, I asked her if she would offer an opinion on UFOs and alien technology. 'You can't tell the people,' she said. I asked if she was referring to UFOs, it seems that word always puts the wind up. At that moment she raised herself from her seat and said, 'UFOs!' No wonder her Special Branch bodyguards moved forward a few steps. Determined to pursue the questioning I stood facing her and, in almost a whisper, I said, 'UFOs and alien technology, Lady Thatcher.' 'You must get your facts right,' she answered. 'What facts?' I wanted to know. In a worried tone of voice, but with her usual composure, she repeated, 'You must have the facts and you can't tell the people.' It was the last statement she made. I shook her hand, thanked her for talking to me and stood aside as Dennis Thatcher moved forward to escort his wife out of the room, followed by her entourage of bodyguards. It was then that I realized Margaret Thatcher had actually taken the conversation seriously.

So had my instinct been right after all, is the former Prime Minister aware of the UFO phenomenon and, if so, how much does she know? What were the facts she was referring to and, even more importantly, why would she insist that the people should not be told about UFOs? For anyone who thinks Baroness Thatcher was just being polite, I have it on very good authority that even in her private life she lives up to her public reputation of being a no-nonsense sort of person. Rest assured, if she thought the conversation was verging on the wacky, she would not have stayed interested as long as she did. Not being a particularly humorous woman, she most probably would have terminated the conversation with a constipated, 'You have been watching too many *X Files* episodes, my dear.' Instead, it was a pleasant change not to have to endure another 'It is of no defence significance' type of reply. In all fairness to Baroness Thatcher, I am certain the reason I received such a response is because I caught her completely off guard. Just the same, I could not help feeling somewhat amused at the thought that she would think I was about to expose the UFO/ET secrets on the World Wide Web.

For a brief period in my early twenties, I worked for a private investigator. It was a monotonous job, when more often than not I would spend days watching a premises to see who was coming and going. But one thing my boss taught me was the basics of how to investigate a case – something I never forgot. It was not until I decided to investigate the UFO enigma that I realized how much those skills would come in useful. The most important asset in any investigation is undoubtedly the witnesses, because without them one has a very difficult job. Unfortunately, if the case involves the military, there is often a wall of silence surrounding it, and nowhere is this more prominent than when it involves both the military *and* UFOs.

My old boss taught me never to accept a testimony without first taking it apart and putting it back together again. I had been desperately trying to piece together Larry Warren's testimony, but the pieces most certainly did not fit and this was a problem. Warren was a former airman with the United States Air Force in Europe (USAFE), and whilst stationed in England he claimed he was a first-hand witness to a UFO incident. He also accused the United States Air Force (USAF) of abducting him and taking him to an under-ground facility on a military base, where he was drugged and interrogated in order to silence him. For more than seventeen years he had been telling the world that his commander, Gordon Williams, had also been involved in the incident and, furthermore, Williams had exchanged communication with the alien crew of a landed spaceship. Another lesson my boss taught me was never to take one person's word for it. But how do I get to talk to the general, I thought? No one had ever been able to interview him. Then, one dull January morning, as I was sitting at my computer, I received an electronic mail from a retired major general of the United States Air Force. His name was Gordon Williams. This was the beginning of a journey that led me on a quest to find the truth about one of Britain's most famous unsolved mysteries, the Rendlesham Forest incident.

It was a bitterly cold afternoon when Jacquieline Davis and I arrived in rural Suffolk. My companion had recently written a book entitled *The Circuit*, which told the truth about her career in the police force, and later as the world's top female bodyguard and covert operator. She was glad to be taking a break away from the heavy schedule of media interviews and I was pleased to have a professional of her status along with me on this most unusual trip. As we drove up to the Woodbridge military base, there to meet us was the smiling and rather jolly John Lawrence Briggs, to whom I took an instant liking. Briggs, a six-foot-tall well-built man with more than twenty years' army experience behind him, was in charge of the Ministry of Defence security at Colchester Barracks. Today he was going to escort us on a tour of an old RAF base, which until 1993 had been leased to the United States Air Force. Briggs needed a list of places I wanted to view so that he could arrange for the appropriate keys. I gave him three: the weapons storage area; the murals, which are all over the base; and the underground facilities. Briggs said he was unaware of any underground facilities and asked for their location. That was a question I did not have an answer to. According to the Woodbridge security personnel, they were not aware they existed either. But just as we were about to begin our tour, a guard nervously approached us, explaining that there was a place on the base with steps leading down to an underground bunker, but it was apparently full of rubbish. He gave us instructions and Jacquieline and I scrambled excitedly into Briggs's vehicle.

We began the tour by photographing many of the murals for which the Americans are famous. These consisted of rough graffiti to full-blown works of art, mostly to do with the USAF, although there were a few comic ones in the latrines. So historical are these murals that the Ministry of Defence have photographed and catalogued them for their archives. In a building that had been designated to the 67th Aerospace Rescue and Recovery Squadron (ARRS), I discovered a fascinating piece of work. It featured a circular globe depicting American aircraft throughout the decades, and to complete the cycle, which included a magnificent NASA space rocket, the artist had painted a realistic-looking A-10 tank buster, the last official military aircraft to be deployed at RAF Woodbridge.

Our next stop was the search for the underground facilities. Whilst I was busy examining an outdoor shower structure, Briggs was receiving instructions on his radio for the combination lock to a nuclear fallout shelter. The shelter, which turned out to be the old Command Post, was a maze of vaults and rooms with enormous solid steel doors, many with elaborate combination locks. It was the spookiest place I had ever seen. Amidst the blackness, for there was no electricity connected, Briggs's state-of-the-art torch cut out, and by now we were deep inside the vaults. Thank goodness I had remembered to take my torch along. The complex had the nauseating odour of stale air, which was obviously due to it being tightly sealed for a long period of time. With only one torch between us we were obliged to stay close together, fully aware that if one of the steel doors slammed behind us it could be a very long time before we were rescued. With no oxygen, I did not relish the thought of being buried for too long inside one of those confined units. Once inside the complex, neither our mobile phones or Briggs's radio was functioning, so we had no contact with the outside world.

In a small room at the farthest end of the complex we discovered an old telephone system. It was a PABX4, which according to my British Telecom source was used by the Ministry of Defence until 1992. The reason they continued to use this old system for so long was because it was the most efficient and could not be hacked into. My source was part of a British Telecom team who had special MOD clearance. She would be responsible for checking out the MOD lines, which included underground facilities at Rudloe Manor and Colindale, as well as a secret facility beneath a public house in Hampstead and another accessible from the middle of a field in Redhill. Apparently, there are hundreds of underground bunkers scattered throughout Britain. It could take more than four hours to test and link up the bunkers, and apparently all lines went straight through to the MOD at Whitehall. One perk of being on this special BT team was that every five years they were able to purchase, for a cheap price, the underground food stocks that were being replaced with fresh ones. My source recalls that some of the bunkers were three floors below ground and they stank of diesel oil.

It was a great relief to exit the shelter and Briggs gave us a thrill by driving us down the famous Woodbridge runway. On the way back we stopped near the east-gate exit and he pointed out that this was where the ufologists hang out. Since reports of UFO landings had first made the news, the area has become quite famous among UFO enthusiasts, and the local foresters have taken to conducting tours from the east gate to the suspected landing sites. I spotted a helicopter hovering overhead and my thoughts turned to the days when the runway was used as a crash-landing site in World War Two. How many innocent young souls had given their lives for king and country on this very spot.

Whilst Jacquieline and I were examining numerous odd pipes and what appeared to be air ducts sticking out of the ground, Briggs, somewhat anxiously I thought, moved us on to another building. I could not help wondering if there was a facility under that area, but if there was I could find no visible entrance. Having toured the rest of the base, including the old weapons storage area, it was now time to call it a day; and Briggs had to return to the gate because the civil police were waiting to see him. As we said our farewells a police transport van came through and I learnt that they sometimes held their anti-terrorist training sessions on the base, as did members of the Special Air Service. It had been a fascinating tour, even though we had not found the entrance to any underground facilities – and we had certainly tried.

The next morning, probably one of the coldest days of the year, I visited the old RAF Bentwaters site, which is situated just a few miles from the Woodbridge base. In its heyday, along with Woodbridge, it had been home to the largest single fighter wing in the USAF. By the time Jacquieline and I arrived at the Bentwaters gate we were late for our appointment, only to find we had to be redirected to the domestic site to meet with the security chief, Vernon Drane. We received royal treatment from Drane's secretary, who kindly escorted us to the plush visitors' room and offered us piping-hot coffee, which went down very well on such a cold winter's day. Drane was equally accommodating, and when I cheekily asked for a copy of the huge Bentwaters map that graced his office wall, he willingly obliged. In all the excitement, I had forgotten it was my birthday and I could not have wished for a better gift than a USAF map of the entire Bentwaters complex, which listed and numbered every building above ground.

Vernon Drane had assigned one of his more mature security guards to accompany us on the tour. Derek Barnes was due for retirement soon, so we were lucky to have his expertise. He was a local who had been with Bentwaters security since the Americans had departed, before that he used to service their domestic appliances. Our first stop was the air-traffic control tower and although not that high, it was one hell of a climb on a wet and windy day. The view from the tower was quite amazing, one could see right across the base, over towards the forest. The fittings, which had once held the controls, were still mostly intact, and I could imagine being seated there, watching the A-10s coming in to land. However, this was not the tower I was looking for, that was in the weapons storage area. It was from that particular standpoint that an airman was instructed to keep an eye on low-flying UFOs. Just as I was taking photographs of the panoramic view, an aggressive young security guard came barging in. He thought we were intruders and had charged in with the aim of confronting us. I was now beginning to feel guilty at dragging old Barnes up those slippery metal steps to the tower, if the climb up was difficult in the gale-force wind and heavy rain, the climb down was equally so.

Our next stop was the base headquarters, where the wing commander would have ruled with his commanding officers. It was a large complex, surrounded by overgrown gardens, and at the entrance was a canopy that had obviously protected the officers from the elements as they stepped into their vehicles. I noticed most of the rooms were carpeted, and as we climbed the staircase to the higher echelons' offices they became much grander. We entered a reception area through two huge glass doors: one etched with the emblem of the USAF and the other with that of the 81st Tactical Fighter Wing, the last squadron to occupy the base. The doors led to a spacious reception area, and off to the right was the grandest office of all, the wing commander's. As with some of the other top-floor offices, its walls were a mass of wall-to-ceiling storage cupboards, concealed by sliding doors with no handles. Jacquieline and I had fun trying to figure out how to open them. This particular office had its own private toilet, en-suite shower and small built-in wardrobe: Air Force luxury at its best, I thought. I could not resist a nose around and found myself looking on to an enormous balcony that Barnes said had been used for cocktail parties during the summer months. This is where the wing commander would have entertained the local Anglo/American Social Committee, commonly known as the Mutual Admiration Society. This building was only constructed in the mid-1980s and according to a former wing commander the old place was embarrassingly decrepit and he had often found himself apologizing to visitors.

Adjacent to the headquarters was the Command Post, which was the nerve centre of the installation. This was another nuclear-protected building. We had the spooks about the Woodbridge shelter, but this was far more sophisticated, and much larger, and I could not resist exploring it. I thought Barnes was not so keen but he never once complained. While we waited for him to open the combination locks we spotted more of the strange showers outside the main entrance to the building.

After entering by the heavy door, we had to once again use our torches because there was no electricity inside the unused structures, and of course there were no windows. The door led into a small cubicle, which must have been where a security policeman once stood guard. From there we entered another door that led to a narrow corridor, and on the left-hand side there was a sign with the words DECON 1. This consisted of a small cubicle with a shower unit. We then passed through another heavy door and as we walked down the narrow corridor we passed three more decontamination units, DECON 2, 3 and 4. We realized that in the event of a nuclear attack, personnel would have been required to take an outside shower and go through the decontamination procedures before they entered the main complex. All along the corridor were strange-looking devices that we realized were oxygen vents. One room consisted of enormous pipes which led through the walls to where we did not know, but assumed these would have provided the oxygen. To my right was a small room full of row upon row of decaying telephone switchboards. Obviously, this had been their communications outfit, and I considered whether it would have functioned had there been an all-out nuclear attack. As we continued through the complex we passed other empty rooms and it felt as if we were inside some kind of capsule. It was difficult in the blackness with only torches for light and I almost fell down some steps as I tried to gain my bearings. At the far end of the building was a room that featured two rows of fittings joined end to end; these had, no doubt, housed computers. Barnes accidentally knocked over an empty can of coke and the noise suddenly brought me back to reality. This was some place! Exiting through the other side of the room, we came across another huge door and it occurred to us that we had passed through several of these on the way in. As with the Woodbridge post, we hoped that none of these would close behind us. I slid back a door that seemed to take up the whole of one wall, only to discover there was a sliding panel behind it made out of some type of steel. When I slid back the panel it revealed another of the same, and another, and another, and so on. After sliding all the panels back a solid steel wall was revealed. Moving back into the room I had previously exited, I found that the panels and sealed wall led right along the edge of that room too. It was obviously a nuclear-safe outside wall and it made me realize what little chance we civilians would have stood had there been a nuclear attack. The government information booklet, *Protect and Survive*, which advised its citizens on how to protect themselves from such an attack, seemed preposterous in comparison.

Suddenly we found ourselves in another passageway that led to a small room. At the end of the room was an unusual solid red door that looked very important indeed. It had a small glass pane but was covered in warning signs such as: 'No photographs beyond this point. This is a restricted area,' and 'Warning. Controlled Area. It is unlawful to enter this area without permission of the Installation Commander.' Next to the door was some sort of old security system; unfortunately the door was well and truly locked and Barnes explained that there were no keys for it. I surmised this must have been one of the sensitive areas that Vernon Drane had told me still existed, apparently there were still a few of these on the installation. The door was at the very end of the building, which meant it could not really lead anywhere other than outside or down. But when I looked through the glass pane there was an area three-feet square directly in front of the door which was blocked off by a wall, and the exit which I could not see clearly was off to the left. However, there were no exits on that side of the wall because I checked when I left the building. Besides, it could not have been an exit because the signs clearly indicated it was an entrance to somewhere. We had to conclude that it was most probably the entrance to an underground facility. Disappointed, and knowing that the secret door would stay in my memory forever, we turned back, looking for the way we came in, but we seemed to have found another route. In the dark everything looked so much more confusing. We passed several more vaults and small rooms, and a sign on one of the heavy doors read: 'There are no classified documents in this vault.' Barnes pointed to a round steel contraption that reminded me of a submarine door. Was it an escape route? Did it lead to secret tunnels? Regrettably, I was not about to explore further. We were becoming nauseous at having to inhale the stale trapped air and desperately needed to get some fresh air into our lungs. As we stepped outside I was overwhelmed by a feeling of relief, and found myself thinking how fortunate we were to be able to walk out of that confined space into a world that was free from nuclear fallout.

Our next stop was the weapons storage area. We passed numerous dull buildings on the way, with our tour guide Barnes explaining what they were. I knew from some of my contacts that many of the aircraft shelters were nuclear proof, but what I did not realize was that they were so tough that the only way to demolish them would be to bomb them with a direct hit. According to Barnes, this would take out the whole of the town of Woodbridge, so it looks as if they are here to stay.

As we approached the weapons storage area I was surprised to see how huge it was. I asked Barnes to take us to the sensitive area that was alleged to be inside the larger complex. He knew exactly where I meant, so it seemed my sources were right after all — there was another area. To gain access to the main complex, Barnes had to stop the vehicle and unlock the massive gates. I noticed a set of buildings to my right, which I was told had been a security post. Not only were there high double fences topped with two to three feet of twisted barbed wire, but when the base was active, the perimeters were heavily alarmed. These alarms were so sensitive that even a small animal could trigger them off. There were signs everywhere that this was a restricted area. It felt unreal to be seeing the base as it had been described to me by so many of the former personnel. We were now at the entrance to what some of my contacts had referred to as the sensitive area, and right in front of me was the 'Hot Row' where they had housed the nuclear weapons. Barnes had to unlock yet another set of security gates to gain access. We passed two rows of bunkers, one on either side of a small access road. The buildings on the right-hand side looked much more modern than the others and I noticed they did not appear on the old Bentwaters map. These were most likely the ones I had heard were built in the 1980s. Barnes was clearly shocked to find one of the older bunkers unlocked and immediately alerted the security desk. Of course I was delighted, and whilst he was busy on his radio I decided to explore the opened bunker. It was dark and smelly and full of huge cobwebs. Overhead was some type of pulley, which I thought could have been used to carry the weapons along. The floor had precise, filled-in cracks which might have been concealing an underground storeroom, and I noticed that the heavy bunker doors were fitted with elaborately secure bolts and locks. At the far end of the bunkers we spotted a small shack type of building, but hidden behind it, which was not visible from the front, was a strange vault with a huge steel door. Sadly, it was well and truly sealed. This was obviously another of those sensitive areas for which they had no keys, or so I was told. I had found two such impregnable doors, and the one on building 560 was one of them.

We were now off to tour the rest of the weapons storage area. The weather was getting colder by the minute and I was sorry for Barnes having to struggle with so many keys every time we wanted to access or leave an area or building. The rain had now turned to hail and we were desperate for some hot coffee. I thought about those poor souls who had stood for hours on duty in these cold and dreary winter elements. Straight ahead was a very tall tower and I conceived that this was the structure I had heard so much about. Apart from witnesses viewing UFOs from this location, this was the tower where ghostly footsteps were heard by a security guard. Jacquieline was willing to climb the tower with me, but in the threatening wind and hail I realized it would have been a difficult task. She was trained by former SAS personnel and is qualified in close protection, surveillance and security, but old Barnes and I shrank in horror at the very thought. Unless you know the height of the tower, with its narrow metal steps, you cannot imagine what a climb that is. I was not feeling that brave and scrambled back into the vehicle.

Driving around the site, looking at the dozens of empty weapons storage bunkers, made me realize the enormity of it all. Just as we were about to leave the area I spotted one of the more humorous graffiti on the wall of a building. It read: 'We live so you may die.' Anxious to take a photograph, I stepped out of the vehicle and found myself slipping on a sheet of ice. I might have been able to save myself from the fall but I was more concerned about the camera and all the photographs I had taken in the Command Post. At the thought of having to return to that spooky place to take another film, I settled for the fall. For one moment I could not move and

Jacquieline, who was at my side almost immediately, went into close-protection mode. With one arm holding Barnes back and the other pinning me down, she began firing questions to make sure I had not damaged my spine. Soaking wet from falling through the ice and in much discomfort, I headed for the warmth of the Crown Hotel in Woodbridge. I do not know who was responsible for the graffiti but his humour almost turned out to be real.

Before I left for my Woodbridge trip I had called Adrian Bustinza to ask for directions to the photo laboratory. Bustinza is a former airman who claimed he was taken to this particular building where he was led underground and interrogated about his participation in a UFO incident. He had warned me to be careful about visiting the base, but did not explain why – just that it was not a good place to be. Jacquieline, as down to earth as she is, made a profound comment: 'It's strange that you should have an accident just when you are about to visit one of the very places you came here to see.' I was beginning to think that some unseen mysterious force was watching from the shadows after all. You might wonder what I was doing exploring two old military bases, but it was all part of my investigation into the Rendlesham Forest incident. I wanted to see for myself the places the witnesses had talked about. But how did it all begin?

At approximately 21.00 hrs on Christmas night 1980 people all over England were seeing strange lights in the skies. The emergency desks at RAF West Drayton and Heathrow airport told journalists they had received a flood of calls from as far south as Cornwall and as far north as Yorkshire. The West Drayton Observer Base reported that a mystery object was on a north-easterly course, high in the sky, causing them to make an immediate search for any aircraft in the area. Unable to find a suitable explanation for the mystery, they came to the conclusion that it was almost certainly a meteor breaking up. As these unusual events were taking place, amateur astronomer Roy Panther was out in his garden stargazing when he noticed an object that he identified as a comet. He was so excited about the sighting, apparently the first of its kind in fifteen years, that according to East Anglian press reports he took the credit for its discovery.

Meanwhile, military personnel serving with the United States Air Force at the twin bases of RAF Bentwaters and Woodbridge in Suffolk suddenly found themselves caught up in a phenomenon that would change their lives for ever. Something had landed in the forest, outside the perimeter fence, and those who went out to investigate came face to face with something terrifying. Whatever it was that was lurking in the blackness of the forest, it was not something the airmen were familiar with, and nothing they had been trained for had prepared them for this moment.

For three years the Ministry of Defence denied there had been any such incident, then, in early 1983, American UFO investigators managed to obtain an official document authored by former Deputy Base Commander Colonel Charles I. Halt. The memorandum, which was sent to Britain's Ministry of Defence in early January 1981, revealed that two UFO incidents had occurred in Rendlesham Forest, on the perimeter of a US military base. It involved not only the US security police personnel but also the deputy base commander himself. Following the disclosure of this document, several military and civilian witnesses came forward, some even claimed to have seen alien entities, but both the USAF and the Ministry of Defence denied the incident had any defence significance. The Air Force personnel who witnessed these incredible events were never told the truth of what had happened. As part of the cover-up they claim they were interrogated by special agents and warned that if they talked, 'bullets are cheap'. Some witnesses were drugged and hypnotized in order to silence them, others were given new identities, and there were those who simply disappeared.

I realized early in the day that it was going to be a difficult case to work with, but I did not anticipate that there would be so many obstacles. Apart from the fact that most of the witnesses had long since retired from the Air Force and were scattered over the vast continent of the United States of America, there were other obstacles to deal with. There was the disinformation, the rumours, the warnings when I appeared to be delving too deep, the diverse testimonies, the hoaxers, the debunkers and the sceptics. It was a bewildering and complex network of truths and untruths which often left me emotionally drained. Nevertheless, I have managed to trace many of those who played a part and, against all the odds, my investigation has revealed that there was a major incident in Rendlesham Forest during the month of December 1980.

The incident has been christened 'Britain's Roswell', and it is true there are similarities. Before the Rendlesham Forest case became known, Roswell stood alone as the world's most famous UFO mystery. For those who are not familiar with it, Roswell is a small town in New Mexico where, on a stormy night in July 1947, at least one UFO was alleged to have crashed to earth, scattering debris over the desert floor. The nearby Air Force base was put on immediate alert and the area cordoned off whilst alien bodies and debris were said to have been removed to a top-secret military installation.

The Rendlesham Forest story is one of intrigue which spans two continents, involving the United States Air Force, the Royal Air Force, British and American defence and intelligence agencies and Her Majesty's police force. It has taken a good deal of courage for the witnesses to speak out, and not only the witnesses themselves but also the players who were reluctantly caught up in this extraordinary incident. As courageous as the first-hand witnesses are, there are others who have also had to carry a burden. These are the men and women whose rank and authority have prevented them from speaking openly about this case. I have talked to several of these people at length and know the agony they have suffered at having to withhold that information.

Here then, for the first time, is the true story of the Rendlesham Forest incident.

GEORGINA BRUNI
LONDON

LAYING THE FOUNDATIONS

If this were a fictional mystery I could not have chosen a better location than England's rural Suffolk for the setting. Known for its myths and legends, hauntings and witchcraft, it is a fiction writer's dream – but this story is not fiction. What you are about to read is the result of a three-year investigation into a factual case involving real people and real events.

The incident took place in the county of Suffolk, which is a part of the larger region of East Anglia. It is a rural area blessed with green pastures, rich farmland and beautiful pine forests. The most popular town is Ipswich, but housewives tend to do their daily shopping in the quaint market towns where they can buy freshly baked bread and produce from the local farms. Scattered throughout the region are several picturesque villages with delightful old buildings and welcoming public houses. Approximately four miles east of the small town of Woodbridge sits Rendlesham Forest, home to an abundance of wildlife and Corsican pine trees. Amidst all this beauty, buried away in a corner of the nearby coastline and facing the cruel North Sea, is a desolate marshy terrain called Orfordness. It is often referred to as the Island due to it being separated by a small stretch of water known as the River Ore. The only structure to brighten up this dull unattractive range is a red and white ninety-nine-foot lighthouse station.

Not only did this part of East Anglia witness one of the strangest events of modern times but it was, and probably still is, home to some of Britain's most secret government research facilities. As early as 1915 the Armament Experimental Squadron descended on Orfordness to test their new bombs. Those early pioneers must have thought they were in hell on earth due to the cold and miserable climate. Although high-ranking officers were fortunate to have been accommodated in the comfort and warmth of the Crown and Castle Hotel at nearby Orford, many of the regular troops were housed in makeshift wooden huts situated along the roadside, facing the seafront. It was a dreadful place to be in the middle of a harsh British winter.

During the early 1930s a team of civilian scientists moved to the Island with the aim of conducting various top-secret military experiments at a building called the Orfordness Research Laboratory. For a brief period during the mid-1930s, radar experiments were also carried out. In fact, this part of Suffolk has a long history of being used for radar experiments. In 1915 Scottish meteorologist Robert Watson-Watt began testing radio waves with the purpose of using them to locate thunderstorms, which he hoped would provide an early warning system to RAF pilots. In 1934 Watson-Watt was approached by H. E. Wimperis, Director of Research for the British Air Ministry. Wimperis wanted to know if it was possible to incapacitate enemy aircraft or its crew by using an intense beam of radio waves, in other words a death ray. If Watson-Watt ever managed to produce such a weapon, it was a well-guarded secret. The meteorologist had other ideas and advised the Air Ministry accordingly, suggesting the death ray was impractical and that radio waves might be better used to detect, rather than destroy, enemy aircraft. Hoping to convince the Air Ministry of the need for practical radar research, Watson-Watt, and his assistant Arnold Frederick Wilkins, produced a detailed report entitled *The Detection of Aircraft by Radio Methods*. The report was then presented to Sir Henry Tizard, Chairman of the newly formed Committee for the Scientific Survey of Air Defence.

The first radar trial took place at Daventry in February 1935 and was considered enough of a success to persuade the Air Ministry to finance further research. On 13 May a team of five scientists, led by physicist Edward George Bowen, began setting up a study centre at Orfordness. The inquisitive were told that the purpose of the studies was ionospheric research, but covertly the team were working on experimental ground radar. The project was so secret that even the lighthouse station was reclassified, and the keepers and their families were ordered to evacuate the living quarters. It was soon realized, however, that Orfordness was not a suitable location for the experiments, prompting Watson-Watt to persuade the Air Ministry to purchase Bawdsey Manor in nearby Felixstowe. By December 1935 the team had moved into the large country manor house and renamed it Bawdsey Research Station. Nine months later Watson-Watt became superintendent of the new establishment, and within three years, just in time for World War Two, the Bawdsey team began installing a chain of radar stations all along the east and south coasts of England. The system became known as the Chain Home and was instrumental in helping the RAF win the Battle of Britain.

By 1940 Germany was swiftly advancing through Europe and Churchill realized that in spite of Britain's military force, her knowledge of code breaking and radar, she was still in danger of being invaded. Although America was a strong ally, she was reluctant to be drawn into the conflict, but Britain was prepared to trade some of the country's top defence secrets in exchange for America's assistance. Part of that trade was the radar developments that were first achieved at Orfordness and Bawdsey Research Station. On 8 July 1940 Churchill sent one of his right-hand men, Lord Lothian, on a secret mission to Washington DC to meet with President Roosevelt. A month later the 'Tizard Mission', as it came to be known, headed by Sir Henry Tizard himself and a team of scientists, which included Edward George Bowen, began disclosing Britain's secrets to US Army and Navy experts. Four months later Britain and the United States of America signed an agreement that would provide total exchange of each other's secrets.

Top-secret research continued at Orfordness throughout World War Two, but intelligence reports revealing that the Third Reich was preparing to invade the Suffolk coastline prompted the Air Ministry to erect barbed-wire fences around the Island. Certain unknown lethal defences were installed and eventually, as part of an anti-invasion plan, the surrounding beaches were heavily mined. By 1942 the Island was used more than ever for aircraft experimental work and bomb-dropping exercises. At the same time, large parts of the Suffolk countryside were classed as 'Battle Areas', which resulted in whole villages being evacuated to make way for training grounds.

One of the strangest stories to emerge concerned a small seaside resort called Shingle Street, which is situated just a few miles from Bawdsey. In 1942 the resort was suddenly evacuated overnight with no official explanation given to the concerned residents. Shortly after this incident took place there were rumours that at least one hundred badly burned bodies, presumed to be British servicemen, had been washed up on the shore. Locals speculated that there had been some sort of explosion out at sea and to cover up the disaster the bodies had been buried in the nearby forest. To this day, apart from those in the know, nobody is sure exactly what happened. Whatever it was, it was so secret that the government closed the files on the case for seventy-five years. But rumours of the Shingle Street mystery continued to persist and it is possible the government wanted to quell these because in 1992 they declassified the files – twenty-five years earlier than expected. The files revealed several reasons for the evacuation, which included the laying of a minefield and the testing of new bombs and chemical weapons. But there was no mention of any accident involving British servicemen.

At the close of World War Two Orfordness was still out of bounds to the public. Then in the early 1950s a new station was set up, known as the Atomic Weapons Research Establishment (AWRE), and activities became more secretive than ever. Daily supplies of equipment were delivered and strange buildings were erected. This was followed by the arrival of numerous scientists and specialists. In January 1953 a terrible disaster struck when a gust of wind travelling at 81 mph broke through the riverbanks and flooded the research station. This was to be one of many unusual freak storms to affect the area, but it would be some time before the locals realized that the scientists at Orfordness were carrying out secret weather experiments.

By the mid-1950s the AWRE were testing their most secret atomic devices. According to local historian Gordon Kinsey, in August 1956 the very first major environmental experiment took place in the confines of an earth-shielded building known as the Pagodas or Lab One. A large live object, which was part of an atomic device, was launched with the aim of dropping it on the Australian desert. Whether the 1956 launch achieved its goal is not certain, but scientists were concerned that the components in the object could have been severely damaged by vibration whilst in flight. It is worth noting that Edward George Bowen, one of the original radar researchers at Orfordness, had since become involved in cloud and rain physics. Immediately after the war Bowen had shown an interest in the work initiated by the Americans Langmuir and Schaefer. After spending some time in the United States, he emigrated to the Australian outback where he used his knowledge to try to improve rainfall in that arid climate. It might be that Bowen was involved in the Orfordness/Australian test.

What is extremely curious is that in August 1956, the very same month that Orfordness tested its most secret atomic device, radar operators at the East Anglian USAF bases Bentwaters and Laken-heath reported a series of UFO sightings that lasted for more than six hours. Until the Rendlesham Forest incident became well known, this event was considered Britain's most authentic UFO case. The first sighting was reported at precisely 21.30 hrs on 13 August and continued into the early hours of the morning, with the objects displaying unusual high speeds and amazing manoeuvres. An official USAF report stated that they could not be explained by radar malfunction or unusual weather conditions, and one has to wonder if the Orfordness experiment could have been responsible for attracting these unidentified flying objects.

By 1959 some of the best scientific minds of the time were involved in environmental atomic-weapons research at Orfordness, and in 1963, ten years after the hurricane wind penetrated the Island, Orfordness experienced more freak weather. This time it was a whirlwind, which in only four minutes caused excessive damage to the area. After the storm had passed there was a weird calm, followed by a strange-sounding noise and a build-up of enormous black clouds. Later that year another storm occurred, this time causing extraordinary high tides, which resulted in emergency work having to be carried out by the River Authorities. It was during this period that the research centre attracted the attention of a group of local protesters who felt they had a right to know the nature of the experiments. On 20 June 1964 the group organized a demonstration and attempted to march on the Island, but were halted within three miles of the site. Orfordness, it seems, was not ready to give up her secrets so easily.

In 1971, twenty years after they moved to Orfordness, the AWRE transferred to their headquarters in Aldermaston, Berkshire. Meanwhile, a group of Americans had established a presence on the Island, setting up a research facility on a marshy section of land that had recently been cleared by a British bomb-disposal team. This was land that had been used as a bomb-dumping ground for World War Two pilots ridding their loads before doing emergency landings at RAF Woodbridge. The new site was to be used for a top-secret experimental Over the Horizon project called Cobra Mist. This was a joint effort involving British and US defence departments.

For twenty-five years the Bawdsey station had been operating a secret underground facility. It was not until its closure was announced in 1974 that 'The Hole', as insiders knew it, was revealed to the local press. An Ipswich reporter was invited to view the underground complex and was surprised to find that a small brick building was the entrance to the super-secret facility. After stepping through an ordinary door, he found himself being ushered into a floor-to-ceiling wire cage and, as the bolt on the door closed behind him, he thought it was like something from a science-fiction film. He was then asked to follow the station commander, Group Captain David Rhodes, down a flight of stairs, where he was guided to the radar rooms through a long air-conditioned corridor with deep yellow walls and a shiny linoleum floor.

Bawdsey officially closed in March 1975, when the RAF ensign was lowered and the local rector conducted a simple service. However, in August 1979, four years after its very public closure, the station reopened with several *old* surface-to-air missiles parked on its front lawn. Could this have been a front for other activities? I discovered that during Bawdsey's closure serious work was carried out to extend its underground facility. Gary Collins, a resident of Capel St Andrew, was one of the workers employed in the reconstruction and recalls how huge it was. Gordon Kinsey, who has written extensively on Orfordness and RAF Bawdsey, assured me that the station did reopen, but the underground was reconstructed as an area where the RAF would have launched missiles and no longer operated as a radar station. However, according to a former USAF officer, RAF Bawdsey was still active as a radar station in 1980.

A LITTLE PIECE OF AMERICAN PIE

Sandwiched between Bawdsey and Orfordnesss, and surrounded by miles and miles of thick pine forest, lie the remains of RAF Woodbridge and Bentwaters. Woodbridge, first named Sutton Heath Airfield but known in official circles as the Emergency Landing Ground, was completed in November 1943. It was rumoured that more than a million pine trees were felled to make way for the site, which was to boast one of Britain's widest and longest military runways. Measuring more than 3,000 yards long and 250 yards wide, it covered an area of 159 acres. The site was chosen for its location and fog-free zone (although it was later realized that fog was still a problem), and was intended as one of three wartime emergency airstrips. These were designed specifically to accept damaged and fuel-short fighter planes returning from German raids. In the first two weeks after its completion the new airfield received more than fifty emergency landings. Throughout the rest of the war they used to bulldoze the burning wrecks off the runway as soon as they came to a halt and the remains of the dead pilots were taken to the morgue, which later became the non-commissioned officers' club.

Soon after work began on Woodbridge, construction also began on another airfield less than five miles away. The site was to be officially called RAF Butley and, although work was started in 1942, it was not completed until late 1944. This was due to emergency war work being carried out at other installations throughout the country. During its completion, two buildings known as 'Bentwaters Cottages' were demolished to make way for part of the airfield, and it was recommended that the name Bentwaters be used as it already appeared on the ordnance map. Because of their close proximity, Woodbridge and Bentwaters essentially became part of the same complex and were often referred to as the twin bases.

In 1945 the Woodbridge airfield, having played an important role in World War Two, became a ground for experimental work, with the RAF testing 'Grand Slam' bombs around Orfordness. Four years later its sister base, RAF Bentwaters, which had been used to train pilots to convert from old propeller-driven aircraft to modern Vampire and Meteor jets, formally closed down. Bentwaters would not rest in peace for long, however; within a few years, along with Woodbridge, it would come to life again, only this time it would be home to Uncle Sam's mighty military power – the United States Air Force.

In the summer of 1951 the United States Air Force in Europe began moving into RAF Bentwaters, and within two years they would expand their forces and take over the lease of RAF Woodbridge. The dual complex was to become part of a large group of sophisticated NATO bases scattered throughout the world. In 1979, one year before the Rendlesham Forest incident occurred, seventy-four A-10 tank busters were flown in from Davis-Monthan Air Force Base, Arizona. It was to be the first time the A-10s would be dedicated exclusively to close air support of allied armies. Why did Bentwaters suddenly need so much powerful hardware? Maybe 'Operation Ready Bentwaters', the name given for the massive delivery, offers a clue. But what were they preparing for?

In 1979–80 there was a build-up of extraordinary tensions worldwide and this was of special concern to the United States of America and her allies. It was also the height of the Cold War and everyone was keeping a close eye on the USSR, especially when they invaded Afghanistan on Christmas Day 1979, precisely one year before the UFOs landed in Rendlesham Forest. On 3 June 1980 a US nuclear alert occurred when a computer error indicated a missile attack by the USSR. There were serious problems stirring in Poland and, in early December 1980, just weeks prior to the incident, Prime

Minister Margaret Thatcher warned the USSR not to intervene in the Polish crisis. At the same time the Irish Republican Army was threatening Britain with a Christmas bombing campaign.

Being a NATO installation, it is understandable that Bentwaters would have had its fair share of secrets. According to a reliable military source, the then super-secret stealth F-117 aircraft, which was supposed to still be in test-bed mode, was deployed there during the early 1980s. I was told they would move the A-10 aircraft to the transport ramp and close off the entire east end of the flightline. On these occasions no one was allowed past the mid-field taxiway and all the Tab-V aircraft shelters were closed the whole time they were there. These arrivals and departures would only take place during the night and, apart from those directly involved, no one would be any the wiser (the latter was confirmed by a high-ranking USAF officer). This is interesting considering the existence of F-117s was not made public until they were used overseas on 19 December 1989, when the Americans gave a show of force by briefly invading Panama with the aim of overthrowing General Noriega. It seems the military were very fond of using the month of December for an invasion. The same source also mentioned that an experimental unit (A-7) from Los Angeles Air Station was deployed at the base as a cover for the entire F-117 programme.

However, not everything was what it appeared to be, *Skycrash* (1984), an early book about the Rendlesham Forest incident, featured a photograph of an alleged top-secret missile parked on the side of the Bentwaters airfield. But this was nothing more than a dummy that had been welded together by the base sheet-metal shop. Personnel had ingeniously joined several 50-gallon drums end to end and topped the structure with a white-painted metal cone. No one can blame the authors of *Skycrash* for their error; I understand it looked very realistic when viewed from a distance. Mark Birdsall, editor-in-chief of *Unopened Files*, even sent me a photograph taken in 1984 which featured six of these dummy missiles lined up on a transporter. Apparently, these were situated on the Woodbridge base. Although no one is really sure what their purpose was, it was speculated they were intended to fool spies and partially for local pilots to see as they came into land. Whatever the reason, they were constructed without authorization and the wing commander was heard to yell, 'Get that shit off my runway.' They then disappeared until they got a commander with a better sense of humour.

From their comparatively humble beginnings the twin installation was turned into the equivalent of a small American town. Once on base, one had to drive on the right-hand side of the road and the monetary exchange was strictly US dollars. To the thousands of personnel stationed there, the bases were affectionately referred to as 'a little piece of American pie'.

At the time of the incident the joint installation was under the command of Colonel Gordon E. Williams (later Major General), wing commander of the 81st Tactical Fighter Wing. It is worth mentioning that Colonel Williams' title was misleading to the British because 'wing commander' is recognized as a rank in the Royal Air Force. His deputy was Vice Wing Commander Brian Currie, and under the Wing were four commanders, one for each of the major departments. These consisted of Operations, Maintenance, Rescue Management and the Combat Support Group. Our story revolves around the latter group of personnel who were under the command of Colonel Ted Conrad. The position held by Conrad was commonly known as the base commander because the Combat Support Group's role was basically to manage the housekeeping and take care of security and policing. Lieutenant Colonel Charles I. Halt (later Colonel) was the deputy base commander. There has also been confusion as to the role of Conrad and Halt, especially Halt, who was one of the primary witnesses to the incident. It had erroneously been thought that Halt was deputy in command of the actual operation, but this was not the case, in fact Halt was subordinate to the Wing. The confusion did not escape the United States Air Force, and a few years ago they decided to do something about it: Combat Support Group commanders are now no longer referred to as base commanders. Subordinate to Lieutenant Colonel Halt was the commander of the 81st Security Police and Law

Enforcement Squadron, Major Malcolm F. Zickler (later Lieutenant Colonel).

The 67th Aerospace Rescue and Recovery Squadron, who have since changed their name and are now part of a special operations unit, were tenants of the 81st Tactical Fighter Wing. The squadron had been stationed at RAF Woodbridge since 1969, when they transferred from Moron Air Force Base in Spain. The ARRS were America's equivalent of Britain's elite Special Air Service and were recognized as the world's largest rescue squadron. They were primarily trained to recover space-mission splashdowns in the Atlantic and Indian oceans but, following the cutbacks by NASA and the termination of the lunar missions, they concentrated on carrying out air rescues behind enemy lines. They were also known and praised for their aid in rescuing civilians. A little-known fact, however, is that during the Cold War they also operated from their Icelandic sub-base in Keflavik, where they rescued many a Soviet trawler in distress. The finest of this elite squadron were the para rescues, or PJs as they were called. These were the highly professional men trained to operate in all areas of rescue.

In 1980 they flew the Lockheed HC-130 Hercules, which was fitted with an air-to-air refuelling system and special advanced rescue avionics. They also used the HH-53 helicopter, known as the Jolly Green Giant, which was ideal for sea rescues and lifting crash survivors to safety. Their sophisticated instruments included a special screen that allowed them to see surfaces in all weather conditions. During their tenure on the Woodbridge base, they were known to carry out simulated emergency exercises, and these were often performed during the twilight hours. When alerted for duty, the crew would speedily take off in their Jolly Green Giants, using a special device called the Apollo beacon, a spin-off from the Apollo space shots. This special transmitter would enable the crew to locate troubled or downed military aircraft. Whilst on the Woodbridge base they were sometimes called to assist the RAF with local air and sea rescues.

The Air Force Office of Special Investigations (AFOSI) was also a tenant of the 81st Tactical Fighter Wing. This unit was predominately placed on the Bentwaters installation, next to the Law Enforcement Office. The AFOSI is an agency that polices the USAF and its personnel are called 'special agents'. Although their role is intended to assist commanders in dealing with criminal investigations, they are known to operate through their own means, which more often than not annoys senior officers.

The Combat Support Group was, among other things, responsible for base security, and this was the job of the 81st Security Police and Law Enforcement Squadrons, which also included the fire department. The security police, or SPs as they are known, were seldom seen by the public because they were primarily assigned to protect the sensitive areas, such as the weapons storage area, non-alert parking area (NAPA), the aircraft and the flightlines. Both police squadrons carried weapons, such as the M-16 and a weapon capable of shooting down a helicopter or small aircraft. There was also a special department within the Security Police Squadron, known as Security Police Investigations (SPI), which liaised directly with the AFOSI. The Law Enforcement Squadron, known as LEs, is the military's version of the civilian police. They would be responsible for watching over personnel, keeping an eye out for drugs, girls in the dorms, greeting people on the front gates, traffic control and reporting crimes in general. These squadrons were all under the same leadership and would assist each other whenever there was an emergency or a problem on the installation. The personnel primarily involved in the Rendlesham Forest incident were from the Security Police and Law Enforcement Squadrons.

Many of the young recruits assigned to RAF Bentwaters and Woodbridge had joined the Air Force hoping to make a career out of it. Instead, they were disillusioned to find themselves standing on guard duty for up to eight hours a shift, sometimes even as much as twelve. In the middle of a Suffolk winter, on the perimeter of a dark and spooky forest and with much time to think, it often got to the young airmen. I was alarmed to hear of cases of drug and alcohol abuse, mental breakdowns and attempted suicides among personnel.

However, not all the attempted suicides were genuine. One such incident concerned a young airman who was so distressed he thought that by pretending to kill himself he would be retired from the Air Force. Steve La Plume was a young nineteen-year-old assigned to Law Enforcement from late 1980 to early 1981. Although not involved in the December incident, in early January 1981 he witnessed two UFOs over the Woodbridge base, and from that moment on things seemed to go downhill for Airman La Plume. More often than not he would end up on guard duty at the Woodbridge east gate, which looks out on to the desolate forest. La Plume hated the boring work and was frustrated because he was not doing the job he claims he had enlisted for. After only a few months in the service he began making enquiries on how to get a release on a breach of contract clause, but the Bentwaters legal department offered various reasons why this would not work.

It was during a bout of drinking at Woodbridge 'all ranks' club that La Plume realized a possible way out. Dazed in the stupor of alcohol, he decided that an attempted suicide should do the trick. On returning to his dorm he tore off his jacket and, using his diving knife, proceeded to slit open his belly. But the knife was far too blunt to do a proper job and in desperation he broke open his razor to extract a sharp blade. This seemed to work and, careful not to break open his intestines, he started slashing his belly from one side to the other. At that moment all he could think about was getting out of Bentwaters and going home to his family.

Dragging himself to the wall phone, situated just outside the barracks, La Plume dialled the Law Enforcement desk and shouted down the phone, 'I fucked up.' When a patrol arrived to pick him up, he flipped and ran off towards the soccer field. La Plume was a trained track runner but he was wounded and bleeding and after quite a chase the two patrolmen finally caught up with him. Once he had recovered from his ordeal he was summoned to appear before Major Zickler. La Plume told the commander that he was sick and tired of standing around watching the paint peel and wanted to do what he had been trained for. Just to make sure Zickler understood, he threatened that if he was put back on duty watching the forest, he was going to shoot down an aircraft the first chance he got. That apparently did it, and La Plume was instructed to report immediately to the base psychologist, where he pleaded depression and emotional instability. His release document stated 'failure to conform to military standards', and he received an honourable discharge. La Plume clearly wanted some action and shortly after his release he became a mercenary. If the USAF could not find a war for him to fight, some foreign country could.

Understandably, the USAF does not want to publicize its problems, yet their suicide figures for the last decade are very disturbing indeed. In 1996 General Charles Roadman, the US Air Force Surgeon General, realized there was a problem and formed an integrated team of experts to deal with the large rate of suicides. The team put forward eleven recommendations to the US Air Force Chief of Staff and senior leadership. A report published in their in-house news service for January 1998 revealed a drop in the suicide rate for the first time in years, with the lowest number of active-duty deaths being only forty-five. But, as the good general said, this was still forty-five too many.

Most of those newly assigned to the Security Police and Law Enforcement Squadrons were just teenagers. For the majority of new recruits at Bentwaters and Woodbridge, it was their first time outside the United States of America. Fortunately, they had been born too late to experience the horrors of Vietnam, and for this we must be truly thankful. But for those whose lives were changed for ever, and for those whose nightmares still haunt them, the Rendlesham Forest incident was *their* Vietnam.

THE EARLY YEARS

Brenda Butler and Dot Street are two Suffolk women who have gone down in history as being the first people to take an interest in the Rendlesham Forest incident. In fact, Brenda was on the case within days of it occurring. I was familiar with their early research, which was published in *Skycrash*, co-authored with ufologist Jenny Randles, but little had been heard about them in recent years. This may have been of their own making, because Dot had long since left the area and although Brenda was still intrigued with the case she had made little attempt to make it known. I thought it was time I caught up with them.

Neil Cunningham, a media friend and a keen researcher of the paranormal, had planned to join me on my trip to Woodbridge. We had arranged to meet Brenda Butler and later intended to visit the scene of the UFO landings in Rendlesham Forest. I was looking forward to meeting Brenda and was concerned because we were running one hour late due to traffic hold-ups on the motorway. When we finally arrived at the Wilford Bridge, a typical country public house in the village of Melton, Brenda was sitting outside in the shade with her friend John Hanson. It was a glorious summer's day.

After a late lunch, Brenda and John offered to accompany Neil and me to the landing sites. I was pleased to have Brenda along because at the time all I had to go on were a few drawings and vague instructions from the witnesses. The thought of visiting the forest gave me an eerie feeling, but it was a beautiful sight to see and reminded me of how much I missed the country. As we approached the initial landing site Brenda pointed to an area that had been cleared of trees soon after the incident, which allegedly was due to radiation contamination. There were now healthy young Corsican pines growing, but we could clearly see a prominent bare patch at the precise spot where Brenda said the initial landing had taken place. As we moved through the forest she guided us to a clearing which was another suspected landing site. This appeared to be the exact location where the second landing had occurred. We then moved to a field adjacent to the forest near Capel Green, where Larry Warren believes a landing took place. At the far end of the field were situated three houses, and although it is several miles in the distance at night one can see the Orfordness lighthouse beacon as if in a central position.

Later that day Neil and I met up with Chris Pennington (known in the music business as Chris Penny). Chris and Brenda have shared a home together in the Suffolk village of Leiston for almost twenty years, although they have been friends for much longer. Chris was one of the first civilians to hear about the incident, but right from the beginning had kept a very low profile. In fact his name has never been publicly associated with the case. In 1980 Chris was a country and western musician who was often booked to perform on the American bases. He soon realized, however, that if it were discovered that he had any knowledge of what had occurred in Rendlesham Forest, it would result in him losing his base pass. It eventually did.

On New Year's Eve 1980, Chris had thrown a drinks party at his home and invited some friends from the American bases. It was at this particular gathering that news of the incident would first reach his ears. The lively party was in full swing when Steve Roberts (pseudonym) approached Chris and ushered him into the hall to talk to him privately. Roberts had something important on his mind and he seemed haunted. He shared an incredible story with Chris of how he had witnessed a strange encounter in the forest a few nights earlier, where alien entities were seen repairing their spaceship. Chris listened with interest as the airman recounted a series of events that could have come straight out of the pages of a science-fiction novel.

Although Roberts' integrity was never in question it was still a hard story for Chris to digest. But that was not the only time he would hear of the incident. That same evening, Sam Bowman, who worked as a barman at the Bentwaters officers' club, had overheard a conversation between two officers. Apparently something had landed in the forest, causing the area to be severely scorched. Because of Brenda's interest in the paranormal and UFOs, Chris suggested they each speak to her as soon as possible. Unfortunately, that was the last time they would hear from Bowman, who suddenly disappeared without anyone knowing what had become of him.

After listening to Roberts' story, Brenda telephoned Dot Street. Dot's interest in the case stemmed from her background in UFO research. She had worked with a local group called Borderline Science Investigation and knew the procedures for contacting base officials with regards to enquiries. But when Brenda telephoned her in early January 1981 she was too busy, and it was mid-February before she was able to assist in any field research. However, she did manage to start the ball rolling by making telephone enquiries and Brenda began questioning personnel from the twin bases and putting the word out to the locals. Dot had recently joined another UFO group, the British UFO Research Association (BUFORA) and, realizing it might be a genuine case, coupled with her duty to the cause, she pressured Brenda to agree to let her inform the group of the incident. Brenda was not keen on the idea and for the time being wanted to keep it between the two of them, partly to protect her friend Steve Roberts and partly because she is a very secretive and shy individual. But after much insistence from her colleague, she reluctantly agreed to cooperate. Dot contacted Jenny Randles but apparently she was busy writing a book at the time, so Dot called Bob Easton, who was about to become an investigator coordinator for the eastern region of BUFORA, but although he made several enquiries he failed to come up with any significant evidence to prove that there had been an incident.

As soon as she was able, Dot contacted RAF Bentwaters to arrange an appointment for herself and Brenda to visit the installation. The appointment was made for 18 February. On their arrival, a British secretary approached them insisting they talk to her boss, Squadron Leader Donald Moreland. Dot thought it strange that Moreland's secretary should be so persistent they meet him. It turned out that Moreland was the British liaison officer for the joint installation. Although he greeted them with enthusiasm and did not deny something had occurred, he was reluctant to discuss it, claiming it was a Ministry of Defence issue.

Soon after the Bentwaters visit, Brenda received an anonymous telephone call from an alleged witness, who agreed to talk provided his identity was kept secret. His story was basically the same as Steve Roberts', adding that the object was thirty feet wide and that the following day there were scorch marks on the trees and indentations on the ground where the object had landed. When Brenda asked him about aliens, he denied there were any entities present, claiming that part of the story was merely an invention. On 20 February Brenda received a call from another Bentwaters source. This airman did not claim to have been present at the landing site but had heard the story from someone who had. He described an almost identical account to Roberts', claiming that three small entities had been involved. He also told Brenda that the ground had glowed after the object had taken off and for a few days afterwards the site had been cordoned off to civilians and anyone approaching it was told there had been an air crash. It was a busy day for Brenda because a few hours later another call came through, and this caller had something new to offer. He told her that two days after the incident a local farmer had called the base for a second time, complaining that something flying overhead had caused a strong reaction in his cattle, and that his lights and television had suffered interference. Brenda and Dot traced the farmer to the nearby village of Eyke, where they found Victor Higgins. According to the researchers, Higgins had complained to Bentwaters, requesting compensation for injury to one of his cows. It turned out that a vehicle had hit the animal when it ran on to the road in fear of a low-flying craft. When Higgins first complained he was more or less sent packing, but after hearing about a UFO incident he called the base again. This time, however, he mentioned the UFO and was surprised to receive VIP attention, with the base even sending a car to collect him and take him to Bentwaters to discuss his grievances with the commanders. The researchers later discovered that Higgins had been paid a large sum of money for injury done to his cow. Soon afterwards he left the area and purchased a smallholding in the West Country.

During their investigations Brenda and Dot tried to talk to another man, also called Vic, who lived in one of the houses adjacent to the alleged landing sites. Vic was a local milkman who took care of a small herd of cattle that grazed on the field near his home. The researchers questioned him on several occasions but he always denied any knowledge of the incident. One of my American contacts put me in touch with Masie Pettit, a civilian who had worked at Bentwaters for twenty-five years. At the time of the incident Masie lived not far from the suspected landing site, but has since moved from that location. She remembers there was a problem concerning cattle. 'The man you need to talk to is Victor Cuttings, but he is not on the telephone,' she told me. 'He knows what happened; it was his cattle that were scared. It scared a lot of them. I saw the stampede of cattle myself.' I wondered if this could be the same Vic who Brenda and Dot had referred to in their book *Skycrash*. Brenda confirmed that it was the same person, but pointed out that the man Masie was referring to was Victor Higgins. Now I really was confused! 'It was his cattle who were stampeding, not Vic Cuttings',' said Brenda. 'He [Cuttings] was not a farmer but only took care of the cattle, Dot and I interviewed him several times but he denied there were any problems.' Cuttings would milk the cows around 3 a.m. every morning yet does not recall any unusual activity in the area. Considering his house was one of the three properties adjacent to the alleged landing sites and the cattle had grazed on the field where Larry Warren claims the incident occurred, one would assume Cuttings would have seen or heard something.

David Boast is a local gamekeeper who lives with his wife and family in a farmhouse on the field facing the landing sites. The researchers claim that the first time they spoke to Boast, on 24 February 1981, he mentioned having seen a brightly lit object out in the field, but has since always refused to discuss it with anyone. Almost three years later, in October 1983, Brenda and Dot would take ufologist Jenny Randles to visit the family and, whilst the two women conversed with Mr Boast, Jenny chatted with one of the Boast children. In a radio interview the following year Jenny told listeners that the child had asked her whether she had come across anyone who had seen the little men. She also asked Jenny if she had heard about the UFO, saying, 'It was so big, it should have hit the trees when it came down.' Due to the time lapse, was the child referring to something she had overheard from local rumours, or did she actually witness the incident from her bedroom window during that Christmas week of 1980?

I interviewed Mrs Boast, who assured me that the family knew nothing about any UFO incident. I asked about her daughter's comments, but she was adamant that the child could not have seen anything either. She insisted that if anyone went close to the house, especially at night, the dogs would have been alerted, and if they continued barking her husband would have got out of bed to see what was causing the disturbance. 'There was no disturbance that I recall. The dogs didn't wake us,' she stressed. I explained that some of the US military had reported passing her home during the nights in question and again asked her if she was certain there had been no unusual activity. She pointed out that several media types had contacted them and if they had known anything at all they could have made a fortune by telling their story.

However, some people were convinced that David Boast was hiding the truth and would not discuss it because the Ministry of Defence had approached him. There were even claims that the family had been threatened or bribed by defence officials or by Boast's employer. I decided to contact Sir Edward Greenwell, the landowner who I suspected David Boast worked for. Greenwell gave me his brother's telephone number and suggested I speak to him because it was his property I was referring to. Major James Greenwell was not at home when I called, but his wife was willing to take my questions. She had heard of the incident but knew nothing about the animals being disturbed, and she really could not help me because, according to her, it had not concerned them. Even if a UFO had not landed near the Boast residence, one assumes the dogs would have been disturbed by the patrol that was chasing the lights across the field. Having followed the same route through the forest where Colonel Halt claims to have walked, my party was not even close to the Boast family home when the dogs started barking, and they did not stop until we moved away from the area. It is difficult to imagine that the residents, who were adjacent to the landing sites, neither saw nor heard anything unusual. However, if Major Greenwell was a military officer at the time of the incident he would have been committed to the Official Secrets Act. It is only speculation, but if the Ministry of Defence consulted Greenwell, they might have recommended that he discuss the need for silence with his tenants and employees. According to Dot Street, an American officer from RAF Bentwaters rented the property that lay between Boast's and Cuttings' home.

In the early part of January 1981 investigator of the paranormal Paul Begg was told by a civilian radar operator at RAF Watton in Norfolk that an uncorrelated target was picked up on radar sometime during the last week of December 1980. It appears the target was tracked coming in from the coastal area and was lost somewhere over Rendlesham Forest. Begg's source claimed he had not been on duty when the incident occurred but his colleague had. Begg contacted BUFORA ufologist Jenny Randles, and sometime during February she telephoned Bob Easton hoping he could follow up the lead as it was in his region. It was then that Easton brought up Dot Street's report about the lights seen over Rendlesham Forest. He had also heard about a US airman who had been in touch with American investigator Lucius Farish, claiming he was a witness to an encounter near Woodbridge. The information had come from Norman Oliver, editor of the BUFORA journal. Jenny had not been too impressed with the Watton incident, mostly for lack of sub-

stantial evidence and because Begg's source seemed to be describing
a chain of events that were second or third hand in some instances.
However, after collating the three reports, on 21 February 1981 she
wrote a brief item for *Flying Saucer Review* entitled 'Military Contact
Alleged at Airbase' which was published in volume 26, number 6,
1981.

Some time later, Jenny contacted the Watton source, whom she
named David Potts (as a pseudonym), and he told her that a couple
of days after the tracking, RAF Watton had received a visit from a
group of American Air Force officers, supposedly from intelligence,
who requested to see the radar reports. The Americans told the radar
operators that a metallic UFO had crash-landed in a forest near
Ipswich and the patrols who had gone out to investigate had
experienced difficulty with their vehicle lights and engines cutting
out, thus having to continue on foot. It seems the object had been
on the ground for several hours, during which time entities were
witnessed.

In June 1984, three and a half years after Paul Begg contacted
her, and after an extensive search of her files, Jenny found the
original notes recorded from her first telephone conversation with
David Potts. Although in the meantime she had written two articles
referring to the Watton report, she claims she did not consider the
information relevant at the time. It was not until the publication of
Skycrash that her misplaced notes revealed that the base commander
and several officers had been called out to the forest from a party on
the base. Potts also revealed to Jenny that the base commander was
communicating with alien entities.

Jenny Randles has never disclosed the true identity of David
Potts and I had been unable to locate Paul Begg, from whom I had
hoped to learn more about the mysterious source. RAF Watton had
long since closed and I realized it would be difficult to find an
operator who had been on duty during that time. I was grateful,
therefore, to Nick Pope when he introduced me to Nigel Kerr, a
radio presenter from East Anglia. In 1980 Kerr was a radar operator
stationed at RAF Watton, which was situated approximately

thirty-five miles north of Woodbridge. Unlike Bentwaters and Woodbridge, Watton was home to the Royal Air Force.

It turned out that Nigel Kerr had actually been on duty that week. He recalls the incident happened sometime around the Christmas holidays, during which time there was a skeleton staff on duty. He clearly remembers the call from Bentwaters reporting that there was a 'flashing light in the sky', and although he had received similar reports during his tenure at Watton, he thought the Bentwaters sighting was a bit wild. On checking the radar he realized there was indeed something on their approach line, and at first he thought it was a helicopter. However, it remained stationary long enough for it to show up for three to four sweeps across their screens before it dissipated. He thought no more of it until he read about the incident three years later in *The News of the World* newspaper. Nigel Kerr's story obviously tallies with Paul Begg's report, but Kerr seems to know nothing about the story related to Jenny Randles. This may be due to the fact that his shift rotated – whereby he would work two day shifts, two night shifts, followed by a two-day break. It is therefore possible that when the Americans turned up Kerr was off duty. It is interesting that Kerr cannot recall the incident ever being discussed among the operators. I did not have the impression that Nigel Kerr was holding anything back, on the contrary he was very interested in the case and was as keen as me to know what had happened in Rendlesham Forest.

After getting nowhere fast with her enquiries, Brenda decided to call the Ministry of Defence to see if she could glean any answers from them, but she was told she would need to put her request in writing, which she duly did. Four weeks later she received a reply from Mr Weedon from Defence Secretariat DS8. He informed her that the Ministry of Defence did not have a full-time department for investigating or studying UFOs, and failed to answer any questions relating to the incident. Brenda and Dot continued their enquiries but were told that most of the military witnesses had been transferred to other installations, so there were only the locals to question. But that was to prove a difficult task too, for those who were willing to talk in the first few weeks were suddenly less inclined to discuss the matter.

In October 1981 as the newly appointed Director of Investigations for BUFORA Jenny Randles organized a meeting in London, where she met Dot Street for the first time. The Rendlesham Forest incident was on the agenda and because Jenny had not personally met Brenda she suggested that Dot get together with her colleague and document all their available evidence. For the second time Jenny collated their information with the Watton story and Lucius Farish's mysterious witness, this time writing a more detailed report entitled 'The Rendlesham Forest Mystery'. The paper was circulated to the forty subscribers of her 'Northern UFO Newsletter' and later published in *Flying Saucer Review*, volume 27, number 6, 1982.

I tracked down Lucius Farish, hoping he could shed further light on the US military witness who was supposed to have contacted him in early 1981. Farish told me that the information he had passed on had been somewhat exaggerated when it was featured in *Flying Saucer Review*. Contrary to the story, he said he had not been approached by anyone from the USAF who claimed 'something big' had happened in Woodbridge about the turn of the year. Apparently, he had received the information in some correspondence. It enclosed a letter, alleged to be from an airman's wife, describing a UFO incident on a British base in late December 1980. Sometime in February, Farish had posted a note to Norman Oliver, enclosing the portion of the letter concerning the British incident. The story was later published in *Skycrash*, only this time it had grown somewhat more. In the *Flying Saucer Review* article, Jenny saw fit to point out that the report could have been based on rumours, and when she later approached Norman Oliver, he could not recall the precise details. It seems her report was written based on information received from Bob Easton. One can understand why the case never really got off the ground in those early days: much of it was built up on second- or third-hand information and even the military witnesses were unwilling to be named. In fact, although his identity has never been revealed, the only person to give the case any credibility in the early days was Brenda and Chris's friend Steve Roberts.

After months of being fobbed off by the Ministry of Defence, Brenda and Dot were becoming agitated. Dot decided to telephone them again, only this time she was all set to record the conversation. She need not have bothered, because when she spoke to Peter Watkins, from DS8, he wasted no time in explaining that the Ministry of Defence had no knowledge of the incident she was referring to.

In July 1982 Brenda heard from a farm worker that local landowner and farmer Captain Sheepshanks had called the Bentwaters base to complain about a UFO that had disturbed his livestock on 27 December. As soon as Dot heard the news she telephoned the Sheepshanks' home and spoke to the captain's son Andrew. According to Dot, when she asked him about a UFO sighting, he told her that it was he who had witnessed it and it had indeed disturbed their cattle, which is why they had called the base. Andrew promised to call Dot and arrange a suitable time and place to meet to discuss the incident, but he failed to do so. After a couple of days with no word, Brenda and Dot decided to visit the Sheepshanks' farm unannounced. Captain Sheepshanks was not amused at the intrusion and asked the women to leave the premises immediately. Apart from being a high-profile figure in the local community, Sheepshanks was also a member of the elite Anglo/American Social Committee. I had heard about this committee. The American commanders used to entertain the English with numerous cocktail parties as part of a local public-relations peacekeeping strategy: some of the land surrounding the base belonged to Sheepshanks and, of course, it was always good to keep the locals happy. The leader of this elite little group was the late Grace Agate, a longstanding member of the Suffolk District Council and a local magistrate.

I was familiar with Andrew Sheepshanks; we had met several times at social events. I realized I needed to talk to him but had misplaced his telephone number and was not sure of his location. Having heard that Captain Sheepshanks was a difficult man, especially when it came to discussing the incident, I was reluctant to call him. Much to my surprise, he was extremely polite; when I asked him about the UFO he was not at all offended and gave me his son's telephone number, suggesting I talk to him directly because he was the one who was quoted as having seen it.

Andrew remembered the incident but apologized at having to disappoint me because he had not witnessed anything himself. He recalled that a few years afterwards a Japanese film crew had turned up at the house. They wanted to know about the Sheepshanks' cattle, because they had heard they were late dropping their calves after the incident. Andrew thought it was highly amusing because they only had bulls, and told them so. However, he was sure that the gamekeeper David Boast had seen something in the field, but had later denied it because of the constant pestering by ufologists and curiosity seekers. He reminded me that it was a rural area and the locals were very private people and may have been afraid of ridicule. When I asked him if he had ever seen anything strange in Rendlesham Forest, I was surprised to hear that there was a place near the Woodbridge base that he had found very spooky. The area Andrew was referring to sounded very similar to where the incident had taken place. As a youngster he would often walk his dogs through the forest, but it seems they would never go anywhere near this particular spot.

In 1982 Jenny Randles discussed the incident with one of her BUFORA colleagues, Bristol-based investigator Ian Mrzyglod, who in turn contacted the Swindon Centre for UFO Research (SCUFORI). The group decided to visit Woodbridge and set about making arrangements with Dot to spend a weekend camping in Rendlesham Forest. Their plans to research the case were not a great success because most of the military witnesses had now been stationed elsewhere – or so they thought – and the locals were refusing to discuss the incident with anyone. The group settled on examining the landing site for radiation, but Dot claims that much to her annoyance they examined the wrong site. It probably would not have made much difference as it was now twenty months after the incident and it was unlikely they would have found much evidence of radiation contamination. Needless to say, SCUFORI's report was negative, which is understandable considering the obstacles put before them and, of course, there is not much that can be achieved in a weekend. Their findings, which were published in the journal *Probe Report*, were sceptical in the extreme. Not only did they claim there was insufficient evidence to support the case, but their proposal, that it be filed away and forgotten as there would be little prospect of any such proof being uncovered, was very disappointing, especially to Brenda and Dot. The two researchers, who had spent considerable time investigating the case and were positively convinced that an unusual event had taken place, decided it was time to get back to normal living. Their domestic lives had certainly suffered in recent times, and Dot blamed the case for the breakdown of her marriage. Probably sharing in their disappointment, Jenny suggested they write a book about the case, but the women had already considered the idea and did not think there was enough evidence to support such a venture. It would be some time before things would hot up.

In February 1983 American reporters following up an article in *OMNI* contacted Jenny, who was told that the journal had published an interview with Colonel Ted Conrad, with comments from Squadron Leader Moreland. Jenny put the reporters in touch with Brenda and Dot, but not having read the article they made a decision to stay silent, thus the media lost interest. After several attempts at questioning the Ministry of Defence and receiving constant denials that there was such an incident, the researchers had all but given up. But later that month Jenny received confirmation from the Ministry of Defence that USAF personnel at RAF Woodbridge had seen unusual lights, but no explanation for the occurrence was forthcoming. Jenny suspected that the release of this information might have been prompted by Moreland's comments going on record. A few weeks later she received a letter from Barry

Greenwood, an American investigator with Citizens Against UFO Secrecy (CAUS). Greenwood had seen her name mentioned in the *OMNI* article and read her report in *Flying Saucer Review*. It turned out that his colleague Larry Fawcett had been contacted by a witness just prior to the *OMNI* article and was now convinced it was a genuine case. Enclosed with the letter was a witness statement by Art Wallace, the pseudonym used by Larry Warren. Jenny informed Dot about the new witness and she immediately called Larry Fawcett. The retired American civil police officer from Connecticut told her about the witness, explaining that the young man, who was afraid for his life, had talked about his nightmare involvement in the Bentwaters incident. Warren was claiming he had been one of a number of airmen to witness a huge UFO landing and he wanted the story to be told. For the next few months Dot communicated by telephone with Fawcett and Warren, and for the first time in ages it seemed they were progressing with the case.

The big breakthrough came in July 1983 when Larry Fawcett sent Dot a copy of an official memorandum composed by the deputy base commander, Lieutenant Colonel Charles I. Halt. The document, which had been sent to the Ministry of Defence, confirmed that there had been not one but two unusual events, one involving a mechanical UFO. With the new-found document in her possession, Dot called RAF Bentwaters on 11 August to speak to its author. Having personally listened to the recorded conversation between Dot and Lieutenant Colonel Halt, I can confirm that after Dot told him she had a copy of the document there was a long silence. When Halt finally responded, he wanted to know what document and incident she was referring to. He asked her if she was the person who had caused trouble a year earlier – something to do with talking to the local press about nuclear weapons allegedly being on the base. Dot denied it was anything to do with her. He then fired a number of questions at the researcher, but she was not prepared to discuss anything on the telephone and suggested they meet in person. Halt was clearly concerned and explained that he did not want this to be an issue that might interfere with his job. 'I gave that to an RAF officer to be passed to the Ministry of Defence. They assured me it would never be released,' he told her.

The next day Brenda and Dot met with Lieutenant Colonel Halt, and the first question he asked was did they have a tape recorder with them. Apparently, someone had tipped him off that Dot had recorded his conversation of the previous day. Having assured him they did not have a recorder, the meeting began. The researchers showed him the memorandum and he confirmed it was genuine but was anxious to know where they had acquired it. He appeared to be extremely upset that it was in the public domain but refused to discuss the matter further. Dot, still seemingly very let down about losing a proper audience with Halt, told me how ufologist and solicitor Harry Harris later admitted he had alerted the commander to the fact that she had recorded his conversation. This all seemed very odd considering the Manchester-based solicitor was supposedly acting as an advisor to the researchers. Although Harris later apologized, Dot still feels she was betrayed. In a 1999 interview she told me:

> He [Halt] flatly refused to talk to us because of the tip-off he had received from Harry Harris, spilling the beans that I had recorded his conversation. He [Halt] warned me it was illegal, but I only used a microphone taped to my telephone, there was no bug in the phone as I expect Halt thought.

The researchers would later discover that Harris and his colleague Mike Sacks had been invited to Bentwaters to discuss the incident with Halt. Presumably, in exchange for them agreeing to sign a contract of sorts, forbidding them to talk about the incident with anyone, including 'those women', the men were allegedly offered privileged information. When I contacted Harris about his involvement, he insisted that he had played a very minor role in the investigation. That may be so, but in answer to all my questions, I received only negative replies, inasmuch as he claimed to know nothing and could therefore not assist me in my enquiries. According to Brenda, Harris later admitted there was no such deal with Halt.

Colonel Halt had certainly been curious about Brenda and Dot's interest in the incident and had agreed to the meeting in order to find out how much they knew. However, unbeknown to them, he had been told several weeks earlier that the document was to be released through the US Freedom of Information Act. But what he did not probably realize was that the memorandum would find its way back to Woodbridge, Suffolk. This must have been a terrible shock to him at the time.

On 18 August Brenda, Dot and Jenny made an unscheduled visit to the Ministry of Defence Main Building at Whitehall. Not having arranged an appointment, it was some time before Pam Titchmarsh from DS8 turned up at the reception to meet them. When questioned about Halt's memorandum, Titchmarsh admitted they had a copy, or something similar, and that the report had been passed to their 'specialist staffs' who decided it was not a security risk. Titchmarsh assured the researchers that the Ministry of Defence had not instigated the public release of the document, that it had been released by the US authorities under the terms of the Freedom of Information Act. Brenda asked about a covering letter that Squadron Leader Moreland had told her he had sent with Halt's memorandum, and Titchmarsh admitted that there was such a letter. I have often wondered why nobody thought to ask for a copy of Moreland's covering letter. There is a clue, perhaps, in Nicholas Redfern's book *A Covert Agenda*, where he describes how Jenny Randles told him that the letter was simply an endorsement of Halt's credibility. Nonetheless, even though the researchers clearly believed the letter contained nothing of any great significance, it seems somewhat strange that nobody checked this out for themselves.

A week after their visit to the Ministry of Defence, Brenda, Dot, Chris Pennington and Harris attended the International BUFORA Congress in Buckinghamshire, which was chaired by their colleague Jenny Randles. Dot was still somewhat annoyed that BUFORA, Britain's biggest and supposedly most credible UFO organization, had not taken the case seriously, and she aimed to put forward her complaints at the meeting. However, things would take a strange turn, because on this particular day Dot had a big surprise in store for BUFORA. Jenny had not planned to raise the question of the Rendlesham Forest incident because she had now joined Brenda and Dot in writing a book about the subject. But it was at a closed meeting in the early hours of the morning that Dot produced the best available evidence for the case, a copy of Lieutenant Colonel Halt's official memorandum. BUFORA must have wondered what hit them when she threw the document on the table for all to see.

On 31 August Brenda and Dot visited RAF Bentwaters again. This time they wanted to alert Squadron Leader Moreland and Lieutenant Colonel Halt that the press were on to the case. Moreland did not appear to be too perturbed because it was Halt who had signed the memorandum, not he. As far as Moreland was concerned he had only been following protocol. Whilst in his office the researchers made a suggestion that the memorandum might be a fake. Moreland beckoned to his secretary to pass him the 'UFO' file and, after rummaging through a fair amount of paperwork, he produced an identical copy of the document. Before leaving the installation the researchers stopped by to see Halt. They thought it only fair that he too should know that the press were sniffing around. He was very concerned and told the women that he hoped the press would not mention his name because he did not want to hurt his family. Dot pointed out that this would not be easily avoidable because, after all, the memorandum was signed by Halt himself.

The researchers were almost through writing *Skycrash* and were feeling uneasy about the sudden media interest for fear it would interfere with their proposed publication. But it seemed that the story was going to be published with or without their contribution and Harry Harris advised them it was better to assist the newspaper, if only to make sure it was told as accurately as possible. A few months later, on 2 October 1983, *The News of the World* featured a front-page story of the incident.

I was quite surprised to discover that Brenda and Dot had kept all their early notes. When I visited Dot at her home in Hampshire

I saw for myself the work she had put into the case in those early days. It would be much later that Brenda would share some of her files with me. Dot had recorded almost every telephone conversation, including those of military personnel and the Ministry of Defence. I was fortunate to listen to some of the recordings, staying up until the early hours and stopping in between to share a Chinese takeaway with Dot and her partner Howard. Before my arrival, she had warned me that I would need a week to hear them all: she was right, but I listened to what I had time for. I would have the opportunity to listen to more recordings when she visited my home in London a few months later. Dot's reason for recording the telephone conversations was simply because she was not a very speedy writer and she wanted to make sure she had the facts right, rather than to try to recall them through memory. In 1998 an anonymous person had offered her two hundred pounds for the tapes, but she flatly refused. 'I was insulted,' she told me. 'Not only did it cost me more than nine hundred pounds in phone calls, mostly to the United States, but they are part of my personal research material. And besides, it wouldn't be fair on the people who were recorded, so they are not for sale.' I was grateful to be allowed to listen to the tapes and publish some quotes because I understand there are very few people who have had the privilege. Fortunately, Chris Pennington had recently visited her home and labelled them so it was easier to determine the content of each cassette.

There are some highly amusing episodes among the collection and Dot certainly has a sense of humour, which may have contributed to why she was able to gather as much information as she did. One of the most humorous recordings is her half-hour conversation with a Ministry of Defence employee from DS8. When she had no luck with him she insisted on speaking to his boss. 'My boss is not interested in UFOs,' he exclaimed. To which Dot replied, 'Why not, this is the UFO department isn't it?' Even the man from the ministry could not help but find that amusing.

THE MYSTERIOUS STEVE ROBERTS

Steve Roberts plays an important role in this story because he was the first military contact to leak information that would eventually attract worldwide attention. Very little was known about this mysterious player, except that he was an ambitious security police-man based at RAF Bentwaters. Brenda Butler and her boyfriend Chris Pennington had met Roberts a few years earlier at a local public house. Chris was performing and Brenda had gone along to the venue to support him. It was on this particular evening that Steve Roberts had struck up a conversation with her, and it turned out that he was also a keen fan of country and western music. From that chance meeting all three had remained good friends ever since.

It was 2 January 1981 when Roberts told Brenda what had taken place in Rendlesham Forest. Less than forty-eight hours earlier he had mentioned it briefly to Chris, who suggested he talk directly to his girlfriend because of her interest in UFOs. Roberts said an incident had taken place on 27 December, when shards of light had lit up an area where aliens were busy repairing their crashed spacecraft. There were other witnesses too, including the base commander, who had actually communicated with the beings. Roberts claimed to have driven to the landing site in a jeep with three other witnesses. He went on to say that the incident had lasted three hours, during which time the craft had hit a tree. He also told Brenda that photographs had been taken of the UFO. Brenda was not sure what to make of the astonishing story but, like Chris, she trusted her friend. After all, it involved the United States Air Force and she knew Roberts well enough to know that he would not joke about something so serious. Having recounted the amazing incident to Brenda, for the sake of his career, he asked her to keep his name out of it, suggesting she try to contact other witnesses. Meanwhile Brenda telephoned researcher Dot Street and the two women discussed how they should carry out the investigation. Dot had befriended Roberts when she met him at one of Chris's parties in 1979, so he was no stranger to her either. When I questioned whether she thought he was genuine, she replied, 'We had a question mark next to him because he was a bit of a ladies' man. My first thought was that he was an attention seeker.'

Steve Roberts has become something of an enigma in this case, and this is probably because for the last twenty years Brenda, Chris and Dot have gone to great pains to protect his real identity. The only other known civilians to learn the secret were Harry Harris and their co-author Jenny Randles. Dot had always regretted confiding in Harris, the UFO researcher and solicitor who had been introduced to the women as an advisor. No sooner had she told him Roberts' real name than he contacted the witness seeking confirmation of his involvement. This made Roberts feel uneasy and it was some time before he would trust the women with more information. Brenda was also disappointed that Dot had written to Jenny in 1984, offering Roberts' real name, but was glad that she had not found him.

It was during this period that the researchers were beginning to have doubts about Roberts, and this may have prompted him to draw Brenda directions to the alleged landing site. Later she would ask him to draw a picture of the UFO and, as if trying to gain her faith and prove that he had access to important files, Roberts produced a photocopy of an official letter on the reverse of the drawing. Although the letter was in no way connected with the incident, it was an eye-opener for the researchers and, coupled with the drawing of a typical saucer-shaped UFO, it renewed their faith in their friend. The letter was written by Colonel Charles H. Senn, Chief of the Community Relations Division of the Office of Information in Washington DC. It was addressed to Lieutenant General Duward L.

Crow, a retired USAF officer who was then working with NASA. The brief content of the letter refers to an enclosed fact sheet and standard response to UFO public enquiries. In closing, Colonel Senn states: 'I sincerely hope you are successful in preventing a reopening of UFO investigations.' The letter, dated 1 September 1977, proves interesting because it was during this period that Jimmy Carter was attempting to relaunch an enquiry into the subject of UFOs. Carter himself had been a witness to a UFO sighting and had promised the American people that if he were elected for president he would ask NASA to assist in opening the UFO files, but he never did keep his word. Brenda and Dot believe the Senn/Crow letter had something to do with it.

I contacted the USAF and managed to retrieve an impressive biography on Lieutenant General Duward Lowery Crow. I learnt that in 1952 he was stationed at Wright Patterson Air Force Base, Ohio, where he served in the headquarters of Air Materiel Command as chief of the plans and programs division. 1952 was a prominent year for UFO sightings, some UFO enthusiasts link Wright Patterson AFB with the UFO cover-up, suggesting the installation is responsible for retrieving and housing crashed alien space ships and their occupants. In October 1973 Crow was appointed assistant vice chief of staff for the USAF, taking on an additional duty as senior air force member, Military Staff Committee at the United Nations. He separated from the Air Force less than a year later, in August 1974, and although there are no records of his appointments following his retirement, it is not uncommon for retired generals to act as consultants to government and military departments. It is therefore very probable that Crow was involved with NASA and that the document is genuine. However, I did wonder what the letter was doing at Bentwaters. Was it sent with the fact sheet and standard response to UFO public enquiries in order to help personnel deal with the Rendlesham Forest incident?

During my investigation I discovered Steve Roberts' true identity and asked Brenda and Chris if they would care to comment. Although Chris gave me full marks for the detective work, both he and Brenda were concerned that I would go public with his name. The main worry was because Roberts had removed official documents from the Bentwaters installation and passed them to the researchers. I must point out that Steve Roberts' real name has never been published in any literature concerning the case, and none of the aforementioned individuals were responsible for revealing it to me. I came across the information during a conversation with a retired USAF officer. At the time I was not aware that the person we were discussing was in fact Steve Roberts. The officer gave me no hint or suggestion, probably because he did not know either. A couple of weeks later I received a confidential letter from a separate source, which listed several names including Roberts' real name. It was the first time I had seen it in print and although it did not link him to the mysterious Steve Roberts, it was a clue, albeit a well-hidden one, but it was just enough of a lead to go on. Nevertheless, it took me almost a year to track down the elusive Mr Roberts, and I concluded that this was probably because Brenda had alerted him that I was on his trail. Roberts is still in the security business, employed by a government contractor whose role it is to secure classified projects.

Although in January 1981 he told Brenda he had witnessed a landed craft with alien beings, he returned to England in 1987 to inform her that the story had been a hoax perpetrated by the USAF. As Brenda listened attentively, he went on to explain that he and several others had been ordered by their superiors to go out and spread the UFO stories among ufologists. He further explained that something did happen, and one day he would tell her the truth, but it was nothing of any importance and she should waste no more time on the case. Brenda was devastated; after all, he was the only witness she had truly trusted. For seven years she had relied on his word and, when all else seemed hopeless, his testimony alone had inspired both her and Dot to continue their investigations.

During an interview with Roberts, I asked him if he had been a witness to the UFO incident at Woodbridge. He replied, 'Yes, I was.' It was interesting to learn that he was now claiming he had not witnessed a landing, but had seen the object at close range in the sky. I admit I had my suspicions about his alleged involvement in the actual incident and shared my thoughts with Chris Pennington on a number of occasions. Roberts was now insisting there were no aliens present but was adamant that there was a UFO. He refused to discuss his 1987 statement to Brenda concerning the alleged hoax; instead, he suggested I pay special attention to Colonel Halt's record of events because it was 'pretty accurate'. I asked him several questions and although he was polite in his responses he was also very cautious.

G. BRUNI: What incident were you involved in?

S. ROBERTS: I didn't say I was involved.

G. BRUNI: OK, but you say you saw the UFO. How many witnesses were there?

S. ROBERTS: There were only five or six witnesses out there with Halt.

G. BRUNI: I understand there were more personnel further back from the landing site. Were you one of the five or six men with Halt's patrol?

S. ROBERTS: No, I was not one of the five. There were only a few men at the scene. It makes me laugh when I see these TV programmes and hear all these people saying they were involved and talking about all the unusual air traffic coming in immediately afterwards. There was none of that. Bobby Ball's account was pretty accurate; he was there with Halt.

G. BRUNI: But if there were only five people involved, and you were not one of the five, but were a witness, then there were more than five. Who else was with you?

S. ROBERTS: I don't remember who else was there. It was a long time ago and I wasn't paying attention to names.

G. BRUNI: I understand Bob Ball was out there for at least three nights. Was Lieutenant Bruce Englund involved too?

S. ROBERTS: Bruce? Sure, he was out there. Bobby Ball was blinded about it; he was really caught up in it.

G. BRUNI: But you say there were no entities, no aliens involved. Did you see a landed craft?

S. ROBERTS: There were no aliens. I did not see a landed craft.

G. BRUNI: According to the drawing you did for Brenda Butler, the craft was a saucer shape, and if you only saw it in the sky, why was the drawing of a landed craft? [In 1981 Roberts gave Brenda a drawing of a disc-shaped spacecraft with landing legs, which he claimed he had witnessed.]

S. ROBERTS: I am making no comment on that, it was the same as the one described in Halt's record.

G. BRUNI: But Halt's record describes the object as being triangular in shape, and your drawing was of a definite saucer shape.

S. ROBERTS: No comment.

G. BRUNI: Was Adrian Bustinza with Halt's patrol?

S. ROBERTS: Busty? I would say that Busty was pretty reliable. [Note how he does recall names.]

G. BRUNI: Apparently you returned to England in 1987 and turned up at Brenda and Chris's on a motorbike. Were you with Charles Halt on this trip? [This is when he told Brenda the UFO story was a hoax and advised her not to attend a UFO lecture where Colonel Halt was booked to discuss the incident. He explained that Halt was not going to appear due to him attending a meeting at RAF Greenham Common. In fact Halt did cancel the engagement at the last minute.]

S. ROBERTS: No, I was not with Halt. I was on a motorcycle tour.

G. BRUNI: But both you and Halt arrived from Belgium at the same time. Were you stationed in Belgium?

S. ROBERTS: Yes, I came over from Belgium, but I was living in Germany at the time.

G. BRUNI: Were you ever with the AFOSI, or did you have anything to do with them?

S. ROBERTS: No, I wasn't with the OSI, I had something to do with them but, no, I wasn't working with them. There were openings at the time but I never wanted to join them.

G. BRUNI: Were you debriefed by the OSI after the events?

S. ROBERTS: Yes, they questioned me.

G. BRUNI: Did they interrogate you? Were you taken to any underground facilities or do you know of others who were?

S. ROBERTS: No, they did not interrogate me, and I don't know of any others who were interrogated or taken anywhere.

Steve Roberts' answers only added to the confusion; after all, it is not just a case of him changing minor details, over the years he has created several completely different stories. In his initial conversations with Brenda and Chris, he not only described how a craft of some sort had crash-landed near the Woodbridge base, but how little aliens were attempting to repair it. Then after *Skycrash* was published he told Brenda that there were no aliens involved. In fact, when he arrived at Brenda's door in 1987, he assured her that the whole incident had been nothing more than a hoax. Then in 1999 he admitted to me that apart from the encounters with aliens, the UFO story was true. What can we make of this?

According to Brenda and Chris, Steve Roberts was very secretive about his job. All that they knew was that he worked in an office on day shifts. Chris had thought he was a member of the AFOSI, but in fact Roberts was assigned to the Security Police Investigations, a special unit within the Security Police Squadron equipped to deal with local crimes and incidents. Because Roberts worked with the SPI, he would most certainly have liaised with the AFOSI because the SPI were known to report to the agency. He might also have been privy to certain documents, and this is probably how he was able to remove them from the base and obtain details of the incident. Of course, he could have easily been used to pass on disinformation.

Chris had remarked that Roberts was always very careful. 'He would never put himself in an awkward position, and he never accepted a drink or food at my home but always brought his own,' recalled Chris. It is possible that Roberts was encouraged to communicate information to Brenda and Dot with the purpose of tracking down any whistle-blowers. For instance, Sam Bowman mysteriously disappeared after discussing the incident with Brenda and Chris, and Roberts had encouraged Brenda to contact other personnel who were involved. Was this a ploy to keep tabs on the witnesses on behalf of the SPI and the AFOSI, or was Roberts just a ladies' man trying to impress the young researchers?

Based on my interview with Roberts and conversations with Brenda, Chris and Dot, I considered that Roberts might not have been a witness to the actual landing after all. I thought that he could easily have seen the UFO hovering over the base or been one of the many witnesses to have seen the lights in the forest, or even picked up information in the office of the SPI. But then Brenda was to offer some vital undisclosed information, which only fuelled the mystery. Apparently, Roberts had disappeared for three weeks after the incident and on his return he told her that he had been sent away on a special course. But then he later told her that he had been taken to an underground facility where he was shown films of balloons and air ships and interrogated. 'He was under the impression that they were trying to brainwash him into believing it was nothing unusual,' said Brenda. However, his original rough sketch of a typical saucer-shaped UFO with aliens descending in a beam of light was covertly offered to Brenda after his debriefing and 'special course'. Could the fact that he photocopied documents and smuggled them out account for his desire to assist the researchers – or could he have had alternative motives?

It is also curious that Roberts' arrival in England coincided with Halt's, and both were travelling from Belgium. Even more curious is the 'hoax story' that Roberts related to Brenda. This makes me think that he was instructed to carry this message, either by Halt or his own superiors. There is also the possibility, of course, that he was concerned that his identity would be discovered if the investigation continued. If he was not part of a disinformation plan, he may have had concerns about the documents he had removed from the base. It is just too coincidental that Colonel Halt and Steve Roberts arrived in England at the same time, especially as Roberts was based in Germany yet had travelled from Belgium to England. The fact that he told Brenda that Halt was not going to turn up for the conference is also very suspicious. This must surely prove that at least Roberts was aware of Halt's movements, yet Halt has never mentioned Roberts' real name in public. On one of the occasions that I interviewed Charles Halt, I gave him a list of names, including Roberts' real name, and asked him if he knew whether any of them were involved. He told me Roberts worked in an office on the day shift (A Flight) and was definitely not involved but had picked up the story from another witness. He named Jim Penniston. According to Brenda, Roberts had confirmed that he travelled with Halt from Belgium, and that is one part of his story that she is convinced is factual.

If Steve Roberts' original testimony is genuine, it would imply that he was on duty that night, but the day shift only worked night duty during alerts or exercises. However, one witness does claim that he was with members of the day shift (A Flight) who were called out on a night-time exercise. Although the A Flights were known to participate in these exercises on a regular basis, we must remember it was Christmas week and, according to all senior officers, no exercises should have been carried out during that period. In fact, some of the witnesses who were called out on an exercise may have been part of a Red Alert and not aware of it. If Steve Roberts was out in the forest that night he could have witnessed the incident, especially as there were at least thirty military personnel present on the night of the second landing.

What strikes me as very strange is the mention in the 1984 book *Skycrash* where the authors claim that Roberts told them that Gordon Williams was communicating with aliens. In all the press interviews prior to the publication of their book there appears to be no reference to Roberts (or their mysterious witnesses) ever having mentioned the wing commander's name. So did Roberts later agree that Williams was involved and, if so, for what purpose? Steve Roberts' story is so inconsistent that if he decided to stand up and tell the truth today, would anyone really believe him?

According to a former British Intelligence source, the best way to discredit the truth is to create several different stories. This then becomes so confusing that the real facts lie buried among the fiction. Is this what Steve Roberts was involved with? If so, which part of his story is fact and which part is fiction?

THE STORY MAKES HEADLINES

Other than a brief article in the science journal *OMNI* and odd pieces in UFO literature, the media in general shied away from the incident until late 1983. The story first made headlines when Manchester-based *News of the World* journalist Keith Beabey was tipped off about Lieutenant Colonel Halt's memorandum and immediately followed up the lead. Since then, apart from the famous Roswell incident, no similar case has attracted the attention of the world's media quite as much as the Rendlesham Forest case.

In the early 1980s journalists were not so keen to be assigned to UFO reporting because it was considered bottom-of-the-barrel journalism. But the Rendlesham Forest story was different. Reluctantly, the British broadsheets, such as *The Times* and the *The Guardian*, were forced to follow the story due to public interest after it appeared on the front page of Britain's most popular Sunday tabloid, *The News of the World*. The newspaper must have thought it was a good story because the headline alone took up almost half of the front page, followed by an equally impressive section on page three. The actual headline 'UFO LANDS IN SUFFOLK AND THAT'S OFFICIAL' became almost as well known as the case itself.

It was not long before Fleet Street discovered that *The News of the World* were on to something big. On 2 October 1983, the same day the story made front-page headlines, two other Sunday newspapers featured it. *The Sunday Express* crept in with a small article exposing details of Lieutenant Colonel Halt's memorandum, along with a couple of quotes from British notables. Minister of Defence

Sir John Nott remarked of the incident: 'I know nothing about it. Certainly I never saw any report about a UFO landing. I don't believe in UFOs anyway.' Sir Ian Gilmore offered a more aggressive response. 'I should think this is absolute rubbish,' he said. Not having much of a lead, *The Sunday Mirror* dressed up their story by describing a fringed flying saucer with portholes and blue flashing lights, landing on the Woodbridge runway.

On Monday 3 October Britain's most respected broadsheet, *The Times*, trashed the Rendlesham Forest case to pieces. Local Suffolk forester Vince Thurkettle was highly amused when interviewed by journalist Alan Hamilton, who seemed rather more interested in making sure he had the correct name of the forest trees (Corsican pines) and their correct height (75 feet) than whether or not a UFO encounter had actually taken place. Thurkettle, albeit innocently, had set the cement for several 'down to earth' theories and, sadly, by trying to be overly witty, the journalist had made a complete nonsense of the case.

The Daily Express took a different angle (Monday 3 October) and opted for 'UFOs? They're Our Boys Really!' The late Lord Clancarty told reporter John Rydon that he was convinced the UFOs were British and American secret projects. 'I know for sure that such man-powered machines are being used by both the Americans and the British,' said Clancarty. As head of the House of Lords All Party UFO Study Group, Clancarty believed the British and their allies had managed to locate some type of electro-magnetic energy in outer space which powered these crafts. On the same day *The Daily Star* reported 'Spaceship Riddle Deepens', quoting a Ministry of Defence spokesperson as saying they had no record of Halt's memorandum. *The Guardian* claimed 'MOD Quiet on UFO', but the journalist obviously knew how to ask the right questions because the Ministry of Defence spokesman confirmed they had been sent details of an alleged UFO incident, but added that he could not reveal any information. Considering the contents of the memorandum had already been splashed all over the British press, I find it somewhat strange that the Ministry of Defence were still trying to ignore public requests for information. After all, if the incident was of no concern to them, why be covert about it?

On 5 October 1983 the US armed forces publication *Stars and Stripes* bannered the story on their front page. 'Fleet Street whoops it up. British paper reports UFO landing near RAF base,' ran the headlines. When UK bureau chief J. King Cruger questioned Lieutenant Colonel Doug Kennet, director of the Office of Public Affairs at RAF Mildenhall, the officer denied that US Air Force officials had been involved in a cover-up. He explained that they had responded to several Freedom of Information requests and had even tracked down Halt's memorandum and supplied it to CAUS. Captain Kathleen McCollom, chief of public affairs for RAF Bentwaters, confirmed there were sightings of strange lights, but stressed that only a small number of base personnel were involved and they were off duty at the time. Furthermore, she told Cruger that the incident occurred off the base and the sightings had been exaggerated to a comical degree.

Hours before the ink was due to set on *The News of the World* front-page story, Rendlesham Forester Vince Thurkettle received a call from David Jack, a *Sunday People* journalist, who enquired about something unusual that had occurred in the forest. Apparently, one of their spies at *The News of the World* had tipped them off about a UFO incident but having no leads to go on Jack thought the forester would know something. It was too late for *The Sunday People* to run the story and, being a weekly newspaper, they would have to wait until the following Sunday (9 October). By then most of the dailies had picked up on the news, but Jack saw fit to write a small piece entitled 'That UFO was a Lighthouse – and that's official!' The article was based on the forester's theory that the UFO was probably the local lighthouse beacon. It was obviously a sad attempt to debunk their competitors' scoop.

The News of the World must have realized there was still some mileage left in the story because on 9 October they ran a half-page featuring more revelations. This time they interviewed Admiral of the Fleet Lord Hill-Norton, who was the former chief of defence staff (1971–73). 'I must speak out,' he told the journalist, 'the Ministry of Defence know far more than they are prepared to say. But now they have an obligation to tell the nation what occurred that night in a British wood.'

The one broadsheet that seemed totally uninterested in the Rendlesham affair was *The Daily Telegraph*. When it did feature an article on 17 October, journalist Adrian Berry was so critical of *The News of the World* story that the newspaper's editor, Derek Jameson, wrote a letter of protest. On 25 October *The Daily Telegraph* printed the letter without comment, which only added to Jameson's frustrations. He wrote: 'Sir – Mr Adrian Berry (article, Oct 17) is less than fair in his report of UFO sightings when he accuses my newspaper of shameless impudence in reporting that a mysterious object had landed in Suffolk.' Jameson's letter went on to explain the facts of the case based on Halt's memorandum and pointed out the reasons why the UFO could not have been a lighthouse. Berry's article also infuriated seasoned researcher Timothy Good, who wrote to the journalist pointing out that it was 'a disgraceful misrepresentation', but Timothy received no reply from either Berry or the newspaper.

When news of the incident reached Japan, television crews wasted no time in visiting Woodbridge. In fact, the Japanese media were so fascinated by the case that they invited Larry Warren to Tokyo. Warren's visit on 10 October 1983 was heavily publicized inasmuch as he received almost celebrity status. As he was driven from the airport he was surprised to see himself featured on a huge billboard at the top of the television building. Warren had not only made front-page news but had also been interviewed for several television shows, including Japan's version of America's *The Tonight Show*.

In the summer of 1984 American defence and technology journalist Chuck de Caro began making enquiries about the case for CNN's *Special Assignment*. The television show first aired in February 1985 and was dedicated exclusively to the case. Prior to the programme airing, the studio received a memorandum from the

National Security Council, apparently they wanted to review the documentary before it was shown to the public. De Caro related what happened:

> What surprised me was the National Security Council's interest in the programme. A former anchorwoman came in and told me she had received a memo from them. They wanted to send someone over to see me. They sent over a full Air Force colonel. I got the impression they were concerned about the nuclear weapons aspect.

Considering the programme involved one of America's top defence journalists and the report revolved around a NATO airbase that deployed nuclear weapons, it is understandable that the security agencies would be concerned. The programme featured interviews with witnesses and players alike, all of whom except Larry Warren demanded their identity be kept secret and their faces blacked out. Since they are retired from the service it is now safe to name those who appeared on the programme: Ray Gulyas, Bobby Ball, Greg Battram and Larry Warren. It was the first time Chuck de Caro had taken an interest in a UFO case but, as he explained, his investigation was purely from a defence angle. Nevertheless, the programme would make him a household name among ufologists and he would go on to investigate other UFO incidents involving the US military.

I asked de Caro for his opinion of the case:

> I think something went on that they tried to cover up, but you have to eliminate everything else before you can claim it's a real unknown. I tried to do that but I had limited time because we had a programme to make. You have got to get at the paperwork. You need answers from the AFOSI. Why? What did they learn? Why were they so intense? These guys were security police patrolmen. They go off base into a forest carrying weapons and that is a violation. They then turn around and run away. You need to find out how the Air Force does business. If they have something they don't want you to know, sure they'll cover it up.

De Caro had tried to interview the witnesses but most were too afraid to talk to him. He explained the difficulty:

> When I talked to them they were still curious. Larry [Warren] was very much emotionally affected by all of this, but he was too far down the ladder [rank]. I spoke to Lieutenant Englund and he was absolutely terrified. He was stupefied. Stuttering, he said, 'I don't want to talk about it.' I went to see Adrian Bustinza, who had recently married, and his wife told me he still woke up screaming in the middle of the night. He was terrified to talk about it too. I can understand that, you know, if they are threatening you with prison sentences. I spoke to Colonel Halt and saw his plaster cast of the landing marks, others said theirs disappeared. I couldn't get to [General Gordon] Williams. The Air Force protected him from me.

De Caro's interest was causing some concern for the USAF, especially Captain Victor L. Warzinski, the public affairs officer at RAF Bentwaters, who had to respond to de Caro's demanding requests for information. Although he went to the top, by contacting the Pentagon, de Caro's queries were referred back to the head public affairs office at RAF Mildenhall, who in turn contacted RAF Bentwaters. In one of many cables on the subject (August 1984) Warzinski sent the following message to RAF Mildenhall and the Headquarters of USAFE, Ramstein AFB Germany:

> Colonel Halt is currently assigned with AFLC at Tinker AFB, OK. Suggest OSAF/PA discuss his desire to go on record and grant interviews to credible press. He had indicated a desire to do so while assigned here. We discouraged this at the time, feeling it would only fan the fire. Interview now could be advantageous. He would basically say he saw lights he could not explain. Does not mean he's drawn a conclusion in favour of UFOs.

I asked de Caro for his opinion of the UFOs:

> I don't know. Was it an experimental weapon? Electromagnetic pulse maybe? I've looked into radio-frequency weapons. The

British were experimenting with a death ray during the war, then Over the Horizon, they tend to pulse. It could be something left over from that. Was it an infrasound weapons experiment? No one ever followed that up. You need a lot of money for that kind of research. I didn't necessarily believe in UFOs, I was looking at it from a defence angle. A few years ago I stumbled across a security guard who talked about an incident on a base in Alaska. He described seeing some sort of wave in the snow heading towards him. He panicked, vomited, ran off – that sounds like a weapon experiment to me.

What about a hologram? I asked.

The problem with holograms is that it wouldn't explain the static charge. They complained about the hair on their necks standing up, and they said, 'this thing moved and we followed it'. That doesn't sound like a hologram to me.

Whatever his thoughts, de Caro does not believe it had anything to do with a lighthouse. It was science writer Ian Ridpath's public claims that the UFOs were nothing more than the beam from the Orfordness lighthouse that was the most damaging argument against the case. Over the years, both his contribution to BBC TV's *Breakfast Time* and his article in *The Guardian* (5 January 1985), promoting the lighthouse theory, have been used by sceptics and debunkers in an attempt to discredit this already complex case. Referring to *The News of the World* feature in his *Guardian* article, Ian Ridpath points out that the informant was former US airman Art Wallace (Larry Warren). I was convinced this was inaccurate so I checked with the journalist who actually got the tip, Keith Beabey.

G. BRUNI: Keith, can you tell me how you first became interested in the Rendlesham Forest case?

K. BEABEY: I received some information concerning a document, which turned out to be a memorandum written by the base commander.

G. BRUNI: I understand it was Harry Harris who tipped you off.

K. BEABEY: That is correct.

Whilst investigating the story for *The News of the World*, Beabey became frustrated after trying for several days to get an audience with Lieutenant Colonel Halt. The Bentwaters public affairs office had suggested he talk to the British liaison officer, Squadron Leader Moreland, which he did, but it was as if Halt was trying to avoid him at every turn. When Beabey finally managed to talk to him, he realized he was not willing to discuss the case. 'This is a very delicate situation. I have been told very clearly that I could jeopardize my career if I talk to you about it,' Halt told the journalist. However, he did not deny the report was his, and Beabey managed to secure a copy of the memorandum which was the proof of the pudding he needed. I asked his opinion of the case:

> I had no doubt at all that something occurred, but I only had the report to go on. Apart from Halt, all the witnesses had gone back to the United States because it was now almost three years after the incident . . . The story became more complex after we published it. The waters became muddied by people offering all kinds of explanations. Unfortunately, some were only interested in putting themselves in the limelight . . . My argument was that these were experienced airmen, and surely they ought to know the difference between a lighthouse and whatever it was they couldn't conceive . . . I didn't believe that a man of Halt's integrity, a senior officer and the base commander would have written something untrue.

I asked Beabey if he would have followed up the story without the official memorandum to work with. 'Yes, without that we would have still made our enquiries, but that gave us the basis to work with.' I discovered that Beabey is as fascinated as ever with the Rendlesham Forest incident and has not changed his opinion that something very strange occurred during Christmas week 1980.

THE LARRY WARREN STORY

Larry Warren has been connected with the incident since early 1983. Being the first person to go public with the story (using the pseudonym Art Wallace) was not an easy task for this young man, but he was so traumatized by the course of events, he told witness Adrian Bustinza, that he was going to make sure the world knew about it. He lived up to his promise.

In 1997 Larry Warren co-authored *Left at East Gate* with American researcher Peter Robbins. It is an intriguing story of his early life and his misgivings at being caught up in the Rendlesham Forest incident. As gentle and professional as Peter is, there were moments of intense frustration as he tried to make sense of his co-author's case, and equally so for Larry as he desperately tried to prove his story was genuine. This was a difficult task because the years of stress and nightmares had taken their toll, and more than once Larry had contemplated suicide. It was as a result of his story that I became more interested in this case. Indeed, some of his claims were far more exotic than those of other witnesses, and I felt compelled to investigate if only to discover what it was that had or had not intruded on this young man's life.

Over the years Larry has had to suffer the indignity and criticism of sceptics and ufologists, many of whom insist he could not have been involved because his statements did not match those of other witnesses, coupled with the fact that his story has changed over the years. Like others before me, I discovered that there were several grey areas to his testimony, but then it seemed to me that one does not spend so many years trying to prove one's case if it is nothing but a lie in the first place. I figured that if Larry Warren was intentionally lying he would have dropped out of the story long ago, especially as new evidence surfaced. He certainly has not stayed with it for financial gain, on the contrary, it has cost him a small fortune. It also cost him his marriage and very nearly cost him his life.

Lawrence P. Warren was only eighteen years old when he joined the USAF on 22 July 1980. On 1 December he arrived at RAF Bentwaters, having received basic training at Lackland Air Force Base, Texas. When questioned about his Air Force status, Colonel Halt claimed Larry was not on duty at the time of the incident and, furthermore, he was not on the installation. Halt also insisted that he had played no part in the events, and even after Larry produced certain Air Force documents, Halt still had difficulty accepting that he was involved, pointing out that he was not trained for security police duties. Brenda Butler was another person who was sceptical of Larry's involvement. She was inclined to think he might have picked up the story from other witnesses. With this in mind, she once offered him false information about a witness who did not exist. Larry told her that he knew the man and they had discussed the incident in passing. This episode resulted in a damaging stigma to his credibility. I asked him if he would care to comment on the matter:

> I admit it was wrong. I was not altogether sure of everything that had taken place the night of the incident, or who some of the others were. I was still grasping for the truth myself. Looking back, I think I was trying to get her attention. She wanted to believe it happened and I wanted to get the story out because it really did happen. I suppose I wanted her to believe me, so I agreed with everything she said.

Witness Jim Penniston also questioned Larry's involvement, agreeing with Colonel Halt that Larry was not trained to be on duty at the time. However, Penniston admits that soon after the incident he had to caution Larry for discussing it with his fellow airmen. I told Penniston that I had a copy of Larry's certificate of training, which certifies that he successfully completed the Security Specialist Course. The course was conducted at USAF Lackland, Texas, and Edward D. Young, Colonel USAF, Commander of the 3250th Technical Training Wing, signed the document. I gave him the date (28 October 1980) and also pointed out that I had an original document entitled 'Report on Individual Personnel', prepared at 21.16 hrs on 11 December 1980. This document was addressed to the 81st Security Police Squadron, Bentwaters, and was signed by Thomas A. Mosely, TSGT USAF, at Bentwaters Classification and Training School. It proves that Lawrence P. Warren had completed further training (including ground defence) at RAF Bentwaters and was assigned to official duties on 11 December 1980. Having explained the details of Larry's military training to Jim Penniston he had to agree that if the documents were genuine, then there is no doubt that Larry was trained to be on duty at the time of the incident. I also pointed out that Colonel Halt gives credence to witness Edward Cabansag, but Cabansag had only been on official duty for one or two days prior to his involvement in the incident. Surely if Cabansag can be officially assigned to duty and carry an M-16 rifle within two days of completing his training, then why not Larry Warren?

Larry has never been certain of the exact date of his involvement, believing it might have been the first night of his midnight shift with D Flight. This would normally have been 26/27 December, but I have since learnt that the Flights were mixed up due to the Christmas holidays. Based on his testimony, Larry is presumably referring to a later incident. The following is based on his own account of the events with my added comments in parentheses.

It was just after 23.00 hrs when Larry arrived at his posting, which was perimeter post 18, at the furthest end of the flightline on the Bentwaters installation and closest to the Woodbridge base. (This may be an oversight on Larry's part, or it could have changed, but on checking an official Bentwaters map, I noticed that post 18 was not at the perimeter, but was situated in a central position at the mid-way flightline. From what I understand, this was the area where the aircraft were stored, and as such it required special security at all times. Therefore, the guard on duty should not have been removed from his post.) Soon after midnight Larry began hearing radio transmissions coming from the Bentwaters tower and other transmissions between personnel stationed at RAF Woodbridge. The Woodbridge patrol were observing funny lights bobbing up and down over the forest and Airman Warren was becoming nervous at being so alone in the dead of night. Suddenly a truck arrived with three or four personnel, which included Lieutenant Bruce Englund and Sergeant Adrian Bustinza. Airman Warren was instructed to call Central Security Control and announce he was being relieved of duty at his post. Sergeant Bustinza then instructed him to climb into the back of the truck and the patrol headed off to the Bentwaters motor pool to fill some light-alls (generator-mounted light systems). (Adrian Bustinza recalls collecting personnel and having them fill the light-alls but, apart from his superiors, he cannot recall the identities of any of the men he picked up that evening.) After refuelling the light-alls, the patrol then drove to Rendlesham Forest, passing the Woodbridge base by the east gate and taking the next turning left into the logging road.

Brenda Butler, who is familiar with the area, has pointed out that Larry's directions to the landing site are incorrect. But having taken the route myself I can see where the confusion arises. If one were to leave the Woodbridge base, taking the road from the east gate (see map) to the area in question, then one would turn right not left. But Larry's patrol went directly from Bentwaters (Adrian Bustinza has confirmed the patrols took this route) and did not use the short cut through the Woodbridge base. By using the normal route they would have passed the east-gate entrance to the Woodbridge base on their right, they then took the next turning immediately on their left. Therefore Larry's directions are correct when he says, 'We turned left at east gate.'

Larry recalls being at the site with Bustinza when the big UFO landed (Bustinza insists he was not there when the landing took place but arrived soon afterwards. He also refers to an entirely different landing site than Larry) and describes the landing as a red ball of light exploding in a blinding flash, with shards of light and particles falling on to a yellow fog. Larry remembers going numb during the encounter, as if in a state of shock. Right in front of him appeared a huge machine, which at first seemed to be triangular in shape but was constantly distorting. It reminded him of a huge soluble aspirin (Bustinza also mentions that it looked like a soluble aspirin). The object was covered in weird pipes and what looked like little boxes and there was a bank of cobalt blue lights at its base and a glowing reddish light at the top. Larry was of the opinion that it was old and yet advanced at the same time. Numerous personnel were busy surrounding it on all sides, making a broken circle around it. He was now about twenty-five feet in front of the object and could see landing gear that appeared to be three legs protruding from its main body. At this stage Larry was feeling a sense of nausea and the hairs on his neck and body were standing on end. An officer instructed him and another airman to move closer to the object whilst a disaster preparedness officer led the way with a Geiger counter. Larry could see their shadows on its surface, which appeared to be unusually distorted. It was at this moment he claims to have seen three aeronaut entities communicating telepathically with Wing Commander Gordon Williams. The entities, floating in bluish gold balls of light, seemed disturbed by a noise that sounded like a loud bang. Larry and the others backed away from the object as they heard an officer calling to some men who tried to run off over the fence. The commotion appeared to disturb the entities and, as if in fear, they floated back towards the object before moving forward again and continuing their silent communication with the commander. Larry claims that people were filming the UFO and taking photographs during the entire event.

One of the major problems with Larry's story is that he is the only witness to go public claiming Wing Commander Gordon Williams was involved in the incident. In *Left at East Gate* he refers to the CNN documentary, stating that although the faces of the witnesses were blacked out he recognized Captain Mike Verrano, and claims Verrano had verified that Wing Commander Williams had taken a film canister of the incident to a waiting aircraft. Former Senior Master Sergeant Ray Gulyas, who worked alongside Captain Verrano in 1980, pointed out that it was Verrano who had taken the film to the aircraft, not Williams. He was sure that Williams was never mentioned in any of the briefings by Bobby Ball (also a witness), only Halt, and he did not doubt Ball's word. In the same context Larry implied that Gulyas had said he had seen flying objects containing maybe people or different life forms. Gulyas positively denies he saw anything of the kind. 'I was not a witness to the incident and I never heard of there being any aliens or beings out there,' he told me. I asked Larry to comment on Gulyas's statement. He checked the original manuscript and suggested it was a publishing error – that it should have read Bobby Ball and not Ray Gulyas.

Nevertheless, Larry is still convinced that Wing Commander Gordon Williams was out in the forest communicating with the crew of an alien spaceship. But as I explained to him, I needed more evidence because there was no other witness who put Gordon Williams in the picture. It was then he suggested I speak to Lee Speigel. I had been trying to contact Speigel for several months, without success, and was pleased when Larry asked Peter Robbins to put me in touch with him, promising he would confirm that Williams was involved. Lee Speigel was a producer and talk show host who had caught up with Colonel Halt at his home in 1985. According to Larry, Halt had become defensive when Speigel asked him about Gordon Williams and the Colonel had asked him and his crew to step outside. It was then that Halt allegedly admitted that 'Williams and beings' were involved in the incident. This is what Speigel related to me:

> Yes, I did interview Halt at home and he was candid, to a point, but was obviously not telling all the facts. Whether it had more to do with keeping quiet because of national security reasons or perhaps personal reasons, I don't know for sure. When I asked

Halt whether or not it was true that Base Commander Williams [sic] had some sort of very close encounter with alien beings, with a possible communication, Halt didn't get defensive and didn't ask me to have my crew step outside . . . My camera crew never came into Halt's home, just myself and an NBC producer, no one else. So re. Williams, all that Halt said was that he couldn't comment on what happened, not denying it, not confirming it. You can read anything you want into that, but that's what he said, and I've never embellished it beyond that. Halt never told me that beings had been observed on the third night. He simply wouldn't or couldn't confirm it.

According to Peter Robbins, Speigel was interviewing Larry and him for a New York radio show and it was after the show that Williams' name cropped up. Peter remarked on the conversation:

. . . I am not certain whether we were still in the studio or already in the cafe when it came up, but I specifically remember Larry asking Lee, certainly at least in part for my benefit, about Halt telling him that Williams had been involved. And I distinctly remember Lee responding in the affirmative . . .

Clearly there is a disagreement here. It seems strange that Larry would insist I talk to Speigel if he was not certain he would back up his story. However, when I first asked Speigel about his interview with Halt, he gave me a detailed account but there was no mention of Williams. It was only when I asked about Williams' alleged involvement that he offered the aforementioned statement. Could Peter have been mistaken about Speigel's affirmative answer or is it possible that Speigel might have misunderstood the question in the heat of the moment, several years down the line?

Adrian Bustinza disagrees with Larry, and is in no doubt that Williams was not involved, although he does remember Halt mentioning Williams' name during the encounter. Bustinza has no memories of Larry being at the landing site either. He explained the difficulty of trying to follow what was going on at the time:

I don't recall seeing him [Larry] out there, but there was a lot of confusion going on. There was tunnel vision. After the incident Larry was very upset and paranoid, and I had to try to calm him down. He wanted to talk. I remember us walking down the dorm and he was saying, 'I wonder if they are watching us now, if they have cameras watching us.' He got me scared. Even back then he was determined to get the story out. Larry wanted to talk, he was talking to everyone.

Steve La Plume remembers Larry very well. They had first met in a bar in San Antonio, Texas, whilst they were both at the police academy. It was not until the middle of January 1981 that they would meet again. La Plume heard about the major event the morning after it occurred, when some of the witnesses from the night shift walked through the day room on their way to their quarters. At the time, he did not pay too much attention to the witnesses, who were carrying their gear bags over their shoulders and walking with their heads and eyes down as if trying to avoid eye contact with anyone. He recalled how the men in the day room jeered as they passed through. 'Hey, see any little green men? Did you get probed?' One of the men retaliated by shouting 'Fuck you guys! Shut the fuck up.' La Plume does not remember seeing Larry with the group, but a few weeks later Larry discussed the incident with him in his dormitory. As confirmed by Bustinza, it seems Larry had been hunting out fellow witnesses and had heard about La Plume's January sighting and wanted someone to talk to who had had a similar experience. Because it was the first time they met since leaving Texas they did not immediately recognize each other.

La Plume related only what Larry had told him on that first day because he felt that this was the purest form of his story – before any outside influence might have tainted it. Larry told him that something had occurred outside the perimeter fence at RAF Woodbridge. He had been ordered to collect a light-all and fuel it at the gas station. He mentioned that they had trouble, both with filling the light-all with fuel as well as keeping their vehicle running. When Larry's patrol arrived at the forest, they were ordered to secure their weapons and leave them with another patrol. They then made their way to where they saw a craft. Larry also mentioned that at least one airman was taking photographs, probably with a personal camera, which was later confiscated. There was also a video-camera recording of the event which he believed was authorized because it was later flown to Germany. Larry explained that everyone was in a broken circle around the craft and a colonel was communicating with beings. However, he was very straightforward about the fact that they were not talking, just communicating. Larry told La Plume that he also saw the beings, which he described as three feet tall and resembling kids in snowsuits. There were two of the beings outside the craft, and one inside, and they appeared to be floating around as if inspecting it. Larry said that when the craft took off it joined about five other objects that formed into one unit before disappearing. Steve La Plume's story seems to give credence to Larry's, which is also very similar to Steve Roberts' original story.

According to Larry, the morning after the incident, he and several other airmen were instructed to report to Major Zickler. The airmen were lined up and checked over with a Geiger counter, doubtless for radiation, and told they were going to be debriefed concerning what had occurred the night before. They were then ushered into Zickler's office and instructed to sign statements without having the opportunity to read them. Larry managed a quick glance through the statement and realized it was a watered-down version of the actual event. It mentioned only that what he had seen were some unusual lights in the trees.

The witnesses, having been seated in front of a movie screen, were again told by Major Zickler that they would be debriefed and to be sure to give their full cooperation. Zickler then departed and three men in civilian suits entered the room. One was introduced as an officer from Naval Intelligence and the other two men represented the Armed Forces Security Service. After the introductions the naval commander gave them a briefing about UFOs and how the government had been aware of them for a very long time. The airmen were told that numerous 'off-earth' civilizations visited the planet from time to time, and that some had a permanent presence here. They were then instructed not to discuss any aspects of the incident with anyone on the base and if pressed they should just mention they saw lights in the trees. The commander then gave them a pep talk on patriotism before showing them a film, which revolved around the military's encounters with UFOs. According to Larry, the footage consisted of segments from various eras, beginning with World War Two, the Korean War and Vietnam, followed by footage from the US space missions. He claims that it was during this meeting that the men were told their security clearance had been upgraded. Having received no further confirmation, written or otherwise, he was of the opinion that the latter was mentioned only as a ploy to deter the witnesses from discussing the incident.

During a conversation I had with Malcolm Zickler, he confirmed that such a meeting had taken place although he did not offer any details. If you have a problem believing that the USAF educate their personnel on UFO matters, let me relate a similar story that was told to me in early 1997. Bruce Taylor, a Vietnam veteran who resides in Seattle, USA, informed me that before going off to war he and other personnel were summoned to a classroom where they were taught what to do in case they came into close contact with a 'craft of unknown origin'. In the likelihood of an encounter, they were expected to back away whilst observing everything possible, and then report it to their immediate supervisor. Taylor was also shown footage of UFOs in Korea and Vietnam, probably the exact same film that Larry and the other witnesses were shown. Taylor explained how the Air Force deals with this particular subject. 'What was hard for me was that on one hand they were telling me UFOs don't exist, but on the other hand they were telling me what to do if I see one.' I asked him if he had been given any information on extraterrestrials and what they might look like. 'No, they didn't tell me what they might look like because that might be too easy,' he said. He added, 'I believe there are a couple of different races that fly these craft and I don't think it would be easy for the governments of the world to tell people what they look like if they are telling everyone that they don't exist.'

A remarkable part of Larry's story is his recollection of the events whilst under hypnotic regression. The session, which was carried out by ufologist and abduction researcher Budd Hopkins on 15 July 1995, has Larry being taken to an underground facility by two strange men in black civilian suits. This occurred in the early evening following the morning meeting in Zickler's office, and one has to wonder if certain individuals were singled out. Larry was relaxing in his dorm when he was called on the telephone and told to report to the parking lot within twenty minutes. He was very concerned because earlier that day he had called his mother from the base telephone box and was in the middle of telling her about the UFO when he was cut off in mid-sentence. As he made his way towards the vehicle he was very nervous about what was ahead.

During the hypnotic session with Budd Hopkins, who is well known for his work with people who claim to have been abducted by aliens, Larry tried to describe what happened in the parking lot. As he walked towards the vehicle, which he thought was a 1980 Cadillac with New York number plates, he noticed Adrian Bustinza leaving his building and heading in the same direction. There were two men waiting for them, and as Larry tried to climb into the back of the vehicle he was sprayed in the face from something that looked like a deodorant can. He complained that his nose, eyes and mouth were stinging and he was very scared because he could not open his eyes and had trouble breathing.

As the car stopped Larry was pulled out and laid on an icy patch of ground near the Bentwaters flightline. He was then taken through a door and experienced the rapid descent of going down in an elevator. But he was not sure if the elevator was real because suddenly everything became a void. The next moment Larry was in a clinical-type room, sitting upright in a chair having his eyes washed by a man in a white coat, whom he assumed was a military doctor. The room adjoined an office area, but it was not the Bentwaters clinic he recognized. He was then approached by a colonel who ushered him into another room where Adrian Bustinza and six other airmen were seated. At this point Larry was clearly having problems and was very frightened and, according to Budd Hopkins, brought himself abruptly out of the hypnosis. It is certainly an unusual story, but it is the remainder of Larry's underground experience that causes the most concern, the conscious memory without hypnosis.

According to Larry, he was still heavily sedated when he was confronted by two men in black SWAT-type uniforms who led him through a narrow corridor where he passed rooms full of computers and high-tech machines. He recalls the operators were dressed in orange and black uniforms. They then went through a pressurized door and an alarm triggered as the seal was broken. The door slid back into a white tiled wall and revealed a large dimly lit rectangular room which led into a smaller area with full-length windows. Larry stepped into the small space and could see a black liquid floor below, which housed a UFO similar to the one he had seen in Rendlesham Forest. Exiting from the confined space, he was ushered through a large door which led down a long corridor and into another room full of rows of seating. Larry was instructed to be seated, and as he did so he spotted Adrian Bustinza off to his right. Directly ahead was a large translucent screen and as he stared at it he realized he could not move his head. Suddenly he sensed there was a small figure behind it and he realized he was having a telepathic exchange with an alien entity. The voice began discussing Larry's life and, as if waiting for confirmation, it would constantly ask if he could remember. Larry then heard the being say that it was from another place, another reality. He was told that the underground facility under Bentwaters was very deep and had been there since the 1940s. With the aid of human support it had been expanded in the 1960s enabling the beings to travel in their crafts through an extensive tunnel system that exited into the North Sea.

An amazing story but what can we make of it? Those interested in this case have had difficulty accepting Larry's claims of alien beings living underground in rural Suffolk. Most people have simply dismissed it, claiming it is just too weird. Even with a vivid imagination, I find it strange that anyone would want to make up such a bizarre story, especially if they want to come across as credible. One thing that had crossed my mind was that if Larry had seen a UFO underground, could this have been a stealth F-117 aircraft that had been secretly deployed at Bentwaters? The design would most certainly have looked alien to someone who did not know of their existence, and if Larry was drugged it would be even more confusing. According to my source they had been housed in hangars at the far end of the flightline. It is a possibility that the hangars had some sort of lift that would transport the aircraft to a basement area.

Steve La Plume confirms part of Larry's abduction story:

> He also told me he was taken in a black car, that when the car pulled up close a window rolled down, and when he stuck his head in to talk to the occupants he blacked out. I do know for a fact that he said he was debriefed and told to keep quiet because 'bullets are cheap'. He also said he went under the base and there was a parking facility or something like that. He stated that the North Sea was close and they entered the underground base via the North Sea in an underground tunnel or something to that effect. I didn't see him for a few days after this [relating to when Larry spoke to him in mid-January], and when I did he was upset, because we were supposed to go drinking but he never showed up.

A few weeks after the statement from Steve La Plume, I told him about *Left at East Gate*. He reviewed the book and submitted another statement for my perusal.

> Larry never told me that it was Williams who was out there. I only remember him saying that a colonel was present. It was only after we got back to the US [a few years later] and talked about it more that I remember him saying it was actually Williams. He did tell me he was abducted about the same manner that he states in his book. He also mentioned the underground complex under the photo lab. He said the car was big and dark in colour, but never mentioned that there was anyone else with him. I was told this while we were on Bentwaters.

Considering he had had such a dramatic time in the Air Force, I find it strange that Larry decided he wanted to re-enlist so soon after his separation from the service. But in 1981, following several failed attempts, he consulted Congressman Gerald B. Solomon and some months later he received a copy of a letter written by Lieutenant Colonel Thomas M. Alison, addressed to the Honourable Gerald B. Solomon. It turned out that five months after his discharge, the Office of the Surgeon General, USAF, had permanently disqualified him by reason that he could not fully extend his right arm. Larry has always claimed that he did not receive a medical discharge from the USAF even though the Air Force wrote to Solomon and explained the details of his disablement. Steve La Plume comments:

> I remember Larry being assigned to the supply hut, and I distinctly remember that he was getting out of the Air Force due to his wrist, which he showed me would not move correctly. He explained that he was getting out for medical reasons – or breach of contract because they should not have assigned him the job of security to begin with, and should have caught his disability during his physical.

Larry supplied me with a copy of the letter of approval for his separation from the Air Force, which was stamped with Wing Commander Gordon E. Williams' signature. There is no obvious mention of a medical problem (unless it is coded), the separation was agreed on ('Nonfulfilment of Guaranteed Training Enlistee Program Agreement').

It seems as if Larry had a number of concerns whilst at Bentwaters and was under the impression that the AFOSI (known to servicemen as the OSI) were out to get him. Steve La Plume had warned Larry that they were watching him because he had put his name forward with several others for allegedly using drugs. La Plume recalls the incident.

> I was bagged for doing drugs in Amsterdam. They, OSI, could prove it, and guilt on my part knew they could. I was told that if

I cooperate they would not hold up my release from the service. I was already snapped at this time and had already had my sighting. I wanted nothing more than get the fuck out of Bentwaters and the USAF. I was in trouble with my drinking and was just a mind full of mush at this point in my life. I am making no excuses. I was weak and they preyed on that. However, I was the one who suggested they might want to take a look at Larry because I knew he had gone to Amsterdam recently or was about to. I was spouting off every name I could to get me out of this mess and get back home. So it was not like they were out to get him. Not from where I was sitting. Perhaps they picked on me hoping I would give them some dirt on Larry . . .

There were several rumours about Larry being thrown out of the Air Force for being a drug user, and I asked him outright if this was the case, but he absolutely denied it. Edward Cabansag remembers seeing Larry in the supply hut and was told by a fellow airman that Airman Warren was waiting for his release, which was a result of his involvement with drugs. Larry reminded me that he had an honourable discharge from the Air Force (I have a copy of this document) and was never associated with drugs. He believes these rumours were started to discredit him as a witness because the Air Force knew he was talking about the incident. Other personnel told me that sometime during 1980 a huge drugs bust was carried out on the Bentwaters installation. Those involved were members of the Security and Law Enforcement Squadrons and they were immediately sent back to the United States. In fact most of the new recruits at Bentwaters in December 1980 were said to have been replacements for those who were transferred. If Larry had been busted for drugs he would probably have received the same treatment and may even have been discharged. Besides, I have in my possession a copy of a document with the stamp of Wing Commander Gordon E. Williams' signature, which proves that Larry himself requested separation from the Air Force and not the other way around.

Not only did Larry's attempts to re-enlist fail, but when he applied for his passport to be renewed in 1994 he received a letter stating his request had been denied due to the passport being altered or mutilated. He was told he would have to appear before a passport agent or designated court employee with acceptable proof of his US citizenship. He also had to submit a written statement explaining the reason for the condition of the altered/mutilated passport. Larry called the State Department Consular Center in New Hampshire and was told the letter had been sent to him at the behest of the Department of Defense. The reason given for the refusal was that he had been discussing sensitive defence issues on foreign soil. Further attempts to obtain a passport were blocked and Larry discovered that all files relating to him had disappeared from the State Department's computers. He simply did not exist! On 17 October 1994 Peter Robbins wrote to former Attorney General Ramsey Clark, explaining Larry's passport predicament and asking for his assistance in the matter. Apparently Ramsey, who had represented New York police officer Frank Serpico, offered his advice, but things did not go as well as expected and in the spring of 1995 Larry was again refused a passport. According to both Peter and Larry, Ramsey stepped in and suggested they mention his (Ramsey's) name, and one month later Larry received his new passport.

One can see why Larry Warren's story is by far the most controversial. However, Dot Street and Brenda Butler had to admit that, in 1983, he had certain information about the case that was not public knowledge. But had he picked it up from others on the base, or was he actually a witness? Unfortunately alterations in times and dates have occurred throughout the years. He originally claimed there were two hundred witnesses at the site, then changed it to one hundred and more recently it became forty. However odd this may seem, we must never forget what a trauma it was, and Larry is not the only one who has made errors or has changed his story. Nevertheless, his errors are more prominent because his story has changed more often, and this might be where the real problem lies. For instance, in 1983 he told Dot Street that following the incident he had found himself on his bed, fully clothed and covered in mud, with no idea of how he had got there. This story changed until it became obsolete when in 1997 he described walking back to the truck and returning to the base.

When *The News of the World* newspaper interviewed Larry for the 2 October 1983 issue he did not claim to have seen any aliens, but a month later (6 November) he gave the newspaper a different story. Still using the pseudonym Art Wallace, he had since undergone hypnotic regression and was able to offer a full description of the aliens. According to the newspaper article, during his session with two unnamed hypnotists, he discovered he had witnessed General Gordon Williams communicating with the entities. We must consider that until Williams was featured on the front page of *The News of the World* a month earlier, Larry had never mentioned his name, but now he had linked him with the incident. According to *Skycrash*, Fred Max was a behavioural psychologist who had conducted the hypnotic session that apparently helped Larry to recall the names of other witnesses and much more detail of the events. However, this session still sees Larry having blacked out and waking up in his barracks, which is strange considering he has since claimed this did not happen. I found it equally strange that there was no reference to this session, or indeed Fred Max, in *Left at East Gate*, especially as Larry has since trashed the newspaper article. Surely this was important because it would apply to his involvement in the actual incident and would help to quell the accusations that he was not involved. I decided to contact Peter Robbins in New York, who explained that the reason the session with Fred Max was not featured in their book was due to a decision made by Larry. When I pushed Peter for more information, it turned out that for whatever reason Larry was not put under hypnosis but had gone through the motions.

I already knew there were problems with Larry's testimony. Several months earlier I had heard what sounded like a full confession that he had not been involved in the underground incident after all. It was discovered on an old audio cassette tape with a faded name scrawled on it, the name Art Wallace, his pseudonym. The tape revealed details of conversations between Larry and Dot Street.

Dot had paid me a visit and had brought along several audio tapes, and after listening to them most of the day I was just about to finish up when, towards the end of the tape, Larry's voice became very anxious. Unfortunately, the tape ran out so I only heard the first part of his statement, but it was enough to confuse matters even more. He confessed to Dot that the hypnotic session in 1983 had not been genuine because unbeknown to the hypnotist he had not been fully hypnotized. His excuse was that he had gone along with the pretence because someone had paid for the session and they had said words to the effect that, 'it better be good'.

In the conversations with Dot, Larry then went on to explain that he had asked Larry Fawcett and Barry Greenwood to find Adrian Bustinza in order to back up his story. 'I said, get a hold of Bustinza, he'll tell you what happened, I just told them their names and where they came from . . . Once they get a hold of Bustinza, I'll come out. Larry [Fawcett] called me and said, "We finally got a hold of Adrian Bustinza . . ."' However, it seems Bustinza had clammed up and would not discuss the underground facility, or that they were interrogated, and Larry felt let down. The following is taken from my notes of the recording and it is obvious that Larry was confused:

> It's real, Larry's [Fawcett] lost interest with the case. You know this underground stuff; Larry to this day does not believe me. I told Barry [Greenwood] and Larry Fawcett that it didn't happen to me. I'm telling you it did not happen. When I first came out with that, well, I said it did . . . It was March '81. What can we do about it? Bustinza and a few others, we went down to this place. This underground garbage, I've erased that stuff for ever. I didn't even see those space things. I told Larry, the thing is, March '81 I got together with some people. We were all involved, rehashing the whole thing, Bustinza said we were taken down to this . . . Bustinza wouldn't give him [Fawcett] specific details of the underground. If I said I heard it second-hand no one would believe it. Bustinza said we were taken down to an underground base . . . I did some checking, it seemed there was some fact to him. I'd hoped that Busty would tell him what we went through. Busty denied the underground. I had to play devil's advocate.

OK, I did this. I have an ace in the hole, if I get screwed around
by this, it would make . . . [tape cut off]

Just before this bizarre conversation with Dot Street, Larry
claimed he had received a telephone threat from an anonymous
source. Dot had already spoken to Larry's mother, who seemed clearly
concerned for the safety of her son. I listened to part of that recording
and heard Mrs Warren tell Dot that Larry could no longer talk to
anyone, that he had to stop all talking. Apparently, Larry had received
a brief call from someone warning him 'It's OK for people talking
about this, but you've gone too far. You've ruined families. If you keep
this up we'll be in touch.' Larry believed the threat was as a result of
Larry Fawcett's call to Major Malcolm Zickler's residence. The Major
was not at home when Fawcett called but he managed to talk to Mrs
Zickler at great length, which might have upset her husband.
Whoever called Larry might not have approved of him giving out Air
Force personnel details. Could the threatening call have prompted
him to deny his involvement in the underground affair? I asked Larry
to explain why he went off at a tangent, telling Dot Street that the
underground story was a non-event. 'I had just gone public with my
name, thinking other guys would start talking,' he said, 'but when
Adrian denied being in the underground I decided I wasn't going to
talk about it anymore. I just wanted to forget it so I denied I had been
there.' A few days after the conversation with Dot, Larry was flown
to Japan to appear on a television show.
    But the biggest surprise was yet to come. More than fifteen years
ago Larry had told Dot Street that he had an ace in the hole, but
what was that ace? I was about to close this chapter on Larry Warren
– and believe me it was the most difficult one to write – when he
called with important news he wanted to share with me. It was news
I desperately wanted to hear, but it did not come cheap; in fact, it
cost me many a weary night rewriting the details time and time
again as Larry recounted a different set of events with each conversation. At one point I even considered eliminating the story
altogether, but then I knew it had to be told, but only in its entirety.

Early in 1999 I had called and left a message for Larry, who had been visiting Liverpool, where he was staying with Sue McAllister. There were some final details I wanted to check with him; however, I was not prepared for what I was about to hear. He told me that a few months earlier he had been sent some photographs of the actual UFO encountered by Jim Penniston and John Burroughs, which were taken during the initial incident on 25/26 December. I had heard rumours that someone had managed to take pictures and smuggle them out but had never been able to find any evidence to support this story. According to Larry, someone had read the reviews of *Left at East Gate* on the Internet and had sent the photographs to him care of his publishers. Included in the package were negatives, a Bentwaters photograph folder, a map with directions to the landing site and a letter from the witness. Larry would not reveal the contact's full name but gave his Christian name as Mark. The witness was an accountant living with his wife and family in the United States and although he was very nervous about the whole affair and did not want to be named, he had sent Larry the photographs in the hope that it would back up the case.

The witness had been a bystander who was off duty when he and another airman saw lights over the forest from the nearby village of Eyke. He and his friend became curious and drove back to Bentwaters to collect a camera before making their way to the forest. On passing some buildings by the roadside (Foley Cottages), they saw lights moving through the trees and decided to park the vehicle with the aim of investigating them. But Mark's friend was frightened and refused to follow him into the forest. As Mark moved closer to the lights he could see two figures and a triangular UFO sitting in a clearing. At one point he was only five feet away from the UFO, standing behind a tree taking pictures. The UFO then lifted up and began moving through the forest, dipping in and out of the trees. Mark thought the others had been abducted and decided to run for it. On returning to the base he put another film into his camera and shot pictures of the ground. This film was then turned over to his superiors, and he was told that it had come out 'fogged'. Three months later, when he thought it was safe to have the UFO film developed, he risked taking it to the Bentwaters supermarket. A few days later he collected the film, which included pictures of himself and some friends taken prior to the incident. For the rest of his tour, almost two years, he kept them safely hidden on the base, sometimes moving them to other locations when he became nervous. As soon as Mark returned to the United States he placed the negatives and pictures into a safe deposit box and there they remained until they were sent to Larry in late 1998. An incredible story!

Over the course of several weeks, I listened to Larry as he told me about the pictures and how Mark had kept them safe all those years. In an attempt to get the facts correct I would go over the details, only to find that the story changed during these conversations, which of course gave me cause for concern. Then Larry sent me one of the photographs. It was a glossy black picture with a group of coloured lights in the shape of a triangle and a few other coloured balls of light scattered throughout. I eventually had the photograph blown up and lightened and was amazed to find what appeared to be a distorted forest with a triangle of lights hovering over a clearing. Beneath the lights was an azure mist and at ground level there appeared to be a strange yellow mist rising up a few feet off the ground. It certainly looked interesting and, as promised, I sent a blown-up copy back to Larry. I am aware that the photograph could easily be a hoax. However, until it had been enlarged several times and lightened there was nothing to see except blackness and a few lights, so that in itself is interesting. I asked Larry if it were possible that someone might be trying to set him up, but he was adamant that the source was genuine: not only did he know the identity of the witness, but they had exchanged correspondence and talked on the telephone. Besides, the photographs had come not only with the negatives but also with the Bentwaters supermarket folder, and of course there was the map that Mark had sketched, indicating details of the route to the landing site. If these photographs were of the Rendlesham UFO, they were a good piece of evidence, but unless I could talk to the witness, or have something constructive to back them up, I had to remain wary. Larry promised to send me a photocopy of the Bentwaters folder and a negative. Hopefully, if the negative proved to have coding, it would at least date the film.

Imagine my surprise then when a week later I received a call from Larry confessing that he was the person who had taken the photographs. I was dumbfounded. My first question was, without doubt, 'Why did you sit on them for nineteen years?' This was followed by a barrage of questions. I could not believe that he would not use them in his book or even in the early days when he was trying so desperately to prove his case. Peter Robbins was devastated but still had confidence in Larry, blaming it on the incident and the fact that he had been messed with. Meanwhile, Larry confessed to Peter that he had told me the story and given me permission to use the photograph. Obviously Peter felt betrayed, having been his co-author and helped research his story for almost a decade. I felt for Peter, I had only worked with Larry on a chapter and knew how intense it was – there were surprises around every corner. The problem was the way Larry convincingly told the first story – all those details. I thought he deserved an award for an excellent performance.

Larry's new story was, of course, different. He and Mark had driven to Ipswich railway station and parked Mark's car in the car park. They were catching a train to London to meet two German girls, but first they visited a music shop that was situated near the station. I reminded Larry that it was Christmas Day and the shops were most likely closed during that period. He said Arabs owned the shop, but when I suggested that back in 1980 it might have still been the law to close on Christmas Day, he decided it was not open after all. He now explained that some men were delivering merchandise to the shop and he had stopped them to ask about prices. Mark, I was told, was an airman who had top-secret clearance, worked for the National Security Agency and was posted at RAF Martlesham Heath. On their way back to Bentwaters that night they picked up four other airmen, but how they all got into one old car I have no idea. As they approached the Bentwaters base they saw three strange lights in the sky formed into the shape of a triangle that seemed to be making a droning noise. Mark drove to the base, dropped off the other airmen, picked up a camera, and he and Larry headed for Rendlesham Forest. As they approached the cottages they heard Motorola radios and saw a white Law Enforcement vehicle parked on the roadside. Having parked their car close by, they followed the noise of the radios into the forest where they found the UFO, which had three points to its base and looked like a Christmas tree. Apart from the reddish lights, everything was pitch black and as Larry took a photograph the UFO moved up off the ground and the radios became silent. Mark suddenly became very frightened and ran away, hiding on the ground in the forest. Larry saw some figures he could not recognize but thinks they were abducted because as soon as he began taking photographs the men disappeared. On leaving the forest, Larry spotted John Burroughs who was standing beside a truck. Of course, at that stage he did not know who Burroughs was. Mark then fired off a blank roll of film (both films were Cannon 35 mm) and Larry took the canisters back to his dorm for safekeeping.

Larry put the canisters on his windowsill but his roommate was uncomfortable with the situation and told him he should report it. He decided to take only the blank film to his superior, Senior Master Sergeant Lee Swain, who then referred Larry to Major Drury. However, Larry thinks Drury was unaware of what was going on. Later that day he heard that someone called Burroughs had seen a UFO and, realizing there might be a search, he wrapped the canister inside a sock, which he placed in a small canvas bag and took to Steve La Plume. Without explaining what it was, he asked La Plume to look after it in case someone searched his room. But La Plume declined, so he went back to his dorm and hid the canister inside his mattress.

Larry smuggled the pictures out of Bentwaters by placing them in the bottom of a Wedgwood German beer mug, which he had bought on a recent trip to Germany. He posted the parcel to his mother, who knew nothing about the photographs until he returned home a few months later. Once back in the United States he placed the photographs and negatives in his sister's safe deposit box. 'I was very frightened of having the pictures,' he told me. But then he said he had thought of taking them to the newspapers. Larry suggested I contact Steve La Plume, because although he may not be aware of what was inside the sock, he might remember him asking to look after it. But La Plume does not recall the incident and according to his earlier testimony he and Larry never talked until the middle of January 1981. Larry also told me that Adrian Bustinza knew about the photographs, but when I questioned him he denied any knowledge of them.

A year earlier I had discussed Larry's alleged trip to Germany with Peter Robbins. According to *Left at East Gate*, Larry had just arrived back from Germany the day before his encounter in Rendlesham Forest. Peter assured me that was what his co-author had told him, but I was not convinced. If Larry was in Germany, I thought he could not have been a witness because by his own admission and his records he was on D Flight, which meant he should have been on duty during 26/27–28/29. Therefore, if he had been involved in the second landing, he would have already been on duty the day before. However, since then I had discovered that some of the flights were mixed up due to the Christmas holidays. With this in mind, I realized Larry could have been on a different shift that week, but for no reason in particular I had failed to mention my new findings to Larry or Peter.

Just when I thought I had heard everything, Larry had another surprise in store for me. He was now confessing that he had never been in Germany during the Christmas holidays but had used the trip to cover up the fact that he had been involved in the initial incident. He claimed that if researchers thought he was out of the country then they would not connect him with it. I was obviously trying to figure out how anyone could connect him with the photographs or his alleged involvement when nobody had known anything about it anyway. This statement was remarkable, considering he had diligently done everything he could to prove the incident had occurred and especially that he himself was involved. Suddenly,

I was expected to believe that he was trying to cover up his involvement in an earlier encounter. I could have gone on for weeks with my questioning but I felt there was no point. I was burnt out with this latest saga and had already spent far too much time on the Larry Warren story.

However, I did ask Larry if he would send me some evidence to back up his claims. I suggested he send me one of the negatives, a photocopy of the strip of negatives, showing the code numbers, a copy of the Bentwaters folder and a letter admitting he had taken the photographs and had copyright to them. These items were promised to me but Larry claimed he might not be able to locate the folder and instead of the ten photographs he originally had there were now only five. In a previous conversation, when we were discussing the mystery witness, he had told me that some of the photographs had been taken before the incident and featured Mark and his friends. Understandably, I was very sceptical about all of this, and until such time as Larry could prove he took the photographs I would remain so. Unfortunately, albeit innocently, Peter related my concern and disbelief to Larry, who then thought it was not worth pursuing the matter with me. I admit I discussed the situation with Peter because we were both totally confused. I believe we were both looking for some positive answers but Larry seemed to be even more confused than we were.

John Burroughs, who was a witness to two events, offered his opinion of Larry's story to science writer Antonio Huneeus in an interview in 1990:

> Larry Warren has hurt this case quite a bit. The only thing I can say about Larry Warren's testimony, that aliens came out, his excuse was that CNN did a botched-up job and he never described those little men like they were and stuff like that. There was something out there that was intelligent, that (hurt the eyes especially) when there was the blue transparent-type lights that were coming out, and the different things that they were capable of doing. That is my stand on that. Now Larry Warren took it a step further and, as far as I am concerned, there was no contact

between, he called him the base commander, Lieutenant Colonel Williams at the time, and I did not see him out there. I know for a fact that Colonel Halt was out there and there is a small possibility, if I remember, I did see for a brief moment possibly the new base commander, which would have been Colonel Conrad at the time. But there was nothing that I am aware [of] or through talking to other people that would describe what Larry Warren described to CNN, other than there were blue transparent lights that could be possibly – they did act intelligently, some of the stuff they did . . . There was something else that came off the main craft that was able to do different things and flew over the top of us and flew through a pick-up truck and did stuff like that.

Larry always told researchers he had an ace in the hole to play, and he has since told me that the photographs are that ace. But are they? Could it be that he was not involved in the Rendlesham Forest incident after all? Throughout my investigation I have found no witness to back up Larry's story. Whether he was involved in one of the encounters, either standing next to the object or further back in the forest, is open to debate. Did Larry take the photographs of the first encounter or was someone trying to set him up? If a witness really did send the photographs to Larry then it is a real pity, because the story has now become so distorted that unless the witness comes forward there is no way of knowing the truth.

Sue McAllister, who married Larry in Nevada in March 2000, told me in early 1999 that she believed he was genuine. 'He's one of the most courageous people I've ever met,' she told me. Sue recalls the first time she heard Larry talk at a UFO conference. 'The whole audience were mesmerized by him,' she said. 'He comes across as being genuine.' Sue is a member of a small Liverpool UFO group, and apparently Larry showed some of the photographs to them when he visited England. According to Sue, one of the members suggested they might be a set-up. Obviously, at that stage he had not told the group that he had taken the photographs. Peter Robbins has seen one of them and when I asked him if he knew who was responsible for them it turned out that Larry had claimed witness Ed Cabansag had taken them. After almost twenty years of silence from Cabansag, Larry might have thought he would never have gone public. Was Larry doing this to protect the witness named Mark, did he really take the photographs himself or was he trying to paint himself back in the picture?

In 1999 Sue McAllister wrote me a letter pointing out that, among other things, Larry's medical records should be proof enough that he was involved. Larry has produced medical records for an eye problem that he suffered whilst at Bentwaters and another injury that surfaced a few years later. During 1983 he had complained of a burning sensation and bleeding through the skin on his neck and back. On one occasion in 1984 his former wife had rushed him to hospital thinking he had ruptured a blood vessel. According to Larry, the doctors detained him for four hours while they conducted several tests. Finally three doctors entered the room and the most senior of these asked Larry a number of questions. He wanted to know if Larry had ever been in Vietnam or worked around any nuclear devices. When Larry admitted he had worked at a nuclear base, he was told that it was their opinion that he had been exposed to an unshielded nuclear device. The doctor asked Larry if he could recall when this might have happened. Larry explained that he could but he doubted the doctor would believe it. Larry was then told that in normal conditions these effects should not show up for twenty years. Considering Larry did not have clearance to work in the weapons storage area, it is unlikely he was exposed to any of the nuclear devices deployed at Bentwaters. But then if he was standing facing the UFO, why would only his neck and back have been affected, and why was Adrian Bustinza, who was also standing *facing* the object, not affected?

Peter Robbins went to great pains to research the site where Larry claims the second landing had taken place. In 1990 samples of soil were analysed by Matthew Miniz of Springborn Laboratories Inc., Wareham, MA. Miniz concluded that it was a difficult task due to the time lapse and the conditions the samples had been stored under, but nevertheless his professional opinion was in favour of anomalies in the samples, although he expressed a need for further research. Although Larry is the only person to claim the UFO landed in the farmer's field, the analysis tends to show that something affected the soil on that particular site. However, local resident Gary Collins claims the UFO could not have landed in Capel Green, which he says was only a road, or the farmer's field, which was visible from his property. 'I would have been able to see it if that had been the case,' he told me. However, so would the occupants of the three properties that were directly facing the site, but they deny they witnessed anything unusual.

I met Larry Warren in 1997 when he visited my home with Peter Robbins during their promotional tour in England. I found him to be a charming well-mannered individual, albeit that I sensed there was hidden anxiety. Against all the odds, I had believed he was somehow involved in the incident along with numerous other witnesses. At no time did I favour his underground scenario with the alien being, but considered that he was possibly messed with. Always, I asked myself the same question. 'Why stay with it for so long and put up with all the criticism if it was not true?' Was Brenda Butler right, did Larry get the story from someone else? Certainly, he told Dot Street he had heard the underground story from Adrian Bustinza, and had apparently confirmed it with Larry Fawcett and Barry Greenwood. It was the only way to get the truth out, he had told Dot. If he explained that the story was second-hand it would not be believed, so he had to play the devil's advocate. This was the gist of what he told her in 1983. I know because Dot, my mother and I listened to those recordings when Dot visited me in March 1999. However, we all agreed it was probably because he had been threatened.

Adrian Bustinza would eventually admit to having been taken to an underground facility, but his story is different from Larry's. Was Larry tampered with, either by government agents who gave him several memories and trigger words, or by some alien force that we still know so little about? There is no doubt that he is very bitter and blames the USAF for what happened, but we must then question why he was so intent on re-enlisting so soon afterwards. It is not my intention to discredit Larry Warren; in fact I had hoped more than anything to prove his case was genuine. It is difficult to believe that Larry is intentionally lying, but could there also be some confusion there? He has genuinely cooperated, leading me to sources he truly believed would back up his story even when they did not. And he has endured so many years of harassment from all sides and appears to have still managed, sometimes with great difficulty, to hang on to what he believes is right. I have discussed with both Larry and Peter the possibility that Larry could have unknowingly been used to spread confusion and disinformation. Let us also not forget that if he truly was involved in a close encounter of the third kind there are forces out there that would want to silence him. But Larry was not one to keep his mouth shut and, as we know, was already discussing the incident within hours of it happening – even threatening to go public. If Larry Warren could not be silenced he could be discredited. It is very possible that he is a victim of the Rendlesham Forest incident but, like Steve Roberts, Larry's story has become very confusing.

In March 2000 Larry Warren attended a UFO conference in Nevada where he impressed researchers with the story about the UFO photographs. Only this time he did not admit that he had taken them himself but claimed they came to him from a witness. It was a similar story to the one he had originally told me in early 1999. Larry's chopping and changing is so much in line with that of Steve Roberts that it actually bears thinking about. Here are two seemingly intelligent men who over the years have altered their testimony to such an extent that it has surely discredited the case, yet they appear to have played some role in the events. Roberts told his original story regarding the alien presence to Chris and Brenda, and Larry recounted an almost identical story to Steve La Plume a few weeks after the incident. Did something sinister really happen during those debriefings? Could it be that the witnesses were programmed with trigger words or sounds, which every now and again would result in them telling a different story in order to confuse the truth? Larry says, 'Take me out of the story and you still have a case.' That is true, but I don't believe the Larry Warren story will ever go away. It will just change from time to time.

THE ENIGMA OF GENERAL WILLIAMS

Ever since General Gordon Williams was featured in a British tabloid as having conversed with alien entities in Rendlesham Forest, researchers and journalists from all parts of the world have tried to track him down. No doubt I would have been one of those, so imagine my surprise when in the early part of my investigations I received an electronic mail from someone claiming to be General Williams. My first thought was that I was being hoaxed or set up to try to discredit me or lead me off the track. I was certainly not convinced he was who he claimed to be.

The electronic mail was short and to the point. Basically, he identified himself as the USAF wing commander of RAF Bentwaters and Woodbridge during the alleged UFO business and wanted to know what was new on the case. He signed himself GW. I did not reply to his request for some weeks because I wanted to do a little background research on General Williams. I began by checking the white pages, which are the American domestic telephone directories, but he was not listed. I requested an Air Force Freedom of Information biography on the general, which at least gave me the ammunition to question him. In the meantime, I discovered he was a regional president for the West Point Society and later I would learn that he was involved with the Council on Foreign Relations. Although retired from the USAF, he is still very much a high-profile figure who serves as a defence consultant to several major companies.

According to Larry Warren and Peter Robbins, when investigating the case for *Left at East Gate* they were told that General

Williams was in California, but my mystery man was not based at that location. The authors had received the information from a brief interview with Lieutenant Colonel Al Brown in 1988, almost ten years previously – there was still hope. I decided to compose a reply to GW asking him to offer more information about himself, explaining that there were a lot of hoaxers and debunkers on the Internet and I wanted to be sure he was who he claimed to be. When he answered some weeks later, he offered very little information other than he had retired as a major general and during his tenure at the Suffolk bases he had been a fan of the Ipswich football team. I became equally evasive. Was I in for a cat and mouse game with a debunker or a crank or was he the real McCoy? It was only after several months of regular email exchanges, telephone conversations and exchange of postal mail that I was confident I was dealing with the general himself. It turned out that he was new to the Internet, and although I have asked him several times how and why he contacted me, he has never offered any explanation except 'I don't know' or 'I can't recall'. I thought he might have done an Internet search on Bentwaters and discovered an old article I had written on the case, but he made no comment and eventually I just quit asking, but admit I became a little suspicious as to his motives.

Gordon E. Williams was born in November 1935 in Nashua, New Hampshire. He graduated from Alvirne High School, Hudson, in 1953 and earned a Bachelor of Science degree from the United States Military Academy at West Point in 1957. In 1971 he gained a Master of Science degree in systems management from the University of Southern California. His military career is equally impressive. He completed Air Command and Staff College in 1969, National War College in 1975 and Harvard University's executive programme on national and international security in 1983. During his career he completed more than 4,000 flying hours, piloting F-100s, F-4s, A-7s, A-10s and F-15s. The rest of his military achievements, decorations and awards are too numerous to include here but, suffice to say, he earned his stars and stripes. In January 1981 he was selected for promotion to brigadier general and became a major general in 1984. There is no doubt that Gordon Williams would have made it to the very top of the ranks had he not been forced into early retirement due to an incident that caused him temporary ill heath. He retired with two stars on 1 August 1988.

In September 1977 the then Colonel Williams was assigned as vice wing commander to the 81st Tactical Fighter Wing at RAF Bentwaters and Woodbridge, and in August 1979 he was promoted to wing commander. According to Williams this was a glorious time to be in the Air Force, and he remarked that his tour as wing commander of the Suffolk installations was the best time of his Air Force career. During this period the Wing was equipped with A-10 Thunderbolt II tank busters which were operated by six tactical fighter squadrons: four based at Bentwaters and two at Woodbridge. On one day alone the Wing flew 500 sorties, shooting a 30 mm cannon on every flight and even dropping a bomb. I understand that was something the Wing became famous for, but I doubt it pleased the locals. It was during this time that Williams built up several forward operating locations on the Continent. Each small unit was managed by a lieutenant colonel, who commanded a group of fifty permanent personnel whose job it was to take care of pilots and aircraft arriving from the British bases. These locations were put into action as part of the Cold War defence plan and were ideally situated to contain any threat from the Red Army tank force, should they decide to advance from the far side of the Rhine. Williams' call sign was Dragon. He had used this in Vietnam from time to time and had picked it up again when he arrived at Bentwaters. It was well suited because the 81st Tactical Fighter Wing had adopted it for their emblem. In fact, the fiery dragon has been a symbol used since medieval days to intimidate the enemy.

Gordon Williams completed a total of thirty-one years in the USAF, and every officer I have contacted has had nothing but praise for the general, who was known to encourage personnel by giving them a fair chance to succeed. Few people outside the military realize the enormous legal power held by generals. As Commander of the 13th Air Force, General Williams had to approve a twenty-year sentence in Fort Leavenworth (the military prison in Kansas) and a life sentence in a murder case.

The core of the rumour that would identify Gordon Williams as a witness to the Rendlesham Forest incident dates back to 2 January 1981. Brenda Butler and Chris Pennington would hear from their source Steve Roberts that he had witnessed the base commander communicating with aliens from a landed UFO. The next link came from a civilian radar operator at RAF Watton, who reported a similar story. Of course, it was Colonel Ted Conrad who held the position of base commander; no one had even thought of the wing commander's alleged involvement until Larry Warren told *The News of the World* that Williams had communicated with aliens. From that moment on the die was cast.

Larry Warren claims the main reason for believing Williams was involved was because he remembered the commander in the forest as being an extremely tall man, at least six feet five. Not explaining my reasons, I asked Williams how tall he was, he replied instantly that he was six feet one, not an unusual height for an American but one cannot confuse him with Colonel Halt, who was considerably shorter than his boss. Colonel Conrad was also a tall man but, unlike Williams who stems from a reserved New England background and had fair to greyish hair (now grey) and a fair complexion, he was a Texan who was known to wear cowboy boots at every opportunity. He was also olive-skinned and had a head of black hair and bushy black eyebrows. Could Warren have confused Williams with Conrad? Hardly. But let us not forget the confusion in the forest and the fact that Warren talks about strange shadows on the UFO, which would imply a sense of distortion. I asked Warren if it were possible he could have confused Williams with someone else. He had been a guard of honour at the general's change of command ceremony but admitted that when he saw the photograph of Williams in *The News of the World*, it had looked nothing like the man he saw at the ceremony. 'He wasn't as well built as he was in the picture,' said Warren. 'I remember him being much slimmer somehow.' Airman Warren was only on the base a few weeks before the incident occurred and might only have seen Williams on his first day on duty, when the wing commander gave his welcome pep talk to the new recruits, and briefly at the general's ceremony a few months later. So there is every possibility he is mistaken.

General Williams' photograph appeared in the newspaper because the journalist was unable to locate one of Lieutenant Colonel Halt, the author of the famous memorandum, so they published a photograph of the former wing commander instead. They also quoted him as saying, 'I don't know exactly what happened, it is all there. He [Halt] is not a man who would hoax the British Ministry of Defence or the American Air Force Department.' However, Williams claims he was never interviewed by any journalist and has never spoken to anyone about the incident until he contacted me in early January 1998. If that is the case then who did the newspaper talk to?

The Rendlesham Forest case attracted the attention of several high-profile American researchers. Church minister Ray Boeche was one such person. In the early days he and his colleague Scott Colborn made a joint effort to research the case and managed to contact Adrian Bustinza and John Burroughs, but Burroughs was evasive. Their research findings were published in a paper entitled 'Bentwaters – What Do We Do Now?' But due to Burroughs still being in the military and Bustinza afraid for his life, their identities were withheld, so there was very little follow-up. There is no doubt, however, that Boeche thought the case was genuine because he consulted Senator James J. Exon. The senator was willing to assist in his enquiries but needed more proof before he would proceed with an investigation. On the afternoon of 10 April 1985 Boeche placed a call to Charles Halt (now a full colonel) at Tinker AFB, Oklahoma, and managed to persuade him to talk to the senator. It was during the conversation with Halt that Boeche asked him about Gordon Williams' alleged involvement. Ray Boeche confirmed the following:

> I told him I was an independent researcher, but Halt thought I
> was representing Exon. I asked him if it was true that an officer

drove Wing Commander Gordon Williams from the landing site
to a waiting plane with a motion picture of a UFO. He said, 'Yes,
I can verify that for the senator.'

Thirty minutes after the conversation with Colonel Halt,
Boeche attempted to contact Gordon Williams (now a brigadier
general) at Norton AFB, California, but was unable to speak to him
personally. He tried again on 24 April and the only response he
received was from a Major Verke. 'The general has no comment,' he
said. Having now put Halt in touch with Senator Exon, Boeche was
impatient to proceed with the investigation, but Exon had gone cold
and appeared to be avoiding him. After several calls to Exon's office
he was finally told by an aide that Exon and Halt had talked several
times, but a condition of Halt's was that Exon had to agree not to
discuss their conversations with anyone else. Boeche was being shut
out and he knew it. Did Halt confide to Exon the details of
Williams' involvement?

I asked General Williams if he had been in the forest on any of
the nights in question. 'No, I did not participate in any such event.
I was not out there during any of those nights you mention. You
have to understand that I was the wing commander, it was not my
place to go chasing through the forest,' he explained. When I asked
him if he was out in the forest during another reported sighting that
took place in January 1981, he replied, 'I can't be sure about that.' I
introduced the general to some of Nick Pope's regular web articles,
and he showed an interest, so I managed to have Nick sign copies of
his books which I sent to him. Nick had mentioned the Rendlesham
Forest incident and Williams made the following comment:

> I have already turned to page 146 of *Open Skies, Closed Minds* and
> find my name there, wherein Larry Warren claims I met briefly
> with three creatures with large heads and dark eyes. It just isn't so!
> His [Warren's] credibility is nil from my perspective.

According to Gordon Williams, if he had been in the forest he
would have remembered it because it would have been very unusual

for him to go anywhere other than in his official vehicle, a sedan staff car with the latest communications equipment. He pointed out that if such an incident occurred, he would have recalled it as a one-off sort of thing. I admit there are problems with his answers simply because witnesses claim he definitely turned up for a January 1981 sighting, having left his staff car at the east-gate post to go into the forest in a jeep with a patrol of officers. Halt has publicly denied that Williams was a witness to the December incident, but confirmed he was involved in the January sightings. Charles Halt recalls that Williams eagerly followed him over to Woodbridge in his staff car. It seems he had been disappointed to have missed the earlier events and had expressed an interest in being involved if anything should happen in the future.

Because of the confusion over ranks, it is known that Gordon Williams was sometimes mistaken for the base commander so, that being the case, Colonel Ted Conrad might be Larry Warren's mystery man. Conrad is a name that has escaped the limelight in this case and yet should be of major importance. If any of the commanders were out there that night, surely it would have been the base commander. After all, he was overall commander of the Security Police and Law Enforcement Squadrons who, it must be remembered, were the prime witnesses in this incident. It has not been easy to gather information on Conrad, and it is not for the lack of trying. What I have learnt is that he had only been in the position of base commander a few weeks prior to the incident and was promoted to vice wing commander almost immediately afterwards. I thought it was very unusual to receive two promotions so close together, and of course having been appointed vice wing commander he should have been in line for wing commander on his next tour. According to Williams that can be a general-making position, but Conrad retired! Why would he suddenly retire when he was doing so well? Williams told me that Ted Conrad was pushed into the vice wing position by default as a quick replacement for Brian Currie, who had been re-allocated for breaking Air Force etiquette. Apparently Conrad was uncomfortable in his new role, preferring the position of base commander. Other commanders have told me that although he was a fine man, he and his wife seemed somewhat bitter and disillusioned with the Air Force. It seems unusual that an officer of his category would have such thoughts. Could he have been another victim of the Rendlesham Forest incident?

The first time Conrad's name was mentioned in this case was in the March 1983 issue of *OMNI*. The article, entitled 'Anti Matter', not only referred to a UFO landing but featured an interview with Conrad himself. In 1987 Colonel Charles Halt, who was now based in Belgium, sent a recorded message to an American researcher and, referring to the incident, he said, 'When contact was made with the base commander, it wasn't Colonel Williams; contact was actually made with myself and Colonel Ted Conrad.' The latter seems to imply that there was indeed some sort of contact, but Halt publicly denies he witnessed a landed UFO or that there was an alien crew.

OMNI journalist Eric Mishera was offered a private account of the event by Conrad, provided it was a one-off interview. Mishera's published article with Conrad revealed details of the first incident involving Penniston and Burroughs, but no names were mentioned. There are errors in Conrad's version, however, which appears to be a combination of the two major events that he claimed took place on 30 December. However, he did confirm (a) the men were con-fronted by a large craft mounted on tripod legs, which had no windows and was covered in red and blue lights; (b) it demonstrated intelligent control; (c) for almost an hour the men gave chase after the object when it took off; (d) Conrad himself mounted an investigation the following day and personally went into the forest and found a triangular set of marks evidently formed by the legs of the craft; (e) Conrad interviewed the witnesses and stated, 'Those lads certainly saw something, but I don't know what it was.' But Conrad debunked the alien contact story as being an exaggeration of the events. He also claimed there was no investigation apart from his involvement in checking out the site the following day. However, the latter is in contradiction to witness testimonies. The fact that

Conrad denied there was an investigation, when he must have been privy to that information, is somewhat misleading.

Also worth mentioning is that three of the senior officers at RAF Bentwaters received what some might term 'convenient promotions'. Although General Williams claims there was nothing unusual about these, let us examine them just the same. Lieutenant Colonel Halt received a promotion to full colonel immediately after the case made headlines in 1983, and one has to agree that it looks rather suspicious considering his memorandum had caused such embarrassment for the USAF. Colonel Conrad, who I am to understand did not want the job in the first place, nevertheless was promoted to vice wing commander. Gordon Williams claims he needed someone he could trust to urgently to fill the role, having previously lost two vice wing commanders in a very short period of time. Colonel Williams, although no doubt due for promotion, was promoted to brigadier general almost immediately after the incident (early January 1981), which according to one of the base secretaries was very unusual indeed. She thought the date of rank should have been April or May and could not understand why everything was so rushed or why Williams had to dash off to Mildenhall to receive his promotion. However, Williams points out that there was no conspiracy here because the list would normally come out around Christmas.

Brenda Butler recalls asking Steve Roberts about Colonel Conrad, and Roberts' reply was, 'I knew you would find out sooner or later without me telling you.' But he offered no further information and Conrad disappeared into the woodwork. I have discussed at length with Larry Warren his belief that Gordon Williams was involved in the actual incident. I showed him a fulllength photograph of the general and asked if he could identify him as the person he saw in the forest. He admitted that the photograph resembled the man in *The News of the World* and realized that the man he recalls was more like the person he recognized at the changeof-command ceremony. Warren then supplied me with pictures of several officers taken at a base function. He had written on the back of one: 'Is this Gordon Williams?' I explained that it was definitely not. However, we should not be too hard on Warren if the man he refers to was not Williams. After all, it was a confusing time and, as Adrian Bustinza recalls, 'You had tunnel vision out there.'

More often than not, it is the first recollection of events that is the most credible, from then onwards the story can become exaggerated and distorted. Of course, the first news to surface was that the base commander was communicating with alien beings. As weird as that may seem, it should not be dismissed as complete nonsense. If there was a craft of some sort then there might also have been a crew. Was the base commander summoned and did he go into the forest and communicate with the visitors? General Williams thinks the idea is preposterous, but what if something like this actually happened and he was not privy to it. Although Williams would have been notified, I understand it was not the job of the wing commander to get involved because, although he was in charge of the installations, his primary concern was the flying missions, not investigations. There is no doubt that the incident was compartmentalized immediately and only Colonel Conrad and Major Zickler should have been brought into the loop, inasmuch as they liaised with the AFOSI. By keeping the wing commander out of the investigations they were doing him a favour; besides, he had the day-to-day running of the huge NATO bases to attend to. This is not unreasonable; when it comes to intelligence matters even our prime minister is only briefed on a need-to-know basis. General Williams cannot have it both ways, however; he either knew what was going on, with or without aliens, or he did not.

I asked General Williams why Lieutenant Colonel Halt was allowed to send an important memorandum to the Ministry of Defence without his authorization. 'Honestly, I do not recall,' he said. 'Generally speaking, a wing commander would not let any correspondence go to outside agencies without it being over his signature. But I am sure lots of humdrum paper went back and forth, just so as not to bother the boss. But it was dangerous.' At a later date he confirmed: 'That memo should never have been sent.

If I had known about it I would have tried to retract it.' The fact that Williams would have tried to retract the memorandum is interesting. When I mentioned this to Charles Halt he was not surprised and reminded me that none of the commanders wanted to get involved. Of course, it is possible that Williams was unaware of the memorandum, but Halt would surely have informed the base commander, Colonel Conrad.

One might question where the wing commander was through all of this? According to Halt, Williams knew something had occurred because he was listening to the radio transmissions as they were taking place. Other officers assured me that the wing commander would have been the first person to be notified. However, Williams is very evasive when questioned about the incident, but there is no doubt he knew what was going on even though he may not have been involved in the investigation. He admitted it was possible he may have heard the radio, because although he was not directly linked to the police frequency, he could have easily switched over. I was beginning to understand that, when it came to the incident, Gordon Williams would not offer any straight answers. It was this evasiveness that led me to believe he knew far more than he was willing to discuss.

On Sunday 28 December Gordon Williams was playing golf with Lieutenant Colonel Al Brown. He and Brown were good friends and often played at the local golf club. Brown recounted what he knew about the incident:

> I only heard rumours on the base and at the golf club, but I can tell you that there definitely was not any alert at the time. I know that's been mentioned. The week it happened, I think it was a Friday, I played golf with Gordon Williams on the Sunday. He was a good golfer. I asked him outright, I said, 'Come on, Gordy, tell me what happened.' He said, 'You gotta be kidding me, I know nothing, no one told me anything. Some guys, a bunch of young people got a bit scared in the woods, something scared the hell out of them. That's all I know; but I can tell you that something happened, but what it was, I honestly don't know.' So

something happened and those that were higher rank than me asked and they didn't know. I had heard that an air-traffic controller saw weird lights and things and one of the officers was out there around the Woodbridge base; it wasn't near Bentwaters. I asked Donald Moreland about it but he really didn't know anything much. By the way, the Orfordness lighthouse theory was bullshit!

According to Colonel Halt, Williams had asked him to explain what had occurred during his own visit to the forest. It was then that Halt played him a tape recording of the previous night's event, which he himself was involved in. Williams requested to borrow the tape so he could play it for his boss, General Robert Bazley of 3rd Air Force at RAF Mildenhall. When Williams returned to the base after visiting Mildenhall, he summoned Halt to his office for a briefing. Apparently, when the tape was played for Bazley and his staff, they had no idea what to think of it. I asked Williams to comment, but as usual he was not giving much away.

> I can't recall whether I left the base or not, but I could well have been at a family Christmas thing, I just don't know. I may well have heard the tapes, it seems logically appropriate, but I don't specifically recall it.

It is worth noting that Gordon Williams mentions 'tapes'.

When I pointed out that there might have been a threat to the installations, Williams claimed no one ever suggested to him that that was the case. He explained, 'Everybody would know, all the colonels would know if anything happened because of the command net. There is probably a tape somewhere. There were no secrets.' Of course, I have to disagree with him because my investigation proves that there were secrets surrounding this incident – and many of them.

I realize how difficult it is for General Williams to offer information concerning the incident. Not only did he make the Air Force his lifetime career, but his son is serving as an army captain. His father was also a USAF officer and his stepmother Portia was very well connected in government and military circles. Williams recalls that during his tenure as wing commander at RAF Bentwaters he received a visit from Senator Strom Thurmond, a close friend of Portia's. Thurmond is the longest-serving senator in the United States and a member of the Senate Armed Services Committee. But what is even more interesting is that Thurmond wrote the foreword to Colonel Philip J. Corso's 1997 book, entitled *The Day After Roswell.* The book tells the story of Corso's assignment as the chief of the army's Foreign Technology Division at the Pentagon, and how during that time he was instructed by General Arthur Trudeau to steward alien artefacts to America's industry. These artefacts were allegedly taken from the debris found at the Roswell UFO crash site. After the publication of the book, Thurmond's office took steps to have the foreword removed. One might find nothing unusual about Thurmond's visit to Bentwaters, except that it took place soon after the incident. Is it a coincidence that the senator's name should be linked with the world's two most famous UFO cases? It is interesting that some of the witnesses reported that the Secretary of the Air Force visited the base following the incident, and that he or his aide questioned them. But the only official record of his visit that year was in September. Could they have confused Thurmond for the Secretary of the Air Force?

Gordon Williams was not keen for me to contact his former boss General Bazley, pointing out that he knew nothing about the incident. Robert E. Bazley retired in 1989 as a four-star general. From June 1980 to July 1981 he was commander of the 3rd Air Force at RAF Mildenhall. In early 1981 he was promoted to lieutenant general and in August he was assigned to Ramstein AFB, Germany, as vice commander in chief. It was Bazley who sponsored Gordon Williams, inasmuch as he recommended him for promotion. Williams followed Bazley to Ramstein that same year.

I already knew about General Williams' early retirement, it was no secret in Air Force circles. I will not go into too many details, however, because it would be an intrusion on his privacy, but suffice to say that during his tour in the Philippines in 1985 a mosquito bite almost caused his demise when he contracted encephalitis. This was a terrible shock to a man whose life revolved around his Air Force career, but he was a fighter and was not about to give up easily. After his recovery he was posted to Washington DC and completed his last tour of duty at the European Command Headquarters in Stuttgart, Germany, before retiring in 1988.

In the last few years since Gordon Williams and I have been in touch I have found him to be kindly, humorous and an exceedingly genuine individual. He has been a considerable help in putting me in touch with good contacts, and assisted me in understanding military jargon and many aspects regarding the Suffolk bases and the US Air Force in general. He has filled in many of the missing pieces but has always stayed a far distance from becoming drawn into the Rendlesham Forest incident. Looking back, I realize he has been more than patient with my demands for answers but, although my constant questioning appears to have triggered some old memories, he has not offered any information directly relating to the case. There were times when I became very frustrated, insisting that he must have known something due to the fact that he was the chief of both installations, and I am sure that at these times he was just as annoyed by my constant questioning. But if he knew the truth, he was not telling. He would politely accuse me of being 'testy' and stay clear until I had cooled down. I cannot be absolutely certain that Gordon Williams was not a primary witness to the incident but, so far, I have seen no real evidence to put him in the picture. Williams does not deny knowledge of the events, but his remark that it caused no more than a minor stir at 3rd Air Force Headquarters at RAF Mildenhall, and even less so at the USAFE headquarters at Ramstein in Germany, is questionable. However, when we discussed the UFO, he agreed there are more things in the universe than we may ever know about and was open to the possibility that an advanced civilization could have the technology to cut through time. I could not help wondering if he was trying to tell me something.

I have considered that the encephalitis may have caused a memory problem for the general, and some people might point out

how convenient this is, and no doubt a new conspiracy will be built
up around it. However, Williams seems to be well equipped to
respond to other questions and his high intelligence in other matters
would have me disregard this as an excuse. Because of his former
position and continuing status, General Williams may feel uncomfortable about discussing matters which he may consider taboo. This
is probably the reason he has been so evasive regarding the incident.
Or could it be that he really does not have all the facts and is just
as keen as everyone else to know what happened that December
week? One thing is certain, he is an officer and a gentleman and
abides by the code of honour he was taught in the military, as he
explained to me:

> The truth is important to me. My regard for it all was nurtured at
> West Point with the honour code there. Its importance, and my
> understanding of it, has grown over time. I cannot think of a
> single virtue more important to the continuation of a moral
> society. Without it, over time, we will go the way of the Roman
> Empire.

His words are very refreshing, and I believe they are sincere, but
I am also aware that the very code that taught him to be so honourable in truth may also restrict him from revealing certain truths
concerning this case. I can certainly appreciate the dilemma of being
in such a position.

Although there is a serious side to General Williams, he has often
surprised me with his humour. Having just returned from one of his
frequent trips away, he joked: 'By the way, you will be proud of me.
I bought a cap in a Minneapolis shopping centre that features an
alien on the front with the notation "The truth is out there". On the
back I had embroidered "Bentwaters 1980".'

In October 1999 I was able to meet General Williams in person
when he paid me a visit in London. When he turned up at my
doorstep I was not surprised to see the thoroughly modern major
general sporting his alien hat, which he presented to me as a gift. If
Gordon Williams was not interested in UFOs before I drew him

into my investigation, he certainly was keen to look through my library of books on the subject. He was especially interested in Timothy Good's *Above Top Secret*, so I gave him the book hoping he might think again about the worldwide cover-up.

During his visit I had hoped he would reveal a few secrets, but all he would say is that I should try to find Colonel Ted Conrad; but Conrad had retired from the USAF soon after talking to *OMNI* magazine and all attempts to trace him have so far failed. When I showed Gordon Williams the photograph of the person that Larry Warren believed was him, he explained that it was his vice wing commander, Brian Currie. Did Warren mistake the rather tall Colonel Currie for Williams? Nobody had ever considered that the vice wing commander might have played a role in the incident, and yet it would make perfect sense that Williams' subordinate would be more likely to have been involved, if only to check out the situation for his boss. Colonel Brian Currie did not make it to the rank of general and I imagine he retired soon after he left RAF Bentwaters. According to Malcolm Zickler, one of his Law Enforcement patrols had arrested Currie for his intimate liaison with a female lieutenant on the front lawn of his Bentwaters house. He was ordered to appear before General Williams, who disciplined him, then had him confined to his quarters for five days before sending him back to America. The Bentwaters police log carries an entry of two people being charged with sex offences, but omits their names.

Gordon Williams might not have offered any straight answers regarding the case, but there were clues, and I believe he was sincerely trying to tell me something when he presented me with the baseball hat – 'The truth is out there – Bentwaters 1980'.

THE CIVILIAN WITNESSES

Although the primary witnesses were airmen from the USAF bases, there were also reports from the locals. This is important to the case because their testimonies link up the pattern of events. Since the incident has become well known, several local people have come forward and reported having seen lights in the sky during that time. But a handful of these civilian witnesses have more unusual stories to tell.

One of the first people to come forward was local antiques dealer Roy Webb. Sometime between 01.30 and 02.00 hrs on Boxing Day morning, Webb, his wife and their young daughter Haley were on their way home to Martlesham after spending Christmas Day with their family. They were just approaching Woodbridge when Haley, who was half asleep, alerted her parents to an aerial object that appeared to be following the car. Mrs Webb pulled into a lay-by to take a closer look and, as she did so, the craft also stopped moving. Roy Webb described it as a red globe that was completely silent and suddenly disappeared in an instant. 'One minute it was there, the next it was gone,' he exclaimed. The family continued on their journey unaware of what had been going on in Rendlesham Forest that night.

Another interesting account came to my attention from a local woman who recalls her father's sighting. Pensioner Bertie Coleman lived alone in a small terraced house in the town of Ipswich, about ten miles from Woodbridge. He was a fearless, intelligent old soul who had fought earnestly in the trenches during World War One. Not much frightened him, but something scared the hell out of

Bertie and his faithful dog on Christmas night 1980. Bertie lived alone and usually retired very early. On this particular night he had awoken from sleep to find his distressed dog literally trembling beside the bed. Realizing that something was drastically wrong, and shocked to see his dog in such a state, its hair literally standing on end, he gazed out of the window to see a huge bright object travelling horizontally through the sky. In the morning he recounted the sighting to his family who laughed it off thinking he had been dreaming.

It was not until a few years later, and after Bertie had passed on, that Marjorie Wright realized her father's sighting was probably very real indeed, and might have been related to the Rendlesham Forest incident. Marjorie came to my attention through Dave King, a retired police officer who had visited the forest soon after the incident. An Ipswich newspaper had carried a story on the case, mentioning my forthcoming book and adding King's scepticism, that the UFO was probably the light from the Orfordness lighthouse. Marjorie wanted to talk to him to explain her father's sighting and point out that it could not have been the lighthouse. I spoke to Marjorie at length and realized she was feeling guilty about dismissing her father's sighting as being nothing more than a dream. She wanted it to go on record that he had witnessed something very strange, and hoped it would give more credence to the case. She told me:

> No way could it have been a lighthouse that my father saw, it was not possible for its beam to reach that far. I don't know what it could have been, but he said it was a solid object and it was enough to frighten my father and terrify his dog.

Brenda Butler and Dot Street managed to locate several locals who claimed they had seen lights and even UFOs. One credible witness was Gordon Levitt, a quiet family man from Sudbourne. Levitt was not able to verify the exact date but was sure it was sometime around 28 or 29 December. It was between 19.00 and 20.00 hrs when Levitt was out exercising his dog and looked up to see a glowing green light moving in his direction. Although it made no sound the phenomenon seemed to have a strange reaction on Levitt's dog. During the encounter the animal became very focused on the object and the next day it cowered inside its kennel, refusing to leave it. Levitt described the UFO as mushroom shaped, somewhat rounded and possibly three dimensional. He watched as it travelled towards Woodbridge, about three miles away. For the next twenty-four hours Levitt's dog appeared to be suffering some kind of shock from the encounter. In UFO literature there are reports that Levitt's dog died as a result of the UFO, but in his 17 July 1984 written statement, witnessed and signed by solicitor Harry Harris, there is no mention of the demise of his dog. I spoke to Gordon Levitt myself and he confirmed that the dog did not die as a result of the encounter.

Another local witness was Gerry Harris. He and his wife had arrived home about 23.30 hrs, after visiting friends. Harris told me that he is not absolutely certain what date it was, but believes it was very close to Christmas Day, possibly Boxing Day. The couple were preparing to retire for the night when, walking through his living room to draw the curtains, Harris noticed strange bright lights in the sky. 'Look at those lights!' he shouted to his wife. Mrs Harris walked over to the bedroom window, and on seeing the luminous lights, she commented, 'Oh, it's probably just an aeroplane.' 'No it's not an aeroplane or it would have crashed by now,' he told his wife. Harris watched the amazing spectacle for another thirty minutes, which he described as three bright lights bobbing up and down over the forest. Because his home was close to the Woodbridge airbase he assumed the USAF was responsible for the unusual air show and this was confirmed when he heard voices, as if people were shouting, followed by the sound of vehicles approaching. As Harris watched the lights, one of them suddenly dropped down and disappeared into the trees, returning several minutes later to shoot off at a tremendous speed.

During the ensuing days Harris became strangely interested in the lights he had seen over the forest, and using his local contacts he began to do some quiet detective work. He managed to talk to two local forestry workers and discovered that some trees had been felled in the forest area where the lights had been seen. The trees had been removed and the foresters were warned to stay clear of the area because it was radioactive. Harris also learnt that there was a great deal of daytime activity in the area, lots of people around. He was told that two US aircraft had landed and 'taken things away'.

Gerry Harris owned a garage in Woodbridge which specialized in car maintenance and fifty per cent of his custom came from personnel at the US bases. The garage had been closed over the Christmas period but he was anxious to talk to his American customers in the hope of discovering what the strange lights were. But when he questioned one of them he was told, 'Sorry, I'm not allowed to say anything, it is more than my life is worth.' As the days passed he began to wonder about two automobiles that had been brought in for minor repairs. They both belonged to security police personnel from Bentwaters, but their owners had failed to collect them. A couple of weeks later, two women claiming to be their wives arrived at the garage to claim the vehicles. Harris was told that both men had suddenly been relocated because they had been witnesses to something they should not have seen. The airmen had departed in such a hurry, not only had they left their vehicles behind, but their wives and children too.

Out of the blue I discovered a local witness who has never discussed the incident publicly and yet his story is one of the most fascinating. Gary Collins is a resident of Capel St Andrew and has lived in the area all of his life. In his youth he was a disc jockey at the Bentwaters Panther club and would sometimes work at Woody's bar on the Woodbridge base. During his time as a DJ he met both Gladys Knight and Quincy Jones, who on separate occasions were discreetly flown from the United States to perform at the Panther club. He later became a builder and worked with a construction company on upgrading the Bawdsey underground facility. He also worked on RAF Bentwaters, where he helped build secure bunkers that he says housed short-range nuclear weapons. Gary's relationship with the twin bases became part of his life; not only were they his livelihood, but his best friends were among the USAF Security Police and Law Enforcement personnel. The friends would often meet at the local public house, the Swan in Alderton. One of his old drinking buddies was a security policeman called Wayne, and although he has difficulty remembering Wayne's surname because it sounded foreign, he recalls his friend very well.

It was a usual night out at the Swan, and the four Americans with Gary were off duty and enjoying a beer when later that night their pagers went off and the men were ordered to return to the base immediately. It was a Red Alert. Gary stayed on until closing time, when he made his way back home on his motorcycle. He thinks it was approximately 23.30 hrs when he turned into Lion's Corner, a sharp bend at Capel Green. As he approached the bend he rode straight into a bright illuminated area. Gary describes what he saw next:

> It was intensely bright, like daylight, almost as if the area had been lit up with powerful floodlights. I heard a faint humming sound and looked up to see what appeared to be a thirty-foot object hovering about sixty-foot high above me. I can only describe its underside, which seemed to be triangular shaped, black in colour, but dripping liquid. It was as if fluid was dripping off it. That's the thing I most remember, it was dripping like melted ice. Suddenly it went at an angle, slowly, then took off at tremendous speed and seemed to crash into the forest. I wish I had gone after it, but at the time I was so stunned. I went home and told my mother I had just seen a UFO, but she thought I was drunk. I'm interested in planes, that's why I knew it was a UFO.

The next morning Gary repeated to his mother what he had seen, but she admitted to me that she did not pay much attention to him at the time. However, Gary was still thinking about it later that day and out of curiosity decided to visit the forest to see if there was anything there. All day long he had been hearing planes going over his house, much more than usual, which convinced him that something was wrong. When he arrived at Tangham Road, which led to RAF Woodbridge east gate, the area where he thought the UFO had come down, there was a roadblock. Two US military trucks were parked in the middle of the road and the security police officers refused to allow him to pass. According to Gary, the road belongs to the Ministry of Defence and during the time when both bases were active, although the locals used the road as a short-cut route, it was actually classed as a private road. The two-mile stretch was essentially used by the US military as a route from RAF Bentwaters to Woodbridge. This was the first time I had heard that the Ministry of Defence owned the road, but it certainly made sense and would account for why roadblocks were allowed. Gary does not recall seeing any civilian police officers but was told by the Americans that there had been an aircraft accident. Later that day he talked to the foresters, who told him the trees had been cut down at the very spot where the alleged accident had occurred and the Americans had taken them away. Soon after the incident, he heard from a sergeant at RAF Woodbridge that the residents who lived near the landing site had been told to keep quiet, and if anyone asked questions they should say they had seen nothing.

A couple of days later he met up with his friend Wayne and excitedly told him about the UFO and what had been going on. But Wayne had something even more amazing to tell Gary. After being called back to Bentwaters he had been instructed to collect his guard dog and proceed to the east gate, along with numerous other personnel. When Wayne's patrol arrived at a clearing in the forest they parked their vehicles to continue on foot, but Wayne's dog had refused to leave the truck. Nothing he could do would make the animal budge, and finally he had no choice but to leave it behind. 'Some guard dog,' he told Gary. As Wayne approached the landing site he could see other personnel standing around a huge UFO sitting on the ground. No one could get close due to a kind of force field that surrounded it, but there in front of his eyes were entities that appeared to be repairing what he described as a spacecraft. After confiding to Gary what had happened, Wayne insisted it was not to be repeated to anyone. 'We were told not to talk about it or we would be in deep trouble,' he told his friend. Wayne had also mentioned that the incident lasted for three hours, during which time someone from the base had videotaped the entire event. Gary realized that this must have been the same UFO he had seen on his way home.

That was the last time he would see Wayne or any of the airmen he had become friendly with. In fact, he was supposed to meet Wayne at the Swan a few days later, but he never turned up. Three weeks earlier he had sold Wayne his old motorbike and one day when he was on the base he noticed the bike parked in the car park. When he made enquiries about Wayne he was told that he had been flown back to the United States. The bike was later impounded and Gary recalls that he was very upset because he had not wanted to sell the bike but only did it as a favour to his friend. I asked Gary what happened to Wayne, did he ever hear from him again. Apparently not, and no one else knew what had become of him either. However, Gary does not believe Wayne would have left without his bike or without saying goodbye.

Apart from his immediate family and Wayne, Gary had only ever confided in a couple of local people about his own sighting, and he never told anyone about Wayne's encounter. The reason he decided to speak out now was because I had explained that other witnesses were finally talking about it. It was not until a few years later that Gary heard about the Rendlesham Forest incident and thought it must have been the same one, but like other witnesses he also has a mental block on the date. I found Gary and his mother to be very sincere, and Gary is a very private individual who has a love for the simple life and is certainly not seeking publicity.

THE POLICE FILE

Wherever I turned there were hints that the Suffolk Constabulary were not only involved in the Rendlesham Forest incident but also its cover-up. Researchers and journalists complained at having come up against a wall of silence when trying to question the Woodbridge police, and it was not until years later that one of the police officers spoke publicly, if only to dismiss the 'lights' as being nothing more than the beam from the nearby lighthouse. I was warned that trying to get anywhere with the Woodbridge police might be very difficult. Even veteran defence journalist Chuck de Caro failed to interview the officer who claimed the ground indentations at the landing site were mere animal scratchings. The Suffolk Constabulary wrote to science writer Ian Ridpath suggesting that nothing could be gained by trying to contact the officers concerned. But undeterred, I was going to give it my best shot.

According to local police records, the first reported sighting was received at precisely 04.11 hrs on the morning of 26 December. This was almost five hours after the initial sighting had been reported and the men had long since returned to the base. The call was made to the head office of the Suffolk Constabulary at Martlesham Heath. A staff member from RAF Bentwaters told the officer on duty that there were 'lights in the woods over near Woodbridge', and asked if there were any reports of a downed aircraft. Martlesham Heath checked with Air Traffic Control at West Drayton and was told there was no knowledge of any aircraft in the area to coincide with the current sightings. However, the officer was briefed on earlier sight-ings that had already caused quite a stir in media circles. Martlesham then called the Woodbridge police station, which in turn alerted their night patrol.

On 6 July 1997, almost seventeen years after the call was made to Martlesham Heath Constabulary, a man calling himself Chris Armold contacted the UK UFO Network, run by ufologists Raine and Crow, and claimed that he was the airman who had called the civilian police. Andy Tugby, a.k.a. Crow, explained that Armold had shown up out of the blue claiming they had all been 'well and truly snookered by Halt and his buddies'. I managed to trace Armold, who had obviously read about the case, but when I posed questions to him he was unusually evasive, considering he had made such wild claims to Raine and Crow. I contacted Colonel Halt, who, as the deputy base commander at the time of the incident, might have remembered him. Halt confirmed Armold had been a member of Law Enforcement at RAF Woodbridge but was not involved in the actual incident. From reading Armold's statement it is obvious he has a dislike for some of the witnesses, namely Halt and Burroughs. Armold actually puts himself in the picture by claiming to have been involved in the 'non-event', but his testimony appears to me to be a mix and match of various stories passed down over the years, and not even the sceptics seem prepared to accept it. I certainly cannot take Armold's critique seriously because, apart from his comments on the witnesses, there are several discrepancies which are important enough to question his own alleged involvement.

In the early hours of 26 December PC Dave King and PC Martin Brophy were in their police vehicle heading towards RAF Bentwaters. This was part of their regular nightly visit to the USAF Law Enforcement desk. Being Christmas night it was relatively quiet and they were not expecting much activity, if any, before they went off duty later that morning. So they were surprised when a call came through on their radio instructing them to proceed to RAF Woodbridge to investigate some unexplained lights over Rendlesham Forest. It would take the officers another twenty minutes or so to arrive at the Woodbridge east gate, and it would be coming up to 05.00 hrs before they started trekking through the forest. Dave King recounted what took place during that morning:

> It was the early morning of the 26 December. It was a quiet, mild night and there was nothing going on in the area. I don't know if you are aware of this but, for the police, Christmas Day is the quietest night of the year . . . My partner and I were out on patrol when we received a call to proceed to Woodbridge, the east gate, to check out a report of something going on in the forest. We were actually on our way to visit the Bentwaters Law Enforcement desk when the call came through. When we arrived at the Bentwaters base we were escorted through the back gate to the east-gate sentry post and were then taken to the forest by some security policemen. We had to follow their vehicle. They took us towards the spot where they said the other SPs had gone and we were told they were still out there. We had to park the car and walk on foot. The Americans didn't come with us. We walked about half a mile into the forest toward the direction we were pointed in, but we didn't see any lights out there except the lighthouse and there were no Americans out there, not a soul. We walked for some thirty minutes. If you look on the forest area as being a square foot then we must have covered only a square inch of it . . . We didn't report to the base because when we got back to our car there was no one there so we just left and went home.

I asked King if he had passed any houses or buildings in the forest but he could only remember seeing some cottages beside the Woodbridge flightline. These were most probably Foley Cottages. King explained that this was not his usual patch and although he knew Woodbridge very well, he did not tend to go into the forest. I wondered if he had gone straight ahead, towards the farmer's field near Capel Green, which would have been separated from the forest by wire fencing. But he did not recall seeing any field or fencing.

King and Brophy reported they had not seen anything unusual in the forest and concluded that the Americans had confused the lights with the Orfordness lighthouse. I told King that several witnesses had testified to seeing lights other than the lighthouse, including a craft of some kind. I also pointed out that the first sighting was probably around 23.30 hrs, and wondered if it were possible that something was there before he arrived and had long since gone. 'It's possible. We were called out late and that's five hours after that. I can only report what I saw when I was there,' said King.

When I asked him what the Americans were doing out in the forest in the first place, he agreed that in normal circumstances they would never have investigated off their patch without consulting the police. 'Not one inch,' he told me. When I mentioned that the Americans had later put up roadblocks near the alleged landing site, he was not aware of it, but pointed out that this would have been a private road belonging to the Forestry Commission, and the police would not have been notified had that been the case.

At 10.30 hrs that same morning, RAF Bentwaters called the Suffolk Constabulary headquarters for a second time. They wanted to report that they had found a site where a craft of some sort could have landed. Ian Ridpath, who took an interest in the case in 1983, wrote to the chief constable at Martlesham Heath in November of that year, requesting information on the Suffolk Constabulary's alleged involvement. He received a reply stating that an officer had attended and the area involved did bear three marks of an inde-terminate pattern, but the marks were of no depth and the attending officer thought an animal could have made them.

King recalls seeing the message in the police log:

> When I went on duty the next day I saw another message in the log that had come from RAF Bentwaters at around 10 a.m. on 26 December. It said they thought they had found the place were the UFO had landed. Another police officer went out to the site that morning but he found nothing.

On the second night of the sightings (26/27), PC Dave King and PC Martin Brophy were in the Law Enforcement Office at Bentwaters when the report came in. Dave King recalls the incident:

It was a frosty night. I was doing my routine check with the Law Enforcement desk on RAF Bentwaters. We did that every night. We checked in with them and exchanged information. While I was there another report came in on the radio, a pocket radio, saying that there were lights in the forest at the exact same spot as the previous night. This would now be the early hours of the 27th. I was just about to go and have a look, thinking I might see something this time, when I got an emergency call to attend to a post office break-in about ten miles away at Otley.

I asked King if there was a report filed in the police log for this sighting.

No, we didn't bother with it; we just thought they were bored watching their planes, and besides we had an emergency on. If that happened today the police wouldn't have time to mess around with it. It was a quiet time due to Christmas so there wasn't much going on. There were rumours that the Americans had set up searchlights on that second night waiting for it to return, but I don't believe it.

The fact that PC King did not take the incident seriously enough to at least make a report, resulting in it not being recorded in the police log, is somewhat disturbing. I pointed this out to him, but he considered the post office break-in to be an emergency and the sighting of lights in Rendlesham Forest to be of little consequence. In fact, I was curious to know more about the post office break-in, and why King had been called to an incident ten miles away. I thought, surely there must have been a police station at Otley, where the break-in had occurred, or at least closer to the incident than he was. King agreed this was a distance away, although it was not entirely unusual that Woodbridge police would be called to investigate further afield. Nevertheless, he has confirmed that patrols were off base for a second night, and even though there is no evidence to suggest that a landing of any kind took place that night, we know there were unidentified lights in the sky over Woodbridge.

King and Brophy finished their night shifts on the morning of 27 December, when they went on break for a few days. If, as has been suggested, the Woodbridge police were involved in the second major encounter, it has been a well-kept secret. Through the help of Malcolm Zickler, who was in charge of the police forces at the bases, I was able to contact retired Police Superintendent George Plume, who was the officer in charge of the Woodbridge police station during that period. Plume said he was surprised to hear from me because no one had contacted him about the case in eighteen years. I soon realized, however, that he was not on duty at any time during the events because he only worked the day shift from 08.00-18.00 hrs. Of course, he was aware that something unusual had occurred, but reminded me that it was a long time ago, and in order to assist me he would need the names of the officers concerned.

If George Plume needed names I had to find them. On one of my trips to Woodbridge I decided to pay a visit to the local police station. Being brought up in the country I knew they were always willing to help visitors and were known to be generous with advice. Woodbridge station looked like any other small country police station: you walk into the small reception, ring the bell and out pops the friendly bobby. The officer was indeed very friendly, and when I began asking him about the Rendlesham Forest incident and wanted to know the names of the police officers involved, he seemed familiar with the case and gave me the names of Dave King and Martin Brophy. Having explained that I had already interviewed King and was aware of Brophy, I asked for the names of the other officers involved. Surprisingly, he offered the name of Brian Creswell, and I was told that he had recently retired from the force and was still living locally. The officer could not remember the names of any other policemen who might have been involved, so I asked him if he would enquire of his colleagues. He disappeared into the back office and after what seemed like a very long time, returned with a look of shock on his face. He was positively white! Something had happened in the back office and, whatever it was, it had caused him to clam up. The friendly police officer had suddenly become very aggressive.

'There is no use you trying to contact him because he won't discuss it,' he stated. 'Contact who? Brian Creswell?' I asked. 'He doesn't want to talk about it, so there is no point you trying to get in touch with him,' he continued. I could see he was very agitated and was probably angry because he had already revealed too much. I decided to change the subject slightly and ask if it were possible to view the incident log for that particular period, to which he replied, 'Are you recording this?' I thought this was an odd sort of question. Indeed, why would he be concerned about me recording the conversation? Realizing I was not getting anywhere, I asked if he would summon one of the other officers to talk to me, but he flatly refused, which I found even more odd. After all, it was a quiet police station and I was requesting assistance.

I was not surprised to learn that the log books were no longer available, but according to George Plume, the police force had changed over to computers in 1975 and therefore records of that period should still be stored somewhere. I explained this to the police officer, only to be told that I would need to contact the head office at Martlesham Heath. I had a better idea. Armed with a name, I contacted Plume. He remembered Brian Creswell and told me he was living in Ipswich. Creswell had retired three years earlier, after thirty-three years' honourable service with Her Majesty's police force. Apparently, his colleagues were known to call him 'Monster', probably because he is over six feet tall. Plume suggested I try calling him but I explained that his number was unlisted. He seemed to think it was unusual for a rural police officer, retired or otherwise, to be listed as ex-directory. However, Plume was able to update me on Martin Brophy. PC Brophy had retired a couple of years after the incident and being very ambitious had moved to a civilian job, possibly with a technology company, and was last known to be living near RAF Mildenhall.

George Plume had been a great find, and as a former senior police officer he was able to offer valuable tips that helped with my investigation. But he reminded me of the USAF commanders I had spoken to. They were all very willing to assist in my enquiries, provided I did not ask too many questions about the incident itself. This was very difficult considering that was my main reason for contacting them in the first place. Plume seemed to think I was delving too deep and gave me a friendly warning to be careful. There had been several of these friendly warnings, mostly from USAF commanders, but his was especially interesting, inasmuch as it came from a man who had been in charge of the Woodbridge police when all this was going on. As with the others, his warning was in no way threatening: on the contrary it was very well meant. It was nice to know that so many people were concerned about my welfare, but it only made me realize that something unusual must have occurred, and maybe I really was getting too close for comfort.

I decided to contact Dave King again. I wanted to find out what he knew about Brian Creswell's involvement. Thinking that Cresswell might have been one of the officers called out during the second landing, I was surprised to learn that he was the police officer who had visited the landing site and examined the ground indentations the day after the initial incident. 'He won't talk to you, he refuses to talk to anyone about it,' said King. Where had I heard that before? I asked King why Cresswell was being so secretive. I considered that if he had finished his day shift on the 26th, there was a possibility he might have been one of the officers called out during night duty between 27 and 29 December. King thought it was also possible. It just seemed strange that he would be so evasive if all he did was examine a few rabbit scratchings.

It would take me several months to locate Brian Creswell, and I was not convinced he would not want to talk to me. In spite of warnings that witnesses would not cooperate, most turned out to be very helpful, but I was certainly wrong about Creswell. The lady who answered the telephone took my name and a minute later he was on the line. I had barely introduced myself when he began shouting down the phone in a very determined gruff voice. Now I know why Woodbridge had a low crime rate for so long. You would not want to get on the wrong side of PC Creswell!

I know who you are. I know you have been trying to find me. I know you want to talk to me and I don't want to talk to you. I have nothing to say to you, but I do want to know who gave you my number because I am ex-directory.

When I told him his uncle had given me the number, he would not believe me, and I thought it was just as well he was not aware that I had his work number too, which incidentally was given to me by another retired police officer of the same surname. At this stage I expected him to slam down the receiver, but he wanted me to know that the incident was built up over nothing but rubbish. It was useless trying to ask any questions because these were overpowered by his yelling. Realizing I only had a few seconds with this man, I threw in my ace and told him I had a photograph of a police officer examining the alleged landing site and I had reason to believe it was him. He wanted to know where I had got the photograph, but then he answered his own question by suggesting it must have come from the Americans. I explained that I only wanted to talk to him about his visit to the forest and his conclusion that the ground indentations he had examined were nothing more than animal scratchings. He was clearly not going to discuss it. 'I know what I saw. I know what I did and I'm not giving you any information,' he stated. I apologized for the inconvenience and bid him farewell. A few minutes later he returned my call. There was something he wanted me to know. He had retired from the police force after thirty-three years and, contrary to rumours, had not become an alcoholic but was almost teetotal. I realized he was referring to local rumours and assured him I was not interested in them and they should not concern him either, pointing out that they were related to two officers who had allegedly been involved in the second major incident. With that he offered an apology for the way he had reacted and the call was terminated. In all the time I had been working on this case I had never come across anybody who was so reluctant to talk about it.

According to witness Jim Penniston, the police officer who

investigated the landing site was adamant that he was not going to report anything other than that they were animal scratchings. When Penniston described the UFO to him, the officer refused to write it in his report. From what he told me, Penniston was clearly bothered by what he thought was the police officer's apparent lack of interest in the evidence; I have often wondered what would have happened if a full police report had been written based on Penniston's first-hand encounter with a UFO. I wished there had been an opportunity to discuss this with Cresswell.

Malcolm Zickler assured me there was a British police presence on Bentwaters. He called it a 'subdivision', and he is in no doubt that these officers were fully aware of the incident. It turned out that George Plume was stationed at Bentwaters for several years after his retirement, but was not too happy when I discovered this, which I believe he thought was none of my business. Zickler explained that there were always one or two British police officers on the base, and after-hours they would be called if there were any civilian visitors. Sometimes there were those who drank too much and they apparently had girl problems. Zickler recounted, 'Some of the girls were there to look for husbands, and there were those who were looking for something else – the Colchester lot. So we had to call them if there were problems.'

I met Nick Ryan at a social function I attended at the Bulgarian Ambassador's home in London. Nick was with the elite Air Rescue and Recovery Squadron, based at RAF Woodbridge from 1982 to 1984. I spent the evening drilling him on the Rendlesham Forest incident, the bases and especially the ARRS. He confirmed that at least one British police liaison officer was stationed at Bentwaters during office hours. I asked him if they would have been involved in the incident.

> The British civilian police would not have been notified about this incident until it was over. Under no circumstances would we have involved the civilian police. We would call them afterwards to find out if they had any reports, it was a way of finding out if any civilians were involved. But we would not ask for assistance on

something like this. The MOD Police are responsible for the areas surrounding any USAF bases in Britain. If need be, they would be required to guard the area around the perimeters.

However, Major Edward Drury told me outright that the British civil police were involved in the second incident but could not supply me with names. He even remarked that it was a local police officer he was friendly with who had told him there was a D-Notice slammed on the incident. (A D-Notice is a government instruction given to the press requesting them not to publish because it involves national security.)

Woodbridge resident Gerry Harris had a story to tell about the civilian police. Soon after his own sighting he became curious, and following his conversation with some of the foresters he decided the best way to find out was to visit the area for himself. On 29 December he was passing the east-gate entrance to the Woodbridge base when he noticed a British policeman and an American security policeman guarding the entrance to a forest logging path. After parking his van, he approached the police officer to tell him of his intention to visit the forest to see what was going on. As incredible as it may seem, Harris claims the American refused to allow him access. He argued that it was a public footpath and he had a right to enter but was told, in no uncertain words, 'Go away.' Not easily discouraged, he moved forward only to see the American cock his M-16 rifle and to hear the British policeman warn him, 'You better do as he says.' One burning question has to be, who was the British police officer? If Harris's recollection of events is correct it poses some even more important questions: (a) why was a USAF security policeman guarding British territory? (b) Why was the USAF security policeman armed on British territory? (c) Why was a USAF security policeman allowed to threaten a British citizen on British territory?

It has been a difficult task trying to find the names of the policemen who would have been on night duty during the rest of Christmas week. Over the years the Suffolk Constabulary appear to have gone to great lengths to protect the identity of these officers. As a result, local rumours were invented and these are what appear to have upset Brian Creswell. The gist of the tales is that one of the officers was supposed to have been so disturbed by the incident that he ended up in a mental institution. The other was said to have suffered severe shock and become an alcoholic. I had already checked out these stories and knew they were nothing but nonsense. Whilst I admit that I have not been able to trace either of these men, none of the local policemen I have spoken to appears to know anything about these claims. I realize the police have been very cagey about this case, and it is possible that two local policemen were involved, but I am sure word of them having left the force in such strange circumstances would be known locally. George Plume thought the stories were very amusing, but insisted that there was not a grain of truth to them. 'I would have known if that had happened. None of the men left the force for those reasons,' he exclaimed. I could not help wondering if it was Plume who had forewarned Brian Creswell about these stories and my interest in trying to contact him. Either that or someone was listening in on my phone line.

Dave King does not believe there was any cover-up by the Suffolk Police. He told me:

> I didn't know this was a story until I first heard about that book *Skycrash* a few years later. The reason those researchers never heard from us was because they got the date wrong. They came to the police station saying it was the 27th, but there wasn't a log of it for that day. There was no cover-up from us.

It is very interesting that no further incidents were reported in the Woodbridge police log, especially considering the police visited the bases every night. One would assume that whoever was on duty during the second major incident must have known what was going on. Did they think the same as King, that it was nothing of any importance or are they staying silent for other reasons?

Adrian Bustinza recalls the British police being involved in the second incident. He explained to me what he witnessed:

> The British police weren't there at the beginning. I was on my way back to the forest, after filling the light-all in Woodbridge, and I saw two British policemen blocking the road into the forest. Their vehicle was parked on the road and they were there to make sure no civilians went in.

When I asked him if he had seen any British police officers near the landing site, he was certain they never went near the UFO or into the forest at any time. Apparently, they stayed on the perimeter of the forest, near the road.

Adrian Bustinza's memory of the British police being responsible for keeping civilians out of the way corresponds with the testimony of Gerry Harris, who claims they were blocking the same entrance on 29 December. It stands to reason that the local police would know if there was such an incident taking place. After all, this was a much bigger event than the initial encounter, where only a handful of US personnel were involved. On this particular night, or early morning, we are told that convoys of vehicles were moving through the Suffolk roads heading for Rendlesham Forest. What were the Woodbridge police doing during all of this? With such a large operation going on they must have known about it. So why are they denying it? Could it be that they were under strict orders to stay quiet because the incident was a threat to national security? Or maybe they were told it was a top-secret exercise. According to a police spokesman, there would have been a skeleton staff on duty during the Christmas period, as it was such a quiet time. Could it be that the local police were simply uninformed, or are there police officers out there who know something of the matter but are unable to discuss it because they have signed the Official Secrets Act?

If the Woodbridge police were involved, one wonders what they told the press. Journalists are known to call the local police station every day to pick up the latest news stories. In rural areas they will hear everything from Mrs Jones's cat stuck up a tree to a burglary in the High Street. If there is a serious accident or crime, very often one of the police officers will tip off a journalist whom he is familiar with. So what happened with this particular incident? Why was it not on the front pages of the East Anglian newspapers or mentioned in the national press? Searching through decades of press reports referring to the Suffolk installations, I discovered that several USAF planes had crashed in the area. Surely if the Rendlesham Forest incident involved a plane crash it would have been reported in the local press along with the other reports. But there was no mention of an accident occurring in Woodbridge during that month.

A few months after I spoke to Dave King, the retired police officer visited Rendlesham Forest and retraced his steps of 26 December. He explained that it was nothing like it had been in 1980, when the trees were up to eighty feet tall. Since then, of course, the severe storm of 1987 that hit the British Isles had destroyed a large part of the forest. I was pleased to hear that King had made this trip, and even more so when he told me that he was not so sure it was the lighthouse the witnesses had been referring to after all. This was partly due to the call he had received from Marjorie Wright, a local woman who told him about her father's sighting, explaining that it could not have been a lighthouse. The fact that King had a change of mind was a real breakthrough, because his original lighthouse theory had been damaging to the authenticity of this case. It came as a surprise then that, following my interviews with King, the Suffolk Constabulary had contacted him and were now claiming he was still unconvinced that the 'occurrence' was genuine.

I had decided to write to the chief constable of the Suffolk Police because I wanted to know what their involvement was, if any, and whether Special Branch was aware of the situation. Because it was so long since the incident had occurred, I thought it was necessary to offer as much information as possible. I wanted to make sure they knew my information was not based on rumour.

I received a prompt reply from Inspector Mike Topliss and was very impressed that he had taken the time and trouble to reply in such detail.

28 July 1999
Dear Ms Bruni
INCIDENT IN RENDLESHAM FOREST – DECEMBER 1980

I refer to your letter of 22 July 1999 in relation to a series of unusual events which allegedly occurred outside the perimeter of RAF Woodbridge, Suffolk, during the last week of December 1980.

A great deal of interest has understandably been generated in respect of this story, not least because of the apparent number and standing of witnesses. However, over the intervening years, various reports of the incident(s) seem to have taken on a life of their own to the extent that the 'sighting' details and corroborative evidence have been substantially embellished. This contrasts sharply with the views of local police who attended at the time and did not perceive this occurrence as being anything unusual considering the festive significance of the date and expected high spirits.

Such a perception lends support to the lack of police documentary evidence and one needs to understand the minimalistic nature of rural policing in order to appreciate the answers which I will attempt to give your questions.

(1) Both PC King and PC Brophy have retired from the force but, being a long-standing friend of the former, I have spoken to him recently and at great length in response to similar journalistic enquiries. He does not recall making any official report and there is no evidence that one was made.

(2) Dave King has confirmed that he and PC Brophy were in the Law Enforcement Office at RAF Bentwaters when they were diverted to a 'higher priority' task at Otley post office. As rural night-duty officers they would have sole responsibility for policing a huge territorial area (approx. 400 square miles) and would certainly have treated a post-office burglary as more important than a recurrence of an earlier incident which was seen as somewhat frivolous.

(3) PC Brian Creswell's (also now retired) visit to the alleged landing site would not have generated more than a standard incident log unless he was convinced that something worth reporting had occurred. PC King had discussed the matter with him and it appeared that all three officers were equally unimpressed with the night's events.

(4) Civilian police officers were not employed in guarding the area surrounding the alleged landing site(s) or to deter access, as there was no evidence to indicate that anything of immediate concern to the police had occurred.

(5) There is no documentary evidence that police officers were involved in similar incidents on 27–31 December that year and PC King could not recall any further requests for police attendance.

(6) Special Branch officers should have been aware of the incident(s) through having sight of the incident log(s) but would not have shown an interest unless there was evidence of a potential threat to national security. No such threat was evident.

I have tried to be as objective as possible with the answers provided and, like yourself, would undoubtedly be pleased to see a local incident such as this substantiated as an authentic 'UFO' experience. PC King holds similar views to myself and returned to the forest site in daylight in case he had missed some evidence in the darkness. There was nothing to be seen and he remains unconvinced that the occurrence was genuine. The immediate area was swept by powerful light beams from a landing beacon at RAF Bentwaters and the Orfordness lighthouse. I know from personal experience that at night, in certain weather and cloud conditions, these beams were very pronounced and certainly caused strange visual effects.

If you have any other query in respect of this subject I will be pleased to discuss the issue further. My direct dial telephone number is —.

Yours sincerely
[signed]
Mike Topliss
Inspector – Operations (Planning)

Apart from Dave King's verbal recollection of the 26 December incident, the Suffolk Police claim they were not involved in any further events. As there appears to be no official documentation at Martlesham Heath, Inspector Topliss had interviewed Dave King in order to find answers to my questions. However, King was on his break during the rest of that week and having interviewed him myself I know he has no personal knowledge of what occurred after he went off duty.

I cannot blame Inspector Topliss for thinking there was nothing to the case, especially if there is no documented evidence available in the Martlesham police records for him to refer to. Unless the police officers who were allegedly involved in the incident or its aftermath come forward, then it is unlikely we will progress further in this enquiry. Topliss agrees with Dave King that the Suffolk Constabulary were in no way involved in a cover-up. However, he suggested the officers could be reluctant to discuss the case in general because they are afraid it might be classed as secret, or because they were discouraged to talk to the press.

Also, on 22 July 1999, I wrote to the secretariat of the Ministry of Defence Police. I wanted to know if they were involved in the incident. On 17 August I was surprised to receive a reply from the chief of the department, Paul A. Crowther, whose title is Agency Secretary and Director of Finance and Administration.

D/DMP/36/2/7 (262/99)

17th August 1999

Dear Ms Bruni

Thank you for your letter dated 22nd July 1999, requesting information about an incident in Rendlesham Forest in 1980. With regard to your request, we have been unable to find any reference to the incident in files held by our Operations and CID departments. However, it is worth noting that files of this age are not normally held centrally – they are either destroyed or archived. Several of the more senior officers of the Force have however been contacted with regard to the presence of an MDP detachment at Woodbridge in 1980. It would appear that RAF Woodbridge did not sustain its own detachment; rather it was the subject of infrequent visits by MDP officers stationed elsewhere in Suffolk. There is no recollection of the reporting of such an incident.

The Ministry of Defence Police Agency, like all Government Departments and Agencies, is bound by the Code of Practice on Access to Government Information. This means that we are committed to providing you with the information you require, as long as it is not exempt under the Code. If you wish to make a complaint that your request for information has not been properly dealt with, you should appeal to: Ministry of Defence, OMD14, Room 617, Northumberland House, Northumberland Avenue, London WC2N 5BP.

Yours sincerely

[signed]
P. A. Crowther

I am grateful to Paul Crowther for taking the trouble to investigate and respond to my questions. Nevertheless, the fact that, according to the more senior officers, there was no recollection of such an event does not surprise me. This case is too big, and nobody from the Ministry of Defence, retired or otherwise, is willing to openly discuss it. If any police were involved it might have been the MOD Police. According to local resident Gary Collins, the Ministry of Defence owned the road that separated RAF Woodbridge from the landing sites. This would certainly account for why the Americans were allowed to block the road and guard the perimeter of the forest, because when they leased the bases from the Ministry of Defence, they probably had rights to the road as well. Apart from a different badge, the MOD Police uniform is very similar to the regular force uniform and their vehicles have 'Police' on the side, so witnesses may have confused them with the Suffolk Constabulary.

I read the MOD Police reply to a Ministry of Defence source

whom I have known for many years, and he was surprised to hear that I had received a response from the top man of the department. 'It must be very sensitive to have been considered by the most senior person. You must have worried them. Maybe this case warrants a public enquiry,' he said. Maybe it does.

If Special Branch were involved in the investigation, they certainly cannot admit to it because, by doing so, it would indicate that there had been a threat to national security. As Inspector Topliss points out, Special Branch officers should have been aware if anything had occurred through having sight of the incident log. However, we know that the Woodbridge police log did not record any further incidents; therefore we must consider whether they blundered in this case. The Suffolk Constabulary either took the incident seriously enough to inform Special Branch or, as Topliss suggests, it was dismissed as 'frivolous'. But let us not forget that Prime Minister Margaret Thatcher had just warned Russia to keep out of the Polish crisis, the IRA were threatening to bomb Britain, and unidentified flying objects were playing havoc on the perimeter of a USAF NATO base with Bentwaters armed to its teeth in nuclear weapons. Under the circumstances, are we really expected to believe that Special Branch would not have a reason to investigate? We can forgive the Woodbridge police for thinking that a post-office break-in was far more important than a UFO report near a military base, but surely someone would have been responsible for investigating the incident? Apart from the Ministry of Defence, who claimed to have only checked the radar reports, no government or military department either side of the Atlantic is taking any responsibility for it. The fact that 'unidentifieds' were hovering over RAF Woodbridge for several hours on at least three consecutive nights, even landing in the nearby forest, is, in my opinion, a definite threat to national security. This is especially so when one considers that RAF Bentwaters deployed nuclear weapons.

According to a fact sheet on the Metropolitan Police, Special Branch was formed as 'The Special Irish Branch' in 1883 to combat the threat from the Fenian movement, whose aim was independence in Ireland, and who had been responsible for a series of explosions in London. The Special Irish Branch later became known as the 'Special Branch', and extended work into royalty protection with Queen Victoria's Jubilee. While Special Branch is a division of the police force, in practice it coordinates closely with MI5, and has continued to develop its role as a conduit of information and intelligence for the Metropolitan Police and Security Service.

I wondered if MI5 might have had an interest in the Rendlesham Forest incident. I was in for a surprise, inasmuch as MI5 had a presence at Martlesham Heath for a number of years. Martlesham Heath, just a few miles from Woodbridge, was the headquarters of the Suffolk Constabulary, the headquarters of the Suffolk Special Branch and certain MI5 operations. According to former MI5 agent Peter Wright, the agency had a major post office laboratory based there. In his infamous book, *Spycatcher*, Wright describes how the MI5 infiltrated public mail. The headquarters of this special out-post, known as the 'Post Office Special Investigations Unit', was based near St Paul's in London, where MI5 had a suite of rooms on the first floor run by MI5 agent and ex-military officer Major Denham. This unit specialized in mail tampering and telephone tapping. Apparently, each major sorting office and exchange in the country had, and probably still has, a 'Special Investigations Unit Room'. The headquarters were later moved to Martlesham Heath where a special post office laboratory was set up. Although St Paul's was still in use, if a letter which had been opened needed special attention, it was dispatched by motorcycle courier up to the Suffolk office. It seems there was quite a set-up at Martlesham Heath.

It is worth mentioning that, according to the Bentwaters Staff Judge Advocate, Lieutenant Colonel Arnold I. Persky, the British authorities, including the local police, would have been contacted and expected to accompany the USAF patrols to the scene of the incident. Although Persky was aware that there had been an incident he assured me that if it had concerned an American air crash on British territory someone from his office would have been summoned to investigate, in case the USAF were charged with damages to any property. Persky was sure that the British authorities were alerted and that they went to the forest sometime during the incident. He also thinks that British police were on the scene.

THE WITNESS STATEMENTS

Apart from a brief interview with Colonel Ted Conrad in *OMNI*, the only person willing to speak out publicly in the early days was Larry Warren. It was not until 1984 that researchers Ray Boeche, Scot Colburn and Larry Fawcett managed to interview Adrian Bustinza and Greg Battram. In 1985 defence journalist Chuck de Caro interviewed witnesses for a CNN television show and, apart from Warren, all were filmed in shadow to hide their identities. De Caro traced others, who included Charles Halt, Bruce Englund, Edward Drury and Adrian Bustinza, but they all refused to talk to him on camera. In 1990 science writer Antonio Huneeus published an extensive interview in *Fate* with John Burroughs, and in September 1991 Colonel Charles Halt went public when he and John Burroughs were interviewed by NBC television for a documentary entitled *Unsolved Mysteries*. In 1994 Jim Penniston talked for the first time when he joined Charles Halt and John Burroughs in an interview for the British documentary series *Strange but True?*.

I have since managed to trace other military witnesses and players as well as interviewing those who have already gone public and others who refused to talk in the early days. Their stories are a fascinating account of what actually took place during Christmas week 1980. By collating all their testimonies it has been possible to piece together much of the puzzle – so much so that for the first time in twenty years we now have a much more detailed account of what occurred from the moment of the first reported sighting to the harassment that haunts the first-hand witnesses to this day. However, when reading the witness files, please take into consideration that each of them has different memories and opinions as to what they personally encountered. This might be due to them being involved in a different set of events, being situated at different locations or because of the amount of time that has passed. On a more sinister note, it could also be because they were interrogated using drug-induced hypnosis in order to confuse their recollection of events, or because they really did have an encounter with extra-terrestrial entities which caused them to experience missing time. Many people who have witnessed UFO activity have reported losing time. This can be a matter of minutes or hours. It is interesting that some of the witnesses to the Rendlesham Forest incident have reported losing approximately forty minutes during the UFO encounter: in research circles this is termed 'missing time'.

Although there is no official documentation available concerning the other events of that week, Citizens Against UFO Secrecy (CAUS) were given certain witness statements relating to the initial incident of 25/26 December. CAUS did not receive the documents until some time between 1985 and 1986, and I was interested to know why these were never offered to other researchers or, indeed, made public by CAUS themselves. Undoubtedly, CAUS investigator Larry Fawcett was unhappy with the authors of *Skycrash* because he suspected that Brenda Butler, Dot Street and Jenny Randles were responsible for selling the Rendlesham Forest story to *The News of the World* newspaper in October 1983. This was a story that essentially revolved around the release of Lieutenant Colonel Halt's memorandum. CAUS had managed to locate the document through the Freedom of Information Act and had sent it to the authors in good faith, hoping they would use it as a tool to further their research. Fawcett was also intending to feature the memorandum in his book *Clear Intent*, co-authored with Barry Greenwood. Although the researchers (including Harry Harris and another unnamed person) were said to have been paid a substantial amount of money by *The News of the World*, Brenda, Dot and Jenny told me independently that they were in no way responsible for alerting the press but agreed to cooperate in order to make sure the story was reported accurately.

During a visit to the United States, Dot managed to patch things up with Larry Fawcett, but further disagreements would arise between him and Larry Warren. The reason the statements were not offered to the researchers is probably because of these disagreements or simply because CAUS had lost interest in the case. Whatever the reasons, the statements remained buried in old files and did not surface until recently. Even Chuck de Caro was surprised to hear of their existence.

Copies of the statements came directly to me from the old CAUS files in the United States. They are published here in the witness files, and are explained in their entirety for the first time. When I contacted Colonel Halt for his opinion on the statements, he confirmed they were the originals, made at his request about a week after the events. However, when I pointed out that there were handwritten comments on the statements and one was signed with the initial 'H', Halt denied this was his handwriting and suggested they might be fakes. This sudden change of mind intrigued me, but more about that later. I contacted researcher Barry Greenwood, a former member of CAUS, and asked him if he could shed any light on the subject and could he fill me in on their history. Barry did not go into too much detail, but explained they were offered to his colleague Larry Fawcett, and suggested they most probably came via Colonel Halt. Robert Todd, the man responsible for securing Halt's memorandum, does not want to be brought back into the case but confirmed there were no witness statements with the memorandum. Todd has destroyed most of the Rendlesham files he had in his possession because he thought they were worthless, full of denials from various US Air Force and NATO organizations.

Because some of the statements were typed on official USAF Statement of Witness forms, I have included the following information, which is copied from an original form (first page) of that period. The form was in Dot Street's files. A security policeman at RAF Bentwaters had given it to her in the early 1980s and Dot later had it verified by a high-ranking officer. The form in her possession consists of three blank pages, each individually numbered 1168,

1169 and 1170. The first page listed the address of the Uxbridge office of the AFOSI, which was the US Air Force Office of Special Investigations' head office, the very agency that I believe were involved in the cover-up. When Dot showed me the forms I immediately recognized them as being the same as those used by two of the witnesses for their typed statements. As you will see from the statements reproduced in the witness files, the first page (1168) of the official USAF forms was not used, or if it was they were not included with the statements when they were offered to CAUS. Below is a representation of page one of an AFOSI Air Force Statement of Witness form from RAF Bentwaters, circa 1980.

62 UXBRIDGE UK
AFOSI Detachment 6205
RAF BENTWATERS

Statement of Witness

Place _____
Date _____

I, _____, hereby state that
_____ has identified himself to me as
_____ USAF.

(Special Agent AFOSI, Security Police, Other – Specify)

I do hereby voluntarily and of my own free will make the following statement without having been subjected to any coercion, unlawful influence or unlawful inducement.

[This space is used for the statement]

AF FORM 1168

The list of witness statements is as follows:

Fred Buran (no rank listed)
81st Security Police Squadron
A typed (signed) statement on an official USAF 1169 Statement of

Witness form, dated 2 January 1981.

Master Sergeant J. D. Chandler
81st Security Police Squadron
A typed (signed) statement on an official USAF 1169 Statement of
Witness form, dated 2 January 1981.

Airman First Class John F. Burroughs
81st Security Police Squadron
A handwritten statement on plain paper (signed) and undated.

Staff Sergeant Jim Penniston
81st Security Police Squadron
A typed statement on plain paper (unsigned and undated) with a
cover page.

Airman First Class Edward N. Cabansag
81st Security Police Squadron
A typed statement on plain paper (signed) and undated.

It is worth noting that the only two witness statements to be
typed on official Air Force forms are those of the two more senior
personnel, Master Sergeant J. D. Chandler and Fred Buran. Buran's
rank was not stated but I have since discovered that he was a
lieutenant at the time. Both Buran's and Chandler's statements begin
on section two (1169) of the official forms, and not on section one
(1168) that features the details of the AFOSI. There is no doubt that
by the time these statements were taken, most of the witnesses were
coerced into playing down the incident. Buran's, Burroughs' and
Chandler's statements all refer to the incident taking place at 03.00
hrs but, as you will see, witnesses have since claimed that the
incident took place much earlier in the night.

There are large chunks of information missing from the statements and there appears to be a certain amount of disinformation
mixed with facts. But what is interesting is that throughout the

statements there is reference to a mechanical object sighted by Jim Penniston. Buran writes, '. . . and at one point SSgt Penniston stated that it was a definite mechanical object.' Chandler also states, 'On one occasion Penniston relayed that he was close enough to the object to determine that it was definitely a mechanical object.' Penniston's statement reads: 'Positive sighting of object . . . colour of lights and that it was definitely mechanical in nature.'

Penniston and Cabansag have since denied that they typed their statements. It seems apparent that Halt's secretary, or anyone from Halt's office, did not type them either because apart from the bad spelling and typing errors the typewriters used were not as sophisticated as the one used to type out Halt's memorandum a week later. This probably means that the statements were not typed in Halt's office, but were prepared earlier. It must also be noted that the witnesses did not have easy access to these facilities. The typewriter used to type Cabansag's statement is also a different one than that used to type Penniston's. Whoever typed these statements made sure there were enough errors to make it look like the witnesses, who it must be remembered were not adept at using these machines, did them. In fact, police personnel always used notebooks. However, Chandler's and Buran's statements appear to have been typed on the same machine, the only one that was handwritten was Burroughs'.

Assuming Penniston's and Cabansag's typed statements are bogus, then whoever was responsible for them must have had a good reason for going to all that trouble. They appear to be a clever combination of fact coupled with a fair amount of disinformation. A typical exercise carried out by covert agencies in order to confuse the truth? I discussed the matter with Charles Halt, explaining that Penniston and Cabansag deny they were responsible for the statements and it was imperative that I have his comments. Halt suggested, but could not be certain, that the witnesses may have had the statements with them when they turned up to see him because they were not typed in his office. In a 1990 interview with science writer Antonio Huneeus, John Burroughs commented on his statement, which seemed to confirm that Colonel Halt did send them to Larry Fawcett and also that at least Burroughs' statement (the only one which was handwritten) was handed to Halt personally.

> After the third night I had to write a statement and I turned it over to Halt. Also, which is strange, Fawcett wouldn't say for sure, but Halt sent him some different statements that people had written on this, but mine wasn't included on that, which would be awful strange if Halt was willing to give written statements, that my name wasn't included.

Burroughs' statement was in fact with the others I received.

For me, the biggest mystery is why these were the only statements offered to CAUS. Why did they not receive statements by the witnesses to the major incident that occurred a few nights later? One can only speculate, but it seems to me that this particular incident has been played down as being a non-event, when in fact it was far more momentous than the initial event on 25/26 December. There were also credible witnesses involved. According to Adrian Bustinza, statements were taken from the witnesses but as yet these have not surfaced.

THE EVIDENCE OF
TIMOTHY EGERCIC

On a spring morning in 1978 Timothy Egercic left his parents' home in Farrell, Pennsylvania, to train for the USAF. He was eighteen years old. On 23 March 1979 he was transferred to the 81st Security Police Squadron at RAF Bentwaters and during his entire tour he was assigned to D Flight, working under the supervision of flight chiefs Ray Gulyas, Edwin Keaney and Robert F. Ball.

Sometime between 23.00 and 24.00 hrs on 25 December 1980, an airman at RAF Woodbridge reported seeing strange lights in the sky outside the perimeter fence near the flightline. Over at RAF Bentwaters, Airman First Class Egercic was just finishing his last swing shift with D Flight when the call came through from the Woodbridge patrol. Not thinking any more about it, Egercic and his colleagues turned over the report to C Flight, the official shift that was about to relieve them of duty. Little did they know then that what was about to take place during the next few hours would make history. As Egercic made his weary way home he bumped into a drunken airman looking for a fight and was suddenly reminded he had just missed Christmas Day.

Timothy Egercic cannot remember what station he was working on 25 December but during the next three nights of his midnight shifts he was posted on 'Whiskey One', the alarm monitor for the weapons storage area at Bentwaters. Sometime early in his shift, as was the routine, Central Security Control (CSC) turned over command and control of the airways to his post. Egercic would then make the announcement: 'Whiskey One to all posts and patrols, this office is assuming primary duties as CSC. Direct all radio and telephonic communications to and through this office.' The announcement was then followed by a roll-call security check, where each post would respond back with 'all secure'. The roll-call was supposed to be carried out every fifteen minutes but, according to Egercic, they were lucky if it was done every couple of hours. It was his duty to keep a blotter where he would register information hourly. This would comprise building checks of the Hot Row, which were the eight structures in the weapons area that contained the nuclear weapons, any security exercises and any unplanned events, such as Helping Hand. Egercic cannot recall making any entries of the aforementioned alert in the blotter on any of the nights in question and has no recollection of a Broken Arrow. (Helping Hand was a procedure initiated in response to a serious security violation. It was later changed to Covered Wagon. Broken Arrow was a term used for a nuclear security violation.) However, he pointed out that had he known how important this case would turn out to be, he would have documented everything and audio taped the radio transmissions.

During the three nights of his midnight shift, 26/27–28/29 December, between midnight and 02.00 hrs, Egercic received radio calls from the Woodbridge patrols reporting strange lights over the forest. He noticed that his flight chief, Robert Ball, always seemed to be around when the call came in. Just after midnight a patrol would be instructed to open the back gate (Butley Gate) and Master Sergeant Ball and a handful of personnel would make their way over to the Woodbridge base. During these nights Egercic would try his best to keep in contact with Ball as he entered the forest, at times almost losing him because of a weak signal or static interference. But Ball always managed to respond back with 'secure'. Egercic recounts that other non-commissioned officers on duty during Christmas week were Willie B. Williams, Sergeant Coakley and Sergeant Wimbrow, and he remembers that most of the senior staff were working twelve-hour shifts throughout that period.

During the last night's incident, which Egercic believes occurred on the morning of the 29th, a person from communications was sent to the WSA to observe the lights from the tower. Sergeant Willie B. Williams asked Egercic if he wanted to go to the tower also, but he declined because the radio transmissions from the witnesses were more than the previous two nights and he did not want to miss anything. He explained that he was using one of the most powerful radios on the base, which enabled him to talk to the witnesses directly. As the transmissions came in he would repeat them over the air so that personnel at Bentwaters could hear what was being seen by the Woodbridge patrols. Later that night he and his co-worker Bob Sliwowski had stood on sandbags surrounding the Alarm Monitor building in the hope that they too would see the lights over Woodbridge, but there was nothing in sight other than the lights on a nearby building.

As D Flight's shift came to a close so did the radio transmissions. When Egercic returned from his break three days later he learned that no other flights had reported any strange lights. Whilst in guard mount he had asked Master Sergeant Ball what had happened, but his only comment was: 'I can't tell you what we saw, but there was definitely something out there.' Rumours had circulated that an object had left depressions in the ground that formed a perfect triangle, and someone had taken Geiger readings, but then a wall of silence was quickly established.

It was more than ten years later that Egercic realized the importance of what had occurred that week. He had received a long-distance call from Mississippi. It was his old friend Dock Rhodes, who had been with the Law Enforcement Squadron at Bentwaters. Rhodes had seen television previews on the NBC channel for a show entitled *Unsolved Mysteries,* which he said was going to feature a UFO incident that had occurred during their tour of RAF Bentwaters in 1980. Egercic then called Todd Ray, another colleague who had been on the same tour. Ray had also seen the previews; it seems that former personnel were calling each other across America to alert their old friends about the documentary.

It suddenly occurred to Egercic that it was the same incident that Master Sergeant Ball was involved in, and before watching the programme he decided to test his memory by jotting down a few notes which he then forwarded to his friends, he wrote:

1. The UFO sightings occurred on consecutive nights around Christmas 1980.
2. Bob Ball was the flight chief and went into the forest with other Air Force personnel where the strange lights were seen.
3. Three impressions in the ground were found and formed a perfect triangle.
4. Someone was sent out to take radioactive readings of those impressions.

He reported that all of those facts were shown on the programme.

In September 1997, Bob Kozminski, a former security police-man with D Flight and another friend of Egercic, gave him the book *Left at East Gate*, authored by Larry Warren and Peter Robbins. Kozminski had purchased the book after hearing the authors on a radio talk show. Incidentally, Kozminski and another airman, Kirk Myer, were responsible for opening the east gate on one of the nights in question and had also seen the lights.

Timothy Egercic first came to my attention in early 1997. I had heard about him from a former Law Enforcement woman at Bentwaters, Lori Rehfeldt. But it was not until researcher Peter Robbins faxed me his testimony several months later that I began to see where Egercic fitted into the story. Lori had been keen to talk to Larry Warren and asked me to put her in touch with him. At the time he was not on the telephone so I gave her Peter's fax number, which she then passed on to Timothy Egercic.

I have been in touch with Timothy Egercic since March 1998 and he has been a good source of information. It was interesting to hear that apart from the call that came through about sightings of lights on 25 December he was unfamiliar with the first night's event. Eight months after we talked he sent me the duty roster of his last night (19 March 1981) on D Flight at Bentwaters. By counting backwards from that date we were able to confirm that the first night of the four nights of sightings that he recalls was in fact

25/26 December. It was as a result of working with the duty roster that I was able to figure out how the complex flight schedules operated.

Timothy Egercic finished his tour of duty at RAF Bentwaters in 1981 and was posted to Seymour Johnson Air Force Base, North Carolina. He separated from the USAF on 26 November 1982. In January 1984 he attended ATES Technical Institute, Niles, Ohio, and received a diploma in computer programming. Today he is an information associate developer and lives with his wife Cindy and family in Texas.

LIEUTENANT BURAN AND CENTRAL
SECURITY CONTROL

Charles Halt had warned me not to contact certain witnesses, especially Fred Buran, because he wanted nothing to do with the incident and would have a lawyer at my door if I bothered him. Fortunately, I managed to find Fred 'Skip' Buran and, as I expected, he was quite willing to answer my questions and was in fact very helpful.

> I was never hiding from anyone, but simply didn't want to have anyone misconstrue my involvement. It was an interesting incident, but I never left the base, and what was seen or encountered by those I sent to the scene is for them to interpret as they see fit.

Fred Buran had enlisted in the army in 1968 and was a Vietnam veteran. After leaving the army in 1972 he spent five years with the Florida police force. Then in 1978 he was commissioned for the USAF. During his military career he held several key positions, including a joint duty assignment with the US Forces Korea Provost Marshal. He voluntarily retired as a lieutenant colonel.

In 1980 Buran was a first lieutenant with the Security Police Squadron at RAF Bentwaters. On 25/26 December he was the on-duty shift commander at building 679, Central Security Control. He began his shift at 23.00 hrs and finished at 07.00 hrs. In an official typed statement (2 January 1981) he wrote that it was approximately 03.00 hrs when he was first notified about the initial incident concerning Airman First Class John Burroughs. I asked Buran if he could have been mistaken because my investigation suggests the incident took place much earlier, probably closer to midnight. He agreed it was possible that it began much earlier and that is the reason he made a point of writing 'approximately' on his statement.

Buran told me that he was posted at Central Security Control all night because he was in charge of the security for both bases. As soon as the report came through from the Woodbridge patrol Buran informed his superior officers. He then instructed Sergeant Coffey to contact the Bentwaters tower. Apparently the tower had nothing to report so Sergeant Coffey called London Air Traffic Control to see if they had information. Buran considered that a light aircraft might have crashed in the forest. It seems that London Air Traffic Control had some unusual activity on their radar. Buran thinks the Bentwaters Air Traffic Control might have been down that night due to the late hours, and if that was the case then the Bentwaters and Woodbridge traffic would have been handled by London.

According to Timothy Egercic, who was on duty in the Bentwaters weapons storage area during 26/27–28/29, Central Security Control would pass control of the airwaves to Whiskey One early in the midnight shift. Fred Buran confirmed that Whiskey One was one of the fixed security checkpoints and would have served as the back-up CSC should Primary CSC lose power for any reason. He also agreed that CSC would turn over control of the security forces to Whiskey One for an hour or so every night. Whiskey One would then be in charge of directing and monitoring security activity for both bases, whilst still being monitored by CSC. Apparently, this was standard procedure.

However, when the witnesses reported the initial incident, it was, according to them, sometime around midnight. Assuming Central Security Control passed over the airwaves to Whiskey One just after midnight, then whoever was on duty at Whiskey One during 25/26 should have been operating the airwaves. I wondered if that was why the statements referred to the time of the first reported incident as being 03.00. Could Primary CSC not have been aware of what was going on from midnight until 03.00, even though they were monitoring the airwaves? Buran writes in his statement:

> At approximately 03.00 hrs, 26 December 1980, I was on duty at bldg. 679, Central Security Control, when I was notified that A1C Burroughs had sighted some strange lights in the wooded area east of the runway at RAF Woodbridge.

Fred Buran is an honourable man and assured me that he had taken an oath to support and defend the Constitution of the United States and that he made no false statement. He also assured me that making a false statement in regard to any official act could result in court-martial, prison, dismissal from the service and forfeiture of all pay and allowances, including pension. 'An officer is well motivated to be truthful in all matters,' he stressed. He also pointed out that he had a very high level security clearance which he would never have jeopardized. In all truth, apart from the time, which he admits he was not sure about, I believe Buran's statement is fairly accurate. His statement was not taken until 2 January, eight days after the incident, and he even points out that it may be inaccurate due to the time-lapse and the fact that he was not taking notes at the time.

Fred A. Buran's Statement of 2 January 1981

STATEMENT OF WITNESS

Place <u>Bldg 679, RAF Bentwaters</u>
Date <u>2 Jan 1981</u>

I, <u>Fred A. Buran</u>   , hereby state that
       (Special Agent AFOSI, Security Police, Other – Specify)

I do hereby voluntarily and of my own free will make the following statement without having been subjected to any coercion, unlawful influence or unlawful inducement.

The following statement is general in nature and may be inaccurate in some instances due to the time-lapse involved and the fact that I was not taking notes at the time of the occurrence. At approximately 03.00 hrs, 26 December 1980, I was on duty at bldg. 679, Central Security Control, when I was notified that A1C Burroughs had sighted some strange lights in the wooded area east of the runway at RAF Woodbridge.

Shortly after this initial report A1C Burroughs was joined by SSgt Penniston and his rider, AMN Cabansag. SSgt Penniston also reported the strange lights. I directed SSgt Coffey, the on-duty Security Controller, to attempt to ascertain from SSgt Penniston whether or not the lights could be marker lights of some kind, to which SSgt Penniston said that he had never seen lights of this colour or nature in the area before. He described them as red, blue, white and orange.

SSgt Penniston requested permission to investigate. After he had been joined by the Security Flight Chief, MSgt Chandler, and turned his weapon over to him, I directed them to go ahead. SSgt Penniston had previously informed me that the lights appeared to be no further than 100 yds from the road east of the runway.

I monitored their progress (Penniston, Burroughs and Cabansag) as they entered the wooded area. They appeared to get very close to the lights, and at one point SSgt Penniston stated that it was a definite mechanical object. Due to the colors they had reported I alerted them to the fact that they may have been approaching a light aircraft crash scene. I directed SSgt Coffey to check with the tower to see if they could throw some light on the subject. They could not help.

SSgt Penniston reported getting near the 'object' and then all of a sudden said they had gone past it and were looking at a marker beacon that was in the same general direction as the other lights. I asked him, through SSgt Coffey, if he could have been mistaken, to which Penniston replied that had I seen the other lights I would know the difference. SSgt Penniston seemed somewhat agitated at this point.

They continued to look further, to no avail. At approximately 03.54 hrs, I terminated the investigation and ordered all units back to their normal duties.

I directed SSgt Penniston to take notes of the incident when he came in that morning. After talking with him face to face concerning the incident, I am convinced that he saw something out of the realm of explanation for him at that time. I would like to state at this time that SSgt Penniston is a totally reliable and mature individual. He was not overly excited, nor do I think he is subject to overreaction or misinterpretation of circumstances. Later that morning, after conversing with CPT Mike Verrano, the day-shift commander, I discovered that there had been several other sightings. Any further developments I have no direct knowledge of.

AF FORM 1169 PREVIOUS EDITION WILL BE USED Page 1 of 2 Pages
                                        [note: page number is typed]

CONTINUATION SHEET FOR AF FORM 1168 and 1169
[Second page is not used for further statement but features handwritten comments added at later date]

[Handwritten comments]
Fred Buran is a good and reliable person. He might talk if his name were protected.

I further state that I have read this entire statement, initialled all pages and corrections, and signed this statement, and that it is correct and true as written.

WITNESSES [no witness signatures, there should be two]
              [signed, but no rank given] Fred A. Buran
              81st Security Police Squadron
              [No address or date is given]
              [No signature of person administering oath]

AF FORM 1170   Page 2 of 2 Pages
                                [note: page number is typed]

Before I managed to contact Fred Buran, I had asked Charles Halt about Buran's rank but he declined to comment. However, during a

British conference in 1994 Halt let it slip that the officer on duty at Central Security Control – the very officer who refused to enter the incident in the log – was a lieutenant. This made sense, someone was obviously trying to protect the officer, and considering Halt is supposed to have taken Buran's statement it would be down to him to make sure the witness recorded his rank. But why would Halt want to put me off talking to Buran and the others? From my contact with Fred Buran I realized that at the time of the incident he had not wanted to be too involved, he was a career officer and the subject of UFOs in the military was taboo. This could be why Halt was so evasive. Was he trying to protect Buran? According to Buran, he thinks that immediately following the initial incident he was given temporary leave and was not around during the rest of the week when the UFOs returned.

It is also interesting that Buran's statement refers to Captain Mike Verrano, the day-shift commander, as having mentioned other sightings. Because there are no reports of any incident prior to 25/26 December, Verrano might have been referring to other witnesses seeing the lights from different standpoints on the base.

I was curious to know about the witness statements and why the first pages (1168) of the Air Force forms were not used, and if they were used what happened to them. According to Buran, the security police, the AFOSI and any other party who might have cause to take statements from a witness, used these forms. As he recalls the second page was used as a continuation sheet for both witness and suspect statements. In the case of a suspect's statement, the witness blocks would have been signed, but this was not necessary for the statement of a voluntary witness.

There is not much known about Master Sergeant J. D. Chandler but it is certain that he was on duty on the night of 25/26 December. Although Chandler writes in his statement that 'At no time did I observe anything from the time I arrived at RAF Woodbridge,' witness Jim Penniston claims Chandler had confirmed that he too had seen something. This was told to Penniston when he arrived back at Central Security Control.

Master Sergeant J. D. Chandler's typed statement

STATEMENT OF WITNESS

Place _____

Date 2 January 1981 [handwritten]

I, J. D. CHANDLER, MSgt USAF [name handwritten], hereby
state that
(Special Agent AFOSI, Security Police, Other – Specify)
I do hereby voluntarily and of my own free will make the
following statement without having been subjected to any
coercion, unlawful influence or unlawful inducement.

At approximately 03.00 hrs, 26 December 1980, while
conducting security checks on RAF Bentwaters, I monitored a
radio transmission from A1C Burroughs, Law Enforcement
patrol at RAF Woodbridge, stating that he was observing
strange lights in the wooded area just beyond the access road,
leading from the east gate at RAF Woodbridge. SSgt Penniston,
Security Supervisor, was contacted and directed to contact
Burroughs at the east gate. Upon arrival, SSgt Penniston
immediately notified CSC that he too was observing these
lights and requested to make a closer observation. After several
minutes, Penniston requested my presence. I departed RAF
Bentwaters through Butley gate for RAF Woodbridge. When I
arrived, SSgt Penniston, A1C Burroughs and Amn Cabansag
had entered the wooded area just beyond the clearing at the
access road. We set up a radio relay between SSgt Penniston,
myself and CSC. On one occasion Penniston relayed that he
was close enough to the object to determine that it was
definitely a mechanical object. He stated that he was within
approximately 50 meters. He also stated that there was lots of
noises in the area which seemed to be animals running around.
Each time Penniston gave me the indication that he was about
to reach the area where the lights were, he would give an
extended estimated location. He eventually arrived at a 'beacon
light', however, he stated that this was not the light or lights he
had originally observed. He was instructed to return. While on

route [sic] out of the area he reported seeing lights again almost in direct pass [sic] where they had passed earlier. Shortly after this, they reported that the lights were no longer visible. SSgt Penniston returned to RAF Woodbridge. After talking to the three of them, I was sure that they had observed something unusual. At no time did I observe anything from the time I arrived at RAF Woodbridge.

AF FORM 1169 PREVIOUS EDITION WILL BE USED
Page 1 of 2 Pages
[note: page number is typed]

CONTINUATION SHEET FOR AF FORM 1168 and 1169

[Second page is not used for further statement. There are no written comments]

I further state that I have read this entire statement, initialled all pages and corrections, and signed this statement, and that it is correct and true as written.

WITNESSES [no witness signatures, there should be two]
            [signed] J. D. Chandler
            81st Security Police Squadron
            [No address or date is given]
            [No signature of person administering oath]
AF FORM 1170   Page 2 of _ Pages

Chandler's was the only statement without written notes added. Both these statements tell us a great deal about what went on that night but they are also misleading. It is interesting how Chandler emphasizes the 'beacon light' and, along with Buran, refers to the event as having taken place much later than it actually did. I also wondered why there was no statement in the files from Sergeant Coffey. Fred Buran offered a clue:

As far as I know, SSgt Coffey, who was the on-duty security controller, did not leave CSC that first night. If he was involved later on I know nothing of it. I am not aware that Master Sergeant Chandler ever saw anything either.

Fred 'Skip' Buran retired from the Air Force as a lieutenant colonel and is currently employed in a full-time civilian job. He met his wife, also an Air Force officer, at RAF Bentwaters. She is now working in education. The Burans have a son in high school.

THE EVIDENCE OF JOHN BURROUGHS

John F. Burroughs was nineteen years old when he enlisted in the United States Air Force in March 1979, and in July that same year he arrived at RAF Bentwaters where he was assigned to the Law Enforcement Squadron. The six-feet-plus patrolman from Arizona was known to be a serious individual who would not tolerate lawbreaking of any kind. At the time of the incident he had been on the joint installation for a period of seventeen months and knew the area quite well.

John Burroughs first came to the attention of researchers in 1983 when Brenda Butler and Dot Street were told he was a prime witness. On 26 April 1984 American researcher Ray Boeche surprised Burroughs with a telephone call, but he was nervous and told Boeche that because he was still in the military he would need to contact 'somebody up there' before he could talk. 'If I was a civilian that'd be a different story,' he explained. 'Once I left there, I was pretty much told not to say anything.' He promised to get back to Boeche after talking to his superiors, but he never did.

Burroughs' testimony is important because he is the only known person to have been involved in both the major events. He was said to have been the first person to report the initial sighting on 25 December and later that night had witnessed the landing of a UFO. Along with other witnesses involved in the initial incident (25/26 December), his official Air Force statement has recently surfaced. Although undated, it is suspected it was written on 2 January 1981. It is worth noting that Burroughs confirmed it was written after the second event, but nothing is mentioned about the latter. However,

this might be because he was not actually on official duty during that
period, but had gone back to the forest out of curiosity.

Statement by Airman First Class John Burroughs, handwritten on jotter paper

On the night of 25–26 Dec at around 03.00, while on patrol down
at east gate, myself and my partner saw lights coming from the
woods due east of the gate. The lights were red and blue, the red
one above the blue one, and they were flashing on and off.
Because I've never saw [sic] anything like that coming from the
woods before we decided to drive down and see what it was.
We went down east-gate road and took a right at the stop sign
and drove down about 10 to 20 yards to where there is a road
that goes into the forest at the road. I could see a white light
shining into the trees and I could still see the red and blue one
[sic] lights. We decided we better go call it in so we went back
up towards east gate. I was watching the lights and the white
light started coming down the road that lead [sic] into the forest.
We got to the gate and called it in. The whole time I could see
the lights and the white light was almost at the edge of the road
and the blue and red lights were still out in the woods.
    A security unit was sent down to the gate and when they got
there they could see it too. We asked permission to go and see
what it was and they told us to [sic] we could. We took the truck
down the road that lead [sic] into the forest. As we went down
the east-gate road and the road that lead [sic] into the forest,
the lights were moving back and they appeared to stop in
[illegible] bunch of trees. We stopped the truck where the road
stopped and went on foot. We crossed a small open field that led
into the trees where the lights were coming from, and as we
were coming into the trees there were strange noises, like a
woman screaming. Also the woods lit up and you could hear
the farm animals making a lot of noises, and there was a lot of
movement in the woods. All three of us hit the ground and
whatever it was started moving back towards the open field
and after a minute or two we got up and moved into the trees
and the lights moved out into the open field. We got up to a

fence that separated the trees from the open field and you could
see the lights down by a farmer's house. We climbed over the
fence and started walking toward the red and blue lights and
they just disappeared. Once we reached the farmer's house we
could see a beacon going around so we went towards it. We
followed it for about 2 miles before we could [see] it was coming
from a lighthouse. We had just passed a creak [sic] and were
told to come back when we saw a blue light to our left in the
trees. It was only there for a minute and just streaked away.
After that we didn't see anything so we returned to the truck.

[Page 2 shows a drawing of the object and its description.
Referring to the lights on top of the object Burroughs writes] . . .
this would move back and forth, up and down, but the blue and
white and orange would come out when it was sitting in one
place. [Referring to the other lights, he writes] . . . blue lights
would come out of the beam and the white light below. A white
light would come out below the beam in the trees.

[undated]
[Signed] A1C John Burroughs
81SPS SPOL CFL

[Handwritten comments added at a later date]

Burroughs is a straightforward and honest cop. He does have
the ability to take an incident and turn it into a disaster. (He
comes on too strong.) There's no doubt in my mind his
statement is accurate. He really became obsessed with this.
Now he's worried that this might affect his career.

Working with recent information, I have managed to piece
together a more detailed account of what John Burroughs experienced
during Christmas week 1980. Although his witness statement shows
the time around 03.00, he has since claimed the first incident occurred
after midnight, but does not offer a specific time.

Staff Sergeant Bud Steffens and Airman First Class John
Burroughs, both Law Enforcement officers (although in his statement

Burroughs signs himself as a security police officer), were said to have made the first reported sighting. They were patrolling the Woodbridge base at the time and as they approached the east gate Burroughs noticed strange lights over the skyline to the eastern side of the forest. He alerted his supervisor Steffens, and the two men stared at the sky in amazement. The spectacle consisted of coloured flashing lights that appeared to hover over the trees. Steffens instructed Burroughs to open the combination lock on the gate and the two men proceeded to drive down the east-gate road towards the edge of the forest. Burroughs thought there was something eerie about the coloured lights, which made him feel uneasy. As they got closer they could also see a bright white light shining through the trees. The airmen thought they had better report the incident and started to head back to the base when suddenly there was a tense moment as Burroughs turned around and saw the bright white light moving down the road towards them. When they reached the gate post they could still see the two coloured lights hovering over the forest, but the white light seemed to be parked on the edge of the road.

Neither Steffens nor Burroughs made any mention of calling for permission to leave the base at this stage. However, one very good reason for not making an issue out of this would be if the men were armed. Although it is a violation of the Status of Forces Agreement with the United Kingdom to take weapons off a US installation on to British territory, it will be evident that this was the case during the Rendlesham Forest incident. Whenever possible, personnel would use a landline rather than a pocket radio. This was due to the knowledge that scanners could be used to tap into conversations. So on returning to the east-gate post, Burroughs picked up the landline and reported the sighting to the Law Enforcement duty desk sergeant at Bentwaters. Sergeant 'Crash' McCabe did not take Burroughs seriously at first; being the festive season he thought he was joking. Admittedly, it must have sounded odd, especially if Burroughs was trying to explain that a bright white light had chased them. Realizing that Burroughs was having difficulty convincing the sergeant, Steffens took over the receiver and confirmed the report. McCabe suspected an air crash and decided to alert Central Security Control. Meanwhile, Steffens and Burroughs were instructed to wait at the east gate until another patrol reached them. Sometime later Sergeant Jim Penniston turned up and Steffens and Burroughs explained the situation. Burroughs then accompanied Penniston and his driver, Airman First Class Edward Cabansag, into the forest.

In an interview with Antonio Huneeus in December 1990, Burroughs had nervously recalled what happened in Rendlesham Forest:

> . . . we walked for quite a distance, came into a clearing area and that's when we came upon the object that we saw, the object that all three of us saw, all three of us looked at it a little bit differently. We got pretty close to the object, we knew it had the feet on the ground, from there . . .

Burroughs tried to explain how he was feeling:

> . . . that was like everything seemed like it was different when we were in that area, you know what I mean? The sky didn't seem the same, everything seemed different . . . It was like a weird feeling, like everything seemed slower than you were actually doing and stuff, and all of a sudden, when the object was gone, everything was like normal again, [by] normal [that] everything seemed real around you . . . You're looking around and there at a distance you see the lighthouse beacon, you know, the sky looks the same, everything around you seems the same. But when all this was going on everything seemed different.

Huneeus asked Burroughs to describe the object:

> I would describe it as a bank of lights, differently coloured lights and stuff that appeared to be, you know, the main object was just, to me, a bank of lights that threw off an image of, like a craft, you know, I never saw anything metallic or anything hard . . .

Burroughs might not have been able to define that the object was metallic because, according to Jim Penniston, he was further away from it. But it is interesting that Burroughs mentions the object 'had feet on the ground', which would imply it was a solid object. He also recalls that they saw the object in the distance after it took off, and they followed it for about an hour to an hour and a half before they finally lost it.

In a 1994 *Strange but True?* documentary, Burroughs remarked that the phenomenon in the forest reminded him of Christmas lights, like a 'Christmas display'. He described how it felt as if he was moving in slow motion and how the hair on the back of his neck stood up on end. 'You felt like you had very little control over your body . . . I wish I had my weapon because I felt totally defenceless,' he said.

After his shift was finished Burroughs accompanied Jim Penniston to the shift commander's office, where they were debriefed. Both witnesses were instructed to return to the site to see if there was any evidence left behind. Burroughs discovered depressions on the ground and damage to the nearby trees.

John Burroughs was not on duty during the rest of Christmas week, but on the night of the second major encounter (which he believes took place on the third night, 27/28) he had the urge to return to the forest. He had heard that the UFOs were back and managed to secure a lift from two friends who were in one of the patrols heading out to the east gate. Lieutenant Colonel Halt's patrol had already moved into the forest by the time he arrived, and a radio request to join them was denied by Halt. Whilst Burroughs was sitting in the parked truck along with the other patrols that Halt had stationed at the clearing, blue balls of light, which appeared to come away from the main craft, started moving towards them. One of them passed over the vehicles causing a reaction in the defunct light-alls, which suddenly lit up. The light then moved through the open window of a truck causing a panic situation to those inside. As soon as the ball of light had passed over, the light-all went out again. Burroughs was supposed to have chased after it, but he has not confirmed this in any of his interviews that I am aware of. When Huneeus asked him how many people were involved in the third night, Burroughs told him there might have been fifty to sixty people. This included those who were listening to the radios, those watching from the towers, those who were on duty at RAF Woodbridge and those who were stationed in the forest.

One of the points John Burroughs makes was that the UFOs returned for at least three nights in succession. Burroughs seems to think this is very important, especially because it was basically the same event that occurred on all nights, even though there was no evidence that the object had landed on the second night. It is also important to understand that the witnesses, at least those who have spoken out, have a different perception of what the UFOs looked like, which is probably due to their location or the distortion in the atmosphere during the encounters.

Unlike most of the airmen, Burroughs did not live on the base but preferred to reside in the nearby town of Ipswich. He claims this is why personnel thought he was left alone and not involved in the 'rumour controls'. Contrary to speculation, Burroughs was not transferred immediately but left Bentwaters in July 1981 when he had completed his normal rotation.

When Huneeus asked him to explain the incident and his opinion of what happened, Burroughs made a strong point that it was nothing to do with the lighthouse:

> There is no way that many people were fooled by that lighthouse . . . there is just no way that we were fooled, something actually went on out there for the technology, for the government to have the type of technology that went on in early 1980, it would just be hard to believe. You know, people have said it was possibly the government testing stuff. If they had the capabilities and the technology to do what went on that night, it would just be hard to understand. We would be so far advanced in technology that we've been lied to for years. As far as the UFO experience, it's something that, you know, it's strange in the first place. I don't really know in history where something has come back over a three-night period and that many different people have seen it in a row.

Burroughs seems to suggest that attention should be paid to what was going on in Suffolk at the time. He mentions the radar developments that had taken place on the coast, and points out that as a result of local research in this field, and because radar can produce different waves in the atmosphere, the experiments could have caused some kind of 'time door' to open.

As with many of those who were involved, Burroughs is clearly annoyed at the way the Air Force have dealt with the case. He points out that there is enough proof to support that an incident occurred and the public should pay attention to it. The proof he refers to are the military witnesses and Lieutenant Colonel Halt's official memorandum. The most profound part of his interview with Huneeus is when he sums up how the incident affected him personally:

> It really confuses me. If you look at it, what is the status of the world? You know, you can go along your life and basically you believe in God; you believe in your country; you believe in your government; you believe everything is under control. In the back of your mind you hear about UFOs, you think, well, there is a possibility, but is it really possible? But then you actually see something like that and then have it handled the way the government handled it . . . You wonder what's going on in the world, and you're really interested in knowing, but the American people, do the American people really want to know? Does the world want to know? I began to wonder sometimes because nothing is done about it. I am not saying nothing has been attempted . . . but the overall thing of the American people seems to be, 'yeah, that's interesting', but outer space and this stuff is going on.

Burroughs believes that if more witnesses were to talk about it, then the government would have to answer. After his retirement from the USAF Burroughs did try to get the story into the public domain and agreed to be interviewed by researcher Jim Speiser. But according to Burroughs, Speiser went after another story instead. In his extensive interview with Huneeus, he mentions a taped hypnotic session that he had sent to someone, but no details of this have been made public.

John Burroughs retired as a sergeant from the USAF in February 1988. According to Jim Penniston, Burroughs was being harassed by the AFOSI and his mail was being tampered with. On returning from England after being filmed for the *Strange but True?* television documentary in 1994, he discovered his home had been totally ransacked. The only things missing were his files on Bentwaters and a videotape of the CNN documentary on the incident. Since then nobody has been able to locate him and, according to Penniston, he disappeared from his home in Arizona without a trace. Penniston thinks Burroughs got scared and packed up. All attempts to find him have been fruitless.

James W. Penniston has completed twenty years' service in the USAF. He was only eighteen years old when he joined in July 1973. He was promoted to sergeant when serving at the Strategic Air Command Elite Guard at Offutt Air Force Base, Nebraska, and was then posted to RAF Alconbury in England. Following his tour at Malmstrom Air Force Base in Montana, he arrived at RAF Bentwaters in the summer of 1980 where he was promoted to staff sergeant.

On Christmas night 1980 Staff Sergeant Jim Penniston was the on-duty flight chief for the Woodbridge base. He had been on duty since 18.00 hrs and was enjoying a midnight snack when he received a call from Sergeant Coffey at Central Security Control. Coffey told him that Airman First Class Cabansag was on his way to pick him up and he should head for the east gate and make contact with Police 2, which was Staff Sergeant Bud Steffens and Airman First Class John Burroughs. He thought it unusual that he was given no information about the call-out, but was simply told that Burroughs would brief him on arrival. When Penniston arrived, Steffens informed him that he and Burroughs had seen some funny lights in the woods and that there might be a problem. Penniston thought it might be an air crash; he had been in the Air Force for seven years and had been involved in numerous crash retrievals. Steffens pointed out that there had been no noise as the craft came down, so it could not have been an air crash. 'It didn't crash, Jim. It landed,' he said.

Penniston looked down the perimeter road and could see what appeared to be different coloured lights, and thinking it could be a fire he radioed Central Security Control. Master Sergeant J. D. Chandler, who was the overall flight chief for both bases, asked him to stand by whilst he made enquiries with the control tower at Bentwaters. When Chandler came back on the radio he informed Penniston that the tower had checked with Heathrow airport, RAF Bawdsey and RAF Watton. Apparently a 'bogie' (the USAF term for a UFO) had been tracked and lost fifteen minutes earlier when it had dropped from radar imaging over Woodbridge.

Penniston was still convinced it was a downed aircraft and requested permission to investigate. Chandler contacted the shift commander and a few minutes later Penniston was instructed to select two airmen to accompany him. He decided that Burroughs should stay at the east-gate post and Staff Sergeant Steffens should join his patrol. But whatever was out there, it must have scared the hell out of Steffens because he refused to go back into the forest. Realizing that Steffens was serious, he summoned Burroughs and Cabansag and the patrol drove down the east-gate road towards the forest. From the edge of the road they could see a bright light through the trees and because it was on British territory he again radioed Central Security Control for permission to continue the investigation. Probably sensing there might be a problem, he requested back-up assistance. The patrol then turned right and, taking a sharp left turn, drove up the adjacent logging road into the forest, but due to the rocky terrain they had to abandon the vehicle and proceed on foot. Meanwhile, Master Sergeant Chandler had made his way over to Woodbridge and parked his vehicle on the side of the road near the flightline.

As Penniston's patrol moved in closer to the lights they began experiencing difficulty with their radios, and he instructed Cabansag to stay back at the vehicle to act as a communications relay between the patrol and Chandler. Penniston and Burroughs continued through the forest towards a bright white light which was just sitting in a clearing. It was so intensely bright that it caused them to squint as they stared in its direction. All around them was the commotion of animals and birds that seemed to be in a terrible frenzy, but apart from the noise of the creatures there was no other sound to be heard. Penniston was now 50 metres from the object and had lost all radio contact with Central Security Control, and contact with Cabansag was becoming increasingly difficult. At this stage he instructed Burroughs to stay back at the tree line to act as a radio relay back to Cabansag, but Burroughs had lost his calm and was becoming highly agitated and thus did not acknowledge the order. As a result, that was the last contact anyone had with the patrol until the incident was over.

At a distance of 50 metres Penniston was just close enough to realize it was a metallic-type object, but it was not a conventional craft, not like anything he was familiar with or any prototype he had heard of. The air surrounding it was electrifying, causing him to think he was moving in slow motion and the sensations of his hair and skin gave him the feeling that he was surrounded by static electricity. The birds and animals had scattered and everything was now deathly quiet. Penniston moved to within 20 metres of the phenomenon and could make out a shiny black opaque triangle about nine feet in width and six feet high. At times giving an almost glasslike appearance. He would later describe it as being the size of a tank. White light was mainly emitting from the top portion of the object, with some intense white light visible at its base. From where he was standing, he noticed a bluish light on the left-hand centre side and a red light on the right, both of which were flashing alternately. The lights seemed to be moulded into the very fabric of the object. Personnel normally carried cameras which they used to photograph people who ventured too close to the perimeter, so Penniston removed his camera from its case and bravely began to photograph the object, snapping away as fast as he could and making rough notes in his jotter at the same time.

Having finished the film he moved in closer, to within 10 metres of the object. He then began to examine it, walking around looking for an opening of some kind, but he realized there were no visible seams. Although in awe, he gathered his wits and made an even more courageous move and at one point he actually slid his hand over the surface of the object, which felt warm to the touch. There were raised symbols etched on to its left-hand side, which seemed familiar but he did not know why. The unusual markings measured approximately three to four inches in height and covered an area of about three feet in diameter. There were no obvious life forms, but he sensed there was some sort of life presence within the object. One thing is certain: he was sure it was under intelligent control.

Suddenly there was a tremendous bright flash and both men hit the ground, burying their faces in the dirt to hide their eyes from the intense light. The object lifted silently up to about four feet off the ground and started manoeuvring very slowly and carefully through the trees. Having raised up to a few hundred feet, it hovered momentarily before disappearing in the blink of an eye. The patrol spotted more coloured lights visible about half a mile away and, according to Penniston, they followed them until they too disappeared from sight. There was still no radio contact and the patrol decided to turn around and head back to the base, first stopping on the way to examine the landing site. Burroughs was the first to notice the ground impressions. There were three, all triangular in shape and each appeared to be about three metres apart. The witnesses were now wondering how they were ever going to explain the incident to their superiors. As they made their way back to the base they saw another light flash through the sky. On arriving at Central Security Control, Penniston ran into Master Sergeant Chandler, who told him that they had been very concerned because there was negative contact with the patrol for almost three hours. It seems Chandler had returned to base when he lost contact with the patrol. Penniston told Chandler, 'You're not going to believe what we saw tonight,' to which Chandler replied, 'Yeah, if it's anything to do with what I saw a while ago I would believe you.' At the termination of their shift, the airmen were instructed to report to the shift commander's office.

After being debriefed they were given a history lesson citing the official Blue Book and informed that what they had observed was no longer reportable through Air Force channels. Penniston was told that the Blue Book project was an official Air Force investigation of the UFO phenomenon, which was terminated in 1969, following the conclusion that there was no threat to national security. Penniston and Burroughs were also advised that some things are best left alone and it was suggested that they try to forget what had happened and not discuss the matter with anyone. Penniston says it was this mentality that prompted the shift commander to delete the report from the blotter and replace it with something totally unrelated, such as 'investigated aircraft crash off the installation'. He claims there was an Accident and Complaint Report form (1569) filled out, but this consisted of only a few sentences and there was no mention of an unidentified craft. Penniston is sure that Lieutenant Fred Buran was the night-shift commander on duty. Following this meeting they were debriefed by Captain Mike Verrano, the day-shift commander. He advised them to return to the suspected landing site in daylight to look for any physical evidence. They were then given a six-day official break to get over their ordeal.

After turning in their weapons and signing off duty, Penniston and Burroughs returned to the landing site and found broken branches scattered on the ground. These appeared to be from the canopy of trees where the object had crashed through as it landed. They also found three indentations on the ground, which they realized were the marks left by the UFO. There were also scorch marks on the trees facing the landing site. It was a relief for Penniston who needed some proof to believe that it really had happened, but for Burroughs it was a reminder of something he would rather have forgotten. Penniston then took photographs of the landing site and, along with the ones he had taken of the UFO, delivered them to the base photo laboratory on Bentwaters. He then dropped Burroughs off at his home (they both lived in Ipswich), because apparently he was still very shaken. Penniston went home, changed into civilian clothes and visited a British friend, a painter and decorator, where he collected some plaster of Paris. He was going to return to the landing site with the intention of making some casts of the three triangular ground indentations left by the object. This was for his own peace of mind as he desperately wanted some lasting proof of what he had witnessed the night before. There was no one at the site when Penniston arrived, so after pouring the plaster into the depressions, he waited about forty minutes for them to mould. He had just finished storing them in the boot of his car when Captain Mike Verrano and Major Edward Drury turned up with a British civilian policeman. Drury wanted to know what Penniston was doing in the forest. 'I'm just looking around,' he said. After he had described the incident to the policeman, Drury advised him to go home and get some sleep. Penniston intended to do just that, but first he had a job to do, which was to seal the plaster casts in plastic wrapping and hide them in a safe place. A point made by Penniston is that the forest terrain was very solid, almost frozen, and even the tyres from military vehicles did not leave much of a depression so the object must have had some weight.

Although Penniston was on official break, he was instructed to report to the base commander at 09.00 hrs the following morning (27 December). Colonel Ted Conrad debriefed him and Penniston was then told to report to the AFOSI, where he met with two special agents. He was told the craft had returned a few hours earlier but it had not landed. He was then debriefed for approximately ninety minutes, and at that stage it seems they were confident that the incident was under control. Penniston did not tell them he had approached the craft or touched it but he did mention he had taken photographs. After processing and reviewing any film, airmen were supposed to turn them over to the AFOSI, but when he later called at the base photo laboratory to collect the films, he was told there were none. Penniston was simply informed that they had come out fogged. He was not convinced, however, because the cameras they carried were good quality military stock. After the UFO returned on the third night, Penniston was again called by the AFOSI. This time he was required to go over every single detail of his own encounter, from the moment he checked in at guard mount until he handed in his weapons and went off duty the following morning.

About a week after the initial incident Penniston was told that a special team would be doing some electronics work on the perimeter of Woodbridge and he was instructed to brief personnel to ignore the activity. He thought it very odd that these people were not wearing military uniforms but were dressed in civilian attire. He later learnt that they were a containment study group from Langley, the CIA research centre.

For years Penniston would hear stories about the incident circulating among military personnel. Many of these tales were erroneous but he never spoke out. He had already tried to do that once when he approached Brenda Butler in 1983. Brenda and her colleague Dot Street had not known his true identity and had given him the pseudonym James Archer. Both researchers had considered him a valuable witness to the case. However, something went wrong and a planned second meeting, when Penniston promised to produce some important evidence, never took place.

It is unfortunate that the meeting did not go as planned because he would turn out to be one of the most important witnesses. It would be more than ten years before he would go public, and in 1999 Penniston finally confessed to me that he was indeed the mysterious James Archer. He also told me a slightly different version of his meeting with Brenda and Dot. Apparently, it did not last very long because one of the women persisted in asking questions about nuclear weapons and wanted to know if there were any deployed on the base. This has always been a sensitive issue and Penniston could have been in serious trouble for even discussing it. He had top-secret clearance and if anyone asked about sensitive issues he was supposed to report it immediately to his superiors. This was often the case if any of the personnel found themselves drinking in an Ipswich public house with a Russian. This could happen when the Russian fleet were in town. Penniston told me what happened during his meeting with Brenda and Dot:

> Here I am trying to offer them the truth of what really happened with the UFO and they wanted to know about whether or not there were nuclear weapons on the base. I had top-secret clearance and couldn't discuss those things. I had no choice but to terminate the meeting there and then. The reason I contacted

them in the first place was because I wasn't happy about *The News of the World* story and wanted to offer them the full facts. They had the first chance to really break this story but they lost that opportunity.

Penniston had been annoyed about a certain witness testimony being featured in the newspaper, namely that of Art Wallace, the pseudonym of Larry Warren, who he claimed was not involved in the incident. Obviously, Penniston's full account would have been a tremendous asset at the time. It is possible that he did have some vital evidence to share with the researchers because he desperately wanted the story to be told. However, he wanted it done discreetly because, after all, he was still in the military.

Not long before his retirement from the USAF the TV documentary *Unsolved Mysteries* was aired, which became a nightmare for Penniston. This was because for the first time ever his name was mentioned in the media. Penniston heard the programme had been featured on national television, but it was only when the Armed Forces Network for Europe (AFNE) got a hold of it that he was called by the AFOSI for yet another debriefing. Penniston was stationed in Bitburg, Germany, at the time and was absolutely stunned that at the precise moment the programme was to be shown on the AFNE, there was a power cut which lasted throughout the duration of the programme and was conveniently restored as soon as it terminated.

However, after his retirement in 1994, Jim Penniston would have the opportunity to put his own case forward when he featured in a British documentary of *Strange but True?*, produced by David Alpin and presented by Michael Aspel. Although there was still a good deal of research to be undertaken, it was considered to be the best documentary on the case so far. Penniston, Halt and Burroughs were flown to the UK to take part in the programme, and researcher Brenda Butler was briefly interviewed.

It was during this visit to England that Brenda realized James Archer was Jim Penniston. They had met briefly at the *Strange But*

True? recording and although the witnesses and the crew met for a drink in a local public house Brenda refrained from joining them, instead staying outside in her car. Penniston thought this was very strange at the time, but on his return to the United States he received an emotional letter from Brenda, explaining that she had recognized him as the man she had tried to interview more than ten years earlier. However, Brenda told me the reason she did not join the witnesses that day was because the film crew had instructed her to stay away from them. According to Brenda, all the witnesses were separated, and in her research papers she mentions that Halt told her that he had to go discreetly to Penniston's and Burroughs' hotel rooms to check which story they were telling.

After fourteen years of trying to come to terms with what he had witnessed, Jim Penniston finally succumbed to hypnotic regression. The nightmares had become less frequent but they were still difficult to deal with, and he had recently been diagnosed as suffering from post-traumatic stress. A professional psychologist who was known to the family carried out the sessions, which were videotaped. The questions to be posed were put together by some of his colleagues, with a suggestion from Penniston that they should not be leading or suggestive. The first of two sessions was carried out in September 1994, with Penniston covering the same memories as he recalled consciously. During the encounter he finds himself beside the craft but the next moment he is further back, standing next to John Burroughs. There is approximately forty-five minutes of missing time. This is interesting because when I asked him if Burroughs was present during the encounter, he replied:

> I don't remember John being there the moment the craft landed, which appeared to be on landing gear. I gave him an order that he disobeyed, that was to stay back at the tree line. It was a confusing time. I don't even know if Cabansag was there. I only cared about what was 180 degrees in front of me, an unidentified. I did a 360-degree walk around it and touched the surface, which was warm to the touch. I do know it was there for about thirty to thirty-five minutes.

Two months later Penniston went through the second hypnotic regression. This time he was taken back to the time he was debriefed by the AFOSI. This session produced an interesting twist to what happened during the debriefing. At some stage the two agents left the room and two other men replaced them, an American and an Englishman. Penniston was told that the American was from the State Department and the Englishman was from the British equivalent. He was then asked if they could give him a shot of sodium Pentothal, the truth serum. They wanted to record the interview and make sure they had all the facts, they told him. Penniston agreed provided it would put an end to it. During the regression Penniston actually lifts his arm as if to take an injection. The two men questioned him repeatedly, mostly about the structure of the object; they were very interested in its speed and how it made its approach. Penniston told them he did not see it land, that it had already landed when he arrived. In my interviews with Penniston, he explained that most of the time was spent doing sketches of the craft. 'Draw what you see,' he was told. After Penniston describes the symbols, the two men start talking among themselves and conclude that there is no point in going any further, that they know what he has seen and the question now is how to contain it.

The most amazing part of the regression deals with an alien encounter at the scene of the incident. When asked about the possibility of beings being present, Penniston begins to talk about 'the visitors'. He describes them as being from our future, a dark and polluted world with many difficulties. He explains that they are visiting in teams and each team is assigned a different task. Apparently, the teams know exactly which people they are to target when they arrive in our time. Penniston reveals that some of them are coming here to take sperm and eggs, which are necessary in order to help their species survive. It seems they have a serious problem with reproduction. This all sounds very familiar, and those who fear they have been victims of alien abduction can certainly relate to it. However, Penniston clearly has problems with this part of the regression, which is not surprising considering his long-term military background.

I asked him if he would give me a transcript of those sessions, but he shied away, saying, 'I don't know, they are very personal.' The hypnotic sessions not only confirmed his recollections of the event, but highlighted names he had long since forgotten, including the names of the American and British agents who interrogated him under drug-induced hypnosis.

Even if we dismiss the information obtained whilst under regression, Penniston's conscious memory of the events is very valid and of great importance to the case. Apart from the initial debriefing, he also recalls meetings with his superiors, including Wing Commander Gordon Williams. In fact, the AFOSI continued to bother Penniston until his retirement from the USAF in 1993. Penniston claims his sleep patterns are often interrupted by terrible nightmares and he blames this partly on the interrogations he suffered at the hands of the AFOSI and other agents.

For as long as the military witnesses remained in the service they were the property of the USAF, and the AFOSI made sure they never forgot it. Jim Penniston claims he was harassed by the agency until just before his retirement. He blames them for a missing plaster cast which he had taken of the ground indentations. When his tour at Bentwaters terminated in 1984, he had packed one of the casts in his household belongings that were shipped back to the United States, and the other two he carried in his hand luggage. When he unpacked the crates there were three boxes missing, which included the box containing the plaster cast. He filed a complaint about missing boxes and it took an incredible nine months for them to arrive. When they finally turned up they were badly damaged and there was no sign of the cast.

During Penniston's 1984 tour at Grissom AFB, Indiana, he accidentally discovered a listening bug in his home, which was situated on the base domestic site. He could not be sure if the bug had been planted to spy on him or if it had been there for some other purpose, maybe involving the person who had lived there before him, but he doubted the latter and he was taking no chances. The device was cleverly positioned inside the living-room wall, close to the telephone socket. The first thing he did was remove it and take it to someone he trusted who was familiar with these gadgets. Not only did it turn out to be a bug but it had a listening range of up to 3,000 feet. Penniston also received harassing telephone calls, which prompted him to change his number. There was mail tampering too, and he confirmed that John Burroughs had received similar harassment. Apparently the mail was often delayed, sometimes for weeks on end, and letters arrived that had been opened and resealed in a fashion that made it obvious they had been tampered with. Since he realized he was under surveillance he always takes precautions.

The following typed statement is part of the file of alleged witness statements that were officially made for Lieutenant Colonel Charles I. Halt in January 1981. When I told Jim Penniston of its existence, he told me, 'My statement was handwritten, if the one you have is typed then it was not done by me.' After sending him a copy of the typed statement, he responded, 'Statement seems original in content, however, original was not typed. I think Halt summarized statement.'

Typed statement allegedly by Staff Sergeant Jim Penniston, typed on plain paper, unsigned

Received dispatch from CSC to rendezvous with Police 4 AIC Burroughs, and Police 5 SSgt Steffens at east gate Woodbridge. Upon arriving at east gate directly to the east about 1½ miles in a large wooded area. A large yellow glowing light was emitting above the trees. [Refer diagram 1] In the centre of the lighted area directly in the centre ground level, there was a red light blinking on and off 5 to 10 sec intervals. And a blue light that was being for the most part steady. After receiving permission from CSC, we proceeded off base pass [sic] east gate, down an old logging road. Left vehicle, proceeded on foot. Burroughs and I were approx. 15–20 meters apart and proceeding on a true east direction from logging road. The area in front of us was lighting up a 30 meter area. When we got within a 50 meter distance. The object was producing red and blue light. The blue light was steady and projecting under the object. It was lighting

up the area directly extending a meter or two out. At this point
of positive identification I relayed to CSC, SSgt Coffey. A
positive sighting of the object . . . 1 . . . colour of lights and that
it was definitely mechanical in nature. This is the closest point
that I was near the object at any point. We then proceeded after
it. It moved in a zig-zagging manner back through the woods,
then lost sight of it. On the way back we encountered a blue
streaking light to the left lasting only a few seconds. After 45
min walk arrived at our vehicle.

Included with the statement were sketches of a map of the area,
details of where the UFO was located and a sketch of the UFO. In
separate files there were drawings of the UFO and the symbols that
Penniston saw on the object.

Handwritten comments added at a later date:

Sgt Penniston has a lot to contribute. He promised me a plaster
cast + photos but never delivered. I think he's holding out to 'sell'
a story. He is, however, a very competent individual and can be
trusted. I'm convinced his story is as he says. He was so shuck [sic]
he had to have a week off to recover.

It is interesting that Penniston's alleged statement implies that
the closest point he was to the craft was at a 50 metre distance, but
note that there appear to be missing words in the preceding sentence
('object . . . 1 . . . colour'). If a copy of his handwritten statement
were required, surely Halt would have asked his secretary to type it,
or at least someone with more experience in such matters. Assuming
Penniston is telling the truth, that he was not responsible for the
typed statement, then who is?

Referring to the handwritten comments on Penniston's statement: 'He promised me a plaster cast + photos but never delivered.'
Penniston told me in conversation that Halt had requested a plaster
cast and he had eventually given one to him. This was probably the
cast that Halt carried with him when he attended a UFO seminar

during his trip to England in 1994. Referring to the photographs, Penniston does claim to have a photograph of the landing site, which he managed to coax from an AFOSI special agent. The written comments also state: 'I'm convinced his story is as he says. He was so shuck [sic] he had to have a week off to recover.' Charles Halt had previously confirmed that Penniston was so shaken by what had happened that he had asked to be transferred to another base as soon as possible.

Probably the best part of these documents are the drawings by Penniston and Burroughs. Penniston has confirmed that he did numerous drawings, many for the AFOSI. One of the drawings shows a map of the area depicting the route taken from the east gate to the landing site and, on a separate page, there is a drawing of the forest area, the UFO and the positions of himself and Burroughs. In the corner of the page Penniston has done a rough sketch of the UFO, which is just an oblong-type box, showing landing legs and three coloured lights. The description of the lights are as follows: blue glow from underneath the object, bluish light in the central position and a large red light at the top (probably due to the passing of time he would later describe the top and bottom lights as being white). Penniston later sketched a set of symbols, which he says he copied from his original jotter. These were the raised symbols he saw on the UFO the night of the incident. He also drew three pictures of the UFO. These drawings are an excellent description of the triangular object, which can be viewed from three different angles.

At the time of the incident, Jim Penniston was a trained observer with seven years' military experience behind him. He had also been involved in several downed-aircraft retrievals. He explains that the reason he kept silent for so long was because he was still serving in the USAF. He had been told early in the day that the incident was not officially classified but that it was in his best interests not to discuss it.

It is worth remembering that following the incident Penniston was debriefed more than any other witness. This included meetings with Wing Commander Gordon Williams, Vice Wing Commander

Brian Currie, Base Commander Ted Conrad, Lieutenant Colonel Charles Halt, Major Malcolm Zickler, Major Edward Drury, Captain Mike Verrano, Lieutenant Fred Buran, the AFOSI special agents, and a British and American agent. The debriefings with the commanders were fairly standard-type procedures where he would make a report, give statements and submit his notes. But the AFOSI debriefings were tape recorded and the ones with the British and American agents were carried out using drug-induced hypnosis.

Jim Penniston retired from active duty in 1993 with twenty-seven military honours. He also received a letter of appreciation from the President of the United States. As one of the more senior witnesses, he had served in Vietnam and would later be involved in the Gulf War conflict. He is now settled with his wife and family in a small American town and is currently employed as a human resources director for a manufacturing company.

It is my opinion that Jim Penniston is a most reliable witness. During my conversations with him, he never changed his story and always answered my questions intelligently. He is willing to be challenged by the sceptics who have publicly claimed that his experience cannot be genuine because he did not discuss it in the early years. Yet not one sceptic has gone to the trouble to locate and interview him. If they had done so they would realize that Penniston did try to talk discreetly to researchers as early as 1983 but was unable to go public because until 1993 he was still serving in the USAF.

Over the years he has searched for a meaning as to what happened in Rendlesham Forest that Christmas in 1980, but has never come to any conclusion. He does not expect the US Government to admit it was extraterrestrial for even he does not know what it was. However, he would like some answers and, rather than the denials, he would be satisfied if the government would admit that it was 'a craft of unknown origin' and they are unable to explain it. Jim Penniston sums it up when he says 'the incident was of biblical proportion'.

THE EVIDENCE OF EDWARD CABANSAG

Nineteen-year-old Edward N. Cabansag was among the latest recruits to arrive at RAF Bentwaters during the month of December 1980. He was fresh out of training school and recalls it was only the first or second day of his official duty at the base when he was unknowingly caught up in Britain's greatest UFO mystery. Cabansag, of Hawaiian parents, is best remembered for his light-hearted sense of humour and dedication to duty. Because he was the third primary witness to the initial event, I was sure his contribution would add greatly to the testimony of Penniston and Burroughs, but Cabansag had never gone public. At a British UFO conference in 1994 Charles Halt told the audience that Cabansag would not talk to anybody because he was in a sensitive position with the government and he did not want to risk his job. Halt told me a similar story in 1998, but when I spoke to Cabansag myself he assured me that at no time since leaving the military in the mid-1980s had he been in a sensitive position and, what is more, he was quite willing to discuss the incident. When Cabansag made contact with me, having read an early article I wrote on the case, he was ready to talk. Basically, he had been told to keep quiet about what he had witnessed, but now that others were talking he was prepared to do the same. Nobody had heard of Cabansag, at least by name, until Colonel Halt mentioned him at the UFO conference. Unfortunately, because it is an unusual name, ufologists picking up on Halt's words misspelt it as Kavanasac, which is the correct pronunciation, but locating him proved a difficult task. The first thing I did was draft him a copy of his alleged statement and ask for his opinion. The following typed statement was signed by Edward N. Cabansag and was from the original CAUS files.

1981 Statement by Airman First Class Edward N. Cabansag, typed on plain paper

On 26 Dec 80, SSgt Penningston [sic] and I were on Security #6 at Woodbridge Base. I was the member. We were patrolling Delta NAPA when we received a call over the radio. It stated that Police #4 had seen some strange lights out past the east gate and we were to respond. SSgt Penningston [sic] and I left Delta NAPA, heading for the east gate code two. When we got there SSgt Steffens and A1C Burroughs were on patrol. They told us they had seen some funny lights out in the woods. We notified CSC and we asked permission to investigate further. They gave us the go-ahead. We left our weapons with SSgt Steffens who remained at the gate. Thus the three of us went out to investigate. We stopped the Security Police vehicle about 100 metres from the gate. Due to the terrain we had to go on by foot. We kept in constant contact with CSC. While we walked, each of us would see the lights. Blue, red, white, and yellow. The beacon light turned out to be the yellow light. We would see them periodically, but not in a specific pattern. As we approached, the lights would seem to be at the edge of the forest. We were about 100 meters from the edge of the forest when I saw a quick movement, it look visible for a moment [sic]. It look like it spun left a quarter of a turn [sic], then it was gone. I'd advised SSgt Pennington [sic] and A1C Burroughs. We advised CSC and proceeded in extreme caution. When we got about 75–50 meters, MSgt Chandler/Flight Chief, was on the scene. CSC was not reading our transmissions very well, so we used MSgt Chandler as a go-between. He remained back at our vehicle. As we entered the forest, the blue and red lights were not visible anymore. Only the beacon light was still blinking. We figured the lights were coming from past the forest, since nothing was visible when we past [sic] through the woody forest. We would see a glowing light near the beacon light, but as we got closer we found it to be a lit-up farm house. After we passed through the forest we thought it had to be an aircraft accident. So did CSC as well. But we ran and walked a good 2 miles past our vehicle, until we got to a vantage point where we could determine that what we were chasing was only a beacon light off in the distance. Our route through the forest and field was a direct one, straight towards the light. We informed CSC that the light beacon was farther than we thought, so CSC terminated our investigation. A1C Burroughs and I took a road, while SSgt Penningston [sic] walked straight back from where we came. A1C Burroughs saw the light again, this time it was coming from the left of us, as we were walking back to our patrol vehicle. We got in contact with SSgt Penningston [sic] and we took a walk through where we saw the lights. Nothing. Finally, we made it back to our vehicle, after making contact with the PCs and informing them of what we saw. After that we met MSgt Chandler and we went in service again after termination of the sighting.

[Signed]
EDWARD N. CABANSAG, A1C, USAF
81st Security Police Sq.
[Undated]

[Handwritten comments added at a later date]

I'm convinced this is a 'cleaned-up' version of what happened. I talked with Amn Cabansag and can say he was shook up to the point he didn't want to talk. From talking with Chuck Decarlo (C&N) [sic] I can say he is still working today. He might talk if approached right. [signed] H

The statement is not the full story, however.

Airman First Class Cabansag had just completed guard mount at the Bentwaters installation when he was instructed to collect Staff Sergeant Jim Penniston. He was to be assigned as the member, which meant that he was to be Penniston's driver. Cabansag was not given any information at this stage and just assumed he would be working a normal patrol. When he reached Penniston, he was directed to drive to the east gate at Woodbridge, where they were to investigate a possible air crash in the forest. After talking to Staff Sergeant Steffens and Airman Burroughs, Penniston consulted Central Security Control and was given permission to proceed with an investigation. Penniston then instructed Cabansag to drive him and Burroughs to the forest. Cabansag's statement claims the patrol left their weapons with Staff Sergeant Steffens, but he told me that was incorrect, that he had handed his weapon over to Master Sergeant Chandler who was stationed near the flightline. Lieutenant Fred Buran's statement also confirms that weapons were turned over to Chandler:

> SSgt Penniston requested permission to investigate. After he had been joined by the Security Flight Chief, MSgt Chandler, and turned his weapon over to him.

Chandler's statement tells us that the patrol was on British property when he arrived, which would imply that they were in violation of the Status of Forces Agreement by taking weapons off the installation. It is worth noting the different testimonies regarding who turned weapons over to whom. This only confirms that there are errors in the statements. Could it be that the men did not turn their weapons over to anyone but actually took them into the forest?

> When I arrived, SSgt Penniston, A1C Burroughs and Amn Cabansag had entered the wooded area just beyond the clearing at the access road. We set up a radio relay between SSgt Penniston, myself and CSC.

As they moved through the forest Cabansag recalls seeing unusual coloured lights and it soon became evident that there were difficulties with their standard military Motorola radios. It was during this time that Penniston claims he instructed Cabansag to stay back near the vehicle where he was to act as a relay communications between the patrol and Chandler, but Cabansag does not recall separating from the patrol.

Cabansag's statement, more than any of the others, points out that the men were following a lighthouse beacon. I thought it entirely possible that after the encounter with a landed object, the men may have momentarily mistaken the lighthouse for the UFO, but the witnesses deny that the lighthouse played any part in the encounter. Let us examine Cabansag's statement more closely. (a) It states that he and Penniston were patrolling the Woodbridge base when they received the call, but according to Penniston's recent testimony he was taking a midnight snack at Woodbridge when he received the report and Cabansag claims he was still at Bentwaters when he was instructed to join Penniston at the Woodbridge base. (b) The statement refers to Police 4 having seen some strange lights, but Penniston says Burroughs and Steffens were assigned to Police 2, and both Penniston and Cabansag have since confirmed they were Police 1. (c) Cabansag's statement makes a definite point that they were in constant contact with Central Security Control, but the witnesses claim they lost contact with CSC, which is exactly why Cabansag and Chandler were performing a relay. (d) There is a reference to PCs. The letter P is somewhat messy because it has been typed over another letter, but the initials PC do not stand for anything in the USAF that I am familiar with, therefore I can only assume it means police constable. This, of course, would point to the two British policemen who were sent into the forest, but this is questionable because Cabansag writes, 'Finally, we made it back to our vehicle after making contact with the PCs and informing them of what we saw.' This would imply that he made contact with the PCs while they were still in the forest. However, PC Dave King states, 'There were no Americans out there, not a soul. We didn't report to the base because when we got back to our car there was no one there so we just left and went home.' Is this the story Cabansag was advised to tell? Apparently, he was so nervous at being brought before Lieutenant Colonel Halt that he signed a document without even looking at it. I asked him to explain:

> The only thing that I signed was for Colonel Halt. I didn't type anything out. Maybe someone else did it and asked me to sign it.

Besides, I couldn't type, I had never used a typewriter before. I don't even remember what I signed. I was so nervous, I just signed it. I don't remember talking to Halt, I remember sitting in his office in fear of Halt. I was fresh from school.

I wondered if he knew what a PC was and if he recalled seeing any PCs in the forest.

Yes, I know what they are, but I didn't see any PCs in the forest and I never talked to any of them . . . I never spoke to any British policemen.

Cabansag's statement reports the following:

After we passed through the forest we thought it had to be an aircraft accident. So did CSC as well. But we ran and walked a good 2 miles past our vehicle, until we got to a vantage point where we could determine that what we were chasing was only a beacon light off in the distance.

However, in a recent interview he denied he walked a distance of two miles or anything close to it. He also denies that he mistook the lighthouse for the UFO. Here is Cabansag's own story of what he believes occurred that night.

Because I was new, and probably green, I thought it was some sort of prank or a fraternity thing like they do in college. I recall being assigned to Security One, driving Penniston over to the east gate and meeting up with Burroughs and Steffens. We thought it was going to be a downed aircraft. It was Burroughs who made the report. We had to wait for Master Sergeant Chandler to meet us because we had to hand our weapons over to him and get permission to proceed further. I've read all that stuff about me being a com-link, but I can't remember any of that. I remember being with Penniston and Burroughs, there were only three of us, Sergeant Chandler stayed back with the jeep. We all saw something, and I kept thinking this was a joke, but as we got closer and closer we could see a light, and our radio transmissions were cutting out. I remember what I saw; it was to the right of the lighthouse. It was cone-shaped – egg-shaped, with lights running around its belt from left to right. They were blue, white and red lights, flashing, sometimes rapid, sometimes slow. Then we saw flakes of metal coming from it. It is difficult to describe. We were all trying to make sure what we'd seen . . . It wasn't the lighthouse. I saw the lighthouse, this wasn't it, it was to the right of the lighthouse.

Cabansag does not remember seeing a landed object in the forest or chasing an object for two miles. He explained:

You know, I don't remember any of that. It seems like I have a blank there somewhere. I don't recall walking the two miles either. I would have remembered that. It couldn't have been two miles; it was cold out there. I know what they're saying, but I can't recall, maybe I was told not to discuss it, maybe they blocked it, I don't know.

Cabansag was concerned after reading Jim Penniston's account of what had occurred, and it was obvious he had a complete blank of what had taken place after they entered the forest until they saw the object to the right of the lighthouse.

I'm very confused. I may have been with Chandler, but then I can't remember separating from Burroughs and Penniston. Why do I just recall? – I have a blank. I really don't remember anything about the thing landing. The next day, or a couple of days later, I heard Lieutenant Englund or someone had gone out with Geiger counters, and some people were saying, 'How could it get in the small space between the trees?' But this was all second-hand information. I wasn't involved in any of the other nights and I didn't know what else went on. I carried on with work as usual. It was never discussed, I remember that.

Whatever I was expecting to hear from Eddie Cabansag, it was not that he had experienced missing time. But as you will see, all the

evidence points to there having been an incident involving a
triangular object that landed in Rendlesham Forest. There is no
doubt that he was out with the patrol that night, his name is firmly
linked with the incident. Of course, there is a possibility that he is
knowingly holding back information, but I doubt he would want to
discredit Penniston and Burroughs, and I certainly did not consider
him to be dishonest in his recollection of what had occurred. But
what really concerned me was that, as he was telling his story, I
realized he was recounting the before and after, but was not discussing what happened in-between. It is as if there is a chunk of time
missing from his memory.

It is possible that Cabansag was not a witness to the actual
landing. In his statements, Penniston points out that due to the
radio transmissions breaking up, he stationed Cabansag back at the
jeep to act as a communications relay. But Cabansag believes he was
with Penniston and Burroughs the whole time. However, Penniston
does not suggest that Cabansag was with him during the encounter
with a landed object. He told me that Burroughs and he had headed
on foot towards the tree line, which was approximately fifty metres
away from the object. At this stage, Penniston seems to have lost all
radio contact with Cabansag. It was not until he was put under
hypnotic regression that Penniston discovered he had experienced
forty-five minutes of missing time, and apparently Burroughs also
experienced the same. If all three men are reporting the exact same
phenomenon then we must seriously consider if they were involved
in something even more sinister than witnessing a UFO. Were they
abducted or were they somehow locked in a different time or
dimension?

It is interesting that Cabansag does not remember getting into
the vehicle and returning to the base but recalls that he and
Penniston went back on patrol immediately after the incident. One
of his concerns at the time was why they would allow a new recruit
to go out on patrol and not know what the patrol was all about.
When I asked him if he was absolutely certain they were not carrying
weapons in the forest, he confirmed they had handed over their M-

16 rifles but that John Burroughs was still carrying a sidearm. Lieutenant Colonel Halt did not coerce him into denying the incident but he admits that 'they' made out it was the lighthouse beacon. 'I had, and still have, better than average vision. There was no fog, it was a clear night and I could see something moving which was silver in colour with lights,' he said.

Although Penniston and Burroughs were given a six-day break, Cabansag was not given any time off but instead was promoted to a day job. Usually day shifts are carried out by the A Flights, but although he worked permanent days he was still officially assigned with C Flight. It seems that some of the witnesses were moved to day duties following the incident. Was it because they were now afraid of night duties or was it to keep an eye on them?

Not all the military statements are dated and according to Halt he interviewed the witnesses about a week later. However, Cabansag claims he was instructed to report to Lieutenant Colonel Halt on the morning of 26 December, a few hours after he had gone off duty. This being the case it means that Halt was involved in the debriefings from day one. Before he was summoned to Halt's office, Cabansag had been in the showers and it was there that his colleagues suggested he should go along with what he was told. 'Just go along with what the officers tell you, then you don't think about it anymore, that way you don't get into trouble,' they advised. 'That morning everyone was talking about it, but it soon went quiet,' said Cabansag. He claims he was never interviewed by the AFOSI but Lieutenant Colonel Halt told him it was 'very hush-hush' and advised him not to talk about it on the base. Cabansag says he was left alone and not bothered by the AFOSI agents. He believes this was because he followed advice and played dumb.

Let us examine the handwritten notes on Cabansag's statement: 'I'm convinced this is a "cleaned-up" version of what happened.' Whoever wrote this may not have seen the original statements made to the flight commander on the morning immediately following the events, or they might have been aware of the nature of the event but pretended they were uninformed. One message reads: 'I talked with

Amn Cabansag and can say he was shook up to the point he didn't want to talk.' Cabansag told me, 'I don't remember talking to Halt. I remember sitting in his office in fear of Halt. I was fresh from school. I didn't give any statement.' There is mention of talking to the CNN defence journalist Chuck de Caro, who had carried out research on the case for a TV documentary. The message reads: 'From talking with Chuck Decarlo (C&N) [sic] I can say he [Cabansag] is still working today. He might talk if approached right. [signed] H.' We must consider who would be in a position to have these statements in their possession – someone who talked with de Caro with the initial H. The only person I can imagine who would have had access to those statements with the initial H is Charles Halt, who was indeed contacted by CNN and did correspond with Larry Fawcett of CAUS. Halt also admits the statements were made at his request, but denies he is responsible for the written comments.

The fact that Cabansag signed a statement he did not even read may seem somewhat naive to the average person. However, if you can imagine that the youngster, fresh out of training school, was facing a lieutenant colonel who also happened to be the deputy base commander, you can understand how nervous he must have been. Most Security Police and Law Enforcement personnel, especially new recruits, would not expect to have an audience with a commander of Halt's status. The highest-ranking officer who would have interviewed them under normal circumstances would probably have been Major Malcolm Zickler.

The problem now facing Cabansag is the realization that he experienced missing time during the encounter. This has clearly bothered him and he can find no solution as to what happened to him during that period. The remarkable thing is that he has unknowingly lived with it all these years, and it was only when I asked him to piece together his story that he realized there was a blank in his memory. It is certain that this missing time took place during Penniston and Burroughs' encounter with the UFO and, although he was not in close range to the object, it is just possible that he was also drawn into the encounter.

Edward Cabansag was promoted to senior airman soon after the incident and completed a two-year tour at RAF Bentwaters. Six months after leaving England he retired as a security policeman, then spent four years with a combat team stationed at army bases. Since retiring in 1985 he has become a marshal arts expert. He lives with his wife and children in California.

THE EVIDENCE OF ADRIAN BUSTINZA

Adrian Bustinza joined the USAF in 1977 and after basic training he was assigned to Mather Air Force Base, California. It was in the course of this tour that he encountered a UFO incident, which occurred during a midnight shift when he and other personnel witnessed the object hovering over the base near the weapons storage area. But nothing more was said about the incident and he was not debriefed. Before arriving at Bentwaters in 1980, he had been stationed in Alaska on temporary duty. During his tour at Bentwaters he was promoted to sergeant.

Bustinza is not exactly sure what night he was involved in the incident, but thinks it was probably 29 December because he specifically remembers it was the last night of his midnight shift with D Flight before he went on his three-day break. Due to the Christmas holidays, there was a skeleton staff on duty and he was the only non-commissioned officer assigned to the Woodbridge base. When the report came in around midnight he was still in the alert area at Bentwaters, preparing to make his way over to Woodbridge. The airman on duty at the east-gate post did not describe exactly what he saw but thought it looked like a fire in the forest. Sergeant Bustinza immediately alerted his acting commander, Second Lieutenant Bruce Englund, who in turn contacted Lieutenant Colonel Halt. Englund was instructed to check out the situation and, with Bustinza acting as his driver, they collected Master Sergeant Bobby Ball. Ball was on his break, having worked the long Christmas and Boxing Day shifts, and when the patrol arrived at his home on the domestic site (751-C Woodbridge) he was not in uniform and they had to wait for him to change.

The men then drove to the forest to meet with patrols who were already on site. As they approached, a group of airmen rushed out of the forest and told Englund that they had encountered a bright light which was surrounded by a strange yellow mist. Englund reported the matter to his superiors and was instructed to round up more personnel and collect some light-alls. Englund's patrol then headed for Bentwaters to carry out the orders, leaving the patrols in the forest. Instead of taking the short cut they took the usual route back to Woodbridge, through the country roads. Bustinza remembers Englund cautioning him to drive carefully because there was a lot of commotion with the wildlife, and deer and rabbits were running out of the forest. Whilst Englund was dashing all over the installations, other patrols had arrived in the forest and they seemed to be without any form of supervision. There were problems with the vehicle engines, which would not start, and arguments were breaking out as to whether they had gas in them or not. It was then that Lieutenant Colonel Halt arrived. The replacement light-alls were not functioning properly but Halt was becoming bored waiting for more replacements and, according to Bustinza, he selected several officers to accompany him on a search for the UFO. As they moved through the forest, equipped with only a starscope (an image intensifier), they found triangular indentations burned into the ground at three different standpoints. Bustinza commented that it must have been a heavy object that had made these marks. Halt was instructing Sergeant Nevilles to take readings of the indentations with a Geiger counter and Bustinza was instructed to radio Central Security Control to arrange for more light-alls. It was during this period that Bustinza recalls someone had reported seeing the UFO on the ground. Bustinza was having problems trying to contact CSC for replacement light-alls, the static was getting much worse and finally Halt ordered him to the Woodbridge base to collect replacements. Bustinza explained the situation: 'Everything was malfunctioning, people were excited, all running in different directions.'

When Bustinza returned to the edge of the forest there was a British police car parked on the roadside and two police officers were guarding the entrance to the logging road. Whilst trying to catch up with Halt's patrol he saw lights moving through the trees and the forest was bathed in a yellow mist rising about two to three feet off the ground, almost to knee height. As he drew nearer to the lights he realized it was some sort of object that seemed to be hovering about 20 feet off the ground, literally bobbing up and down. When he caught up with the patrol he found twenty to thirty personnel, including Lieutenant Colonel Halt, surrounding a huge UFO which was parked in a clearing near the farmer's field. Bustinza remarked how amazed he was that such a huge craft could have landed in such a small area.

As soon as Bustinza arrived at the clearing Lieutenant Colonel Halt instructed him to join the other men who were surrounding the object. Bustinza was in awe as he stared at the circular craft with its rainbow flashing lights and recalls feeling completely helpless. At that point he noticed two men dressed in black military uniforms, who he thinks were there to investigate the incident. 'They were just standing back watching what was going on,' he explained. He remembers their uniforms were unlike anything he was familiar with. There were also two civilians standing close by who were taking photographs of the craft, and Lieutenant Colonel Halt ordered Bustinza and another airman to confiscate their cameras. He also recalls seeing other people taking photographs and filming the event.

Adrian Bustinza is adamant that Lieutenant Colonel Halt was in charge of the patrol that night. But originally Halt had denied Bustinza was present. The following is edited from my interviews with the witness.

G. BRUNI: Can you tell me what happened in the forest that night?

A. BUSTINZA: At the beginning we had radio contact because we were getting directions. I think my call sign was Alpha One, but it's been a long time. At the time I was the only non-commissioned officer in charge at Woodbridge, there were only six of us on duty at the Woodbridge base that night. Although in the forest there was a staff sergeant, and we had a lieutenant. Nevilles was out there, I remember him getting some Geiger readings that were impressive. I remember saying, 'Oh shit, there's radiation there,' because at one stage I was standing right next to Nevilles.

G. BRUNI: Colonel Halt denied you were with his patrol.

A. BUSTINZA: Halt was there! I remember him because he was giving me orders, but later he denied that anything happened. We were in the woods towards the direction . . . [nervous tension as he describes the events] everything was moving . . . Colonel Halt later tried to tell us it was our imagination. I remember he approached myself and another, and ordered us to confiscate cameras from some British nationals. I went over and took their cameras and gave them to Colonel Halt. He put them into bags and told us that they would be dealt with at a higher level.

G. BRUNI: Can you specify if it was a craft out there, or was it just lights you saw?

A. BUSTINZA: There was a landed craft. There was a yellowish haze on the ground; it came up to about knee level, like a low fog, it was very yellow. Everything was so weird, animals were acting strange and nobody had a sense of direction. People had camera equipment, not the normal equipment, and there was a lot of it.

G. BRUNI: Was Halt was out there when it landed?

A. BUSTINZA: Let me think. Yeah, when this thing landed, Colonel Halt was already there. You see, I didn't see it land; it had already landed. I saw it take off; it kind of hovered at first, and then took off. When I arrived it was going in and out through the trees, and at one stage it was hovering. Then it went over to a clearing at the edge of the forest. By the time we got to the clearing it had already landed.

G. BRUNI: Do you think it was under some kind of intelligent control?

A. BUSTINZA: In my opinion, at that time, I thought we were dealing with extraterrestrial visitation . . . I can't say I saw beings, but I saw the outlines of something.

Larry Warren claims Major Zickler was out in the forest and recalled seeing him step out of his vehicle and fall in some mud. I asked Bustinza if he could remember seeing Zickler at the site. Not only was he sure Zickler was not present, but during one of my conversations with Bustinza he explained that it was not Zickler who had fallen in the mud, but himself. It occurred after the UFO had taken off when Halt's patrol were chasing it through the forest. Apparently, he had slipped on a pile of manure and the men had made fun of him for days afterwards. It seems it was one of the few parts of the incident they felt comfortable discussing, probably because it had some reality to it. I wondered if this had happened in the farmer's field, but he said he knew there were cattle in the field adjacent to the forest but this had taken place inside the forest itself.

Bustinza is not sure how long the UFO was sitting in the clearing, and although it seemed like a very long time he thinks it was probably only between fifteen and thirty minutes. It was obviously a much larger object than that witnessed by Penniston and Burroughs earlier that week. He claims it was huge, at least 30 feet wide, with strange markings on its body. It was difficult to define its shape because it was constantly distorting, but he recalls it being like a soluble aspirin, and at times like a mushroom, with a thickness to its middle. As it lifted off there was no sound but he felt a cool blast, like a breeze. The object then separated into three different lights, which went off in different directions. During the encounter he is sure there were twenty to thirty personnel surrounding the craft and other people further back with the trucks, which were still not functioning.

One interesting twist to the Rendlesham Forest puzzle is Adrian Bustinza's conversation with CAUS investigator Larry Fawcett in early 1984. When 'Busty', as his friends know him, was discussing the incident, he told Fawcett he had seen Lieutenant Colonel Halt talking to somebody or something and he thought he heard Halt say he would contact the electronics division and they would try to get a part from another world.

I was interested to know what he meant by 'a part from another world', but although he recalls something to do with an 'electronics division' he cannot recall mentioning anything about 'another world'. Of course, it is possible that Bustinza is trying to play down the alien connection because of what it represents and, although he is in agreement with most of Larry Fawcett and Ray Boeche's interviews, he challenges other points concerning Larry Warren and General Gordon Williams.

Major General Gordon Williams does not believe the episode Bustinza refers to ever happened. With this in mind I asked him if the USAF had such a division. He explained that the 'Electronics Division' was probably the Electronics Systems Division (ESD). This is one of the principal product divisions of what used to be the Air Force Systems Command (AFSC). Headed by a four-star general, AFSC was responsible for Research and Development and initial procurement of weapons systems, in fact anything that needed to be developed or tested. ESD looked after developing all things electronic such as the Aeronautical Systems Division (ASD) and aircraft. It was also involved in the Cobra Mist Over the Horizon project on Orfordness which closed down in 1973. A few years ago AFSC merged with the Air Force Logistics Command (AFLC) and according to an air force source, it is now part of the Air Materiel Command. Could this be what Adrian Bustinza was referring to? I asked Williams if a security police officer would know anything about this division. He replied, 'A security guard at Bentwaters, bright or not, would have a one in a million chance of knowing about ESD/ASD.' So was the craft in trouble, did it need repairs and, more importantly, did its crew need help from the USAF? If so, then are we expected to believe they were aliens! Or was this indeed an experiment being carried out by the USAF.

Adrian Bustinza had emphasized how confusing it was during the encounter with the UFO, but he positively recalls Lieutenant Colonel Halt was standing facing the object and talking directly at it or to something that he could not define. If Halt was involved in this encounter he could have been talking into his pocket recorder, and that might be what Bustinza heard. But then why would he be talking about getting parts from the electronics division? If an alien encounter was involved, were they communicating messages to Halt, who in turn was making verbal notes on his recorder? It is difficult to imagine that the radios were functioning at that moment due to the static that seemed to be prominent during the encounter.

It had been a long night for Sergeant Bustinza but the drama was not over yet. Later that morning he was instructed to report to Major Zickler's office for a debriefing on what had occurred in the forest. He would also be required to report to the base commander, Colonel Ted Conrad. But Bustinza's worst experience was when he was collected outside his dormitory and whisked off in a black Cadillac by two mysterious men in black.

In the mid-1980s he gave interviews to American researchers, and although he was prepared to discuss part of his involvement in the actual incident he denied government agents ever interrogated him. UFO investigator Larry Fawcett talked to Bustinza on 20 April 1984 and questioned him on a briefing that was supposed to have taken place. He told Fawcett that he was debriefed by Major Zickler, Lieutenant Colonel Halt and the base commander. When Fawcett asked him if he remembered any of the witnesses being threatened, he said no that they had just warned him. He concluded it was the work of the CIA.

Adrian Bustinza was in fact interrogated, but the reason he refused to discuss it with Larry Fawcett at the time was because he was afraid for his life and his family. I talked to him on several occasions and finally, eighteen years after the incident, he agreed to talk about his experience at the hands of his interrogators. The following is part of that interview:

G. BRUNI: Adrian, can you tell me what happened immediately after the incident? I know it is difficult for you to talk about. I only want the truth, nothing more and nothing less. Can you tell me about the interrogations? Where did these take place?

A. BUSTINZA: I was debriefed in Major Zickler's office the first time, but later I remember being picked up in a car. I know this is going to sound like science-fiction, but these men were your typical 'men in black', black suits, white collar and tie, RayBan type dark glasses. It was very scary and confusing because I didn't know where they were taking me. They were very intimidating.

G. BRUNI: Where did they take you?

A. BUSTINZA: I was taken to the security area near where the metal bunkers are. I think it was the photo lab, but I can't remember leaving it. We went underground, down some stairs into a tunnel. We walked through the tunnels and there were light bulbs hanging on the side of the walls. I was taken into a small room and ordered to sit on a wooden chair, which was very uncomfortable. I was told to look directly ahead, neither left nor right, but straight ahead. It was difficult because someone was shining a light bulb in front of my face and it was blinding me. I was really scared and confused and thought I had done something wrong; remember I was very young at the time. I remember thinking, where is my staff sergeant, where is my lieutenant, why am I the only one here going through this? I felt completely helpless. They asked me repetitive questions. They told me I would later be debriefed by my superiors, I was. They asked the same questions over and over again. I wasn't allowed to ask any questions and they threatened me by mentioning some government code. I told them I worked for the government too. They told me I mustn't talk to no one about this. A tall man, I could only see his shadow, moved forward and said, 'Bullets are cheap, a dime a dozen.' It was very scary.

G. BRUNI: What kind of questions did they ask you?

A. BUSTINZA: They asked me what I saw. I told them. And they asked me if anyone had filmed it, was anyone taking pictures of it? They asked me who I had talked to, who I had told.

G. BRUNI: Was it the same men who picked you up who interviewed you?

A. BUSTINZA: At about that time everything was fuzzy, but I remember the two men who had picked me up led me into the room then left. There were two or three men in the room but I couldn't see their faces because of the bright light shining at me.

I could only see shadows, but the man asking the questions wore a black overall-type uniform.

G. BRUNI: How long were you in the room?

A. BUSTINZA: Forever! They just kept on asking repetitive questions. They told me I had been chasing lights. I kept saying, 'No, we saw something else,' but they kept repeating, 'You don't get the picture, do you? You saw a light and that light was a lighthouse beacon.' I said, 'No, it wasn't a beacon,' and that's the moment the guy came over to tell me 'Bullets are cheap and a dime a dozen.' At that stage I just wanted to get out of there so I said, 'OK, it was a beacon.' They then said, 'Let's go over this again.' They wanted to make sure I knew it was a beacon.

G. BRUNI: Can you describe the tunnels you were in: were they narrow or wide?

A. BUSTINZA: They were wide enough to get a truck through. There were tunnels all over that base but we weren't supposed to talk about them. They would take you from point A to point B. They were accessible through the security area.

G. BRUNI: What were they used for; did any lead to the North Sea?

A. BUSTINZA: As far as I know they had been built in case of a nuclear attack or for an emergency. They were escape routes. I don't know where they all led to.

G. BRUNI: What happened after you were released from the interrogations?

A. BUSTINZA: I was upset after being treated so bad, I mean I was a sergeant with the United States Air Force. I considered going AWOL. The only comfort I got was when Major Zickler called us into his office and briefed us. He said that any information we gave would be confidential. I felt comfortable with him and my lieutenant. Not one of us would talk about it afterwards. Sometimes we would get ridiculed, guys going on about UFOs, but we had to take it, we couldn't discuss it. There was a gag order on that incident and we were told that what we saw was a lighthouse beacon. There were many nightmares after that.

During the ensuing days Bustinza was debriefed by Base Commander Colonel Ted Conrad and summoned before Wing Commander Colonel Gordon Williams. Conrad gave him a lesson on how to deal with the press, should they start asking questions, and Williams apparently told him that he did not want to personally know anything about what had happened and informed him that it was a matter for the people who were dealing with it. Of course, Colonel Williams had to be careful that he did not get caught up in the drama, it was in his best interest to leave it to the AFOSI to investigate.

When Bustinza returned to his duties three days later, he was assigned to the swing shift with D Flight. It was during this time that his patrol was assigned to guard a C-130 aircraft that had landed on the Woodbridge base. It was not unusual for C-130s to land at Woodbridge, they were constantly arriving and departing, but they seldom needed top-aid security. This was presumed to be the very aircraft that was alleged to have transported the video film and photographs of the UFO to the USAFE headquarters at Ramstein Airbase in Germany. Former Master Sergeant Ray Gulyas told me: 'Captain Verrano was given a video film taken by a military wife living on Woodbridge base. He was instructed to give it to the pilot of a plane that was waiting for it.' Of course, whilst Bustinza was on his three-day break other flights had arrived which needed security. These aeroplanes were said to have flown in from Washington with the purpose of transporting specialists to investigate the landing sites. It seems that the evidence was quickly removed from Britain to the safety of the headquarters in Germany, later to be transported to the Pentagon. One wonders if Britain's defence departments were ever informed of these goings-on.

Not long after the incident, Adrian Bustinza was sent on temporary duty assignments to other bases around the world. On his return to Bentwaters he joined a special team as a guard of honour for Major General Walter H. Baxter, who replaced Lieutenant General Bazley as commander of RAF Mildenhall. After the incident most of the witnesses appear to have been transferred to other bases on temporary duty. According to an Air Force source, this was normal procedure. Military personnel witnessing these kinds of incidents, or anything they should not have been privy to, were intimidated and immediately moved to another flight and, as soon as it was possible, transferred to other bases. In some cases, an agent would befriend them with the purpose of finding out if they talked about the incident, and if they did, steps would be taken to intimidate them further. It seems the Air Force did not want personnel spreading stories about UFO encounters; it was not good for the morale. The 81st Security Police Squadron at RAF Woodbridge and Bentwaters was already low on morale. There had been the big drugs bust, and the week of UFO events and its aftermath did not help matters. However, in 1981 the squadron received a big boost to their morale when they were awarded an 'Outstanding Evaluation' and won the USAFE title for best squadron.

But did Adrian Bustinza talk? He has since complained of being harassed by the AFOSI. When he left RAF Bentwaters he was posted to Malmstrom AFB, Montana, where he had a very difficult time. He told me: 'I had nothing but problems with my superiors at Malmstrom. I was stripped of a star and put back as an airman senior first class – demoted from sergeant.' It is worth noting that Bustinza was a good security policeman. His skills were recognized by his commanding officer Major Zickler, inasmuch as he had Bustinza promoted to sergeant before his time. Zickler told me himself that Sergeant Bustinza was worthy of his promotion. Was the USAF trying to pressure him into retirement because he was talking? General Gordon Williams told me that it was a serious matter to strip an airman of his rank and there had to be a very good reason for it. Bustinza claimed that for years after he left the service he was under surveillance. 'I had a call from RAF Bentwaters,' he told me. 'I knew I was being watched after I left the service, little things were noticeable. I'm in security so I know about these things.' His mother told me that he had a briefcase full of material relating to the incident, but Bustinza claims he has since destroyed it.

Larry Fawcett sent me Halt's tape recording of the incident. The
tape is edited. I was worried about keeping it and Larry told me to
dispose of it. I disposed of the briefcase. I took everything out and
burnt it in the garden . . . I was concerned for my family, my
parents, especially for my father who works for the government.

Adrian Bustinza retired from the Air Force in 1982 and is now a
supervisor working on criminal investigations with the State Justice
Department. He lives with his wife from a second marriage and his
children in the United States.

Does he have anything to add to what happened?

People have exaggerated on this case. If you're not going to deal
with the truth, then don't deal with it at all. I still can't believe it
happened. I can tell you, I will never forget the interrogation and
the threat, 'Bullets are cheap, a dime a dozen.' That stuck in my
mind.

I asked him if he would confirm Larry Warren's story that there
were small aliens present at the landing site. I realized this was a
difficult question for him because he was clearly uncomfortable with
it. But he answered as best he could:

We were in denial. We went through a denial stage on this. I'm
not ready to talk about it. I know Larry was upset because he
thinks I let him down by not talking about the underground, but
I'm not ready to talk about this.

EXAMINING THE HALT EVIDENCE

Ever since his famous memorandum was made public, Colonel Charles Halt has been a major player in the Rendlesham Forest incident, even more so since his retirement from the USAF when he began lecturing on the UFO conference circuit. The real problem with Halt's testimony is that he has not been consistent with times or dates, but my investigation has revealed that he was in a position to know these facts when he composed his memorandum on 13 January 1981. Since then he has admitted that the night he was involved was not 29 December but 27/28.

Lieutenant Colonel Halt was not on the base when the initial event occurred. It was approximately 05.30 hrs on the morning of the 26th when he walked into the Law Enforcement Office at Bentwaters. Halt might have been involved had he been on hand, because even though his duties revolved around a regular day shift, he always insisted on being called should there be any unusual activities on the base. In fact, if there was a problem Halt would have been contacted on his direct phone line at home, which was known as the 'red line'. However, it was Christmas night, and earlier that evening he had been in the town of Ipswich celebrating. According to one source, Halt was called on his radio, which the officers carried with them at all times, even when they were off duty, but he told the caller that he would deal with the situation on his return. When I questioned Halt about this he could not be certain he had been contacted but admitted it was possible. When Halt checked the incident report log in the Law Enforcement Office, he was told by the duty desk sergeant (who started to laugh) that a couple of guys had been out chasing UFOs. Halt thought it was a joke, but Sergeant McCabe told him about his conversation with the shift commander over at Central Security Control, who apparently had not written a report, so McCabe had not entered the incident in the log either. 'Sergeant McCabe didn't know what to write and I suggested he write "lights in the sky", explaining that something needed to be logged in case there was a query about it at a later date,' recounted Halt.

It was not long before Halt realized that something extraordinary had occurred in Rendlesham Forest. Later that morning he summoned Airman First Class Edward Cabansag to his office. Cabansag was the only witness on the base because Staff Sergeant Penniston and Airman First Class Burroughs had been given an official six-day break and it would be 2 January before he could talk to them. Cabansag was terrified as he faced the commander and Halt was unable to get him to talk about the incident. Before Cabansag left Halt's office he was asked to sign a statement which, according to Cabansag, he did not compose.

Halt was not involved on the second night, 26/27, but he was a major player in one of the events, which he now believes was on 27/28. According to his recollection, he and other officers, including Base Commander Colonel Ted Conrad, were attending a Combat Support Group awards dinner at Woody's Bar on the Woodbridge base. During the evening Lieutenant Bruce Englund turned up looking as white as a sheet. The shocked Lieutenant told Conrad and Halt that there had been more sightings in the forest and that it was back. 'What's back?' enquired Halt. 'The UFO is back,' replied Englund. Colonel Conrad then instructed Halt to assemble a group of personnel and investigate with the aim of debunking the saga once and for all. Apparently, the officers felt it was now getting out of control.

Before leaving the party Halt made a call to the Disaster Preparedness and spoke to the chief of the department, Captain Sue Jones, who told him that the officer on stand-by was Sergeant Munroe Nevilles. When Halt reached Nevilles, a keen amateur photographer (although Halt claims he was a professional), he instructed him on what equipment to gather and reminded him to take along his camera. Nevilles was a part-time barman at the non-commissioned officers' club, and apart from his involvement in this case he is best remembered for accidentally driving into, and semi-demolishing, Master Sergeant Buckholt's house on the Woodbridge domestic site. Apparently, Nevilles went right through Buckholt's son's bedroom. Fortunately the teenager, although obviously shocked, was not injured. Nevilles was working twelve-hour shifts at the time, which of course included his part-time work as a barman, and he was obviously very tired. One wonders why the poor man was allowed to take on extra work when he was employed in the Disaster Preparedness Department. It seems he did not even have time to repair his equipment because during the incident he told Lieutenant Colonel Halt that the headpiece on the Geiger counter he was using was broken.

Having instructed Englund to collect Master Sergeant Ball and arranged to meet Nevilles, Lieutenant Colonel Halt made his way to his office to pick up his pocket recorder, a fresh set of batteries, utility earphones and a couple of miniature audio cassette tapes. He then jumped into his sports car, taking the short cut to his home at the Bentwaters domestic site, where he changed into his military field attire. As far as I can ascertain, Master Sergeant Ball collected Halt and Sergeant Nevilles and drove them to Rendlesham Forest. At this time Halt's only concern was to debunk whatever it was that seemed to be causing havoc among the men, but little did he know what was out in the forest until he himself became a witness. By the time Halt's patrol arrived in Rendlesham Forest there were already numerous personnel and vehicles in the area, and the men were running about all over the place.

None of the light-alls appeared to be functioning and Halt, having sent another patrol to refill them, was getting tired of waiting, so he summoned all the senior personnel to accompany him on his recce. The men he names as being part of his team are Lieutenant Englund, Master Sergeant Ball and Sergeant Nevilles. I thought it was unusual that Lieutenant Colonel Halt would leave several patrols back at the clearing with the vehicles and weapons, without any senior supervision. At least no other officer is named as taking control of the confused patrols and Halt admitted to me that he was the officer in charge who ordered them to stay at the clearing. It was not until later that Sergeant Frail appears to have turned up, and there is no evidence to say that he was with the patrols that Halt had left behind at the clearing. His voice can be heard on the tape recording of the incident, which means he must have been in close range to Halt's patrol.

For whatever reason, Halt decided to make his way to the initial landing site, which he explained was difficult to find in the dark, and apparently it took some time before they managed to reach it. While waiting for the fresh light-alls to arrive, the patrol decided to take Geiger readings of the three ground indentations and the burn marks on the trees. Interestingly, Halt admitted that the place where they took the readings was the same place that they had seen a glow from earlier that night.

The refuelled light-alls were still not functioning properly but Halt's patrol were managing to get by with a starscope and their torches. Nevertheless, the light-all situation was becoming a major problem and vehicle engines were also affected. As the patrol moved through the forest, Halt spotted a glowing red object that looked like a red eye with a black pupil, which seemed to be winking and dripping what he could only describe as molten metal. He decided they should approach it as it moved in and out through the trees, but at one point the light startled them as it turned and headed towards them, before receding and moving back again through the forest. Halt makes no mention of a landed object but claims they pursued the light as it moved in the direction of the adjacent farmer's field. He recalls that as they neared the fence line, which separated the forest from the field, they noticed that one of the houses appeared to be glowing as if on fire. Halt was concerned for the occupants but decided it was not a good idea to alert them as the patrol were in uniform and they were not supposed to be on British territory. He also thought they might be frightened at that time of night if US airmen knocked on their door.

The patrol continued to follow the lights across the farmer's field towards a ploughed area, and as they waded through the terrain Lieutenant Englund noticed three objects to the north that were performing strange manoeuvres. These eventually turned into a full circle. Master Sergeant Ball thought they were doing a grid search. Over to the south, travelling at tremendous speed, another object came into view, which, according to Halt, stopped about 2,000 to 4,000 feet above their heads. Halt was amazed as it sent down a laser-type beam that hit the ground within feet of where he was standing. As fast as it had appeared, the beam suddenly switched off, but the object was still in the sky and was now sending out beams to other locations. Halt was under the impression that one of the beams had penetrated the Bentwaters weapons storage area, but none of the wit-nesses I have spoken to, including those who were on duty at the weapons storage area, are aware that this took place. After several hours of chasing the UFOs, the men were feeling hungry, cold and miserable and Halt gave the order to return to the base.

There is official documented evidence to support that there was an incident in the early morning of the 28th. It is on record that RAF Bentwaters contacted RAF Watton to report UFO sightings in the area. The report was confirmed to researcher Nicholas Redfern, who wrote to RAF Watton Eastern Radar in 1989 and received this reply:

> Thank you for your letter requesting further information about the UFO report on 28 December 1980. I am afraid we are unable to provide you with copies of our log books. However, I can offer you a verbatim statement of the only entry regarding the subject incident in the log for that period. The entry is timed at 0325 on 28 December 1980 and states:
> 'Bentwaters Command Post contacted Eastern Radar and requested information of aircraft in the area – UA37 traffic southbound FL370 – UFO sightings at Bentwaters. They are taking reporting action.'

UA37 means the Upper Air Route Upper Amber 37 which runs approximately North/South some 40 miles east of Bentwaters and is used by civilian airliners. FL370 means 37,000 feet in altitude.

This informative letter reveals that Bentwaters was experiencing more than mere lights in the sky, in fact, they were referring to UFOs coming in from the east of Bentwaters. We might wonder why, if the sightings were reported much earlier as the witnesses claim, Bentwaters waited until 03.25 hrs before contacting RAF Watton.

Colonel Halt believes he was involved on the night of 27/28, but RAF Watton Eastern Radar timed the Bentwaters entry for that night at 03.25 hrs stating that: 'They are taking reporting action.' Halt made a tape recording of the event which begins hours earlier and terminates at 04.00 hrs. In fact, at 03.30 hrs, five minutes after Bentwaters reported the incident to RAF Watton, Halt's patrol were heading back to the base. Halt records: '3.30, and the objects are still in the sky, although the one to the south looks like it's losing a little bit of altitude. We're turning around and heading back toward the base. The object to the south is still beaming down lights to the ground.' Either Halt's patrol were out on a different night or they did not report the incident until they had completed their investigation. Of course, this would not be the first time that Bentwaters delayed reporting the incident to British authorities, or so it seems.

Approximately one week after the incident, Halt informed the British Liaison officer, Squadron Leader Donald Moreland, of what had taken place on British property. Moreland had been on his Christmas holidays and had just returned to the base. After listening to Halt's evidence, he asked to see the suspected landing site. Halt took him to the forest where they examined the initial landing site concerning the incident with Penniston and Burroughs. Moreland then asked Halt to write a memorandum, which he would dispatch to the Ministry of Defence and which was released through the US Freedom of Information Act in 1983.

Without doubt, Halt's memorandum is an important document, and because of its official status it has been accepted in most circles as highly credible. Of course, it was only a brief summary but, nevertheless, the dates are wrong. Why would an officer, serving with the United States Air Force stationed in Britain, compose an erroneous report intended for Her Majesty's Government? I have spent countless hours analysing this document and feel there are several issues that need to be addressed.

It is indisputable that the first incident occurred on 25/26, and not on 27 December as is stated in the memorandum. The Bentwaters report was recorded in the Suffolk Constabulary log at 04.11 hrs on 26 December. The date was confirmed by American journalist Chuck de Caro, who inspected the civil police log when he investigated the case for CNN's *Special Assignment* programme, which aired in 1985. The Suffolk Constabulary headquarters at Martlesham Heath also confirmed the report when they responded to requests for information from researcher Nicholas Redfern and science writer Ian Ridpath. It has since been established that when Lieutenant Colonel Halt wrote the memorandum he was not aware that the local police had been informed of the initial event. The following is part of a letter to Ian Ridpath, dated 23 November 1983. The letter, though it appears to have been signed by the chief constable of the Suffolk Constabulary, was, according to retired Police Superintendent George Plume, signed by the *deputy* chief constable, Barry Kitson:

SIGHTING OF UNUSUAL LIGHTS IN THE SKY AT WOODBRIDGE ON 26 DECEMBER 80
With reference to your letter dated 5 November 83, which related to the above mentioned incident. Police knowledge of this matter is limited to a telephone report of the alleged incident timed at 4.11 a.m. on 26 December and received from a person at RAF Bentwaters.

The following is part of a letter to Nicholas Redfern, supposedly from Superintendent S. M. Pearce at the Felixstowe office, dated 27

October 1988. According to George Plume, S. M. Pearce was a female administrator at the time:

> I can inform you that, at shortly after 4 a.m. on 26th December 1980, the police did receive a call reporting unusual lights being seen in the sky near RAF Woodbridge.

Although it has not been challenged before, I believe there is also an error in the memorandum regarding the time of the first incident. It states that the patrolmen saw the unusual lights at approximately 0300L, but according to Timothy Egercic's testimony, his patrol received the first call during shift change, which occurred between 23.00 and midnight. This is more than three hours' time difference. Egercic's testimony, along with other witnesses, is also in accordance with the time recorded by Staff Sergeant Jim Penniston, who claims he was contacted at precisely two minutes past midnight. By the time the airmen at RAF Woodbridge had checked out the sighting, reported it to the Law Enforcement desk, which in turn was reported to Central Security Control and Egercic's patrol, it would certainly have been around midnight when SSgt Penniston was alerted. What is more, the events of the first night appear to have been terminated before the local police arrived, because PC Dave King, having turned up at approximately 04.30, reported that there were no military men in the forest. Besides, the patrolmen went a fair distance on foot and, having personally walked that route and in view of the witnesses' accounts of the event, it would have been difficult but not impossible to complete those tasks within ninety minutes. Let us also consider the following: (a) the time taken for Penniston to arrive at the east gate and exchange data with the Woodbridge patrol and Central Security Control and receive permission to proceed with the investigation; (b) drive from the east gate, park the vehicle and walk through the forest at night; (c) circle an object for at least thirty minutes and check out the surrounding area; (d) chase the object through the farmer's field, walk back to the vehicle and return to base before the British police arrived.

At a Quest UFO conference in 1994 Colonel Halt told the

audience that Penniston's patrol walked towards the coast for one or two miles and were not contactable for around one and a half hours. He also stated that the desk sergeant, Crash McCabe, referred to the time of the incident as being 'sometime around midnight'. In view of the aforementioned I conclude that the time of 03.00 hrs for the initial sighting is incorrect.

Also, in paragraph one of the memorandum, it states: 'The object was hovering or on legs. As the patrolmen approached the object, it manoeuvred through the trees and disappeared.' Was the object hovering or was it standing on legs? Halt seems undecided, yet in paragraph two he ascertains that an actual landing took place. 'The next day, three depressions 1½' deep and 7' in diameter were found where the object had been sighted on the ground.' According to the witnesses the object actually landed, and Penniston claims to have had direct physical contact with it, but there is no mention of this close encounter in the memorandum. However, Penniston might not have told Halt about his physical contact with the craft, because he did not mention it at the debriefing with Lieutenant Buran. In fact, Buran exclaimed how shocked he was to hear that Penniston had actually touched the object.

In paragraph two of the memorandum there is another erroneous date: 'The following night (29 Dec 80) the area was checked for radiation.' In this instance, the following night being referred to would have been 27/28 and not the 29th. But the actual date (the following night) was 26/27. One wonders why there would be a need to check for radiation two nights after the initial encounter, when it is known for a fact that USAF personnel carried out official investigations in daylight hours during the morning of 26 December. There is also documented evidence that the British civil police were called out to investigate the landing site. The following extract is taken from the aforementioned letter addressed to Ian Ridpath, dated 23 November 83:

SIGHTING OF UNUSUAL LIGHTS IN THE SKY AT WOODBRIDGE ON 26 DECEMBER 80

. . . A further report was received at 10.30 a.m. on 26 December 80 from a staff member at RAF Bentwaters indicating that a place had been found where a craft of some sort could have landed. An officer attended and the area involved did bear three marks of an indeterminate pattern . . .

In paragraph three of the memorandum, it reads: 'Numerous individuals, including the undersigned, witnessed the activities in paragraphs 2 and 3.' This is confusing because until recently Colonel Halt has always claimed there were only four or five men who accompanied him into the forest, but here he mentions 'numerous individuals'. In a radio interview on 13 May 1997, seventeen years after the incident took place, he told radio presenter A. J. S. Rayl that there were probably twenty-five or thirty security policemen in the forest. In a later conversation with me, he claimed he had ordered a group of men to stay back where the vehicles were parked and had taken only four senior personnel into the forest with him.

Admittedly, without the memorandum there may never have been any official evidence, but it has still proved a huge obstacle in trying to solve this case. The fact that its author has admitted the dates were wrong, this being after such a long period of time, is curious. When I asked Halt if he was coerced into writing an incorrect version, either by the AFOSI or by his superiors, he insisted this was not the case. In an earlier conversation he strongly denied he was ever questioned or debriefed by either the Wing or any agency. In fact, he mentioned that he was 'best friends' with the chief of AFOSI on the Bentwaters installation, and that somehow the chief had ignored his involvement. 'You find that difficult to believe, don't you?' he said. One could accept that the AFOSI would treat commanders with a great deal more respect than they would treat their subordinates and, after all, Charles Halt was a lieutenant colonel and the deputy base commander. Part of a mission statement for the AFOSI sheds light on their commitment to work with Air Force commanders:

The office is responsible for providing commanders of all Air Force activities independent professional investigative services regarding fraud, counterintelligence and major criminal matters using a worldwide network of military and civilian agents stationed at all major Air Force installations and a variety of special operating locations.

After his retirement from the USAF, Halt was introduced to the international UFO conference circuit. It was at a Fund for UFO Research (FUROR) seminar in August 1997 when Halt told the audience that no AFOSI personnel had ever investigated him but he knew of others who had been investigated by them. He went on to say that witnesses were subjected to special treatment and injections. A FUROR statement refers to the seminar and quotes: 'unidentified intelligence personnel, probably including the Air Force Office of Special Investigations (OSI) worked around him [Halt] and the base commander to gather information.'

During a conversation with Colonel Halt, in October 1986, researcher Timothy Good asked if the memorandum was legitimate. 'It certainly is,' Halt affirmed. In the same conversation he then goes on to say, 'There are a lot of things that are not in my memo . . .' Halt has since explained to me that the reason he did not reveal everything in the memorandum was that he was afraid of the reaction it might have had in official circles. However, I would soon discover that the memorandum was not exclusively the work of Lieutenant Colonel Halt. Jim Penniston told me that he and John Burroughs were discreetly summoned to Halt's office for an unofficial meeting. It seems Halt was concerned because the British liaison officer, Squadron Leader Donald Moreland, had asked him to write a memorandum for the Ministry of Defence. Penniston asked Halt not to mention their names and to keep the report as brief as possible because they were concerned for their careers.

It was not their first meeting with Lieutenant Colonel Halt, Penniston and Burroughs had been called a week earlier, six days after the incident, when Halt had ushered the men across the corridor to see Wing Commander Gordon Williams. Penniston told me it was like going through the back door, which I took to mean that it was not supposed to look obvious that Williams was interviewing the witnesses. Halt apparently told them, 'We need to talk to the old man.' Penniston said he had been more open with the base commander, Colonel Conrad, and his deputy, Lieutenant Colonel Halt, but after the meeting in Halt's office it was decided they would give a watered down version to the wing commander. 'I talked to Williams,' Penniston told me. 'Halt, John and I sat in Williams' office and we told him what happened. He listened to everything we were saying, but asked no questions. After we'd finished, he thanked us for the information and that was that.' No questions? Here we have two security police officers telling their commander that they had witnessed a UFO landing within a short distance of the installations and the commander does not ask one single question! Of course, Williams could not be seen to be interested in the incident, but I was still amazed to hear this, so I sought to obtain some answers from the commander himself, but General Williams claimed he could not recall the meeting with the witnesses.

Halt did not want to write the memorandum but was pressured by Squadron Leader Donald Moreland. All USAF installations in Britain maintain a British RAF officer to act as a liaison between the USAF and the Ministry of Defence; he is commonly and politely referred to as the British base commander. Moreland had missed all the excitement of the past week, but within hours of returning to his Bentwaters office he had received a visit from Halt. The Colonel seemed agitated; he had something to discuss and the matter was of a serious nature. When I first spoke to Moreland he told me he had not talked about the case since the early 1980s. He was annoyed because he believed he had been misrepresented by the press and UFO researchers alike, and had since refused to talk to anyone. However, he soon relaxed when I assured him I was only interested in getting to the truth, which was for a book I was writing on the case. I explained that I had heard comments he had allegedly made and I wanted to confirm these with him. Below is the transcript of my 31 August 1998 interview with Squadron Leader Donald Moreland (ret.):

G. BRUNI: Squadron Leader Moreland, can you tell me what happened when you first heard about the Rendlesham Forest incident?

SQUADRON LEADER MORELAND: As soon as I returned from my two-week Christmas leave, the first thing that happened was that Halt came to see me straightaway, said it was a serious matter. He told me about the incident and I suggested he write a memo. I thought it only right that I should inform the MOD. He wouldn't have done the memo, but I told him that the MOD should be informed if there was an unusual occurrence on the base.

G. BRUNI: Did Halt explain the details of what took place?

SQUADRON LEADER MORELAND: He said there had been an unusual occurrence on the base, out in the forest. Halt, it appears, was called out to join the men, it was a quick decision. I think it was decided that it was nothing more than a lighthouse or something.

G. BRUNI: Did Halt say it was a lighthouse?

SQUADRON LEADER MORELAND: No, it was a non-event for two years until the press got hold of it. It was then that someone put it down to being a lighthouse.

G. BRUNI: Were the Americans given permission to be on British property: I refer to Rendlesham Forest?

SQUADRON LEADER MORELAND: No, they got permission from the base commander. They shouldn't have gone on to private land. That was British territory and they had no permission to go out there.

G. BRUNI: Did you investigate the incident on your return?

SQUADRON LEADER MORELAND: I went out to the site with Halt but I saw nothing. I don't know what they did on the American side, but we didn't investigate it.

G. BRUNI: So you sent Halt's memo off to the Ministry of Defence. Was there more than one memo or letter sent to them?

SQUADRON LEADER MORELAND: Yes, Halt went away to write the memo, I whisked it off with a cover note to the MOD. There was only one memo. They didn't reply, they didn't even reply to the radar report, but eventually said it had been investigated and they had not found anything. I thought it was odd that I didn't receive a written reply from the MOD. I phoned several times. I was quite annoyed.

G. BRUNI: Did you know there was a recording of one of the events? Have you listened to it?

SQUADRON LEADER MORELAND: I never heard the tape, I was incurious. I'm a Christian. *The News of the World* came out and asked me if I believed in the supernatural. I told them I was a Christian. I was misquoted by the newspapers.

G. BRUNI: According to some witnesses, the bases were on alert during the December incident. I know you were on leave, but do you know if there might be any truth to that?

SQUADRON LEADER MORELAND: I didn't know the bases were on alert. I'm amazed, I would have been told had that been the case.

G. BRUNI: Were you aware that there were Flash calls being made during and after the December incident?

SQUADRON LEADER MORELAND: Flash, priority calls are not uncommon during an exercise.

G. BRUNI: In all the years that you were flying, have you ever witnessed anything unusual?

SQUADRON LEADER MORELAND: Yes, I flew in the Air Force for years. I've seen flashes. I'm sure the Americans investigate UFOs, but I don't think we do.

Considering Halt thought the matter 'serious' one wonders why he and his superiors would wait until Moreland's return to report the incident to British officials – or did they? Halt assured me that the incident was discussed through their own channels, but because it took place off the installations it was left to the British to deal with. Yet in a tape-recorded conversation with researcher Dot Street, in 1984, a staff member from DS8 at the Ministry of Defence assured her that their department did not investigate the incident but the Americans did. Moreland points out that Halt was not keen to write the memorandum, but having made it clear to him that the Ministry of Defence should be informed, he then whisks it off to them. For something that was so serious a matter, it is worth noting that it was not until two days after Halt's secretary, Peggy Ross, typed out the memorandum that Moreland's covering letter was typed by his secretary. During our conversation, Moreland also mentioned a radar report, and the apparent lack of interest the Ministry of Defence took concerning this. Only when he put the pressure on did they finally offer a verbal response to his request concerning the radar tracking of the UFOs, and only then to inform him that they had investigated it and had found nothing unusual. This is nonsense because we know that there was at least one radar report from RAF Watton Eastern Radar.

Moreland was clearly baffled as to why he had received no written response to his covering letter or indeed Halt's memorandum. Was the Ministry of Defence trying to avoid a paper trail? Although the famous memorandum was released in the public domain in 1983, researchers never retrieved Moreland's covering letter. In October 1998 I wrote to Gaynor South at the Ministry of Defence requesting a copy and received a prompt reply with Moreland's covering letter attached.

> Miss G. F. South, Secretariat (Air Staff) 2a, Room 8245
> MINISTRY OF DEFENCE
> Main Building, Whitehall, London SW1A 2HB
>
> Dear Ms Bruni
>
> Thank you for your letter of 20 October in which you asked
> for a copy of the covering letter under which Lt Col Halt's
> memorandum concerning strange lights in Rendlesham Forest
> was sent to the Ministry of Defence in January 1981.
> I have attached a copy of the letter as requested.
>
> Yours sincerely
>
> [Signed]
> Gaynor South

Moreland's cover letter reads as follows:

RAF LIAISON OFFICE
Royal Air Force Bentwaters Woodbridge Suffolk IP12 2RQ

Telephone Woodbridge 3737 ext XXX 2257

MOD (DS8a)   Your reference
                             Our reference BENT/019/76/AIR
                             Date 15 January 1981

UNIDENTIFIED FLYING OBJECTS (UFOs)

I attach a copy of a report I have received from the Deputy Base
Commander at RAF Bentwaters concerning some mysterious
sightings in the Rendlesham Forest near RAF Woodbridge. The
report is forwarded for your information and action as
considered necessary.
[signed]
D. H. MORELAND
Squadron Leader
RAF Commander

Copy to:
SRAFLO, RAF Mildenhall

I admit I was not expecting to find anything of great significance
in Moreland's covering letter to the Ministry of Defence, but the
heading was certainly a surprise: 'UNIDENTIFIED FLYING
OBJECTS (UFOs)'. It is quite different from the heading on the
accompanying memorandum, which only mentions 'unexplained
lights'. According to Colonel Bent's forwarding letter to CAUS, the
81st Tactical Fighter Wing no longer kept any records relating to the
incident, but Her Majesty's Government had kindly provided a copy
of the memorandum. On reading Bent's letter, one automatically
assumes the document would have been released through DS8a, the
department that essentially dealt with this type of request at the

Ministry of Defence. However, DS8a, later changed to Sec (AS) 2a, have always denied they were responsible for releasing the memorandum. Moreland's covering letter reveals that he sent a copy to his Senior RAF Liaison Officer (SRAFLO) at Third Air Force, RAF Mildenhall. In a taped conversation with American researcher Peter Robbins, on 23 June 1992, Colonel Halt discussed the details of how the memorandum came to be released.

> What happened was the copy went to the MOD, but Don Moreland sent a copy – we would call it a bootleg copy – sent it to, or through, I don't know which, his superior, who was the 3rd Air Force. Somehow a copy had stayed in 3rd Air Force, either in his superior's office or in some curiosity seeker's office, and resurfaced several years later, and somebody talked to somebody who talked to somebody. 3rd Air Force called me and said, what should we do? I said, my personal suggestion is, burn the thing. I don't want all the publicity . . . I said, do me a favour, burn it, and he said, no, we have to release it under the Freedom of Information Act.

The memorandum was certainly released through the United States Freedom of Information Act, and may have been dealt with through the senior RAF liaison officer at Mildenhall, and not directly with DS8a at the Ministry of Defence. Because the memorandum was officially an American document, one assumes that the Ministry of Defence would not have had much say about its release, but as a courtesy it is most likely they were informed of the matter. CAUS are well known for their expertise in obtaining Freedom of Information files, and on receiving their request Colonel Bent may have pushed for its release believing he was doing the right thing at the time. Little did he know then what an embarrassment it would become for the United States Air Force, and it still haunts many of the senior officers today. Lieutenant Colonel Bernard E. Donahue, the base lawyer who actually read the entry in the Law Enforcement blotter, remarked that the entire incident was an embarrassment to everyone at Bentwaters.

Command Post, RAF
Bentwaters (1999)
© *Georgina Bruni*

Right: East Gate Road
leading to RAF Woodbridge
(1999) © *Georgina Bruni*

Below: Bawdsey
underground facility known
as 'The Hole' (1974)
courtesy Gordon Kinsey

Above: Mural depicting aircraft throughout the decades, ARRS station RAF Woodbridge (1999) © *Georgina Bruni*

John F. Burroughs (circa 1990) *courtesy Quest International*

Steve R. La Plume (circa 1981) *courtesy Steve La Plume*

Former commander of RAF Bentwaters/
Woodbridge, General Gordon E.
Williams (1981) *courtesy USAF*

Anthony Johnson at
RAF Woodbridge (circa 1982)
courtesy Anthony Johnson

Timothy Egercic and fellow
airman, RAF Bentwaters 1981
courtesy Timothy Egercic

Jim Penniston (circa 1995)
courtesy Jim Penniston

Former deputy base commander
Charles I. Halt (circa 1994)
courtesy Quest International

Larry Warren (1997)
© *Nick Pope*

Major General Gordon E. Williams (ret.) with Georgina Bruni, London 1999
© *Nick Pope*

TOP LEFT: Brenda Butler and Chris Pennington, the first known civilians to hear about the Rendlesham Forest incident © *Georgina Bruni*

MIDDLE LEFT: Major General Gordon E. Williams (right) with General Petr. S. Deynekin, the former Commander in Chief of the Russian Air Force (centre) and General Merrill Anthony McPeak, the former Chief of Staff of the United States Air Force (left) circa 1996 *courtesy Gordon Williams*

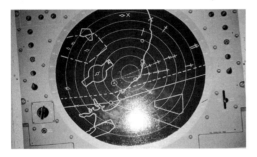

BOTTOM LEFT: Mural depicting the radar screen (probably for training purposes) RAF Woodbridge (1999) © *Georgina Bruni*

BELOW: The control tower in the weapons storage area, RAF Bentwaters (1999) © *Georgina Bruni*

Rendlesham Forest as seen from the East Gate; taken by Adrian Bustinza a week after the incident (January 1981) © *Adrian Bustinza*

Rendlesham Forest, path leading to the landing sites (1999) © *Georgina Bruni*

LEFT: Site of the initial landing site, Rendlesham Forest (1999) © *Georgina Bruni*

BELOW: Close up of the initial landing site showing barren area, Rendlesham Forest (1999) © *Georgina Bruni*

Enlargement of photo 1 showing British police officer and Captain Mike Verrano (USAF) *courtesy Ray Gulyas*. Photo 2 of contact strip: British police officer and Captain Mike Verrano (USAF) examining the initial landing site the morning after the incident (26 December 1980) *courtesy Ray Gulyas*. Photo 3 of contact strip: initial landing site showing the scuffed-up area as explained by Lt Col Halt: also shows three indentations in a triangular shape which are marked by three twigs (26 December 1980) *courtesy Ray Gulyas*. Photo 4 of contact strip: initial landing site *courtesy Ray Gulyas*. Photo 5 of contact strip: initial landing site showing indentation marked by a twig *courtesy Ray Gulyas*. Photo 6 of contact strip: initial landing site showing indentation marked by a twig *courtesy Ray Gulyas*. Photo 7 of contact strip: initial landing site showing indentation marked by a twig *courtesy Ray Gulyas*

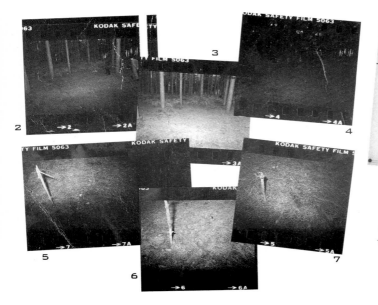

ABOVE: Sign on the entrances to the command posts at RAF Woodbridge/Bentwaters © *Georgina Bruni*

Having received a copy of Donald Moreland's covering letter, I was interested in what he had to say about it.

G. BRUNI: Squadron Leader Moreland, can you explain why you titled your covering letter 'Unidentified Flying Objects (UFOs)'?

SQUADRON LEADER MORELAND: That's what Halt said they were. He called them UFOs.

G. BRUNI: If it was so urgent why did it take two days for you to write your covering letter (dated 15th January) after you received Halt's memorandum, which was dated 13 January?

SQUADRON LEADER MORELAND: Well, I wrote it as soon as I received his memo. It probably took that time to reach me.

G. BRUNI: Why would that be?

SQUADRON LEADER MORELAND: I have no idea.

G. BRUNI: You mentioned that Halt approached you as soon as you returned to your office after your holiday break. I realize it has been a long time but would that possibly have been Monday 12 January?

SQUADRON LEADER MORELAND: That is confusing because I think I would have returned a week earlier. I usually took two weeks' Christmas break, but I'm sure I would not have been away until the 12th. It would have been a week earlier.

G. BRUNI: That would be Monday 6 January.

SQUADRON LEADER MORELAND: That seems more like it. I would not have been away until the 12th.

G. BRUNI: Did any of the other officers discuss the incident with you?

SQUADRON LEADER MORELAND: Sam Morgan did and the police officer Major Zickler.

I was pleased that I had spoken to Squadron Leader Moreland about the dates because I had always wondered how Halt could have put the memorandum together in such a short period of time. Of course, nothing is ever easy in this case, and now instead of being concerned about how quickly he had composed the memorandum, I suddenly realized that it took him eight days. This is a considerable length of time to alert the Ministry of Defence considering it was supposed to be so urgent.

In a conversation with Halt on 28 August 1999 I asked him why he had given the wrong dates in his memorandum and I was surprised to hear him explain that they were typing errors. I find that very difficult to accept, considering the nature of the memorandum and its destination. When I told Halt that his boss Gordon Williams claimed he would have attempted to stop the memorandum leaving the installation, had he known of its existence, Halt pointed out that none of the commanders wanted to get involved and he was sure Williams had not discussed the incident with me.

When Halt wrote his memo soon after the events, little did he know that less than three years later, on Sunday 2 October 1983, it would turn up on the front page of the British tabloid *The News of the World*. The day after the story broke, the base was hounded by journalists seeking an audience with the author of the memorandum. It was too late because he had discreetly left the base on a military flight to Washington DC. Before leaving, however, he had consulted with his superiors and the Public Affairs Office and had stopped by to see the secretary of the officers' club to ask her to renew his membership. When Halt entered her office she was busy reading *The News of the World*. When she showed Halt the headlines, he informed her that he had already seen it, and she recalls he didn't appear to be too perturbed by the front-page story. I asked the lady, a British citizen now living in the United States, if she had ever heard the incident being discussed among the officers. She insisted that she had been totally unaware of it until she went to work that morning and was handed a copy of the newspaper by one of the kitchen staff.

According to Halt, his trip to the US was of a personal nature which involved his presence at a court case. When I questioned him further about whether or not he was on duty at any time during his trip to the US, he did remember using military transport to take him to another destination, but would not go into detail about the nature of this trip. When Halt returned to Suffolk, he did so with a promotion to full colonel, not bad considering his memorandum had just caused a major headache for the USAF. But in all fairness to Halt, he had no role in the memorandum's release; as far as he was concerned the document would remain in the files of the Ministry of Defence at Whitehall. That is what he was promised.

Another interesting item that conveniently found its way into the hands of researchers was the audio tape recording of one of the actual events, recorded on military equipment by Lieutenant Colonel Charles Halt. The recording has caused even more controversy than Halt's famous memorandum, partly due to it covering only eighteen minutes of an event that lasted several hours. The tape was made public in 1984 when it was first given to researchers Harry Harris and Dot Street. Since then there have been numerous copies, all very bad due to second, third and fourth-generation recordings.

With an introduction from General Williams, I managed to contact Colonel Sam Morgan, a fighter pilot who was posted to RAF Bentwaters and Woodbridge in 1980. Colonel Sam Morgan and General Gordon Williams have been close friends for many years. On arriving at the joint installation, Morgan was assigned to deputy chief of maintenance. When Colonel Conrad received his promotion to vice wing commander, Morgan moved into Conrad's position, taking over the role of combat support group commander, commonly known as the base commander. During the changeover, when Conrad vacated his office, Lieutenant Colonel Halt had used it for a few weeks whilst assuming the position of temporary base commander. Colonel Morgan's involvement in the Rendlesham affair comes about because he was the person responsible for stewarding Halt's tape to various researchers in 1984/5. No one is really sure why he took it upon himself to do this, including Halt. Morgan claims he found the tape in his desk when he was assigned to the Combat Support Group as their new commander.

I was rummaging through the trash in the desk and came across a small cassette-type tape. I played the tape and it was a recording of Halt chasing lights through the forest . . . After I left England I was assigned to Hill AFB, Utah, where I was the director of maintenance for the Air Logistics Center. While there I copied the tape to a regular cassette . . . I left Utah in 1984 for an assignment to NORAD and Air Force Space Command in Colorado Springs, Colorado. At the time I received calls from a number of people, including the fellow you mentioned [Harry Harris], and a woman named Dot Street. Some of them seemed to think there was a connection between the incident in the forest and my position in Space Command and they were sure I was not being totally forthcoming, but that was not the case.

I did send copies of the tape to several people . . . I understand one person sold the tape to a Japanese TV station for a considerable amount, but I never got a penny out of it . . . Making copies of the tape, as well as the expense of mailing the tapes, became a bit of a burden and I was getting behind in my mailing . . . Then I began to get snarly calls demanding a copy . . . Then I got a letter from a UFO buff in Oregon, demanding I send him the tape immediately and threatening me with legal action if I didn't respond. I was so offended by that idiot that I quit responding to all requests for the tape. I still have the little cassette somewhere and a regular cassette copy of it . . . I don't think he [Halt] or the other people rehearsed the tape so I tend to interpret it as indicating they saw something they did not totally understand . . .

Having read several different versions of the transcript, in 1997 I decided to make one of my own. This was a painstaking task, due to the tape being copied from a second- or third-generation recording. I played the tape on several machines, including re-recording it to bring to the fore the background conversations, and I was confident that my transcript was the most accurate version available. However, when I heard that Sam Morgan still had the original copy taken from the miniature cassette, I asked if he would send it to me. He promised he would but was moving house at the time. Meanwhile, he and General Gordon Williams were in communication and Williams managed to receive the tape before I did. After months of pleading, Gordon Williams finally sent me the cassette, on condition I send it back to Sam Morgan when I was finished with it. This was much clearer than any of the others I had heard and I immediately set about rewriting the transcript. I realized there was much more information on this copy than on the copies which were in the public domain. I also managed to slow the recording down, enabling me to interpret much of the background conversations, which was virtually impossible on the other copies. On this particular tape, after Halt's episode concludes, it continues with officers discussing, over coffee, the base housekeeping, the need for full-time secretaries and the garbage situation. Halt's recording has obviously been recorded over the latter. On the reverse side is an interview with a witness to an aircraft accident conducted by Colonel Morgan. The recording was made when Halt and his party ventured into Rendlesham Forest, following reports of a further encounter with a UFO. The first part deals with the patrol taking Geiger-counter readings for radiation. The second part records the patrol chasing lights through the forest. The voice-overs are interruptions in the recording made at a later date and are unrelated to the incident itself. I asked Colonel Morgan to offer his opinion on the tape recording. Apparently, he had questioned Halt about it soon after moving into his new position as base commander, but Halt was evasive. Out of frustration Morgan told him, 'I'm not asking you to volunteer the information, I am ordering you to tell me the story.' Morgan then coordinated Halt's account with Donald Moreland's, who assured him he had reported the incident to the Ministry of Defence, but he did not think there was much evidence to back up Halt's story. I asked Morgan if it was normal practice for personnel to carry tape recorders while on duty. He said it was not uncommon for some commanders to carry small pocket recorders. These were ideal when touring the bases and were used to report minor incidents, such as vehicle problems and lights being left on during daylight hours. On returning to their office, the tape would be played by their secretary who would then type out the report for the commander.

I was interested in why Halt had begun the tape recording without stating a date or time, especially considering there were references to the time at various intervals throughout. Halt said he did not usually make a point of starting his recordings in that way. I thought this odd considering his dedication to detail. Morgan thinks there may have been about twenty minutes' recording time on each side of the micro-cassette tapes. When I asked Halt if he had taken more than one tape with him into the forest, he replied, 'I may have put another one in my pocket.' Apparently, he did. On a British lecture tour in the early nineties Halt told the audience that he had picked up the tape recorder, a fresh set of batteries and two tapes which he dropped into his pocket. This confirmed my suspicions that there were at least two cassette tapes used that night. If Halt had two tapes on his person, and each tape was approximately twenty minutes each side, that means there could have been up to eighty minutes of recording time. At the very least, forty minutes if the tapes only recorded on one side. When I asked Halt what happened to the other tape, he said, 'I can't say what became of it.' Yet in an interview with Jonathon Dillon, for *Sightings* magazine in 1997, he makes no mention of the other tape.

> My pocket recorder only holds about twenty minutes or so, of audiotape, so how did I manage to tape over four hours of commentary? Sure, the tape recording shows over two hours have elapsed but that's because I had to be as brief as possible because I didn't have more tape with me.

Six months after I first questioned Halt about the tapes, he admitted that he did take two tapes with him, but that he only used one. When I asked him why he had not used the other cassette tape, he said, 'I don't know why.' Halt has always claimed that the recording is genuine and reminded me that the CNN Network TV channel in the United States had done their own analysis when they became interested in the case. When I queried this with Chuck de Caro, who was responsible for the CNN programme, he was not aware that the company had done any such analysis, although he did recall they had considered it at the time. From what I gather, the analysis would only have confirmed that the voice stresses of the people concerned could not have been fabricated, and not whether the tape was edited or not. Colonel Morgan has since confirmed that the voice-overs on the tape, such as 'It took this long to document', belong to the then base commander, Colonel Ted Conrad, and have absolutely nothing to do with the incident. One has to wonder why, if the AFOSI took so much trouble to silence the witnesses, would they allow this prime piece of evidence to escape their notice and fall into the hands of ufologists. There are a number of other important issues which need to be addressed regarding Halt's tape recording.

Soon after the incident, certain details of the recording came to the attention of Brenda Butler. She had heard about it from her contacts on the base, and both Lieutenant Colonel Halt and Squadron Leader Donald Moreland had confirmed its existence before it was released into the public domain. Moreland told Brenda and her colleague Dot Street about the tape in August 1983, and although Halt was less forthcoming, he confirmed its existence on at least one occasion. More importantly, the women claimed that the memorandum underplayed the tape recording, which picked up the amazement and terror encountered by personnel. They were clearly convinced that what Halt and his patrol saw that night was a machine. Several people told Brenda that at one stage in the recording Halt called out something like 'Oh my God, it's a m . . .' It was speculated that what he actually said was 'a machine' but the tape was erased at that precise point, followed by a blank space before recording continued. It is worth mentioning that in some of my conversations with Adrian Bustinza, he also referred to it being a *machine* and he is adamant that the tape is edited. There was also mention of a light being beamed from the craft, which narrowly missed Halt. This was later confirmed by Halt himself. One might dismiss these accounts as hearsay, were it not for the fact that a recording of some sort eventually surfaced.

Fifteen years after the incident Brenda decided the tape was not genuine after all. She concluded that it must have been made inside a building because there were no background noises to be heard, such as when the patrol was tramping through the forest. It is obvious that Brenda had heard a bad recording because these sounds can be clearly heard on the cassette tape that Colonel Morgan allowed me to copy, and it is my opinion that the recording is genuine, inasmuch as it was made in the forest. However, I am not convinced it is the full account of what happened that night. Of course, it was only eighteen minutes out of a period of time that lasted at least four hours, and much could have taken place during those hours or indeed after the last recorded data.

Just after a possible break in the tape, at around 01.48 hrs, Halt states, 'We just bumped into the first light we've seen.' However, sometime before that, we can faintly hear Lieutenant Englund say, 'It's still flying around,' which by anyone's estimation means that the object must have been seen earlier. At 04.00 hrs, Halt records that one object was still hovering over the Woodbridge base. At one point in the tape there is a record of the time being 01.25. The next mention of time is recorded by Halt at 01.48. During those twenty-three minutes there are an estimated twelve breaks in the tape. Even dismissing the number of breaks, the men miraculously managed to take Geiger readings of the trees, make a sweep around the whole area, bottle samples and take photographs. All this in less than twenty-three minutes in the middle of the night with light-all problems.

As early as 1984 Adrian Bustinza conversed with researchers Ray Boeche and Scott Colborn. They had called him on 15 April, five days before Larry Fawcett interviewed him. Bustinza explained that while searching for the object someone had spotted it, as if sitting on the ground, and as they searched they came across triangular tripods burned into the ground at three different standpoints and they took radiation readings of these indentations. Was the patrol taking readings of the original landing site or a fresh one? Halt told me that they were investigating the former but that they had trouble finding it in the dark.

According to several witnesses, the object appeared to be moving through the trees. The tape makes numerous references to trees, and one particular tree is mentioned four times, but this is supposed to be the site where the UFO landed on a previous night – or is it?

'It looks like an abrasion on the tree.'
'We are getting readings on the tree . . .'
'That's the strongest point on the tree.'
'Getting a definite heat reflection off the tree.'

The second landing also involved a close encounter with unidentified, highly advanced flying objects. Some witnesses have claimed that aeronaut entities of some kind were also present. Most of the witnesses to this incident continually point to this night as being either 27/28 or 28/29 December. The problem with being involved in this particular event means one might have to admit to having had a close encounter of the third kind. It is one thing admitting to seeing lights in the sky, but quite another admitting to seeing alien entities in any shape or form.

Halt has stated that, including himself, there were only four or five men in the original patrol. He claims the men were all senior officers he knew on a first-name basis. The names he originally referred to are as follows: Lieutenant Bruce Englund, Master Sergeant Bobby Ball and Sergeant Munroe Nevilles. What of the other man or men? I asked Halt to reveal the identity of the other individual(s) but he said he could not remember. Having reminded him of his previous statements, made to others and myself, that being as he knew the men on a first-name basis he surely must know their identity. He replied, 'No one has ever asked me that question before.' I told him I had recently interviewed Adrian Bustinza and had reason to believe that he may have been one of the men in his patrol. Halt said he could have been. Less than a month earlier I had asked him the very same question and had been told that Bustinza was not with his patrol but could have been further back in the forest. The very fact that Halt was now prepared to admit that Bustinza could have been with his original patrol was indeed a breakthrough.

It was only later, when I heard the master copy of the tape, that I was absolutely sure Bustinza was there. He had vaguely remembered his call sign as being Alpha One but was not sure because of the time lapse. On the tape a sergeant, who is talking on the radio, gives his call sign as Alpha Two. Three times he gives his name as Sergeant Bustinza. I also discovered other names on the tape, which have not been heard before, namely John Burroughs and Sergeant Frail. With this new-found information I called Halt and, having explained that Bustinza's name is mentioned on the tape three times, he admitted Bustinza was with his patrol and claimed he had never denied he was not. When I questioned Halt again on whether he had witnessed a landed object, stating that Bustinza claims he did, he denied it. He then again suggested that Bustinza was further back, which is possible because he was in the background. However, he was close enough to be heard on Halt's pocket recorder so he could not have been that far out of range. It is possible that the reason Halt has always had problems with Adrian Bustinza being one of his patrol is because of Bustinza's testimony regarding a landed UFO. Bustinza was the youngest member of the patrol and had far less to lose than the other seasoned officers. He was also the only one who retired from the Air Force within a couple of years, this being because he was stripped of his rank for no apparent reason. Of course, we cannot count Nevilles, who is said to have disappeared and been given a new identity.

However, there is another witness who confirmed the patrol had encountered a landed UFO, at least according to former Senior Master Sergeant Ray Gulyas. Bobby Ball and Ray Gulyas were both flight chiefs. Gulyas told me that Ball had briefed him on a daily basis as to what occurred in the forest. Ball said he had been involved for three consecutive nights. This would have begun on 26/27 and ended on 28/29. Although Ball never suggested that Gordon Williams was involved, he confirmed he was with Halt's patrol on the third night and it was during this particular night that they saw an object. At first they tried to follow it as it moved through the trees, almost touching the ground. Then it landed! He also confirmed there was someone in the tower keeping an eye on the object. If Ball was referring to the third night that he was on duty, that would mean Halt's patrol were in the forest on 28/29, one night later than he now claims he was involved. Halt's date on the memorandum is also confusing because he mentions only the 29th, but it is assumed that means 29/30 and not 28/29. Ball's evidence corresponds with other witnesses who all claim it was the last night of their midnight shift with D Flight, and all three give the date as 28/29. This would imply that there were four nights of events.

In late 1999 Charles Halt admitted to me that he had four or five hours of tape, which I would never be allowed to hear. I asked him to explain but he just repeated that I would never be allowed to hear them. It would not surprise me if Halt had made more tape of the incident; it is exactly what I would have expected the officer to do. However, what would be surprising is that he personally has kept the recordings. I have always believed there was more tape than that which has been made public and have asked Halt on several occasions to confirm this. If they do exist and are in his possession, he has attended UFO conferences and appeared on television shows promoting only a segment of tape. My conclusion is that he did make more tape at the time of the incident, but that these were confiscated by the AFOSI and an edited version was conveniently placed in the public domain to coincide with the release of *Skycrash*. Considering the book covers speculation that the tapes did exist, it would have been a perfect piece of disinformation to quell stories that the men were so terrified of what was taking place that they ran from the scene in panic. I am not accusing any individuals of perpetrating this conspiracy, but I am in no doubt that the segment of tape in the public domain is there for a specific reason. Ufologists and sceptics have spent the last sixteen years debating this piece of evidence. Sceptic Ian Ridpath has made much of the fact that the flashing light referred to in the recording matches the exact timing of the flashing light of the Orfordness lighthouse beacon, which it surely does. Let us not forget, however, that the AFOSI's role was to convince (under pressure) the witnesses that it was the lighthouse beacon they saw.

If Halt really does have these important tapes, it may be that he copied them before they got into the hands of the AFOSI, in which case it would be difficult to make them public without possible repercussions. But if there was an encounter with a landed UFO and its crew, then he would want to keep this under wraps for obvious reasons. Maybe one day Colonel Halt will tell us what he really witnessed in Rendlesham Forest in December 1980.

According to radio presenter Lee Speigel, Halt confided in him that he did not think the public were totally ready to hear all the facts about the case. He said what he and others had experienced out in Rendlesham Forest was so extraordinary that if the public were made fully aware of the circumstances, it would completely change the way people look at reality and the nature of the universe.

Colonel Halt had a long and successful career in the USAF, which included several tours in Southeast Asia. He was eventually promoted to base commander for RAF Bentwaters and completed several tours in Europe, the US and Korea before he retired in 1991. He is now a manager with a real estate company and lives with his wife by a second marriage and their young daughter in Woodbridge, Virginia.

MORE BASE PERSONNEL
SPEAK OUT

Airman First Class Gregory Battram was assigned to the Program and Planning Department, working day shifts with A Flight. Once or twice a month Battram's unit were required to participate in alert exercises, and this included being posted on guard duty on either the swing or mid shifts. Battram was on one such exercise during the night the second UFO landed. He and three other security policemen were driving around, patrolling the perimeter of the Woodbridge base when they spotted some unusual lights in the sky. After a while the lights disappeared into the forest and, realizing there might be a problem, the patrol contacted Central Security Control for permission to investigate. They were instructed to go ahead and meanwhile CSC would alert the fire department and the British authorities. The four men drove towards the scene of the lights and, after parking their jeep on the side of the road, headed through the forest on foot. (It is worth noting that Battram's patrol were still carrying their weapons during this time.) As they neared the object they could hear a humming sound and the area seemed to be full of static electricity, making the hair on their necks and arms stand up, and the closer they got to the object, the worse the static became. There was also a strange yellow mist, which looked like a ground fog surrounding the object. This phenomenon measured about one hundred feet across, with a denser section inside measuring between thirty to fifty feet. There appeared to be pulsating lights emitting from the object but it was difficult to determine exactly what it was. The men suddenly became frightened and decided to make a run for it, and as they did so they ran straight into a patrol. Battram remembers Lieutenant Englund as being the only officer he recognized. Having explained the situation to Englund, Battram and his colleagues were instructed to return to the base. On the way out of the forest they bumped into another patrol of about twenty men, some carrying light-alls with them.

Battram remembers being debriefed the next day. He told Larry Fawcett in February 1984 that they were told not to discuss it with anyone. He remembers all the commanders were in attendance and some people he had never seen before, who he thought were from Washington DC.

Malcolm Zickler's name has been linked with the Rendlesham Forest incident since the early 1980s, when he first came to the attention of researchers Brenda Butler and Dot Street. Because he was in charge of the police squadrons, Dot and Brenda were convinced he was involved in the actual incident. Unfortunately, Zickler had never gone on record and no researcher had ever managed to interview him, consequently several rumours were started and these became a part of the story itself. The gist of Major Zickler's participation was that he was out in the forest during the third night's event.

I caught up with Malcolm and Linda Zickler on 11 June 1998. Here is part of my first interview with the now retired lieutenant colonel concerning the actual incident:

G. BRUNI: Were you involved in the incident? Were you out in the forest on any of the nights?

M. ZICKLER: No, I wasn't there on any night. I was called on a number of occasions but I wasn't out there. I was advised on what they saw – an object – but I went to the woods during the day and saw none of those things out there.

G. BRUNI: So you were not involved in the incident?

M. ZICKLER: When I knew Halt was out there, I chose not to go. I heard he was out there, I heard his radio call, Bravo Charlie 2. Halt and I didn't see eye to eye. I was subordinate to him in rank but I didn't work directly for him, I worked for the base commander.

G. BRUNI: What do you think happened in the forest?

M. ZICKLER: I don't know, Halt seemed to think this was a major problem. I know he did a report but I was not privy to that and I've no idea of the response to it.

G. BRUNI: What about Gordon Williams, was he out in the forest on any of those nights?

M. ZICKLER: That would be unusual for him because he would leave it in my hands unless he was called for any reason. I was in charge of the police and security. Gordon Williams gave me a free hand.

Lieutenant Colonel Zickler retired from the USAF in 1989. He lives with his wife Linda in Florida and runs a business called Woodbridge Engineering.

The fear imposed upon those individuals connected with the incident is still embedded deep in their minds. Major Edward Drury remembers exactly how he was silenced. I first spoke to Drury's mother, who was very polite and welcomed a conversation with me. I told her I wanted to talk to her son about RAF Bentwaters. Ms Drury updated me on his career, explaining that he was in a good civilian job which involved top-secret security. She also talked proudly of her English grandchildren and suggested I contact her son and also talk to his ex-wife, an Englishwoman who still lives in Woodbridge, Suffolk. I did not discuss the Rendlesham Forest incident with Ms Drury, but when I briefly mentioned my forthcoming book on the case, there was a sudden change in her attitude. 'No, I can't talk about that, he was told to be quiet. He won't talk to you about it either because he is in security,' she said nervously. I called his ex-wife Ann. She was very curious about my call but was also unwilling to discuss the incident, reminding me about the system and how she was glad to be out of it. 'I don't think he'll talk to you because he was ordered to keep quiet. He was in security and was contacted by the State Department at the time. I can tell you he wasn't involved but was called about it.' Ann told me that her ex-husband had never discussed the incident with her because he was not allowed to.

Fortunately, Edward Drury was more forthcoming. He had been contacted in 1985 by CNN journalist Chuck de Caro, but had been reluctant to speak publicly at the time because he was on a liability programme and was in command of a missile squadron. Apparently, he was the youngest major in the USAF when he first received his promotion, and as a young officer he had high ambitions but was disappointed that he had not made it to colonel. He blamed one of his superiors at Bentwaters for giving him a bad efficiency report, which may have been based on his interest in the incident. Nevertheless, this did not affect his civilian career because when he retired from the USAF in 1986 he was offered employment with one of America's foremost government contractors (a company that have strong links to the infamous Area 51) and has been on their payroll ever since.

Drury recalled how the cover-up first began. After he had read the witness statements he realized that something very unusual had occurred and started asking questions around the base. Forty-eight hours later he received a sharp call from the more senior Major Zickler who gave him a direct order to 'shut up'. It turned out that the order had originated from the AFOSI. From that moment on Drury was out of the loop.

Although Drury was not technically on duty, he had been contacted on his radio earlier that night and was in the shift com-mander's office when Jim Penniston and John Burroughs were being debriefed. Drury expressed his opinions: 'I read their statements. It was normal procedure to take statements if something unusual happened. What I noticed from them was that they were very serious. I got right in their face. "No sir," they said, "we are serious."' When I asked Drury what became of the statements, he said, 'That's a point.' Drury had originally thought the men were joking and were getting their own back because he had recently put them through 'some pretty heavy exercises'. After reading the statements, however, he decided to contact the Bentwaters Command Post, who confirmed they had picked something up on radar. He then called RAF Bawdsey who validated that they too had tracked the UFO.

I asked Drury if he could recall what had occurred on that first night.

> I was not on duty, technically that is, but I remember being called on my radio. We carried them all the time even when we were off duty. I honestly thought it was a joke they were playing on me. I told them, 'Hey, it's Christmas,' and I went back to whatever I was doing at the time. Later that morning I was in the shift commander's office when some of them were making their statements. There was a pile of them because I recall going through them. On reading the statements I understood that it wasn't very big [the object] but it was bigger than a mini. There were marks on the trees, quite high up and someone said they'd walked up to it [the object] and it had left depressions. I went out during the day and saw the marks on the trees and the ground depressions, which weren't that deep, well defined and I suggested we send someone out there to do some readings [Geiger-counter readings].

Sergeant Rick Bobo was assigned to the alarm systems and stationed in the Bentwaters tower, which was situated in the weapons storage area. In an interview, he described to me what he could see from where he was located. He thinks the incident took place on the morning of 29 December.

> R. BOBO: I think I was the first to report the sighting that night. I was on the tower at Bentwaters; you get a good view from up there. There were several lights and there was this huge ship over the forest. It seemed to be very low with lots of red and blue lights on it and I saw something come away from it and land in amongst the trees.
>
> G. BRUNI: Can you describe the object?
>
> R. BOBO: I'd say it looked circular but, remember, I was over at Bentwaters and this was happening over at Woodbridge. I was

instructed to watch it and can tell you it was up there for about five hours, just hovering. I would say it was quite low in the sky.

G. BRUNI: Were you alone in the tower?

R. BOBO: Someone came to the tower and watched it through a scope. I don't know who he was, he was from a different department. I wasn't told anything and I didn't get to look through the scope.

G. BRUNI: Could you hear the radio transmissions from your location in the Bentwaters tower?

R. BOBO: I heard some of the radio transmissions, not all of them, you understand, because there were different frequencies. I heard over the radio that London had spotted something on their radar. I heard some of the radio transmissions from the men who were out there. They were reporting a light going through the woods, it had bumped into a tree and they were getting radioactive readings from the area. They were discussing three impressions and stuff moving through the woods towards Woodbridge. They kept switching to different frequencies so I couldn't hear everything. I know there was a colonel with them.

G. BRUNI: Rick, did you hear anything about a landed object being out there?

R. BOBO: No, the conversations were steady at first, then they got less. There could have been other conversations on different frequencies though.

G. BRUNI: I heard rumours that the tower was full of airmen trying to look at the UFOs through binoculars. Do you remember that?

R. BOBO: Absolutely not. That would mean taking people off their posts. This was in the weapons storage area. There might have been people in the Woodbridge tower, but that didn't happen the night I was on duty, not at Bentwaters anyway.

Immediately after the incident, there was an unusual amount of communications activity going on. From late November 1980 until February 1981, Sergeant William A. Kirk Jr was posted on temporary duty to RAF Bentwaters. Kirk was a technical controller with the telecommunications department and his actual duty site was RAF Martlesham Heath, Suffolk. He informed me that at the time the big communications group was breaking up and Bentwaters was about to become the major communications base. During his TDY he was assigned to the communications centre on Bentwaters, which was located directly adjacent to the commander's office. Immediately after the incident, Kirk noticed massive communications traffic, so much so that the radio lines to the main switch at RAF Martlesham Heath were jammed, and switchboard operators were complaining about the traffic. Thinking there was a communications failure, he began monitoring the lines and making enquiries. On contacting the telecommunications technicians at Martlesham Heath, he discovered that the majority of traffic were Flash calls. He also noticed a large number of personnel around the headquarters. According to Kirk, there were twenty-four lines on the radio system between RAF Bentwaters and RAF Martlesham Heath. This was the serving telephone switch and was called the Gateway to Europe; RAF Hillington being the Gateway to the United States. All twenty-four lines were in constant use for several days after the incident, and users were complaining that they couldn't get through or were being bumped off. Kirk explains that the traffic was much higher than normal and he was taking complaints from personnel who were authorized to use Priority. It became a real problem when even he could not get through to RAF Martlesham Heath and was ordered to use Immediate. Because Kirk was new to Bentwaters, he thought the excess traffic was due to an exercise in progress. In fact, why he remembers this incident so well was that during later exercises he never once experienced telecommunications traffic that ever came close to that level of usage. When hearing the scuttlebutt about the UFO story, he recalls saying to a fellow sergeant, with a wry smile on his face, 'Well, that probably explains it.' I posed some questions to Kirk, asking him if he would explain the priority telecommunications jargon used that week, so that I might understand it in layman's terms.

Priority traffic: imagine a standard touch-tone phone, but on the left of the numbers 1, 4, 7 and the star symbol are four more buttons. To make an ordinary call you would pick up and just dial the number. If the number was busy and your call was important, you might hang up, pick up again, push the button next to the number 1, which was labelled P, and dial the number again. Provided the number that was busy was connected by ordinary traffic, you would BUMP the callers off the line. The person you wanted to call would get a special tone in his ear, he would hang up, get a special ring of the bell, and, bingo, you were talking. The P stood for Priority, next to the number 4 was the letter I, which stood for Immediate. Next to the number 7 was the letter F, for Flash, and finally, next to the star button was FO, which stood for Flash Override. Very few people had anything over Priority, and most traffic was ordinary. Only communications and commanders had the power to use Immediate or Flash. Flash Override being reserved for the highest authority only. It works like this: think of a call going to the president. ORDINARY: 'I understand that the Russians may declare war.' Bumped by a Priority call: 'Mr President, not only have the Russians declared war, but they have just launched . . .' Bumped by a Flash call: 'The Russians have launched all ICBMs but we are not sure of their target.' Bumped by Flash Override: 'Mr President, this is the Vice President here at Cheyenne Mountain, the Russians have declared war and have launched a full ICBM strike aimed at New York.'

If the majority of calls going backwards and forwards during and following the Rendlesham Forest incident were Flash calls, it surely suggests there was a major problem. If the enormous amount of Flash calls were classed in a similar mode to Kirk's description, that being 'The Russians have launched all ICBMs but we are not sure of their target,' then the Flash calls must have been of vital importance to national security and, if so, must certainly have been of interest to the Ministry of Defence. Yet we are constantly being told that it was of no defence significance.

Airman Tony Brisciano was on duty at the desk of the Fuels Management Branch, located at the Bentwaters site. It was in the early hours of the morning when he received a call informing him that there were several emergency vehicles at Woodbridge needing fuel urgently. In those days the person on this particular duty had to cover both bases, so Brisciano had to drive over to the Woodbridge pumps. Because the situation was urgent he decided to take the back gate, which was much quicker than the normal route, but three minutes into the drive something in his head seemed to say 'Do not go this way.' The message was so strong that he turned around and proceeded to head for the front-gate route. Brisciano recalls what happened next:

> When I reached the military gas pumps at Woodbridge, I never saw so many police vehicles and equipment waiting for fuel. It was especially unusual to see this as it was in the early hours of the morning. The vehicles were mostly pick-ups with light-alls attached, and there were a few police cars. I was having a difficult time with Lieutenant Colonel Halt, the deputy base commander. He was in a hell of a hurry and was bitching at me to snap it up and get the pumps going. After that I drove back to Bentwaters and didn't think any more about it until rumours started to circulate about UFOs, and a few days later when an SP told me he'd seen a UFO out in the forest, I was glad I followed my conscience and didn't take the back road to Woodbridge that night.

I asked Brisciano if he was absolutely certain it was Lieutenant Colonel Halt who was with the patrol, and could it have been another officer? He seemed confident it was Halt, and confirmed that he was on duty between 26/27 and 28/29 December. He believes this incident took place on 27/28. I thought it was possible that Halt stopped off at the Woodbridge gas pumps on his way into the forest, but Halt denies it was him.

Brisciano also recalls an odd incident that took place when two security policemen stopped by to refuel their trucks a couple of days after the incident. It seems the cover-up threats were already working.

I remember in early January, I got a call from Maintenance Operating Control Center to open up the pumps for some SP vehicles on the Bentwaters site. Time frame was early morning. Two vehicles came down and after the first one left the other vehicle took gas. There were two cops; one stayed indoors with me to fill out the forms and chat and the other went outside to pump the gas. This cop asked me if I believed in UFOs. I said, I think so. He appeared to have something on his mind; I guess that's why he told me this. But why me? He then proceeded to tell me an interesting story that I didn't believe. He said that one had landed at Woodbridge a while back and that I should keep an eye on the sky and look for lights. He said he saw some beings that almost looked like small children dressed in snow suits/bunny suits, running around in the forest, but they posed no harm or threat. At that moment the other cop walked in and told him to shut up and reminded him that they were told not to discuss anything. I thought it sure was a strange story to tell somebody you don't know, but that last comment really got my attention.

Thanks to Captain Mike Martin, who was stationed at RAF Bentwaters from 1980 to 1983, I was able to contact a couple of British secretaries who were employed at the base. Martin told me that, unless it was classified, the wives and secretaries knew almost everything that went on and suggested the ladies would be a source of reliable information. I managed to trace an ex-Ministry of Defence employee; due to her not wanting to divulge her name publicly I am giving her the pseudonym of Betty Garfield. Betty worked at RAF Bentwaters for more than twenty years and had secret clearance with the Ministry of Defence. She has allowed me to name one of her bosses, whom she says was very involved in the incident, and she was the contact who put me in touch with local witness Gary Collins. Betty began working at the base in 1971, and in 1980 she was the secretary to Lieutenant Colonel Richard C. Spring, who had been the Chief of Base Operations and Training since July 1979. I asked Betty to explain Spring's involvement.

I must be careful what I say because I was with the MOD, but I can tell you that Colonel Spring was very much involved. I remember he suddenly disappeared from his office at short notice to meet the police. I think they were from Hull, but can't be sure about that. I think they had a similar incident up there and that was the reason for their visit – to compare notes. Colonel Spring went to the station to meet them.

Betty pointed out that the visitors were British civilian police and even the chief of police for Hull, or wherever they were from, was among the group. She insists there were no MOD police stationed at the bases, and she does not recall seeing any visit the base during that time. When I pushed her further, she replied, 'They sent people away and gave them new identities. Some were sent to RAF Lakenheath, others further afield.' I was surprised to hear that Sergeant Nevilles was sent back to the United States the day after the incident. I had not mentioned Nevilles' name to Betty, but she asked me if I had heard of him. Nevilles was the sergeant who accompanied Lieutenant Colonel Halt into the forest on the night he was involved. Betty told me that he had not only been sent away, but his name had also been changed. Apparently, his wife left soon afterwards. All attempts to contact Nevilles or his former boss, Captain Coplin, have been fruitless.

Betty did not explain how Lieutenant Colonel Spring was involved but confirmed he was the Chief of Operations. Because Lieutenant Colonel Spring was in charge of base operations he would no doubt have been informed of the incident and would most likely have played an important role in what happened after the events. Betty offered her own opinions about the incident, which I found very interesting, especially the part about electricity – was she trying to tell me something?

It was all very hush-hush at the time. I do believe it happened. The universe is massive and there must be others more advanced than we are. We don't know enough about electricity. I think they can transform themselves by using electricity. A tremendous amount

went on, it was all very hushed up. I had secret clearance but that
didn't include American clearance. I never had that in all the time
I was on the base. I can tell you there was a lot of radiation activity,
a lot of coming and going.

Betty was friendly with Lieutenant Colonel Halt's secretary,
Peggy Ross, who stayed behind in England for a time before returning to the United States. Apparently, the encounter really disturbed
Halt. Betty also confirmed that one of the base photographers went
out to the forest and took photographs of the event. This corresponds
with reports of the second landing where witnesses claim military
photographers were at the site. She put me in touch with Bob
Higgins, who was involved with the photo laboratory on Bentwaters,
and named Gary Tomoysu, who was one of the base photographers
sent out to photograph the incident. I contacted Higgins who is now
based in Hawaii. He was not stationed at RAF Bentwaters in 1980
but knew of the incident involving Lieutenant Colonel Halt. Higgins
confirmed Tomoysu was the photographer at Bentwaters during that
time frame and he was also now based in Hawaii. Higgins promised
to speak to him, and if Tomoysu agreed to talk to me he would call
back with his telephone number. But Higgins never did. I called
several times but only ever managed to speak to his daughter. From
what I understand, both Higgins and Tomoysu are still in the Air
Force, and Higgins' wife was a British officer with the RAF. Although
I did not manage to talk to Tomoysu, I have no reason to doubt that
Betty is telling the truth about photographs being taken at the
landing site. She also mentioned that the chief of publishing for the
base magazine *Forum* had confirmed there were photographs.
However, the USAF has denied it. In a letter addressed to the then
assistant director of CAUS, Larry Fawcett, the commander at RAF
Bentwaters in 1983, Colonel Cochran, wrote, 'No photos of the
alleged craft were taken by the Air Force.'

I asked Betty if she could recall any suicides on the base at that
time, because Larry Warren alleges that a security policeman had
killed himself after being involved in the UFO encounter. She could

not recall that incident but commented that there were more suicides than there ought to have been. 'Bentwaters wasn't a good place,' she told me. She did remember seeing the body of a pilot hanging from a tree near the Bentwaters installation, but that was a long time prior to the 1980 incident. According to former Bentwaters officer Lieutenant Colonel Park Simms, who worked in administration, there was a suicide on average every other year. This was confirmed by the civilian police officer in charge of Woodbridge police station, George Plume, and one of the Bentwaters lawyers, Lieutenant Colonel Bernard E. Donahue.

Another interesting snippet of information came from Betty. She suggested I contact the civilian electrician who was apparently called out on a job immediately following the incident. Brenda Butler and Chris Pennington had mentioned that a local electrician had been summoned to repair the lights over the Woodbridge flightline. According to Brenda, the UFO had crashed into them before it had landed in the forest. Neither Brenda nor Chris could offer any name for the electrician and I had to abandon my search, but then Betty came up with the information. Betty explained that there were two local electricians who were contracted by Bentwaters. One of the men, who owned a small electrical business in Felixstowe, had become friendly with Gordon Williams. His name was Cook and, according to Betty, 'he had his fingers in every pie'. The other electrician, Keith Stuart, has since moved from the area. Betty thinks it was Stuart who made repairs to the Woodbridge flightline.

Another woman I spoke to allowed me to use her real name. Mary Everest was also with the Ministry of Defence and was in charge of British personnel at the installations. She told me:

> There was a lot of speculation, but it was nothing to do with Bentwaters. It was probably related to military testing. There were lots of different military installations in East Anglia and they were always testing something new. I don't think you'll ever find out what happened because they will never admit to it. It was really kept very, very quiet. I think it will remain a mystery.

There has been speculation that the 67th Aerospace Rescue and Recovery Squadron were part of the cover-up operation, and there are rumours that the team had scrambled helicopters and were flying over the landing site at the time of the incident. Nick Ryan had been a member of the elite 67th ARRS stationed at RAF Woodbridge from 1982 to 1984 and I asked him if it were possible they were involved:

> I wasn't there at the time, but I can tell you that we were not involved. I would have been told about that because we were a close-knit team. What you must realize is that we are trained to go behind enemy lines. We would never have taken a helicopter up to go half a mile down the road. That would be the job of the security police. Here's what would happen in a situation like that. The first person to be contacted would be the base commander. He would then order a patrol to the area, which would be instructed to surround the object or whatever. There would also be another group to keep people away from entering the actual site. Even though this was on British property, we had an agreement, if you like, that the land surrounding the bases was not off limits to the USAF. After all, these were NATO installations and we had to keep an eye on what was happening outside the perimeters. The AFOSI would not get involved during the incident, but they would carry out an investigation afterwards.

I knew that the 67th ARRS had assisted in local rescues and pointed this out to Nick.

> Yes, that's correct. We helped the RAF with rescues over the North Sea and other areas, and we assisted the 81st Tactical Fighter Wing with the same, but we would not be required to assist with a local incident that occurred so close to the base, that was definitely the job of the Security Police Squadron.

Although the unit were allowed to practise off the base, this would have taken place in a field that directly adjoined the left side of the Woodbridge base. If they had been in the forest they were certainly not practising.

In 1999 researcher Peter Robbins was a guest on the popular American radio show *Sightings* and had told the presenter Jeff Rense that I was investigating the Rendlesham Forest case. The day before the show aired Jeff called to tell me that a new witness, an officer's wife, was going to speak on the show and would I like to get involved. I was keen to ask the lady some questions but it was doubtful she would talk to me privately. During the show Jeff contacted me to tell me that another witness had called in and the following day, thanks to Jeff and Peter, I was able to interview the witness.

Jerry Valdes-Sanchez, who at the time of the incident had been an airman first class with the Law Enforcement Squadron, had retired from the USAF in 1992 as a sergeant. Before speaking to him I logged on to the *Sightings* archives on the Internet and listened to the three-hour radio show. I certainly had some questions for the witness. Sanchez claimed that on the night of 25 December he was working the last swing shift with B Flight at the Woodbridge base when he witnessed unusual lights in the sky. Because it was Christmas week, some personnel were given special leave to be with their families, thus a combination of flights were on duty, so it is possible that Sanchez was at Woodbridge. He thinks he was supposed to have been relieved from duty at 23.00 hrs, but it was well after 07.00 the following morning before he got off duty, which means he must have worked a double shift. He certainly recalls being exhausted the next day.

According to Sanchez, the first sighting was around 22.30 to 23.00 hrs and continued for several hours afterwards. I asked him if he was absolutely sure it was the night of 25/26, and he seemed reasonably certain it was. But there are problems with Sanchez's story simply because it does not tie in with the pattern of events. According to him, it was not John Burroughs who reported the first sighting but another Law Enforcement officer by the name of Mark Beaucham. Sanchez says Beaucham was due to be relieved of duty because the east gate was not always manned after 22.30 and sometimes much earlier. He distinctly remembers listening in on the radio frequency and hearing Beaucham report that he was seeing coloured lights in the sky over the forest. Central Security Control did not take the call seriously at first; they thought he was 'screwing around'. But suddenly the radio reception was becoming more difficult and CSC must have thought something was wrong because they sent a patrol out looking for him, but Beaucham was nowhere to be seen. The airman had simply disappeared from his post (the closest to the forest area) without a trace. The patrol went out in search of him, but they too disappeared. CSC then sent out another patrol searching for the missing personnel, but apparently they went missing too. Sanchez remembers that all three radio frequencies were experiencing bad reception during the night. If his testimony is true then there were several missing airmen that night. Sanchez is adamant that the airman who made the first call was Beaucham, and not Steffens or Burroughs, although he is sure Burroughs was involved.

Until Jerry Valdes-Sanchez came forward, no one had heard of Airman Beaucham and it was always assumed that Staff Sergeant Bud Steffens and Airman First Class John Burroughs were the first to report the incident. I admit this had bothered me because, according to Timothy Egercic, the first call came in during shift change, between 23.00 hrs and midnight. Egercic thinks it was closer to 23.00 hrs. This is confusing because John Burroughs was definitely with C Flight that night and his shift began at approximately 23.00 hrs. The fact that Burroughs was with C Flight is recorded in his handwritten statement to that effect. Of course, it is known that during shift change there is a period when shifts overlap. Sanchez points out that Beaucham was stationed on the east gate and was due to be relieved, which would mean he could have been working the swing shift with D Flight. If Timothy Egercic and Sanchez are right about the time of the first report then it is possible that Burroughs and Steffens were the second patrol to become involved in the incident and, if this is the case, then the established story of the first night's events in Rendlesham Forest changes dramatically.

However, based on information offered by Sanchez, I am

inclined to think he was referring to another night, and not the initial event. For instance, Sanchez was not aware that there was more than one event. He talks of seeing men in long white overcoats, who he thought could have been scientists, standing near the edge of Rendlesham Forest the morning after the incident. There is no doubt that investigations were going on but these did not take place until later in the week. He also points out that when he finished his shift that morning, he asked his shift commander, Lieutenant Bruce Englund, what was going on. Apparently, Englund warned him to be quiet, threatening him with a court-martial. But, as far as I am aware, Englund was not on duty on the morning of 26 December. Sanchez names other personnel who were stationed at the Woodbridge base that night, and assures me that they saw the lights hovering over the tree tops and heard the break-up of the three radio transmissions. Several years later Sanchez bumped into Mark Beaucham at another airbase, but when he asked him about what had happened Beaucham claimed he had no idea what he was talking about. It is interesting that Sanchez also named Sergeant Frail as one of the officers involved. Frail was on duty that week, but not on 25/26. In fact, Frail can be heard, albeit faintly, on Halt's audio recording, which must confirm that Sanchez was referring to a later event. Surprisingly, Larry Warren mentioned years ago that an airman had disappeared the night he was involved. Could that have been Mark Beaucham?

In all the evidence presented for the case, there seemed to be very little mention of the fire department being involved in the incident, yet Jim Penniston, who was one of the primary witnesses, initially believed it was a fire in the forest or a crashed aircraft. In 1998 I was given the name of an individual who was a fireman with the USAF based at Bentwaters in 1980. When I called him he was absolutely terrified. He told me: 'I saw the results and I don't want to talk about it. There was a cover-up, something went down.' I managed to persuade him to meet me, promising not to reveal his identity. He had married an Englishwoman and was now living in East Anglia, and I was under the impression that he was afraid to upset the

British authorities. I spent several hours interviewing him, but if he was privy to any 'results' he could not furnish me with the details. I did learn, however, that he was not on duty when the Bentwaters fire department was put on standby. When he returned to duty a couple of days later, he attended a meeting where he and other firemen were told that there had been an alleged UFO incident, but were warned not to go around spreading rumours. According to the fireman, nobody from the Bentwaters fire department was involved in the incident but he could not be sure if the Woodbridge department were sent out to the site.

Considering that the incident had occurred on British territory, I wondered if the Suffolk fire department would have been notified. It seems they were. In the early 1990s Brenda Butler received a call from a local who told her that his brother-in-law had been on duty at the Ipswich fire department in 1980 when they received a call to attend an incident in Rendlesham Forest, Woodbridge. The firemen were already on their way when another call came in from the Bentwaters base explaining that their services were not needed because it was just a minor incident and the USAF fire department were dealing with it.

In 1990 Ben Jamison, a professor of science and maths from New York, was working with John Burroughs' story, with the idea of writing a book. During that period he was contacted by an A-10 pilot who insisted on remaining anonymous; Jamison gave him the pseudonym Major Everett. According to Brenda Butler, who met Jamison in 1991, the officer told him that he had been present at a meeting called by Wing Commander Gordon Williams. Apparently, Williams informed the officers that there had been an incident involving a UFO which had landed on 25/26 and 29/30 December. Jamison interviewed the pilot five times and accepted his testimony as credible. In April 1990 Jamison managed to obtain a copy of the police log (October 1980 to March 1981), a copy of which he gave to Brenda and she later gave to me. The log was retrieved from the files of the 'History of the 81st Tactical Fighter Wing' supplied by Maxwell Air Force Base, Alabama. There are several incidents recorded, such as drugs offences and three attempted suicides, but there is no mention of an incident concerning a UFO or aircraft accident during that time. A copy of a letter to Jamison from Richard R. Kyle states that the history of the 81st Tactical Fighter Wing for October to December 1980 did not record any unusual events such as the 'lights' Jamison had mentioned. This is interesting, considering Colonel Halt claims to have instructed Sergeant McCabe to write 'unexplained lights' in the log, and one of the base lawyers, Lieutenant Colonel Donahue, recalls seeing the incident noted in the log for that week. So why did the USAF delete the entry if it was nothing more than unidentified lights? Considering the information came from the historical records of the 81st Tactical Fighter Wing, we must question who was responsible for removing this important piece of information from the log. Indeed, who in the USAF had the authority to change history?

SPECIAL AGENT PERSINGER AND THE AFOSI

What happened immediately after the incident is as important as the events themselves. In an attempt to cover up the previous week's activities, witnesses were thoroughly debriefed by government agents, several of whom were specifically flown in from Washington to do the job. Indeed, some witnesses have complained that the debriefings were so intense they were more like interrogations.

Colonel Charles Halt believes there are at least five American agencies and one British agency all competing with each other for a piece of the action, and only sharing information if and when it suits them. Halt might be right about the competition, the USAF alone created several new agencies in 1993, and the United States government probably has more intelligence-related agencies than the rest of the world put together. However, the one I was primarily concerned with was the Air Force Office of Special Investigations (AFOSI), or the OSI as it is referred to in Air Force circles. Based on my suspicions, I turned again to the claims of certain witnesses: that they were interrogated, some possibly with the aid of drug-induced hypnosis.

Officially, the AFOSI have denied they ever investigated the Rendlesham Forest case. Their denial was logged on file with the public affairs office at 3rd Air Force, Mildenhall, and reproduced by the Bentwaters public affairs officer, Captain Victor Warzinski. In August 1984, he wired the following information to the USAFE headquarters at Ramstein Airbase, Germany: '3AF/PA has a letter on file from AFOSI Commander during period of incident saying AFOSI did *not* do any investigation.' During the course of my own investigation I have learnt not to trust the USAF public affairs office because it is obvious they only repeat what they are instructed to. In November the same year, defence journalist Chuck de Caro, on behalf of CNN, received a letter from the office of the Secretary of the Air Force in response to his questions about the case. Referring to the AFOSI, the office confirmed that the agency did not do an investigation. It is obvious from the paper trail that the information given to de Caro came from the Air Force public affairs office at Mildenhall, and that they were fed false information by the AFOSI. Whilst in conversation with Malcolm Zickler, I asked him what had taken place following the incident. I mentioned there had been reports of civilians arriving from Washington DC who had apparently debriefed the witnesses. I was surprised by his reply, especially as I had not referred to the AFOSI at any time during our conversation.

> The consensus of those who investigated it – the AFOSI, Office of Special Investigations – came to the conclusion that something happened, but there was insufficient evidence.

Considering the AFOSI officially denied they participated in the investigation, this was music to my ears. The witnesses recall the meeting with plain-clothes agents that took place in Zickler's office, so it stands to reason that he would know about it, and I was to learn that the AFOSI agents do in fact wear plain clothes.

Very little has been reported about the AFOSI's involvement in the aftermath of the incident, but there is no doubt that they played an important role in keeping it suppressed. It was Jim Penniston's testimony concerning the drug-induced hypnosis that intrigued me most. Would the AFOSI go to such lengths to silence the witnesses? It is not easy to find information on this agency but I have a copy of a twenty-page paper entitled 'Air Force Intelligence and Security Doctrine', dated 22 July 1994. The paper covered an abundance of information on the workings of the AFOSI, and under the heading 'Specialized Investigative Services' was listed 'Forensic Hypnosis'.

The document states: 'Any person who wants to use hypnosis or drug-induced interviews for investigative or administrative purposes must contact the closest AFOSI office, which processes the request.' This begs the question – who has the authority to request permission from the agency to drug military personnel during an investigation? The witnesses argue that 'there were a lot of plain clothes about'. Could these include CIA agents? I believe so. And if the CIA were involved in the interrogations, which included drug-induced hypnosis, then my next question is: Why was it necessary if nothing of any significance occurred?

One reason for the AFOSI's involvement would be if there was a threat to the installation or mission, which in this case would have been RAF Bentwaters and Woodbridge. It makes sense that the events of December 1980 would be considered a threat to the Suffolk installations, especially as it was the height of the Cold War and, due to the tensions in Iran and Poland, there had to be concern. From reading the 'Air Force Intelligence and Security Doctrine', I also learnt that the AFOSI were involved in numerous covert activities, including providing counter-intelligence support for the US defence agencies, which included intercepting wire, oral and electronic communications. The Air Force document[1] reports on the agency's activities for the USAF, their work on 'Counter-intelligence Investigations, Operations, Collections and Activities'. In the United States the AFOSI coordinates these activities with the FBI. Outside the United States the AFOSI coordinates these activities with the Central Intelligence Agency.

I gathered it was not until twenty-four hours after the initial event in Rendlesham Forest that the AFOSI began taking a serious interest. They were aware of what had occurred but were hoping it was reasonably contained. At that stage they were confident it was just an isolated case involving just a few security personnel. It was not the first time the agency were forced to deal with UFO reports, but most of them were just sightings in the sky, and the military

[1]Air Force Intelligence and Security Doctrine. By order of the Air Force Instruction 71–101. Volume 1, Secretary of the Air Force: 22 July 1994 (Special Investigations).

witnesses were usually briefed and told to forget about it if they knew what was good for their careers. The AFOSI on Bentwaters was a small unit, which consisted of only a handful of special agents who liaised with their head office at Uxbridge and other units scattered throughout the UK. During Christmas week there was an even smaller staff at Bentwaters, only two agents on official duty.

For two years I had tried desperately to find information on the special agents involved in the initial investigations. The USAF denied the AFOSI had played any part whatsoever, the AFOSI denied they did an investigation, the Air Force commanders claimed they had forgotten the names of the special agents and were reluctant to discuss the matter. I thought I would never get anywhere, but eventually my ferreting paid off. Through the help of Lieutenant Colonel Park Simms, a former Bentwaters officer, a name was passed to me. However, Simms informed me that the agent had long since died. But with a name and his last location to work with, I aimed to try to find a family member who might confirm his identity and maybe offer more information. To my surprise Wayne Persinger was still very much alive and residing in England with his British wife Diana. The confusion over his alleged demise had come about because he had worked with his brother-in-law in a family business, and his brother-in-law had been killed in a car accident several years earlier. Lieutenant Colonel Simms had been mistaken, and I often wonder if he would have parted with the information had he known Persinger was still alive.

Special Agent Wayne Persinger was the deputy commander of the AFOSI at RAF Bentwaters during the time of the incident. Having heard the most awful allegations about how they treated the witnesses, it was difficult to imagine that this friendly and humorous individual was someone who could have once instilled fear into Air Force personnel. But by his own admission he has mellowed over the years. Persinger was a veteran of the agency, having served as an intelligence officer in Vietnam. He was then allocated to RAF Lakenheath, where he started up an AFOSI unit with just two special agents, then to RAF Mildenhall and finally RAF Bentwaters.

I already knew the AFOSI had certain rights, but after listening to Persinger I realized they were more powerful than I had first imagined. The special agents could walk into just about any area on the installations without permission from base personnel, including the wing commander. They could not be suppressed by senior commanders and their significant rights allowed them access to classified information. In fact, they did not have to answer to anyone but the Secretary of the Air Force in Washington DC. Persinger confirmed their role covered security investigations, which included checking the personal details of new recruits, keeping an eye on cash-funding facilities, Air Force criminal offences, counter-intelligence and espionage. Persinger also confirmed their connection with the Federal Bureau of Investigation and the Central Intelligence Agency, adding that they also liaised with Britain's Special Branch and on occasion with MI5.

On the Bentwaters installation, the AFOSI worked alongside the Security Police Investigation Department, a small unit within the Security Police Squadron itself. It seems there was a thin line that separated the two departments, and if anything crossed over that line then the AFOSI would take over the investigation. He explained that the AFOSI head office for Bentwaters was stationed at Uxbridge. Persinger also pointed out that special agents seldom wear uniform and they never reveal their rank. When I asked him if they would ever wear black overall-type uniforms (which is what Adrian Bustinza recalls), he admitted this would be the uniform worn in a covert operation. The agency employ both civilian and military agents, and although Persinger has been retired since 1981 he refused to discuss his rank or whether he was a civilian or military special agent with the AFOSI. But I heard from one of the Air Force commanding officers that he was in fact a senior sergeant.

I was pleased with myself at having tracked down Persinger, and I only wish I had known about him earlier in my investigations. I could have done with his expertise as an investigator for the USAF and told him so. He is obviously a very intelligent man and certainly knew his business, and it must have been strange for him that I should be the one questioning him about a USAF incident. His wife Diana was very concerned that I would write terrible things about her husband and the AFOSI and I admitted that to my mind, judging from my investigation, they had a lot to answer to. It was not the first time I would be told that someone was just doing his job.

General Gordon Williams remembers Persinger well and remarked on what a hard man he was. Apparently, the men were terrified of the six-foot-plus special agent, and Williams had pitied anyone who got on the wrong side of him. I asked Persinger why the AFOSI were so terrifying. 'Some people were frightened to death of us, but there was nothing to fear if they hadn't committed any crimes,' he said. I could not help wondering what crimes the poor witnesses had committed that they had to be interrogated in such a fashion.

It has been almost twenty years since Wayne Persinger retired from the agency and settled in England. Whatever his secret past was, today he is an ordinary civilian running a successful local business and happily married to his English wife Diana, whom he calls 'Princess'. There is no doubt that Persinger served his country well, especially during his covert operations in Vietnam, so it is understandable that he would deny any responsibility for the investigation of the Rendlesham affair. 'I put my hand on my heart to tell you I was not involved in the investigation,' he assured me. It is possible that he was not directly associated with it because at the time he was being down-phased ready for his retirement in August 1981, eight months after the incident. He also claims he was not on duty during the first part of Christmas week because he and Diana spent the holidays at his in-laws. Diana told me:

> We always spent Christmas Day and Boxing Day with my family. We would leave at around 11 a.m. on Christmas Day and travel back on the day after Boxing Day. If anything happened Wayne may not have been told, even though he was second in command, because they never talked about their work among themselves. I think the investigation would have been packed up quickly and hushed up.

This means that Special Agent Persinger was not on the base during the first two nights of events, but it does not take him out of the picture for the rest of the incident. If the Bentwaters deputy commander of the AFOSI was not on the case, then who was? Persinger named the commander as Chuck Matthews, who was also based at the installation. However, when I mentioned Chuck Matthews to General Williams, he informed me that he was not Persinger's boss, but a lawyer on the base, and that the chief of Bentwaters AFOSI was at another location. This was very interesting – who was I to believe, the wing commander or the deputy commander of AFOSI? Gordon Williams is still very friendly with Matthews, so I suggested he approach his friend and ask him if he was the chief of the Bentwaters AFOSI. I received a rather amusing reply from Williams:

> If there was an OSI agent there by that name, then eighteen intervening years has erased him. Or the aliens have been seriously screwing with my mind! Or we had two Chuck Matthews at Bentwaters! I give up!

The Persingers did offer the name of one special agent who was involved in the investigation. I asked Persinger if other agents were involved in the debriefings besides the AFOSI. He responded: 'Usually if a Fed agency came in we liaised with them. Although sometimes inspection teams would come in unannounced to test alert preparedness, and not even we would know until they wanted to land.' I am, however, still of the opinion that another agency, either the CIA or agents from another AFOSI unit – or both – took over the investigations.

Although Persinger claimed not to have been involved with the investigation I wondered if he would care to comment on the witness statements. After examining a copy of Lieutenant Fred Buran's typed testimony he offered the following information:

> AFOSI would always take handwritten statements because that way the witness couldn't say we forged them. This looks like a

genuine AFOSI Statement of Witness form but there should be a page with AFOSI's details [1168]. I don't know what Halt was doing taking these statements or who typed them. I notice it's dated 2 January. There doesn't seem much point in taking statements a week after the events were said to have happened. I can't see the point. You need to take them when they are fresh in the memory.

He asked me what the base commander was doing whilst all this was going on. I told him that during one of the events he was supposed to be at an awards dinner party on the Woodbridge base, and this is why his deputy commander was instructed to investigate. Persinger thought it was highly questionable that the base commander would continue to hand out awards when there was supposed to be a crisis on. I asked him if he would oblige me by giving a rundown on what procedures would be taken if such an incident had occurred (my comments in parentheses). According to Persinger, if there was a report of a 'hostile invasion or a craft that had come down', the base commander (Colonel Ted Conrad) would have dropped everything and put his police and fire departments on alert. The wing commander (then Colonel Gordon Williams) would have been notified immediately. The commander in charge of the Bentwaters AFOSI (Chuck Matthews) would have been informed and special agents (possibly John Wolfe and Steve Smith) would have been put on alert notification and would probably have gone out to investigate. The major in charge of security police (Malcolm Zickler) would have alerted his men and called in those on stand-by. He would then have had the patrols surround the craft and guard the surrounding area. ARRS would normally have been called if there was an aircraft down, but due to the close proximity of the base they would not have been involved. The British authorities, such as the Ministry of Defence Police and Special Branch, would have been informed, and of course the CIA.

So did the AFOSI investigate, I wanted to know? According to Diana Persinger, a few years after her husband's retirement they received a visit from Special Agent Steve Smith. He was a fairly new recruit in 1980, having served only seven months in the agency at the time of the incident. Smith was trained in technical security with Defence Logistics and had been stationed in Britain a long time. The Persingers were casually chatting about Bentwaters, and when Diana brought up the subject of the UFOs Smith told her he had been involved in the investigation. However, he refused to discuss the matter in any detail, except to say that the information was 'buried' in Washington. Persinger told me that the AFOSI files were never stored at any installations they worked on, and personal files on the AFOSI special agents and the agency's manuals were kept at Randolf Air Force Base, Texas, along with all Air Force personnel files. Thanks to Wayne and Diana Persinger, the puzzle was beginning to fit into place. At least there was confirmation that the AFOSI did do an investigation.

What was to be even more surprising was that Diana Persinger had also encountered a UFO during that Christmas week. She described what happened when she was driving home from a late shopping trip with her young daughter:

> I was driving up the road towards the Woodbridge base, we lived on Woodbridge, and I saw this big UFO. It was suddenly on the top of me, over the car. It was very low, with lights all around. I couldn't define the shape but it seemed to be round. I pulled off the road to have a look, but it just disappeared. The next day I told some of the wives. There was an officer's wife, I can't recall her name, but she went out there with some people, camping in the forest looking for them. After that I never heard anything until I saw the TV programme and read about it in the paper. I was quite pleased because it confirmed my sighting. Even though it was me who saw it, Wayne refuses to accept that's what it was. He said it was a helicopter. I suppose it's all right to talk about it today as it's been a long time now.

Amazing! The wife of the deputy commander of the Bentwaters AFOSI was a witness to one of the UFOs and her husband tells her it was a helicopter. It seems none of the wives were in the loop. However, Diana still believes it was a UFO, and considering she lived on a military base, surely she would know the difference between a helicopter and a UFO. Thanks to documents collected by seasoned researcher Francis L. Ridge, I learnt that the USAF have used the helicopter term for a number of UFO sightings. Ridge had taken an interest in declassified UFO Freedom of Information files and had discovered several military documents that referred to 'unidentified helicopters'. As one reads through the files, in some instances the words 'unidentified helicopters' later become 'UFOs'. The reports are clearly UFO sightings but have been disguised by substituting the word 'helicopter'. For example: 'October 27. Loring AFB, Maine. "Unidentified helicopter" penetrated the base perimeter and on one occasion came within approximately 300 yards of the weapons storage area . . .' It is interesting that all these incidents occurred on installations known to deploy nuclear weapons. What is even more interesting is how the USAF has a problem identifying a helicopter. Persinger's rationale was that there really are some very secret helicopters that are used for covert operations. In fact, he told me about one he had seen in Vietnam that had the capability of throwing down a beam of light which could light up an entire area.

When I asked Wayne Persinger what the AFOSI would term an investigation like the Rendlesham Forest incident, he said they would call it 'Damage Assessment'. He also left me with some cryptic clues. Having told him I believed the AFOSI and the CIA were responsible for silencing the witnesses, he surprised me by replying: 'Well, it worked didn't it.' When I asked him about the UFO, he answered me with a question that gave me the impression he knew the answer. He asked, 'Did they track it when it left?' I suddenly realized that there was no information about the UFOs being tracked when they left Rendlesham Forest, and that had me thinking. Although there are rumours that the USAF retrieved one of the UFOs, I am not convinced. Nicholas Redfern's 1999 book, entitled *Cosmic Crashes*, covers these theories. Possibly one reason why it was not tracked is because they did not leave in the normal sense. After all, the witnesses make a strong point of saying the UFOs just disappeared in the blink of an eye.

CHALLENGING THE SCEPTICS

With all the information laid before us it seems obvious that the witnesses are claiming the objects were UFOs, but that does not necessarily mean they were extraterrestrial in origin. An unidentified flying object could mean any number of things the witnesses were unfamiliar with. We must also keep in mind that these were military men, educated in military hardware, and yet to this day they are still trying to understand what it was that landed in Rendlesham Forest in December 1980. With the extraterrestrial theory very prominent, the case has attracted its fair share of researchers, ufologists, sceptics, debunkers and, as journalist Keith Beabey pointed out, those who just want to make a name for themselves.

Drugged and Drunken Airmen?

American media sceptic Philip Klass has challenged ufologists with his remarks concerning the Rendlesham Forest incident. At a British conference in London a few years ago, he infuriated much of his audience when he suggested the witnesses could have been hallucinating on dope. High-ranking Air Force commanders have suggested the same, until I reminded them that these men were employed to guard a NATO base and it would not look too good for them to claim personnel were taking drugs. Needless to say, they all withdrew their arguments and admitted I had a point. When an Ipswich *Evening Star* journalist asked former Bentwaters commander Colonel Rudolph Wacker his opinion of the incident, he suggested that because it was the festive season, many of the guys had had 'quite a lot to drink'. It seems any excuse, even claiming security guards were drunk or drugged, is better than admitting they actually encountered a UFO. Let us not forget that this was a base that deployed nuclear weapons, and if the USAF allows their personnel to get drunk or take drugs whilst on duty then the Ministry of Defence ought to be employing more suitable British liaison officers to keep an eye on them. But I do not believe that the USAF allows this to go on. I know that both security police and law enforcement personnel are checked for drink and drugs at guard mount before going on duty. One point worth mentioning came from witness Jim Penniston. He suggested that if the commanders thought the men were drunk or on drugs, they should have checked this during the debriefing. According to Penniston, nobody was checked for either.

The Lighthouse Theory Explained

Ian Ridpath is still very sceptical about the 'landed objects', dismissing them entirely in favour of alternative theories for the lights in the sky. With all due respect to Ian, this is a typical sceptic move. It amazes me how sceptics can take one or two fragments of a case and claim to have solved it. Ian has offered various theories for the phenomenon. These include meteors, stars, a lightship and a beam from a nearby lighthouse. Having sceptics add their opinions to such an interesting case is certainly welcome, but when it borders on stonewalling it can be extremely annoying to those with a serious interest. Ian Ridpath is not alone in his belief that the Orfordness lighthouse was the main culprit; several sceptics, including the Suffolk Constabulary, back up his claims. Jenny Randles, who has offered several theories for the case over the years, has since become very sceptical. In *The UFOs that Never Were*, published in March 2000, she wrote a chapter entitled *Rendle Shame Forest*. Jenny concludes that some major elements of the case can be explained as mundane phenomena and tends to support Ian Ridpath's theories, crediting him for his foresight in suggesting the airmen had witnessed nothing more than the Orfordness lighthouse and heavenly stars. She even suggests the light from the far-off lightship was a contributing factor. Over the last twenty years, hundreds of hours have been spent debating the lighthouse theory as the obvious solution to what the UFO represented and rabbit scratchings as the cause for the landing marks. In my opinion, flying lighthouses and radioactive rabbit scrapings as the possible cause for the encounters are even more incredible than the encounters themselves. It is for this reason that I am sceptical of the sceptics.

The long-standing lighthouse theory first entered the public forum when Vince Thurkettle made it fashionable in 1983. Vince was a young forester caring for the Rendlesham and Tangham forests when he invited the press into his normally peaceful life almost three years after the incident occurred. At the time he had no idea his throwaway comment, that the UFO was probably nothing more than the beam from the Orfordness lighthouse, would become so valued by the world's sceptics. Aware that the witnesses had been led into signing statements and admitting that the UFO was the lighthouse beacon, I wondered if the media had been fed this untruth by the USAF or other official sources, or was it just Vince Thurkettle's theory? Without revealing my thoughts on the subject I managed to talk to the forester. Expecting to hear his well-publicized views, I was pleasantly surprised to learn that he was not amused by it at all. 'They take a cluster of facts and only pick up those that suit the situation,' he told me. It is refreshing to know that Vince is no longer so sure that the lighthouse was responsible for the incident. Indeed, he was never really sure to begin with. It was just a theory, after all.

I realized it was time I checked out the lighthouse theory for myself. Jacquieline Davis, one of the world's top female bodyguards, joined me on this trip, and I could not have wished for a better person to protect me against whatever might be lurking in the forest. Besides, should the occasion arise, she had promised to throw herself in front of a UFO to save me from being abducted by aliens. Whilst

I was not keen on the idea of being abducted, I may have secretly hoped to encounter a UFO. However, if it scared the hell out of dozens of military personnel, we would not stand a chance. Just the same, it was good to have her company.

We were invited to stay with Lieutenant Colonel Al Brown and his English wife Sally at their lovely home in Eyke near Woodbridge. Al is an American and long-time friend of General Gordon Williams, who, along with the general, was stationed at RAF Bentwaters during the 1980 incident. Gordon Williams had suggested I contact the couple if I intended to visit the area, but when I called Sally she insisted we stay at their home. Sally had prepared a delightful supper and, over coffee and dessert, Jacquieline and I listened to the highlights of Al's long military career and Sally's escapades as a young woman travelling the world. After supper we planned our midnight recce to Rendlesham Forest. I had no luck in persuading Al to join us, but Sally was certainly enthusiastic. Having filled a flask with hot coffee and changed into Al's old military clothes, I was ready for our mission. Now I know why Halt took time to change into proper field attire, those outfits certainly keep you warm.

The idea was to do a reconstruction by following the exact same route the witnesses had taken. When we arrived at the east gate we had to park the car beside the logging road because there was a barricade blocking the entrance. As we began walking into the forest we could clearly see the blue beam of the Orfordness lighthouse as it circled the sky. Admittedly, since 1980 many of the mature pine trees have gone, either through logging or due to the terrible storm of 1987 which demolished a large part of the forest. However, the route leading up to the site was still abundant with mature pines. As we approached the farmer's field on the edge of the forest – the area which is associated with the lighthouse theory – we spotted a bright shining object which pulsated every few seconds. The white star-like light, which appeared to be at ground level, was obviously the beam from the lighthouse. We then continued to walk towards the left of the field, as witness Colonel Halt claims he did, and noticed the white light had disappeared from our view and the flash of the blue beam appeared to change direction. When Colonel Halt and I discussed his whereabouts on the night he was involved, he explained that he was on the far left-hand side of the farmer's field, near a farmhouse. From this angle it is very obvious, by the way the beam hits the sky, that it is nothing more than the lighthouse beacon. It is also not possible to see the bright star-like light from this position.

Vince Thurkettle and I both agreed that if the men were looking for an object they had seen earlier in the forest they might have mistaken the bright pulsating light of the lighthouse for the UFO as they made their way towards the field. However, we also agreed that the men could not have attempted to chase this same light for any distance before realizing what it was. Ironically, Vince's earlier conclusions, that it was probably the lighthouse beacon the men saw, were backed up based on information that the incident occurred on 27/28 December, which was allegedly a misty night. Yet, according to Colonel Halt the night he was involved, which he now thinks was 27/28, was a very clear night. Of course, in those days nobody was certain that there was more than one night involved. Vince explained that on a misty night the lighthouse might give off a reddish orange glow, but it was usually a white pulsing light that would disappear as you walked down the hill towards it. Based on all the evidence I have presented for the case, I am not even going to discuss suggestions that the UFOs were lights from a National Security Agency building, the faint light from the *Shipwash* lightship, lights from a nearby police car or celestial stars. Sceptics may accuse me of trying to get out of explaining these objects, but the truth of the matter is far too much time has already been spent debating these theories, which I believe are of no significance whatsoever when one considers the case as a whole.

I would hope there is now enough of a reason to dispel the theory that the lighthouse was the culprit. Having been presented with more facts, both Vince Thurkettle and former policeman Dave King have reconsidered their original theory and have now admitted they are no longer certain that it was the lighthouse the witnesses saw. Let us also consider the testimonies of the witnesses themselves.

Adrian Bustinza was forced into agreeing it was the lighthouse when interrogated by special agents. Edward Cabansag denies he typed the witness statement, which claims they were chasing a lighthouse beacon. Charles Halt, Jim Penniston, John Burroughs and others are in no doubt that the lighthouse was not what they saw. Therefore, it looks as if the sceptics will have to turn to the AFOSI for support on this matter.

Rabbit Scratchings or Landing Marks?

Another famous quote Vince Thurkettle has been associated with was his comment that the ground indentations from the initial landed craft were nothing more than rabbit scratchings. I wanted to know how he came to this conclusion because it was approximately six weeks after the incident when he visited the alleged landing site. Vince explained that he was prompted to examine the area after a series of events made him more and more curious. The first occurred just before New Year 1980, when he was approached by two strangers asking unusual questions. He is not certain what day it was, but local rumours circulated that two men visited the area on New Year's Day, questioning everyone living near the forest. The spin on this story is that it must have been very important for the strangers to turn out on one of the most important holidays of the year. Vince disagrees with the rumours and confirmed the following. 'It could not have been New Year's Day because I would have been with my family, not out chopping wood for my fire.' Apparently, he was startled when the two civilian-suited men approached him because it was unusual to see smartly dressed people walking through the forest. The visitors wanted to know if he had been out in the forest the night before or at any time over the last four nights. The fact that they referred to four nights is very interesting, especially if we count from 25 December, it is a clue that the men were visiting on 29 December and not New Year's Day. Vince was told there had been a story going around that there were coloured lights in the sky and they were questioning the local residents to see if they had seen or heard anything unusual. Vince was not aware there had been any activity and was intrigued by the questions. I asked him if they had identified themselves.

> No, strange isn't it? I didn't think to ask who they were at the time because I was, I suppose, intrigued at what they were asking. I thought they might have been from the press but I never saw anything reported, so I realized later that they were not newsmen.

But why did he decide to visit the site six weeks after the events, I wanted to know?

> I was excited for about two weeks after the two men visited me. I was expecting something to happen but nothing did. After about four weeks one of the guys working in the forest asked me about a burned area out there and if I'd seen it. Apparently, his wife was out shopping with one of the commanders' wives and she told the forester's wife that there had been a lot of fuss because there was a burnt area in the forest. So he checked with me. That got me interested. Then a local saw-miller talked about there being a burnt area, so I enquired at the Forestry Commissioner's Office. They told me they didn't want the story to get out, but that it was now out anyway. This wasn't an official statement, we were talking informally. It was six weeks later, this is the pivotal bit, there were vehicle marks and Pepsi cans.

So now we learn that the Forestry Commission was somehow involved in the cover-up. I asked how he knew this was the site and wondered if he had seen the burnt area.

> I didn't. I assumed it was because of the military vehicle marks and the Pepsi cans. Americans always drink Pepsi, and of course there was the ring of sticks . . . No, I never saw the burnt area. It was a great disappointment to me because I was expecting to see something. There were three marks but they weren't all at the same angles. They seemed like ordinary depressions, like rabbit marks.

I asked him if he was sure he had visited the right spot because it was now six weeks after the event and it was known that the men had been partying in the forest since the encounters had taken place. Some of the officers' wives and teenage children were actually camping out in the forest, looking for UFOs, so the site he mentioned could have been a camp site – but it was the ring of sticks which would later intrigue me. Vince was not aware that several people had visited the site immediately after the event, or that plaster casts of the indentations had been made. I pointed out that by the time he had found it the site would have been trampled on and interfered with, and he agreed that this was possible. There were even reports that a false landing site had been prepared with an arrow marking the way.

Probably the best available evidence to prove that the markings at the initial landing site were not animal scratchings came to me unexpectedly from Ray Gulyas. Senior Master Sergeant Gulyas had enlisted in the United States Air Force on Friday 13 March 1959. He retired in 1963 after serving at a missile base during the Cuban crisis and for the next few years he was employed as a civilian policeman until he was recalled for active duty in 1966. He retired in 1982, moved to Alaska and now works for the government in a civilian job. Ray told me that he and Captain Mike Verrano investigated the initial landing site on 26 December. Armed with a camera and measuring instruments, the two officers followed instructions and found the site in a clearing inside the forest. Ray took photographs of the area, the indentations where the craft had landed and the marks on the trees. He also measured the width from each ground indentation, which he recalls being twelve feet centre to centre. The marks on the tree were measured with a ruler and were found to be five feet off the ground. Ray shot a roll of film, which he later gave, along with the measurements, to Captain Verrano. He believed Verrano passed the information to others in the chain of command. Ray was told that the film had come out completely fogged and he assumed this was due to radiation. Forty-eight hours later he returned to the site and took more photographs, as well as taking plaster casts of the indentations for his own curiosity. Only this time he decided to have a friend develop the film instead of turning them over to Verrano or the base photo laboratory.

It was early January before Ray was able to deliver the film to his English friend Richard Nunn. Fortunately, the film turned out fine and showed details of three indentations as well as the markings on the tree. Ironically, the film, negatives and plaster casts disappeared from his personal possessions when he was transferred to the United States in the spring of 1981. Ray gave me contact details for Richard Nunn, whom he said would confirm that there had been such a film, but it was unlikely he would have retained copies of the photographs after all this time. I trusted Ray and his wife Maryann, but we all agreed that there is nothing like hard evidence.

Richard Nunn had moved house twice since 1980 but it did not take too long to find him. This was made much easier thanks to an elderly gentleman called Fred Nunn who, by a twist of fate, was living in the very same street that Richard had lived in before leaving the area. Fred kindly offered to visit the local residents to try to find his namesake and fortunately managed to locate Richard's mother who still lived in the same family home. Mrs Nunn gave her son's telephone number to Fred, who in turn passed it on to me. When he called to say he had Richard's business telephone number, I was elated, but it was a bank holiday weekend and I would have to wait three days before I could talk to him. The suspense was killing.

It turned out that Richard Nunn was now living in Norwich where he owned a small photography business. He remembered Ray and Maryann Gulyas; they had been good friends back in 1980. When I enquired about the photographs, explaining how important they were, he knew what I was talking about and thought there might be a chance he still had the contact strip and promised to search through his old stock. A week later I was to learn that he had indeed kept a contact strip, six shots in all had been buried in his files for the last nineteen years. This was to be the first real evidence that pictures were taken of the landing site. It seems that the AFOSI had blundered on this one. Two weeks later I received a compact disc and the original black and white contact strip, which consisted of six pictures of a forest area. The strip revealed that it was Kodak Safety Film 5063. I contacted Kodak in London and spoke to Martin Wood who informed me that this particular film had been available since 1954 and is still being used today. I was rather hoping the code numbers would date the film more accurately, but was told that I would need to have the original negatives before any such research could be undertaken. However, that was no longer possible due to the fact that they had disappeared from Ray's personal belongings many years ago. Maybe the AFOSI had done a good job after all.

As with everything about this case, there is a twist to this story. Featured on one of the photographs is an exceptionally tall man in uniform. When the picture was blown up it looked very much like a British police officer. Ray could not recall the policeman, although he did suggest it had been a long time since he had taken the film. However, he told me originally that these pictures were taken forty-eight hours after he had shot the first film. This meant there should not have been a British policeman at the site because he had visited it on the morning of the 26th – or had he? On checking the original source of information, the 1983 Martlesham Heath Constabulary's letter to Ian Ridpath, I realized there was no mention of when PC Creswell had visited the site, only reference to a call from RAF Bentwaters and an officer attending, but no time or date was given for the visit. Could it be that the police thought it so unimportant that they waited forty-eight hours before checking it out? It was only when Jim Penniston confirmed he had spoken to the policeman on 26 December that I realized the officer must have visited the site that day. So who was the policeman? The other mystery was that Captain Verrano was also on the film. Of course, Ray could have been mistaken about when he took the photographs or may even have mixed it up with the original because it is a military standard film. Like he says, 'It's been a long time.' But then I asked him about the twigs that had been placed next to each depression and were clearly visible on the photographs: he was positive he had not put them there and could not remember them. Jim Penniston does not recall any twigs marking the site either, but it dawned on me that Vince Thurkettle had mentioned there being sticks at the site he visited six weeks later. But what was even more intriguing was that Colonel Halt had also referred to markers in his audio tape recording of the event. Halt: 'Let's, let's, let's identify that as point number one. That stake there. So you all know where it is if we have to sketch it. You got that Sergeant Nevilles?' Did Halt put the markers there or were they already in position when he investigated the site a few days later? I am just grateful we have the pictures to prove that there was a landing site. Of course, the sceptics will always argue that these photographs prove nothing but, knowing their history and the route it took to find them, I have no reason to doubt Ray Gulyas or Richard Nunn.

The following are descriptions of the six photographs after I had them enlarged. Unfortunately the close-up photographs of the marks on the tree were not among them.

1. Landing site. Photo slightly damaged (cracked) on right-hand side. Picture shows a clearing marked by twigs and a marking of a cross can be seen in the soil next to one of the twigs. There are two male figures in the picture. One is a tall man dressed in a dark uniform with a flat-rimmed hat showing a blurred light band. The other is a shorter man wearing a much lighter-coloured uniform and fits the description of Captain Mike Verrano. Neither man is wearing a winter jacket. The tall man, who is staring at one of the indentations, looks like a British policeman. I checked with former superintendent of Woodbridge police, George Plume, who told me that if the bobbies were driving they would have worn the flat hat, but would have changed into the traditional helmet when dealing with the public. However, he thinks that the officer who visited the forest would probably have left on his flat hat. The man in the lighter-coloured uniform is walking with his hands behind his back (Prince Charles fashion) and is several paces behind the other figure. It looks as if Ray was trying to photograph the centre of the landing site. There is a scuffed-up patch just off the centre which fits the

exact description and position to that mentioned in Colonel Halt's tape recording. A light can be seen through the trees showing that the photographs were taken during daylight.

2. Landing site. Picture features a clearing showing three twigs marking the indentations. Background view shows tall pines and ferns. Daylight can be seen through the top of the trees.

3. Forest area but too dark to identify.

4. Picture features a twig marking a triangular indentation. When the picture is blown up it is better viewed from a distance.

5. Picture shows a twig marking a triangular indentation.

6. Picture shows a twig marking a triangular indentation. This one is not so clear and might show traces of plaster because the edges are lighter coloured.

Tree Damage and Radiation

Although I have seen no photographs of the marks on the tree, I think there are enough witnesses to support that these were caused by something crashing against it. This is especially evident in Halt's tape recording. The overhead damage to the trees, as if something had fallen or crashed through them on landing, is not always discussed by the sceptics. Maybe this is because there is very little explanation for it other than the aforementioned. Ian Ridpath argues that the alleged burn marks on the trees were axe cuts in the bark made by the foresters themselves as a sign that the trees were ready to be felled. Vince Thurkettle pointed out that this is how they would test the trees to see if they were healthy. 'We would take out the weak trees. We would chip a bit off the bark to see if it was strong. I think that's what Halt was referring to on the tape,' he explained. It is very possible that Halt's patrol mistook the foresters' cuts for the marks made by the UFO. But if one refers to the tape recording made by Halt's patrol, it proves that there were stronger Geiger readings on the trees facing the suspected landing site and not on the back of the trees.

There has been considerable debate about the radiation readings recorded by Lieutenant Colonel Halt at the scene of the landing site. Ian Ridpath and Nick Pope continue to agree to disagree on the matter. Ian believes there is no evidence to support that the readings were anything unusual and questions the equipment used by Colonel Halt's patrol. Nick responded to Ian's concerns, agreeing on some legitimate doubts about the suitability of the equipment used to record the radiation levels, and further suggested that Halt may even have misread the dial on the Geiger counter. According to Halt's memorandum there were beta/gamma readings of 0.1 milliroentgens, with peak readings centred on the three depressions. Part of the damaged tree facing the depressions had moderate readings of .05–.07. My own concern about the readings is that because they were supposedly recorded a few days after the initial landing took place any radiation that might have been present would surely have depleted to some extent.

In April 1994 Nick Pope sought a professional opinion by contacting Giles Cowling at the Defence Radiological Protection Service, which is attached to Hasler, the Institute of Naval Medicine in Gosport. Having described the data in Halt's memorandum, he was informed that the readings were ten times higher than normal, but posed no threat to anyone who had been in the vicinity. Nick also asked Cowling if the readings could have been faked. Cowling confirmed it was possible, not at school level, but certainly at college or university level. Ian did not entirely agree with Nick's results and decided to write to Cowling himself. Cowling wrote back, explaining that it was difficult to judge the readings unless they knew what type of equipment was used. Nick accepted the valid points but expressed that he was working on information provided by the only source available, namely Halt's memorandum. He further explained that setting aside any debate about the precise level of the readings – on the basis that the readings can only be considered in their proper context – we still had to consider the events collectively, not individually. I have to agree with Nick when he points out the following:

> We have a sighting of a UFO, coupled with tree damage and indentations in the very same clearing in which the UFO was seen. Then we have radiation readings which, irrespective of how high they were, just happened to peak where the trees were damaged and in the very centre of the indentations. We should also remember the fact that Halt's memo explains how 'the animals on a nearby farm went into a frenzy' when the object was seen. While none of this proves that the UFO was of extraterrestrial origin, it seems clear that there was an object of some sort involved, which had an effect on the surrounding environment.

Considering that nothing unusual was supposed to have occurred, an incredible number of people were interested in the landing site. Later that morning several senior staff members visited the spot, and measurements, photographs and radiation readings were officially taken. The Americans must have thought it was a very real event, or why would they contact the Suffolk Constabulary at Martlesham to report that they had found a place where a craft of some sort had landed? It is unlikely that the USAF would waste valuable police time on something that was supposed to have been a 'non-event' and nothing more than a lighthouse that the witnesses had seen. One has to ask how a lighthouse could fly through the forest, smashing through the trees and leaving indentations in the forest floor. Some of the individuals who checked out the landing site were Colonel Ted Conrad, Colonel William Sawyer, Lieutenant Colonel Charles Halt, Captain Mike Verrano, Major Malcolm Zickler, Major Edward Drury, Master Sergeant Ray Gulyas, Master Sergeant Bobby Ball, Staff Sergeant Jim Penniston, Airman First Class John Burroughs, Squadron Leader Don Moreland (a week later), Lieutenant Englund, Sergeant Nevilles and a British police officer, to name but a few.

PANDORA'S BOX

As with all mysteries, the Rendlesham Forest incident has been a magnet for theories and rumours. Many of these have been bandied about for years, often exaggerated and written into UFO literature, then taken for fact by those unfamiliar with the case. Having already realized that there was no truth to the tale that Gordon Levitt's dog had died as a result of its encounter with the UFO, I also found no evidence that one local policeman had become an alcoholic or that another had been certified insane after their contact with the UFO. I came across several of these stories during my investigations and thought it a good idea to explain some of the more popular ones.

The Mysterious Officer's Wife

I mention this story because the officer's wife has turned up a few times in the life of this case, and she has become quite an enigma. It all started with Dot Street's visit to Larry Fawcett's home in the United States. Dot was sure Major Malcolm Zickler was involved and persuaded Fawcett to call him. Zickler was not at home but Fawcett managed to question his wife. She was aware of the incident and thought Fawcett should talk to Colonel Sawyer, who, she suggested, had been involved in the incident. Colonel Sawyer was not at home either, but Mrs Sawyer was very helpful and confirmed that her husband had indeed been involved. She talked of the first event as occurring on 26 December, followed by others around the

New Year. She recalled an incident with a damaged tree and told of her own frequent trips to the forest, which went on well into early January 1981. Apparently, Mrs Sawyer and a group of people, which included Colonel Ted Conrad's son, had made a trip to the forest in the early part of January when she had taken a movie film of a light through the trees. Fawcett asked to see the film but this seemed to cause Mrs Sawyer some nervousness and although she promised to send it, it never arrived.

The officer's wife was first brought to my attention during my interviews with Rendlesham forester Vince Thurkettle. Unfortunately, he could not give me a full account due to the lapse in time, but from what he recalled an officer's wife was out shopping with one of the foresters' wives soon after the incident and had described a scorched area in the forest where something had taken place.

Then, a couple of months later, Ray Gulyas told me about a video film which had been taken by one of the officers' wives. The wife, whose name he could not recall, had been watching the spectacle and decided to run home and grab her video camera and film the incident. The film was immediately confiscated and a couple of days later Captain Verrano was tasked with the job of delivering it to a waiting aircraft which was destined for Ramstein Air Force Base in Germany. This information was vital because as far back as 1984 Adrian Bustinza told a similar story to investigator Larry Fawcett and, more recently, confirmed it with me. According to Bustinza, he was responsible for arranging the security for the aircraft which had landed at the Woodbridge base.

In 1999 I listened to an officer's wife talk on a recording of the American *Sightings* radio programme presented by Jeff Rense. The woman did not reveal her full name but called herself Paula. She said she was the wife of a retired Air Force officer who had been the director of personnel at RAF Bentwaters during 1980. Paula claimed not only to have been involved in one of the December events but said she was actually with Halt's patrol, and that he had allowed her to look at the objects through a starscope. She then went on to tell listeners that she had taken a movie film of the lights and still had it in her possession. Bells began to ring. Who was this woman and where have I heard that story before? I checked with some of the former commanding officers and was told that the director of personnel had been Colonel Bill Sawyer, the same Colonel Sawyer who Larry Fawcett had tried to contact.

I have reason to believe that Mrs Sawyer and Paula are the same person, and could even be the woman Vince Thurkettle was referring to. Assuming I am correct, it is interesting to see how her story has changed over the years. Mrs Sawyer told Larry Fawcett she had visited the site in early January, but the mysterious Paula claimed it was December. I do know there was an officer's wife with a group of people who went out into the forest in early January. This group also included General Gordon Williams, Lieutenant Colonel Charles Halt, Lieutenant Bruce Englund and a teenage boy. It was interesting to hear Paula mention that she had gone out to the forest on several occasions after the initial events and that her husband had joined her on one of these nights. 'He had already been there with the official group,' she told Jeff Rense. The fact that Paula talks of her husband joining her on one of the nights in question but mentions that he had previously been with the official group, implies that she was not involved in the incident. But some female certainly seems to have been filming the event because we hear this story from credible people. There is no evidence that Colonel Sawyer was involved in any of the night-time events, but I was informed that he visited the landing site the day after the initial event. Considering he was the director of personnel, it is understandable that he would be interested, if only because it concerned base personnel. Jeff Rense was unable to supply me with Paula's telephone number or address because she requested to remain anonymous. However, I did manage to locate a Mrs Bill Sawyer and the lady who answered the telephone sounded very much like the lady on the radio show, but she denied it was her.

Part of a UFO or part of a Bomb?

One story to surface in the early days concerned a report that an object, possibly cylinder shaped, had been removed from Rendlesham Forest by a group of British soldiers. Certain ufologists theorized that this could have been something to do with the UFO incident, and for a long time it became part of the story. My own investigation has found no clues to substantiate this story. However, sometime in early December, British bomb-disposal experts were called to the Bentwaters installation to remove an unexploded shell weighing 70lb. The shell, no doubt dropped during World War Two, had been discovered on the new domestic site that was being built at the time. A few weeks later, on 22 December, just three days prior to the initial incident, another shell was discovered, and the bomb-disposal team were again called back to remove it. One might wonder if this could have had something to do with the object that was removed in Rendlesham Forest. Considering the danger of diffusing the shell on a NATO installation which housed nuclear weapons, is it possible that the shells were transported to a safer location – Rendlesham Forest maybe?

Malcolm Scurrah's Connection

Malcolm Scurrah is a systems analyst for the West Yorkshire Police, but in March 1979 he was stationed at RAF Coltishall in Norfolk. During his tenure at Coltishall he was often assigned on temporary duty at the highly sensitive radar site RAF Neatishead. It was on one of these assignments that Scurrah was involved in monitoring an unknown target at a height of 5,000 feet. Sometime after 20.00 hrs an unknown object came to their attention, primarily because it was not carrying an Identification Friend or Foe signal, and was capable of climbing at tremendous speed. The operators realized that this was an unknown because the only aircraft able to reach such heights was the American spy plane Lockheed SR-71 Blackbird, but even that was only capable of a steady climb. However, this object was achieving unusual manoeuvres which defied known conventional aircraft and at least one Phantom jet pilot was instructed to investigate. The pilot encountered a very bright light that disappeared at tremendous speed when he came to within half a mile of it. The following day two senior controllers, who were on duty the previous night, were quizzed by high-ranking RAF officers who had travelled from London specifically to debrief them. Following the debriefing other senior RAF officers turned up and confiscated the radar tapes for that particular incident. Scurrah told me that the only reason any radar tapes would be taken in this fashion is if they were needed for investigation, such as an aircraft crash, near miss, loss of aircraft and loss of lives. During this whole incident video images had been transmitted directly to West Drayton. A very interesting story, but what has it got to do with the Rendlesham Forest case? Well, although it has been directly linked to the December 1980 sightings, the incident did not in fact occur at that time, but happened earlier that year, in either October or November.

Scurrah was annoyed to find himself misquoted by UFO researchers, journalists and even the Thames Television *Strange but True?* documentary which aired in 1994. He claims he offered the programme's researcher the names of other witnesses to back up his story, but these were ignored in favour of linking the incident with the famous Rendlesham Forest case. Scurrah assured me he had never suggested the incident took place in December 1980. Ironically, even after the British *UFO Magazine* published Scurrah's story in their May/June 1995 issue, Malcolm Scurrah's testimony is still being linked to the 1980 Rendlesham Forest incident.

Alleged Death of a Witness

The rumour that the tragic death of teenager Michael Simms was as a result of him witnessing the Rendlesham Forest incident is questionable. Michael was the son of Lieutenant Colonel Simms, an officer who was based at RAF Bentwaters for eight years. I received an introduction to Colonel Simms from General Gordon Williams, who spoke very highly of the former Air Force officer. My conversation with Simms was strictly about the incident itself, which he was very sceptical about and which did not concern his son. According to rumour though, Michael had befriended some locals and shown an interest in UFOs, and it has been suggested that he personally witnessed one of the December sightings. This may have been true, but it is more likely that he was with one of the officers' wives who took some of the teenagers on trips to the forest, searching for UFOs following the initial events. Nevertheless, based on his alleged encounter with a UFO at Woodbridge, he was apparently murdered in his hotel room by the FBI during a brief visit to the United States. According to General Williams, this story is nonsense. Apparently young Michael was studying medicine in England and during the summer holidays had decided to take a back-packing holiday to the United States to visit long lost relatives. It was during this trip, whilst hitch-hiking from El Paso to Colorado, that he was tragically murdered. I believe there is no connection to the Rendlesham Forest incident whatsoever, and for the sake of his family it is high time this rumour was put to rest.

British Army Confront American Airmen in Rendlesham Forest?

I had heard a report that British UFO researcher Tony Dodd was informed by 'an impeccable source' that during the incident USAF personnel had had a 'stand-off' with British Army personnel from Colchester. The British Army chaps, having discovered the Americans were armed on British territory, had raised their weapons, with the Americans doing the same, in what could have become a dangerous confrontation. I asked Tony Dodd to verify the report. He confirmed it came from a good contact but was unable to supply me with the name or check further details because he had lost touch with the source. I have found no evidence to back up this story and, apart from Larry Warren mentioning it, none of the other witnesses recalls seeing any British military personnel in the forest. However, that does not mean it did not happen, but I wondered if Dodd's source could have confused it with another incident.

According to Major Edward Drury a similar situation did take place, but it was not connected with the Rendlesham Forest incident, and it did not occur in the forest area but actually on RAF Bentwaters. Drury read me the report from an American Air Force journal, which included his name. In August 1980, just four months prior to the incident, the Special Air Service were carrying out one of their exercises, attempting to covertly access the USAF base, when (unusual for them) they were caught and confronted by armed US security police. Could it be that Dodd's source had misunderstood the SAS exercise thinking it was linked to the famous incident?

DEFENDING THE REALM

Unidentified flying objects penetrating British airspace would be a matter for the Ministry of Defence, or so one would expect. However, the department does not admit that these incidents are cause for concern but, to put it bluntly, they insist they are of no defence significance whatsoever.

The Rendlesham Forest incident may have occurred on British soil but the airspace it penetrated was leased to the United States Air Force, so officially the UFOs over Woodbridge were not intruding British airspace. It certainly seems logical, but it was a point I had missed until the Americans brought it to my attention. Nevertheless, that does not account for the many UFOs that do in fact penetrate British airspace, and of course Lieutenant Colonel Halt's memorandum explicitly refers to an object that was hovering or on legs, which by anyone's estimation is low enough for it to be on British territory. It therefore stands to reason that our British defence departments would – or should – have investigated the matter. Yet the USAF was in Rendlesham Forest poking around and taking radiation readings when it should not have concerned them. Are we to believe that the Americans were allowed to carry out these investigations without permission from British authorities? It is understandable they would be in a hurry to investigate the first sighting, obviously thinking it could have been an aircraft that had crash-landed close to their installation. But that does not account for why they would continue investigating the incident for several days without permission from British authorities? But who would have given that permission and, what is more, was Britain involved in the investigation?

Britain and America had already sealed their friendship when they signed an agreement in 1940 which stipulated that they would share their secrets with each other. It was during the early 1940s that Britain's secret Government Code and Cipher School reorganized itself and changed its name to the Government Communications Headquarters (GCHQ), as it is still known today. Following this changeover another momentous deal was made between Britain and America. This was known as the BRUSA Agreement, an intimate pact that would further cement relations between the two countries and would require joint cooperation in handling super-sensitive material. In 1947 it became known as the UK/USA Agreement, and the Canadian, Australian and New Zealand code-breaking agencies were invited to become second parties. Britain's GCHQ was now a first party with the National Security Agency (NSA). As both agencies specialized in intercepting and decoding communications worldwide, part of the special agreement was that they had the right to set up listening posts on each other's territory. Indeed, soon after GCHQ moved into their new home in Cheltenham, the NSA moved next door. The NSA also set up offices in London. By 1951 they had seven establishments in British-controlled territories. Meanwhile, Britain's GCHQ set up a unit in Washington DC.

The UK/USA Agreement proves that Britain and the United States of America work closely together when it comes to international security. But what is important is that the agreement is between two very secret agencies, the National Security Agency on the American side and the Government Communications Headquarters on the British side. It stands to reason, therefore, that the Rendlesham Forest incident, which involved the USAF in Britain, would surely be of interest to both agencies.

Having realized the significant role of GCHQ, I learnt that Robin D. Cole, head of investigations for the Gloucestershire UFO Group, had come to the conclusion that this same agency are involved in the UFO agenda. Cole lives in Cheltenham, only a few miles from GCHQ. In August 1997 his detailed report on a UK UFO incident, alleging interest from GCHQ, went out live on the television main evening news. At 9 a.m. the following morning Cole received a telephone call from Cheltenham Special Branch asking if they could pay him a visit. Within ten minutes they arrived at his door, barely giving him time to set up a recorder that he managed to hide from view. 'I thought no one would believe me,' he said. Apparently, the reason given for their visit was to enquire about the activities of certain British UFO researchers. They wanted to know where they got their funding, and if they had terrorist connections. In other words, were terrorist groups funding them? Cole was not convinced that this was the real reason for their visit and suggested it was due to his public reference to GCHQ.

GCHQ are very much concerned with government intelligence operations but deny any involvement with UFOs. Cole discovered that Martin Redmond MP had addressed GCHQ's possible monitoring of UFOs in a Questions and Answers debate in the House of Commons. Redmond asked the Right Honourable David Davis, Minister of State for Foreign and Commonwealth Affairs

> If he will list by month for each of the last ten years and this year [1996] the number of occasions on which the Government Communications Headquarters has monitored unidentified flying objects.

Unfortunately, Redmond died a few weeks later and consequently a reply was not forthcoming. Cole wrote to Ministry of Defence employee Nick Pope, who during 1991–94 was appointed to secretariat (Air Staff) 2a. Cole wanted to know if he had had any liaison with GCHQ on any matters relating to UFOs. On 11 February 1997 Nick Pope replied:

> As you may know, it has been the long-standing policy of successive Governments not to comment on the operations of the intelligence and security agencies. I intend to maintain that policy. I am sorry to have to send what I know will be a disappointing reply, but I am sure you will appreciate that this can be my only response on such matters.

In his quest for the truth Cole also wrote to the director of GCHQ, Mr D. B. Omand, asking what tasks GCHQ had undertaken with regards to the UFO phenomenon. Surprisingly, Omand's response (dated 15 January 1997) was considerably more informative. Cole paid special attention to Omand's words '. . . we hold no information from our *normal* work which would shed any light on the debate whether UFOs have or have not ever been detected.'

> I would not normally reply to a letter of this kind, given it is our firm policy not to comment on intelligence operations. In this case, however, I would not want to leave you with any impression that we are concealing work on UFOs. We are not engaged in any way whatsoever in any monitoring for suspected UFOs, and we hold no information from our normal work which would shed any light on the debate whether UFOs have or have not ever been detected. So a nil return from us.

As with America's NSA, the GCHQ are an intelligence-gathering unit who supply information to other government departments, which include MI5 and MI6. Because they work so closely with the NSA, one would assume they would be aware if there was any breach of security resulting from unidentified aircraft. But if the very mention of their name prompts a visit from Special Branch, it is no wonder that government employees refuse to be coerced into discussing GCHQ business. Cole questions why, with the end of the Cold War, would GCHQ be expanding their operations. I do not think this is directly related to the UFO situation for although the Cold War is over the threat of terrorism is greater than ever. Whilst I am against a cover-up concerning the UFO agenda, I am equally glad we have an intelligence force capable of suppressing terrorism. However, Cole is positively convinced GCHQ are involved in investigating UFOs, and claims to have been given inside information to that effect. If this is the case, then that would account for the Ministry of Defence's lack of interest in the matter.

One has to imagine what reaction Lieutenant Colonel Halt's

memorandum must have had on the Ministry of Defence employee when he received it that morning. This was not the usual civilian UFO report from Mr and Mrs Average that inevitably arrived on his desk from time to time. This was an official report signed by a deputy base commander serving with the USAF at an RAF installation in Britain. Surely the employee in DS8 would think it important, if only because it was accompanied by a covering letter from an RAF officer, who clearly made a point that they were UFOs. It is obvious that the recipient of this memorandum would not simply file it away without checking with a higher department. The question is, what was that department? There had only ever been vague references to a department dealing with air-defence matters of this nature, namely DI-55, but it has never been officially acknowledged by the MOD.

Whoever was in charge of assessing the Rendlesham Forest incident at the Ministry of Defence must have thought it was too important to follow it up with Lieutenant Colonel Charles Halt or Squadron Leader Donald Moreland. In a situation as delicate as this, the most logical step would be to contact the wing commander at RAF Bentwaters or, if the incident was of greater concern, his superior at RAF Mildenhall. If, on the other hand, the matter was of little concern, Moreland might have received a courtesy reply to his letter, if only to inform him that it was of no defence significance. But the Ministry of Defence continue to remind us that it was more than two weeks after the events when Halt wrote the memorandum. Why did it take two weeks to consult the Ministry of Defence? You would think that the wing commander would have contacted Her Majesty's Government immediately, rather than wait for the lower ranks to deal with it. But Colonel Halt claims the reason the events were not reported to the Ministry of Defence sooner was because the British liaison officer, Squadron Leader Donald Moreland, was on holiday. But that seems like a lame excuse because Moreland has since confirmed that he returned to the base approximately seven days prior to the memorandum being written.

In Nicholas Redfern's book *A Covert Agenda* there is a conversation with Nick Pope, which took place in 1994 while Pope was still working in Sec (AS) 2a (commonly known as the UFO desk) at the Ministry of Defence. Pope told Redfern that there were very few official papers on the Rendlesham Forest incident and intimated that the file started not in 1980, after the incident, but in 1983 following *The News of the World* article. This seemed unlikely so I checked with Nick Pope, who told me:

> I think I can see where the confusion has arisen. The earliest papers that the Ministry of Defence has on this incident are, of course, Halt's memorandum itself and Moreland's covering letter. However, the Ministry of Defence underwent a major administrative reorganization in 1985. It was at this time that DS8 ceased to exist and that responsibility for investigating the UFO phenomenon passed to the newly formed Sec (AS) 2a. This was an administrative nightmare and involved old files being closed and new ones opened. To further complicate the situation, the Rendlesham Forest papers had originally been placed on a general file containing details of various other UFO sightings. But at some later date all the papers on the incident were extracted from the file and placed on a new file dealing exclusively with the Rendlesham affair. The upshot of this is that although there were various copies of Halt's memorandum and Moreland's letter on the file, the first paper was, as I told Redfern, *The News of the World* report. In other words, the papers had gone out of order and the originals had probably been left on the general sightings file. I'm not sure why I would have told Redfern that I hadn't seen Moreland's letter, I can only assume that for whatever reason I made a mistake. I can appreciate that this complex sequence of events sounds a bit sinister, but in fact it's nothing more than MOD bureaucracy in action. Any civil servant will be able to tell you that this sort of thing goes on all the time.

I admit I was surprised to hear this explanation, but realized that one of his predecessors, Pam Titchmarsh, had used a similar excuse. When researcher Dot Street asked Titchmarsh why she had been told that the Ministry of Defence had no file on the case, Titchmarsh's response had been that she was not with the department in

1981 when Dot made the call, and suggested that the file might have been temporarily mislaid, adding, 'things sometimes get filed in the wrong place'. I find it interesting how often the Rendlesham Forest files seemed to have been misplaced by the Ministry of Defence.

However, I can confirm that Nick Pope was aware of Squadron Leader Donald Moreland's letter being in the MOD files. Having spoken to Moreland and discussed the item with him, I mentioned this to Nick, who suggested that I request a copy under the terms of the Code of Practice on Access to Government Information. I was glad I followed this advice because Moreland's covering letter turned out to be a valuable document. Not only does it prove that the Ministry of Defence were sent a copy of the memorandum on 15 January 1981, but it also revealed that an RAF officer refers to 'unidentified flying objects' and not mere lights in the sky.

I wrote to Ms Gaynor South at the Ministry of Defence, this time requesting information and documents pertaining to their interest in the case – or lack of it. I wanted to know about a letter that they had sent to the public affairs office at Bentwaters and Mildenhall which in part stated: 'the incident was not considered to indicate anything of defence interest'. Reference to this letter was mentioned in a Bentwaters cable, dated 6 November 1984, sent to Ramstein Air Force Base, Germany, and RAF Mildenhall. I asked about documents pertaining to the results of the assessment for the Rendlesham Forest incident. Reference to this report was made by Nicholas Soames on 24 July 1996 and by Lord Gilbert on 14 October 1997. I also asked Ms South to supply me with the name of the department responsible for carrying out the assessment.

On 23 July 1999 I received a reply.

Dear Ms Bruni

Thank you for your letter of 29 June regarding the alleged incident at Rendlesham Forest.

When the Ministry of Defence was informed of the events that are alleged to have occurred at Rendlesham Forest/RAF

Woodbridge in December 1980, all available substantiated
evidence was looked at in the usual manner by those within the
MOD/RAF with responsibility for air defence matters. I believe
the Directorate of Air Defence would have looked into the case
but this branch no longer exists. The judgement was that there
was no indication that a breach of the United Kingdom's air
defences had occurred on the nights in question. As there was
no evidence to substantiate an event of defence concern no
further investigation into the matter was necessary. Although a
number of allegations have subsequently been made about
these reported events, nothing has emerged over the last
nineteen years which has given us reason to believe that the
original assessment made by this department was incorrect.

Yours sincerely

[signed]
Gaynor South

Ms South only responded to the last question and totally ignored the
first two. But it seems there was a Ministry of Defence department
that looked into the case, the Directorate of Air Defence. By far the
most outrageous denial by the Ministry of Defence came, not from
a civil servant but from a man important enough to know better.
Researchers on this case have never forgiven Michael Heseltine when
he wrote to the Right Honourable Merlyn Rees MP, in response to
a request made by one of Rees's constituents, Mr Philip Mantle,
himself a researcher on this subject. In relation to the Rendlesham
Forest case, Heseltine stated categorically that there was no unidentified object seen on radar. According to my MOD source, the
Directorate of Air Defence was only concerned with radar reports,
but the fact that the Ministry of Defence admit that one of their
departments did look into the incident is contradictory to what they
originally told the USAF at RAF Bentwaters and Mildenhall. The
Bentwaters public affairs officer, Captain Victor Warzinski, who
seemed to have worked overtime denying this case, sent a telegram
(August 1984) to Ramstein Airbase, Germany:

Matter was referred to British MOD who would have juris-
diction. I have another letter from MOD saying they did not
investigate the incident, saying the incident 'was not considered to
indicate anything of defence interest'.

I have pondered long and hard on the response of the Ministry
of Defence to this case. One does not want to believe they would lie,
and one cannot blame them for being evasive or offering cryptic
replies when it comes to defence issues. But considering they allude
to the incident as not being a defence issue, one questions their
record of early denial that they had no files on the case in 1981 when
in fact they did. Ms South's letter to me is also cause for concern,
especially when she refers to the 'alleged' incident. Considering she
had access to the Rendlesham Forest files (at least the minor ones),
Ms South should know that there is no such thing as it being an
'alleged' incident. This is surely an insult to former military officers,
Colonel Charles Halt and Squadron Leader Donald Moreland, who
wrote to the Ministry of Defence referring to the incident. One only
has to read the contents of these documents to know that it did take
place. Therefore, Ms South's assumption that it was an 'alleged'
incident is grossly erroneous. But Ms South is from a long line of
MOD employees who have played down the Rendlesham Forest
incident, some of whom require lessons on how to deal with requests
from researchers.

On 19 June 1984 Mr A. Mathewson, a civil servant in DS8 at
the Ministry of Defence, wrote a response to investigative journalist
Mark Birdsall. He suggested Mark pay attention to the press reports,
stating, 'If you followed the press articles on the Woodbridge
incident you will have seen the results of a good deal of investigative
journalism which turned out quite rational and down to earth
explanations for what was seen.' Needless to say, he was not referring
to *The News of the World* article which, strangely, turned out to be
closer to the facts. He continued: '. . . as I recall, one favourite explanation was the light from the Orfordness lighthouse.' Mathewson
then points out: '. . . we do not attempt to investigate reports to a

point at which a positive explanation can be made. I can assure you, though, that there is no question of anything having intruded into British airspace and "landed" near Woodbridge.' It seems to me that if the Ministry of Defence have to refer to the press for information, and do not investigate these cases to a point where a positive explanation is made, how then can they conclude that a UFO did not land near Woodbridge?

Nick Pope suggests the Ministry of Defence did not investigate the incident, but some department certainly did, for I do not believe Britain would allow the United States complete control over an incident that occurred on British territory. However, witness Jim Penniston, who had top-secret clearance when he was stationed at RAF Bentwaters, informed me that Britain was unaware of 99 per cent of what the Americans got up to on the Suffolk bases. According to some locals who lived near the installations the Americans did as they pleased.

As early as 24 October 1983, Member of Parliament Sir Patrick Wall addressed the Secretary of State for Defence regarding Lieutenant Colonel Halt's memorandum and its release. One question he asked Minister John Stanley in a written Parliamentary Question was whether he would now release reports and documents concerning similar unexplained incidents in the United Kingdom. Needless to say, Stanley's reply, though long-winded, basically referred to these reports as being of no concern from a defence standpoint. Since then, of course, there have been several parliamentary questions asked about the Rendlesham Forest incident.

On 24 July 1996 Labour MP Mr Martin Redmond asked Her Majesty's Government to respond to questions about the Rendlesham Forest incident:

> Mr Redmond: To ask the Secretary of State for Defence (1) what responses his Department made to the report submitted by Lieutenant Colonel Charles Halt relating to events in Rendlesham forest in December 1980; what interviews were held; and if he will make a statement. (2) Who assessed that the events around RAF Woodbridge and RAF Bentwaters in December

1980, which were reported to his Department by Lieutenant Colonel Charles Halt, were of no defence significance; on what evidence the assessment was made; what analysis of events was carried out; and if he will make a statement.[2]

Nicholas Soames, Minister of State for the Armed Forces at the Ministry of Defence, replied: 'The report was assessed by the staff in my Department responsible for air defence matters. Since the judgement was that it contained nothing of defence significance no further action was taken.'

Should there be an incident involving UFO activity, especially if it concerns military personnel, we know that certain government agencies are interested, but what about world leaders, where do they come in, are they in the loop? One would certainly imagine so. However, as a result of my investigations on this subject, I am convinced the majority of world leaders are not briefed about the full nature of the UFO/ET situation – if at all. Most Western leaders usually serve only one or two terms in office and as such it would not be necessary to burden them with ET politics. File PREM 11/855, obtainable from the Public Record Office, proves that not even Winston Churchill was in the loop. The Prime Minister's personal minute dated 28 July 1952 is directed to the Secretary of State for Air, Lord Cherwell. Churchill queried:

What does all this stuff about flying saucers amount to? What can it mean? What is the truth? Let me have a report at your convenience.

It took ten days for the Air Ministry to reply to Churchill's concerned request, and the reply did not come directly from Cherwell himself, although he wrote privately to the Prime Minister agreeing with the following report.

[2] WA 423.

Prime Minister
The various reports about unidentified flying objects described
by the Press as 'Flying Saucers', were the subject of a full
Intelligence study in 1951. The conclusions reached (based
upon William of Occam's Razor) were that all the incidents
reported could be explained by one or other of the following
causes:
(a) Known astronomical or meteorological phenomena
(b) Mistaken identification of conventional aircraft, balloons,
birds, etc.
(c) Optical illusions and psychological delusions
(d) Deliberate hoaxes
2. The Americans, who carried out a similar investigation in
1948/9, reached a similar conclusion.
3. Nothing has happened since 1951 to make the Air Staff
change their opinion, and, to judge from recent Press
statements, the same is true in America.
4. I am sending a copy of this to Lord Cherwell.

Unlike most prime ministers, who tend to leave the intelligence
agencies to get on with it, Margaret Thatcher wanted to be on the
inside. Indeed, her interest in Britain's intelligence matters goes back
to well before she actually became Prime Minister, and it is known
that she was regularly briefed by both MI5 and MI6. Once elected,
she became the first British Prime Minister to sit on the top-secret
Joint Intelligence Committee meetings. Even today, it is suggested
that she continues to act as a liaison in intelligence matters between
the United Kingdom and her allies.

Margaret Thatcher had already pointed out to me that the UFO
phenomenon is not something the people should know about. She
is not alone in her concern over keeping this information out of the
public domain, and one might speculate that there are very good
reasons for doing so. One of the major concerns being the Church,
others are a close second behind and include fear of a stock-market
crisis, revolutions and anarchy. So are we being protected from the
truth for our own benefit or are our protectors doing it for theirs, or
is it a bit of both? Even supposing they are aware, what leader would

have the courage to stand up and announce to his/her citizens that we have been visited by UFOs or, worse, have made contact with aliens.

Of course, there are other reasons for not making a fuss about the Rendlesham Forest case. If the weapons storage area at RAF Bentwaters secretly deployed a stockpile of nuclear weapons then it was in the UK/US's interest to keep it from becoming an issue. It was one thing to have to fob off a bunch of local ufologists, but it was quite another to bring to attention an incident involving unknown aircraft penetrating the airspace of a nuclear weapons NATO base. Better to dismiss it as a non-event, that way questions do not need to be addressed.

Between 1950 and 1980 there were an astonishing thirty-two reported accidents involving nuclear weapons on British installations. In 1998 *The Sunday Telegraph* newspaper revealed how Britain had come close to disaster when an atomic-bomb accident occurred at RAF Lakenheath on 16 January 1961. The information did not derive from the Ministry of Defence but was obtained through the American Freedom of Information Act, because Lakenheath was, and still is, leased to the USAF. The journalists also managed to recover 'secret telegrams' sent from the US Embassy in London to the State Department in Washington DC.

The incident occurred when a warplane, loaded with a bomb, caught fire on the runway. Fortunately for all our sakes the fire was extinguished, but not before the bomb had become scorched and blistered. The US Embassy reported that the bomb had remained intact and there was no radiation release in the area. Nevertheless, the casing on the bomb had begun to deteriorate under the intense heat and had the bomb exploded it could have caused a Chernobyl type disaster, contaminating the Suffolk countryside for hundreds, maybe thousands, of years to come. *The Telegraph* also revealed other accidents that were equally alarming.

Five years earlier, at 14.39 hrs on 27 July 1956, just two weeks prior to the Lakenheath and Bentwaters UFO incident, RAF Lakenheath had a serious accident when a B-47 bomber with no weapons on board went out of control during a training session. The plane, piloted by Captain Russell Bowling, slid off the runway, crashing into a bomb dump containing three nuclear weapons. All three bombs were showered with burning fuel from the exploding fuel tanks, and a cable reporting the incident said it was a miracle that one of the bombs with 'exposed detonators' did not explode. Needless to say, better precautions were taken following these events. But so serious was the accident that the base fire department were ordered to ignore the burning B-47 with its four badly burnt crewmen and concentrate on dowsing the flames engulfing the Mark 6 nuclear bombs. Terrified base personnel fled the area in panic, but the local community was not warned of the impending danger. Had the bomb exploded, thousands of people would have been killed and the entire area of Suffolk turned into a desert.

In 1996, after *The Telegraph* first exposed accidents involving nuclear weapons on British bases, the US Embassy in London was flooded with media and public demands for information. The American Ambassador, William Crowe, wired Washington for details of the incidents and advice on how to deal with the numerous enquires. The telegrams revealed that the press and public should be informed that there was 'no evidence that there had been a nuclear-weapon accident or incident involving US forces or weapons in the UK which has resulted in a release of radioactivity to the environment'. However, it was still a denial because there had indeed been an incident involving US forces and weapons in the UK. Apparently, a Freedom of Information report revealed that the US State Department had prepared a more detailed statement about nuclear incidents in Britain, which included a Greenham Common accident. In this instance two British scientists from Aldermaston were called to the installation and found radiation around the base, which they concluded could only have been caused by a nuclear accident. However, it appears the Ministry of Defence prevented the release of this file.

It is interesting that although there were reports that the United States Embassy in London had sent a naval representative to investigate the Rendlesham Forest incident, the Embassy denied any knowledge of it. On 13 August and 22 August 1984 respectively, Mark Birdsall received written replies to his requests for information from the Embassy's chief warrant officer, A. B. Rowley, US Navy Operations Coordinator, to this effect. Since the US Embassy was instructed to deny the near-nuclear accidents, it stands to reason we cannot trust their denial in this matter.

Not even the former Chief of Defence Staff, Lord Hill-Norton, was privy to information regarding the Rendlesham Forest incident. When he tabled a written question to the House of Lords on 14 October 1997, concerning Halt's memorandum and a landed craft in Rendlesham Forest, Lord Gilbert responded with the following: 'The memorandum, which reported observations of unusual lights in the sky, was assessed by staff at the MOD responsible for air defence matters. Since the judgement was that it contained nothing of defence significance, no further action was taken.'[3]

It is worth noting that Lord Gilbert refers only to 'unusual lights in the sky' when in fact Colonel Halt's memorandum mentions an actual metallic object. How the Ministry of Defence dismisses the Rendlesham Forest incident as having no defence significance remains a complete mystery. (a) We either have a very stupid defence system; (b) they do not know how to deal with it; (c) the Americans were/are in control of the situation; (d) another British department is overseeing the UFO agenda; or (e) the evidence is being suppressed for other reasons. I am not convinced that our great British defence system would fall into category (a). Therefore, it leaves little doubt that it must fall into one of the other categories or all of them for that matter.

On 28 October 1997 Lord Hill-Norton asked Her Majesty's Government to respond as to whether allegations to the effect that nuclear weapons had been stored at RAF Bentwaters and RAF Woodbridge in violation of UK/US treaty were true. Lord Gilbert replied, 'It has always been the policy of this and previous

[3]WA 169.

governments neither to confirm nor deny where nuclear weapons are located either in the UK or elsewhere, in the past or at the present time. Such information would be withheld under exemption (1) of the Code of Practice on Access to Government Information.'[4]

In the same Questions and Answers session Lord Hill-Norton asked Her Majesty's Government if reports that a UFO had allegedly aimed a beam at the nuclear weapons area on the Suffolk installations were true. Unfortunately, Hill-Norton erred in his question by referring to RAF Woodbridge and not its sister base RAF Bentwaters. In 1980 there were no nuclear weapons stored on the Woodbridge installation. Lord Gilbert replied, 'There is no evidence to suggest that the Ministry of Defence received any such reports.'

It is clear that Lord Hill-Norton either suspects, or more likely knows, that nuclear weapons were stored at the installation. Indeed, when commenting on the Rendlesham Forest incident on a network first ITV documentary on UFOs, he actually called it a *nuclear base*. Could this be one reason there is such secrecy surrounding the incident?

> It seems to me that something physical took place. I have no doubt that something landed . . . either large numbers of people were hallucinating, and for an American Air Force nuclear base this is extremely dangerous, or what they say happened did happen, and in either of those circumstances there can only be one answer, and that is, that it was of extreme defence interest . . .

When I asked General Gordon Williams if he would comment on whether nuclear weapons were deployed on RAF Bentwaters, he replied:

> This is a tender area . . . the long-established policy to 'neither confirm nor deny' has stood up well. In fact, inadvertently, it's been brilliant.

[4]WA 232.

It certainly has stood up well; I received similar responses from other senior officers who served at the base during that period. Lieutenant Colonel Malcolm Zickler, then the major in charge of the Security Police and Law Enforcement Squadrons, apologetically replied with the official line. Nevertheless, several of the men who served under Zickler's command have insisted there were 'nukes' on Bentwaters, and they should know considering it was their job to guard them.

In October 1998 an interesting declassified top-secret Ministry of Defence document was released through the Public Records Office, which proves that USAF installations in Britain were harbouring nuclear weapons as far back as the 1950s. The document, which was part of a file marked 'Nuclear Retaliation Procedures' and dated 13 March 1961, revealed how Britain would respond should a nuclear attack wipe out the United States of America. In order to retaliate, Britain would need to have secured the nuclear weapons deployed on the US bases in Britain. But in the event that the Americans refused to cooperate for lack of orders from their now defunct higher command, senior civil servants recommended that the British Army should be instructed to shoot the US officers in order to seize the weapons. The MOD briefing document states: 'In any case, we could get hold of the bombs even if it meant shooting the American officers concerned.' Frank Mottershead, the deputy permanent secretary of state at the Ministry of Defence, approved the paper.

Of course, at that time the government may not have been aware that the USSR had secretly placed nuclear weapons in East Germany to target Britain. The operation was discovered by Dr Matthias Uhl who was recently given access to Russian military archives. The weapons had a payload of 300 kilotons of TNT, more than twenty times the force of the bomb dropped on Hiroshima. In fact, the weapons only had a range of 750 miles, so America was safer than Britain in those early days.

It is no secret that US cruise missiles were deployed at the Greenham Common and Molesworth bases. Once word was out, however, the Greenham Common site, then leased to the USAFE, was surrounded by hundreds of women and children who began living in disgustingly filthy conditions at a makeshift peace camp situated outside the perimeter fence. Top bodyguard and covert operator Jacquieline Davis spent several weeks under-cover at Greenham Common. She recalls being disturbed in the middle of the night by a Ministry of Defence police officer urinating on her face. It seems this was one way they relieved their boredom, another was to smear faeces on the tent poles. There has been much specula-tion that Greenham Common was none other than a front for Bentwaters, where the real missiles were stored. One wonders just how different the Rendlesham Forest case might have turned out had the forest surrounding the Suffolk bases been overrun by the Greenham Common protesters.

Lord Lewin, Admiral of the Fleet and the Chief of Defence Staff in 1980, was a great supporter of the United States Air Force in Europe. In fact, Lord Lewin visited RAF Bentwaters on several occasions and eventually retired to live near Woodbridge, where he died a couple of years ago. Apparently Lewin was also a supporter of nuclear weapons and argued the need for Britain's cooperation with NATO on this very subject.

Although no high-ranking American officer will openly admit that nuclear weapons were deployed at Bentwaters, there is a clue perhaps: it seems that RAF Bentwaters carried out exercises that still remain classified. On 30 June 1998 Member of Parliament Matthew Taylor posed a question to the House of Commons regarding the USAF and an exercise carried out in the United Kingdom:

> MR MATTHEW TAYLOR: To ask the Secretary of State for Defence what was the scenario of the exercise, Proper Watch, in 1989; on what dates and where it took place; if the United States Department of Defense took part; and if he will place a copy of the results of the exercise in the Library.[5]

[5] Written Answers 130.

DR REID: Exercise Proper Watch took place at RAF Bentwaters in May 1989. The exercise tested the procedures in place for responding to the crash of a US transport aircraft carrying nuclear weapons. The United States response forces participated in this exercise. A classified report on the exercise does exist, but for the reasons my hon friend the Under-Secretary of State for Defence gave to the hon Member on 31 July 1997, Official Report, column 470, and under Exemption 2 of the Code of Practice of Access to Government Information, I am not prepared to release the report.

Based on all the evidence it seems obvious that there is a continuing cover-up to hide the details of the Rendlesham Forest incident. Could it be because there really was a threat to the nuclear weapons? I asked Nick Pope if he thought the incident was a defence issue.

The Ministry of Defence has consistently said that these events were of no defence significance. As somebody who has researched and investigated UFOs for the MOD I can tell you that I regard this whole business as being of extreme defence significance.

Much has been made of the radiation readings concerning the initial incident, but what if there was a threat more terrible than an isolated case of radiation?

George Wild is a resident of Osset, a small market town in West Yorkshire. Several years ago he told UFO researchers he had heard that Highpoint Prison in Suffolk was to be evacuated on the night of 27 December 1980. Before his retirement Wild had been a senior prison officer at Armley Prison in Leeds, and it was during a prison officers' seminar that he first heard the story. Apparently, he had struck up a conversation with a prison officer from Highpoint who claimed to have received instructions that they might have to evacuate the building due to a possible incident that could occur late that night. Furthermore, the officers were told it was a matter of national security. The evacuation never took place but the report attracted the attention of Lord Hill-Norton who posed a question in the House of Lords.

On 23 October 1997 Hill-Norton asked Her Majesty's Government:

> Whether staff at Highpoint Prison in Suffolk received instructions to prepare for a possible evacuation of the prison at some time between 25 and 30 December 1980 and, if so, why these instructions were issued.[6]

Lord Williams of Mostyn replied:

> I regret to advise the Noble Lord that I am unable to answer his Question, as records for Highpoint Prison relating to the period concerned are no longer available. The governor's journal is the record in which a written note is made of significant events concerning the establishment on a daily basis. It has not proved possible to locate that journal.

According to a local police spokesman, Highpoint Prison used to be an RAF training camp before it became a prison. Initially, it was known for its sloppy security and was notorious for many prison escapes, but since then the security has been stepped up. I could not understand why the government would want to evacuate a prison, but realized it had to involve something of major importance for the government to risk transporting hundreds of prisoners to another location. But was it anything to do with the Rendlesham Forest incident? I decided it was time to talk to George Wild.

Wild not only confirmed the story, but also added that Highpoint was not the only prison to receive the briefing. It turned out that another Suffolk prison was also put on standby for an evacuation. This was the Hollesey youth correction centre, a few miles from Woodbridge. Wild explained that these were ideal establishments to use in an emergency because they are so well isolated,

[6] QA 216.

especially Highpoint. If there was any danger to the area, surely the locals would have been informed, after all one would think their safety was as important as the prisoners'.

It was only later, when I read Brenda Butler's files, which she kindly sent to me, that I found there were more references to the prison evacuations. As early as February 1982 Brenda had heard from a friend of hers, a local police officer, that Hollesey correction centre were told to be prepared for evacuation on 27 December. The alert concerned something happening at RAF Woodbridge which might affect national security. Following this report Brenda received a letter from a prisoner at Blundeston prison near Lowestoft. He claimed to have seen a silver object from his prison cell window at approximately 9 p.m. on the night of 27 December. He also wrote that the prison was on a standby alert and promised to contact Brenda on his release because he had managed to get access to the prison officers' files. But Brenda never heard from him again.

George Wild specifically pointed out that the night of the standby was 27 December. This is interesting because, assuming it is connected with the Rendlesham Forest incident, it means that the government were not expecting the visitors on the first or second night, but were obviously preparing in case another incident occurred on the third. But it still did not make sense. Why would they need to evacuate the local prisons? Were they expecting an invasion or an attack? If that was the case then the establishments would be ideal for prisoner of war camps. But would it not be more sensible to secure prisoners in the USAF bases or in one of the many RAF installations scattered throughout East Anglia? I concluded they were preparing for the worst – a possible biological hazard posed by alien contact. In the event of such a threat, the prisons would be used as isolation units.

Bentwaters and Woodbridge were not the only bases to be experiencing unusual activity during December 1980. RAF Watton, approximately thirty-five miles north of Rendlesham Forest, was home to the Royal Air Force. The installation was closed down several years ago, but in the late 1970s and early 1980s it was the busiest area-radar unit in Europe. It was responsible for handling all the USAF movements in and out of Lakenheath, Mildenhall, Bentwaters, Woodbridge, Alconbury and Upper Heyford. One former RAF officer recalls how hectic it used to be when Lakenheath were practising procedures, such as Surge, Launch and Recovery. They would think nothing of sending eighty F1-11s up at the same time, and that was the easy part, getting them back again was a real challenge. With that level of USAF activity it was considered important to have a USAF liaison officer around to smooth things out if the going got tough. There was also a Royal Navy controller assigned to RAF Watton.

On 27/28 December 1980, two RAF police-dog handlers were on night shift when sometime around midnight they were tasked to investigate strange lights coming in from the north, near the airfield fence to the west of RAF Watton. Less than ten minutes prior to their assignment, both ground and air radar had picked up (as it was later called) 'a large moving air target of unknown type', and the station duty officer was in a terrible flap. The two airmen arrived at the fence to discover several figures shining what appeared to be green and blue lights into the sky. The following statement is taken from one of the witnesses, whom I have named Harry Thompson (pseudonym).

> They were about 100–150 yards away from us, and when we turned our searchlight on them they ran off very quickly. We only saw the figures for a little while in the searchlight and these didn't always work. We both got the impression that their clothes were silvery and bulky and appeared to suck in – or not reflect the light after a few seconds. They wore visors which looked like they were split in two halves, like big eyes. We had to use infrared light because we couldn't see them in the normal searchlight. The dogs started going crazy and wouldn't obey the code words, which was 'Trifle' to bite and 'Custard' to stop. Anyway, we made our report and were told to continue our patrol.

The morning after the incident, a high-ranking British officer questioned Thompson and his colleague. The men were advised to forget what they had seen because it was only poachers and it was now a matter for the local police. Neither of the witnesses believed the poacher story and, as Thompson recalls, their notebooks covering that particular night were immediately confiscated. He also claims that the duty log in Operations and the occurrence log went missing. According to Thompson, the loss of one of these logs would result in a major investigation and in the case of RAF police would never happen.

According to Thompson, for several days after the incident Americans visited the forest around the perimeter of the Watton base. Just after the New Year Thompson was at the local public house, and whilst in the company of a couple of civilian police from the area he remembers joking with them about the locals filling their freezers with poached sheep and venison. It appears that the local police were unaware of any poaching activity during the night in question, though it was known that poachers did operate in the area all year round. They were also surprised to hear about the unusual lights and had not been told that Americans were messing around in the forest. Were these the same American scientists who were reported to have been investigating Rendlesham Forest?

Thompson had more to add, explaining that immediately after the Watton incident a team of four British government scientists, supposedly from the Ministry of Defence Research Centre, Porton Down, were driven to the forest by another of his colleagues, also an RAF policeman. Once in the forest, the scientists changed into strange-looking space-type suits with tubes running into air compressors which seemed to be connected to their backs. The police officer was left waiting for them while they wandered off through the trees. On their return they changed back into their clothes, packed their suits and climbed into the vehicle in complete silence. In fact, the only word they spoke during the whole time they were in the police officer's company was a simple 'goodbye' as they speedily departed. One cannot dismiss the possibility that there may be a connection between the Rendlesham Forest incident and RAF Watton. There are obvious similarities between the two: they occurred on the same dates;

the radar tracked a UFO; there were lights in the sky and strange figures in the forest. There was also an interview with a superior officer, suggesting the witnesses forget what they saw, and the government investigators turning up after the events. In fact the only thing missing at Watton was the landing of UFOs.

It is unfortunate that I am not able to supply the names of these witnesses, but Thompson wishes to protect his colleague who is still in the service and nervous of repercussions.

Several personnel at Bentwaters have reported strange visitors turning up after the incident. Colonel Halt, Adrian Bustinza, Greg Battram, John Burroughs and others have mentioned there were visitors arriving in unmarked aircraft. Jim Penniston and other non-commissioned officers were briefed and told to put the word out to their people to ignore any activity on the perimeter fence at Woodbridge. Penniston was told that a team had been brought in to do some electronics work, but he thought it strange because they were not wearing military uniforms. He later discovered they were a containment study team from the CIA's Langley Research Laboratory. I had heard from other personnel that a study team were sent out to investigate the site. But what was a CIA research team doing on British property?

It is interesting the CIA should send in their specialists, considering the USAF have their own, such as the Bioenvironmental Engineering Support Group, which is the equivalent of the Occupational Safety and Health Administration, the Environmental Protection Agency and the Nuclear Regulatory Commission. These specialists, known as Team Aerospace, would be responsible for surveying and evaluating environments and recommending controls to keep the environmental and occupational exposures within acceptable limits. Their primary aim is to promote the health and well-being of all Air Force personnel. Normally employed in the workplace, they use specialized survey instruments and equipment to collect samples and evaluate any hazards which may exist. They also perform environmental sampling such as air, soil, chemical, radiological or bacteriological.

Porton Down Research Centre, situated in Wiltshire, is one of the United Kingdom's most secretive and sensitive sites. Known as the Chemical and Biological Defence Establishment, it was founded in 1916 to combat German gas attacks. If this centre was involved in an investigation, then there is no doubt that the incidents which occurred during Christmas week 1980 were of great concern to both the US and UK defence departments. I also believe that should their results have proved positive then Highpoint Prison, and possibly others like it, would have been used to isolate those suffering with whatever virus or contamination the visitors might have brought with them. This would also indicate that, contrary to their denial, the Ministry of Defence and the CIA not only carried out an investigation but made preparations.

I spoke to a scientist who is familiar with Porton Down Research Centre. She explained that in the event of an unknown threat, all precautions would be taken. When dealing with the unknown, such as objects landing from space, you would aim for the highest level of isolation in case they brought an infectious agent. When I described the men in white suits with tubes attached to their backs, she explained that this attire would most probably have been used as a protection against dealing with an unknown microbiological threat. I had to conclude that if there was a risk of an unknown threat, it would be much easier to evacuate the local community in such a crisis, but the government would want to have the prisoners made more secure in case they later had to deal with a national disaster. The more I looked into the Rendlesham Forest incident as being a possible biological threat, the more I began to believe that this was indeed something that our defence departments were very much concerned about.

Lord Hill-Norton should be congratulated for his diligent efforts in trying to find answers to the Rendlesham Forest incident. In 1997 he wrote to Lord Gilbert at the House of Lords but was furious when Gilbert failed to respond positively to his questions. Hill-Norton replied to Gilbert's letter on 22 September 1997:

I have just received your reply (I presume that the illegible squiggle is your signature) to my Question for Written Answer of 31 July, about Colonel Halt's report on an incident at RAF Woodbridge, in 1981.

You have not answered my question, which was '. . . Did the MOD reply to the Memo from Lt Col Halt . . .', so I shall have to put it down again in a different form. The answer must be, simply, Yes or No. I need the formal reply for the dossier which is being prepared.

You may wish to know that his Memo, which has been in the public domain for 15 years, covers a great deal more than 'lights in the sky'. Five books have been written about the incident, of which the latest, published two months ago, is *Left at East Gate* by one Larry Warren, who was one of the enlisted men sent to investigate the violation of British Air Space.

Lord Gilbert replied to Lord Hill-Norton's letter on 16 October 1997:

Ministry of Defence Whitehall

Dear Lord Hill-Norton,
Thank you for your letter of 22 September concerning the alleged events at Rendlesham Forest of December 1980.

From Departmental records available from that period we have found no evidence to suggest that this Department contacted Lieutenant Colonel Charles Halt following receipt of his memo of January 1981 recording 'Unexplained Lights' in the area in December 1980. Some 16 years after the event we can only conclude, therefore, that it was not considered necessary to make further enquiries in the light of the lack of any evidence to suggest that the UK's Air Defence Region had been compromised by unauthorized foreign military activity.

It was then, and is still, the case that MOD does not routinely contact witnesses who submit reports of 'unexplained' aerial sightings. Follow-up action is only deemed necessary if there is corroborating evidence to suggest an unauthorized incursion of the UK Air Defence Region or other evidence of a matter of defence concern.

I hope this clarifies the position.

On 22 October 1997 Lord Hill-Norton replied to Lord Gilbert's letter:

Thank you for your letter of 16 October (it took five days to get here!) about my Question and Colonel Halt's Memo. It was good of you to take the trouble to reply.

I do not want to go on and on, but because you are new to this particular matter I would like to put you more fully in the picture. Your officials, and those (perhaps the same individuals) of previous Administration, have sought to pretend that Col Halt's report was only about 'unexplained lights in the sky', but as I said in my letter of 22 September it was about a good deal more than that.

So that there is no possibility of further misunderstanding I attach a copy of the Memo in full, and I beg you to read it yourself. From this you will see that he reported that an unidentified object breached UK Air Space and landed in close proximity to the US/RAF Air Base. He gives considerable detail about what happened at the time, and subsequently, together with physical evidence of an intrusion.

My position both privately and publicly expressed over the last dozen years or more, is that there are only two possibilities, either:

a. An intrusion into our Air Space and a landing by unidentified craft took place at Rendlesham, as described.

or

b. The Deputy Commander of an operational, nuclear armed, US Air Force Base in England, and a large number of his enlisted men, were either hallucinating or lying.

Either of these simply must be 'of interest to the Ministry of Defence', which has been repeatedly denied, in precisely those terms. They, or words very like them, are used again in your letter and I believe, in the light of the above, you would not feel inclined to sign your name to them again.

I could give you a great deal more evidence in similar vein, not only about this incident but about many others, but on this occasion I will spare you. I ought, however, in all fairness let you know that the routine denials by the Ministry – usually the ubiquitous Ms Phillips [sic] – will very soon become extremely damaging to its general credibility in this field.

Lord Hill-Norton did not receive a reply.

If it were not so serious one might be amused by Lord Gilbert's reply. The fact that the MOD does not routinely contact witnesses who submit reports of 'unexplained' aerial sightings, unless there is corroborating evidence to suggest it is a matter of defence concern, is preposterous when relating it to the Rendlesham Forest incident. Lord Gilbert seems to have paid no attention to the fact that the report was made by a USAF officer who was referring to an incident that occurred on the perimeter of a NATO base in Britain and – what is more – it contained nuclear weapons! No wonder Lord Hill-Norton lost his patience. It only proves what the ufologists have been saying all along, that the governments of the world will not admit it is of any concern until a UFO lands on the White House lawn.

On 5 July 2000 I questioned former Secretary of State for Defence Michael Portillo on the Rendlesham Forest case. Although he was aware of the incident, he pointed out that it was before his time. When I suggested that due to his former position he must have been briefed about the case and UFOs in general, and asked if there was anything he could tell me, he grinned and said, 'I know a lot but I tell a little.'

THE CIA FILE

When I first began investigating this case I realized there was far more involved than the initial encounters. The witness testimonies were incredibly confusing and there seemed to be so much disinformation at hand. I was beginning to think some of the witnesses might have been given screen memories. This could be achieved by the administration of drugs combined with hypnosis itself. Should the subject begin to recall the events, the created screen memory (false story) would be distorted and would therefore be recalled incorrectly. The other method would be to induce hypnotic amnesia, which causes the subject to forget all he is programmed to. Using either of these methods, the subject may never know that he was meddled with. These programmes are not fictional, they were designed to be used by the Central Intelligence Agency and the US military. Scientists working on these mind-control experiments were aware that the subjects could be deprogrammed at a future date by undergoing hypnotic regression, thus they decided to create multiple memories in order to confuse any attempt at getting to the truth.

Some of the witnesses in this case were required to report to the AFOSI, and there is no doubt that Jim Penniston was drugged. Larry Warren even claims to have been abducted by his interrogators and kept in custody for three days. Adrian Bustinza, John Burroughs and Jim Penniston were recalled more than once by the AFOSI. Could it be that they were victims of some type of mind control? The CIA claims these programmes are no longer operable, but there are indications that CIA/military agencies are still using this kind of agenda. If the Rendlesham Forest incident actually occurred, then it is reasonable to assume that any lengths would be taken to hide the truth.

I contacted British hypnotist David Bonner, who is a full member of the National Register of Hypnotherapists and Psychotherapists. I wanted to ask his advice on the drug sodium Pentothal and whether he had any information that the military might use it and, if so, for what purpose. I was not surprised to hear that it had been used by covert agencies during the Cold War. When the agents asked Jim Penniston if they could administer sodium Pentothal they explained that it was because they wanted to get the facts, and the drug would make sure he had not missed out any important details of his encounter. Penniston was aware that it was 'a truth drug' and agreed. However, he was not aware that he would also be hypnotized: they did not tell him that part. David Bonner explained that sodium Pentothal is not only administered as a truth drug but has various other uses. It can work alongside hypnosis by suppressing or implanting information, overriding the truth, blocking off certain memories and breaking down resistance. He also pointed out that 'trigger' words, sounds and smells can be planted into the mind and used at any time for whatever reason, even years later. According to Bonner, who has worked in those areas, the Secret Service used it for those purposes. It is no wonder then that the witnesses are still confused about what actually happened.

As strange as it might seem, I have wondered if the witnesses are influenced by trigger words or sounds. I discussed this with Bonner, who assured me it is possible. The witnesses claim they were watched for several years after retiring from the Air Force. If this is the case, were they still being controlled? During telephone conversations with some of the witnesses I was amazed to hear noises and voices coming through loud and clear, and in some instances I would find it difficult to hear the witnesses talking. But what was very odd was that they seemed oblivious to the sounds. I noticed though that after these peculiar noises they would clam up or suddenly change the direction of the conversation. It was as if a pattern was emerging, but for fear of worrying them I refrained from mentioning it.

However, I started making mental notes and watching for unusual signs.

I began to wonder if Penniston's, Burroughs' and Cabansag's 'missing time' was not as a result of their encounter with the UFO but the aftermath. Did the agents use drug-induced hypnosis to block off that particular time so that they would not remember? In recent years there has been an increase in alleged alien abduction reports and many of the victims to these strange encounters are claiming there was a military presence involved, and more often than not this is discovered during hypnotic regression. Realizing that it is possible to plant screen memories inside the minds of these people, we ought to question whether this is the work of aliens, government agencies or, for that matter, both. Are the so-called abductees really experiencing military intervention during these abductions in which they claim to have been used for medical experiments, or is it a screen memory planted by an alien force or a military agency to make them think so? I cannot imagine the military covertly and miraculously abducting humans from their bedrooms in the middle of the night and transporting them to some godforsaken place to carry out medical experiments. However, if aliens are the perpetrators of these abductions and a certain government agency is aware of it, then it is possible that the military would want to be involved, if only to keep track of these events and learn what the victims have experienced. After all, if the aliens have such advanced technology then it stands to reason that there is very little our governments or military can do about it but stand back, take notes and count the victims. Unless, of course, there is a joint effort involved. Like something out of an *X Files* episode, countless rumours exist that governments have done deals with certain alien civilizations, allowing them to abduct humans and slaughter cattle for experiments in exchange for advanced alien technology. As far-fetched and unbelievable as these stories appear to be on the surface, they should not be entirely dismissed. Too many retired military personnel are coming out of the closet and talking about their governments working with these projects. Of course we must also be aware of disinformation.

In January 1997 I interviewed retired USAF sergeant Dan Sherman, a man who claims to have been with United States Air Force Intelligence, working on a joint government/alien project called Project Preserve Destiny (PPD). Like most of the Rendlesham witnesses, Sherman began his military career as a security policeman. He was later assigned to the Electronic Intelligence programme and promoted to sergeant before going to work on PPD. Sherman's job with PPD was to sit in front of a computer screen for several hours a day and try to make contact with aliens. According to Sherman, he was contacted by the NSA and interviewed by a USAF Captain who told him that his mother had been abducted by aliens in the 1960s. Furthermore, whilst he was in his mother's womb he had been genetically implanted to enable him to act as an 'intuitive communicator'. Much to Sherman's relief the officer assured him he was not half alien. I interviewed Sherman, who I admit seems an intelligent individual, and he sent me his book, entitled *Above Black*, which tells the full story of his ordeal. It was only when Sherman began receiving abduction data, which he claims was monitored by the NSA, that he realized he could no longer carry on with his work. However, he had to take drastic measures to get a release from the Air Force because, apparently, they would not agree to his separation due to the secrets he had been privy to. For two years Sherman had received numeral data, but only when he became more knowledgeable did he realize the nature of the communications. He would receive information such as 'potentiality for recall', 'residual pain level', 'nerve response', and other such messages, including the latitude and longitude coordinates, and times and dates when the abductions were to take place. Dan Sherman's reason for going public with this information is because he wants other insiders to start talking. He believes PPD is only one of many alien projects that the US government is involved in. Some people may think Sherman's story is too unbelievable and accuse him of being a misinformer, but he has at least produced his Air Force documents and stood up to his critics. What is interesting is that several of the witnesses have had earlier encounters with UFOs. These have all taken place on military bases and although they were only sightings in the sky they are still worth mentioning here. One former Law Enforcement officer with the USAF believes that some members of the Security Police Squadron are being trained for certain covert operations that they are not aware of. According to Sherman, others like him, who were implanted in the 1960s, were expected to join the military.

Dan Sherman reveals that operating under the Black Project programmes are several agencies answerable to America's National Security Agency. The NSA's head office is situated at Fort Meade, and it is probably the most secure building in the world. The corridors of power certainly do exist here – and corridors there are, dozens and dozens of them, all leading to various different departments. In fact, the security measures are so tight in this establishment that in order to gain access to certain offices one is required to pass through state-of-the-art security procedures. These include retina scanners and metal hand-shaped plates capable of reading fingerprints.

According to Sherman the PPD project was so secretive that it was classed as 'above black', and was known to those in the loop as 'grey matter' or 'slant missions'. He points out that PPD and other alien programmes are not classified because on the surface they simply do not exist. He says there is an alien cover-up buried deep within an 'onion effect' – so many layers – and for every alien project there is a black project hiding it. Apart from the image portrayed to the public, there are five levels of security inside the military alone. Level 5, For Official Use Only (FOUO), was created to keep tabs on unclassified information, for should sections of FOUO be pieced together it could form a picture of a higher classified project. Level 4, Secret, protects the unauthorized release of secret information which could cause serious damage to national security. Level 3, Top Secret, is used to compartmentalize the release of information, and by using coded words it also protects black projects/missions. Level 2, Black Missions, is the highest cover for black projects – the latter being high-level covert operations. The existence and operations of Level 2 are known only to a handful of congressmen and the President of the United States. If government officials become inquisitive, they might be made to feel important by being briefed on the black missions and told the need for secrecy. However, unbeknown to the President and others, Level 2 also acts as a cover for Level 1, which is the top level known as the grey area and is exclusively reserved for alien projects. This level is known only to those directly involved, and those serving Level 2 are unaware that their work is a cover for such programmes. To complicate matters even more, Sherman points out that there are different categories within Level 1 which are called steps. These act rather like compartments, with each person in each compartment corresponding on a need-to-know basis. With a system like this, it is little wonder that the so-called alien project is still very much under wraps. If, as some believe, the Rendlesham Forest incident involved an alien agenda, then it is very probable that the evidence and documentation would be buried deep within Level 1.

There is no doubt that something very unusual took place in Rendlesham Forest during the last week of December 1980. We may never learn the full story concerning these extraordinary events but, as a result of my research, I am convinced there is a cover-up of enormous proportions to keep this and similar incidents hidden under a veil of secrecy. Creating a cover-up is no easy task and for something as universal as this it requires a great deal of effort and resources.

The UFO cover-up as we know it spans several generations and it is the most difficult one to penetrate. This may be due to it being so compartmentalized – on a strict need-to-know basis. We hear of people's lives being threatened if they reveal information pertaining to this cover-up. We hear of military personnel staying silent for fear of being set up with phoney offences, court-martialled and thrown out of the service with threats of losing their pension or being imprisoned. Some people would not even talk to me about this subject for fear of receiving a home visit from some agent, and both civilian and military personnel have reported strange encounters with mysterious men after witnessing these unusual events.

But if all this were true, then surely it would need massive funding to pay for such covert activity. Indeed, a covert funding system does exist and is well known to researchers and journalists as 'The Black Project'. No one is absolutely sure where the money for this project is obtained, or where it goes for that matter. Until recently not even congressmen in the US government were aware it even existed. 'The Black Project' is actually an umbrella term used for numerous covert projects: the UFO/alien project might be just one of them. There are many theories and claims as to how this money is acquired, and some of these theories are so gruesome that they go beyond the realms of normal understanding.

Ex CIA agent Gene Tatum was apparently locked up for whistle blowing on his alleged involvement with a CIA drugs run. Although he kept certain documents which he claims prove there was CIA involvement in a Black Project drugs organization, the case has never been tried in any court in the land. Equally disturbing are the revelations by award-winning journalist Gary Webb, who has won nine awards for journalism, including a 1990 Pulitzer Prize. Webb stunned the world in 1996 when he disclosed in a series of articles that America's crack-cocaine epidemic was a result of CIA-backed Nicaraguan contras. Webb later wrote a book entitled *Dark Alliance*, which revealed the full story of his search for the truth and how he was harassed during his investigations.

If true, Tatum and Webb may have discovered a major source of income for America's Black Projects. But the thought of the CIA being involved in such destructive covert operations as putting hard drugs on city streets, thus encouraging youngsters into drug addiction, would shock any sane person. However, both Tatum and Webb named names, and these names are so well known in US government circles that if the accusations are false surely those being accused of such diabolical crimes would have challenged Tatum and Webb. Supposing the role of these operations is to fund certain Black Projects, then there is always a possibility that the UFO/alien project might be funded in such a way. That being the case (and it is merely speculation because although there are whistle-blowers who claim this is true there is no hard evidence), then there can be no uncertainty that whoever is involved in these projects is not doing it for the betterment of mankind.

The CIA was created in 1947 to serve as America's principal government intelligence collection and analytical agency. Its role was to work covertly in foreign countries, influencing events through propaganda or political and economic means. Since then they have been involved in a series of covert activities that break the barriers of their appointed role. MKULTRA was one such project, involving the testing of human behaviour; but the full horror of these experiments will never be known because the CIA purposely destroyed most of the files. In 1994 the then Director of Central Intelligence was urged to establish the Advisory Committee on Human Radiation Experiments, with the purpose of investigating claims that the CIA had used humans in radiation experiments. This came about because of a Freedom of Information request prompted by the 1977 Kennedy hearings and the book by John Marks entitled *The Search for a Manchurian Candidate*. The committee were unable to locate any files on human radiation experiments but managed to uncover more than one hundred and fifty sub-project files that the CIA had no doubt forgot to destroy. These were found in their budget and fiscal records which had not been indexed under the name of MKULTRA.

The enormous power held by the Director of Intelligence for the CIA can be summarized in part of a staff memorandum from the advisory committee staff to members of the advisory committee on human radiation, dated June 1994:

> The head of the CIA is the Director of Central Intelligence (DCI); he is also head of the entire intelligence community, which consists of the intelligence services of the military branches, the Defense Intelligence Agency, the National Security Agency, the National Reconnaissance Office and several others. The CIA is currently divided into four directorates: Operations (DO), Intelligence (DI), Science and Technology (DS&T), and Administration (DA). DS&T was not created until 1962, and

Operations used to be called Plans (DDP). In addition, there are a number of CIA components that come directly under the DCI's control (DCI Area), including the General Counsel, the Inspector General (IG), the Controller, the Office of Congressional Affairs, the National Intelligence Council (which produces National Intelligence Estimates (NIEs)), and the Center for the Study of Intelligence (which includes the CIA Historian).

The CIA's possible involvement in human radiation testing emanates from a reference in a 1963 CIA Inspector General's report on Project MKULTRA. The report states that additional avenues to the control of human behaviour were to include radiation, electroshock, various fields of psychology, sociology, anthropology, graphology, harassment substances and paramilitary devices and materials. The actual report is still classified but its language was referenced in the investigative reports of the Rockefeller Commission and the Senate Church Committee. The CIA admitted that it conducted human experiments using every listed avenue except radiation. Even supposing they did not stoop to using radiation on humans, the admittance that they used every other means is shocking in itself and surely enough to question the ethics of such alarming human experimentation in the so-called civilized Western world. What is more, who were the unfortunate human guinea pigs that were subjected to such immoral tests? One wonders if these laboratories are still in operation, and just how many government agencies are still involved in this kind of illegal research. Although MKULTRA was technically closed in 1964, some of its work was transferred to the Office of Research and Development within the DS&T under the new name of MKSEARCH, and was known to continue well into the 1970s.

On 4 May 1994 an American citizen by the name of Harlan E. Girard, wrote to the United States Senate accusing the intelligence community of causing the deaths of a great number of people as a result of their behavioural neuroscience research. What I found extremely interesting about Girard's claims is his references to the United States Air Force and the CIA working jointly in successfully diverting public attention from the crimes against humanity. Apparently, the proof of these allegations could be found in the accounts of several government agencies including the Air Force Office of Scientific Research and the Office of Special Investigations. I have no idea how much substance there is to Girard's claims except to say that a copy of his letter to the United States Senate came to me with several declassified documents pertaining to MKULTRA research. Having since spoken to Girard personally, I can confirm that he was involved in trying to get justice for the victims of these appalling experiments.

The Americans for Democratic Action seemed to be on the same track as Girard. In a document titled Resolution 412, used in their 1995 convention, they stated that the Intelligence Budget remained hidden in Air Force accounts. We now know that at least one USAF agency, the Air Force Office of Special Investigations, is directly involved with the CIA. Considering the Director of Central Intelligence controls all military intelligence agencies, it is no wonder that witnesses and players in the Rendlesham Forest case mention the CIA's involvement in the aftermath. Records prove that the CIA were involved in early experiments, which were conducted using the army for biological research involving LSD testing. These experiments were carried out for the CIA by the Special Operations Division of the US Army Biological Center at Camp Detrick, Maryland. However, it could not be stated that the CIA were directly involved in this or similar US-based projects because they are statutorily prohibited from engaging in operations within the United States.

It is understandable that the CIA, along with similar agencies, would have progressed in their field of research and become adept at using more sophisticated means. In the mid-1990s I was introduced to an individual who claimed to have been trained by a US intelligence agency as a psychic spy. Kane (an adopted name) is a British subject who is indeed a very clever psychic, and has proved this to my media friends and myself on numerous occasions, but it was his untold story that intrigued me most. According to Kane, several years earlier he had been visiting the United States and was asked by his host, who worked for the United Nations, to meet with some government agents. He was told he could make a lot of money by using his psychic powers to assist them in a certain project. Kane agreed to meet them out of curiosity. They gave him several tests which he passed with flying colours and they made him an offer he could not refuse. He was hired and taken to a special house in New York City where he and five other young men were put through daily mind tests. The house was very simply furnished in pale grey colours, with no pictures on the walls or ornaments around. Apparently this was so as not to clutter up their minds. They rarely left the building, which was highly secured, and when they did they were driven in a black Cadillac with black-tinted windows under the supervision of your typical 'men in black'. With the help of American researchers I was able to pinpoint the exact location of the property, which turned out to be in one of the most exclusive areas of New York City. In fact, one of the neighbouring properties was the residence of the mayor himself.

After several weeks of intensive training Kane was becoming concerned, realizing that something was not quite right. Every weekend the men would receive a visitor, who Kane described as oriental-looking. He always wore black and had a very aggressive character. He seldom spoke, but when he did, he did so in an odd sort of accent that was not familiar. The household staff would be very nervous when he was around. It was during one of these visits that Kane questioned his role in the project. Although he was already a talented psychic, the continuous mind games were beginning to cause him some confusion and seemed to be blocking his powers. Much to his amazement he was to learn that he was being programmed to get inside the minds of others and his first target was to be the president of a large American company. The idea was to plant Kane inside the company to disrupt the target's mind, destabilizing him so that he would have to resign. He would then be replaced by one of their own people.

When Kane realized what they had planned for him, being a

gentle soul, he made up his mind to leave, but realized the only way out was to escape. He fled back to the United Kingdom, which was not an easy task because he had now been given a new identity. Apparently, the agency continued to pester him until he finally left England to live in Europe. Before he disappeared he told me the people he had worked with were interested in UFOs and it had passed through his mind that the oriental-looking man was alien in origin. His eyes, according to Kane, were so penetrating that no one could look directly at them. That did not surprise me; Kane himself had strange yellow eyes. If you think Kane's story is too incredulous to be true, I suggest you read up on the CIA's psychic-spy and remote-viewing programmes. I am not suggesting Kane was working with the CIA, even he did not know the identity of those people, in fact he had his doubts it was the CIA. However, David Morehouse, a former officer with the US Army's Intelligence Security Command and Defense Intelligence Agency, came out of the closet in 1996, claiming he had been used by the CIA as a psychic spy. Morehouse revealed all in his book entitled *Psychic Warrior*. In recent years the CIA have admitted they carried out experiments using psychic spies.

The director of the CIA's Office of Scientific Intelligence (OSI – not to be confused with the AFOSI, known in Air Force circles as the OSI) in the early 1950s was Dr H. Marshall Chadwell. In a series of documents released through the US Freedom of Information Act is a memorandum from Dr Chadwell to General Walter B. Smith, the then Director of the CIA. Chadwell's memo notes the concern over UFO sightings and the security implications. He states '. . . immediate research and development on this subject must be undertaken.' Chadwell was a participant in the Robertson Panel of 1953, which comprised of a scientific advisory panel meeting to discuss unidentified flying objects. The panel was set up by the CIA and convened by the Intelligence Advisory Committee. The latter being composed of the heads of the intelligence agencies with the director of the CIA as chairman. The panel was chaired by H. P. Robertson, hence its name, other members were from military or

intelligence backgrounds. They concluded that UFOs do not con-
stitute a direct physical threat to national security, but any serious
researcher who has studied the subject of UFOs will have come to
their own conclusions and believe that the Robertson Panel was used
as a debunking tool.

Just prior to the public debunking of UFOs, and only months
after the UFO wave in June 1952, the deputy director of Central
Intelligence sent a memorandum to the director. The memo was a
lengthy report concerning the CIA's concern over UFOs, but the
following should prove that UFOs have been penetrating military
installations for at least half a century.

> Sightings of unexplained objects at great altitudes and travelling
> at high speeds in the vicinity of major US defense installations are
> of such a nature that they are not attributable to natural
> phenomena or known types of aerial vehicles.

Based on the contents of this memo alone, it is inconceivable
that the Robertson Panel would come to the conclusion that the
UFOs were of no threat to national security. It seems somewhat
obvious that due to numerous UFO sightings being reported by the
public at the time, some kind of damage control was needed. I have
to agree with UFO researchers who claim the CIA set up a perfect
public relations portfolio on 'How to Debunk UFOs'. This would
also be a perfect solution to hide the fact that investigations into
UFOs are still ongoing and, if this is the case, then the CIA are still
in control of the situation and no doubt they would have been
directly involved in the Rendlesham Forest UFO cover-up.

EXAMINING THE CAUSE

The Rendlesham Forest UFOs were said to have disappeared in a blink of light, somewhat similar to the blip we used to see when switching off old television sets. This really had me interested so I consulted science researcher Dave Pigott, who has a degree in mathematics and physics. Dave is familiar with the Rendlesham Forest case and has an open mind on the subject, and his honest answers were very welcome. I put forward the scenarios witnessed on both the major events and asked him if he could offer an opinion in terms which would not blow me away with science.

A Scientific Evaluation

When I described the yellow mist effect that witnesses say they encountered, he offered the following theories:

> Well, many things can cause this. Marsh gas has a yellowish tinge, and could look even more yellow if illuminated either from the inside or out. Or even localized mist (not uncommon in that area of the country) that has been illuminated with sodium light. Since it was night-time the only way the colour could have been discerned is if there was illumination.

In an earlier correspondence Dave also mentioned that the yellow mist could be sulphur based. His theories on how the hair on their bodies stood on end and the possibility of missing time are equally interesting.

This could imply a massive electrostatic field, but could also point at a warp field. Time and space would be severely distorted. It could also be pure fear on behalf of everybody. Missing time could come about with either fear, memory block or a warp field. If a sufficiently large field were generated, then they may have suffered a sort of static-relativistic effect. I should point out that all of this is pure conjecture. There may be rational explanations for the reported effect . . . Well, except that the reportage is flawed, but one has to give some credibility when multiple witnesses are involved.

In answer to my question about the UFO disappearing in an unusual blip, he suggested:

As to the switching-off effect, well, it was just that – a light switching off – or maybe the conjectured inertialess drive kicking in. One moment it's there, the next it's not. It could leave a residual retinal image that would fade, so it would look like a fading TV tube. The concept behind the inertialess drive is an extension of the ideas proposed by Dr Miguel Alcubierre, formerly of Cardiff University, now a professor at a university in Germany (possibly Munich). The idea is that you 'warp' the space ahead and behind you so that you don't actually move, you're just suddenly somewhere else. Alcubierre's proposal is taken seriously enough that his ideas (and indeed himself) are included in the NASA Breakthrough Propulsion Physics programme. If such a drive is possible (and the energy required is massive, but Zero Point Energy may provide it) then one could extrapolate that it could be scaled down to terrestrial use. It is proposed as a way of getting to other starts without suffering from relativistic effects and without taking years. Interestingly enough, Alcubierre came up with the idea while watching *Star Trek* and wondering 'Now how would a warp drive actually work?' He published his ideas in 1994. Other than that I can't really come up with a scenario that doesn't involve either a mistake (i.e. a lighthouse) or a hoax.

Weather Experiments

American researcher Peter Robbins speculates that some type of cloudbusting experiment may have been the cause of the Rendlesham Forest incident or, at least, was a contributing factor. Peter's research into cloudbusting techniques stems from his interest in Wilhelm Reich's science called orgonomy. Dr Reich, who was a student of Freud, published a paper in the 1950s claiming he had invented an unusual machine which could alter weather patterns. The cloudbuster, a rather basic contraption with pipes and tubes, could create atmospheric movement by drawing down energy from the atmosphere then grounding it in water. In 1954, just two years before the Orfordness research centre experimented with their atomic weather device, Reich began making plans to carry out a test in the Arizona desert. His aim was to determine if it was possible to reverse the deterioration of the desert environment.

Dr Reich's radical research went against conventional physics and led to him being tried and imprisoned for 'fraudulent claims'. His 1957 publication *Contact with Space*, which featured details of his orgone accumulation boxes, was burned by the US Government while he was serving his prison sentence. Reich's studies also involved UFOs, which he termed Eas, energy alpha-primordia. He came to the conclusion that the silence of the UFOs was similar to that of his own invention, the orgone energy motor. The bluish lights that surround the UFOs (as reported by the Rendlesham witnesses) were related to the blue lumination of orgone energy in vacua tubes, and their movements were compatible with the wave motions of orgone energy. He also concluded that the mathematical formula involved was the very same one he had been experimenting with during World War Two.

In the 1950s, Reich's research team at the Orgone Institute, Maine, complained of strange happenings of a negative nature. UFOs were constantly seen over the laboratory, when the atmosphere would be filled with a black gluey substance. The researchers began seeing weird apparitions in the form of gremlin-type creatures and small objects would suddenly disappear and reappear in different places. Some thought it possible that the team were under psychic attack. Tests were carried out which revealed that during these encounters some kind of stagnant air had surrounded the area. This he called Deadly Orgone Radiation. Apparently, it was so destructive, it caused not only trees and shrubs to wither, but drained energy from the researchers themselves.

Reich was convinced he was being harassed by UFOs and decided to find a way to terminate their presence. Using his own inventions, orgone energy and the cloudbuster, which he named the spacegun, he aimed at two UFOs hovering over the laboratory and caused them to fade out, which allegedly disabled their propulsion systems. This bizarre war on UFOs became an obsession with Reich, and prompted him to advise both the US government and the USAF of the battles he was fighting. Reich has been accused of being a cranky scientist, but what if the man was a genius? Followers of Reich claim that as a result of his research into UFOs he was harassed by intelligence agents who threatened his life. Reich died of a heart attack in his prison cell just fourteen days prior to his release.

If Reich's pioneering cloudbusting experiments could cause rain clouds, then we can be sure that the Orfordness atomic weather experiments were capable of causing freak weather conditions. Assuming Reich's experiments also attracted UFOs, it cannot be ruled out that the Orfordness experiments created a similar situation. If so, did they somehow leave open a window that they were unable to close? It has been suggested that a window of some kind exists in the Rendlesham area, and that UFOs are seen there on a regular basis. Indeed, when I visited the forest during the day and photographed the Woodbridge flightline I was surprised to see that the developed photograph showed three white balls of light that were not visible when I looked through the camera lens. Soon after taking the photograph my camera ceased to function and although the pictures I had taken were not damaged, the camera was deemed useless. I took it to camera shop and, without explaining the circumstances, asked the trained assistant to take a look at it. He was convinced there was nothing wrong with the workings of the camera and tried three sets of fresh batteries, all to no avail. He was totally baffled and could find no answer as to why the new batteries appeared to have been drained of power when placed in the camera. My colleague Neil Cunningham also had problems. His film turned out completely black but fortunately his camera was not damaged.

According to Dennis Bardens, the author of several books and articles on the occult, the RAF were indeed experimenting with cloudbusting forty years ago, which is interesting because this time frame fits in with the Orfordness experiments. In his younger years Dennis moved in prominent government circles and came into contact with many interesting people, including foreign scientists. American scientist Jack Sarfatti is convinced Dennis Bardens was an agent with British Intelligence. I have spent many happy hours in the Travellers' Club in Pall Mall, listening to Dennis talk about the paranormal and other related subjects, but I never imagined he had worked for British Intelligence. When I questioned him about this, he admitted he had been involved with the Air Ministry, which was also news to me, but if he had worked in intelligence he would not discuss it. He explained that the weather experiments involved seeding the clouds with silver, which would control rainfall.

On Tuesday 19 August 1997 journalist Judith Keeling reported for the London *Evening Standard* a story that she suggested was worthy of the *X Files*. It involved the 1952 Devon flood, which was considered one of Britain's greatest flood disasters. Keeling was questioning whether scientists had caused the severe damage with their rain-making experiments. North Devon Member of Parliament Nick Harvey was one of those investigating the matter. The theory was that the United States and Britain had attempted to produce rain by flying over the clouds and shooting chemicals into them. Former Member of Parliament Tony Speller, who became suspicious in the 1980s when one of his constituents claimed the flood had been caused by weather experiments, carried out an earlier investigation of his own. When Speller questioned the Environmental Department he was told that they had no knowledge of the matter. However, he was not satisfied and decided to check some old Ministry of Agriculture files where he discovered that, two weeks prior to the flood, aircraft had been involved in experiments near Salisbury Plain. Apparently there were two missing files and Speller concluded they were removed for security reasons and may not be released for fifty years.

Following the *Evening Standard* report, Paul Sieveking, an editor with the *Fortean Times*, wrote an interesting article for *The Sunday Telegraph* (14 September 1997). It also related to the 1952 flood in Lynmouth, Devon, which killed thirty-four people and was rumoured to a have been a weather experiment. Sieveking quotes declassified documents, which confirm that the British government experimented with cloud seeding with the aim of developing a rain weapon to bog down a Soviet invading force. These experiments, which began in 1949 and presumably continued until 1954 and in some cases 1957, were carried out all over the country. This brings me back again to the Orfordness weather experiments and makes me think that the government were doing far more than seeding clouds with silver. Although Dennis Bardens did not admit that the weather experiments were anything to do with defending ourselves from a Soviet invasion, he did mention that a special radar beam was used for similar effects. What else could this radar beam achieve? Was it also capable of shooting down spaceships? Admittedly, it sounds rather extreme, but if we take into account all the available information, we can conclude that these experiments were being carried out at Orfordness, and it is worth paying special attention to Reich's weather experiments. Maybe Dr Reich was not a mad scientist after all. What is also very curious is that both Reich and Nicola Tesla were experimenting with devices that could cause phenomenal weather changes, and both had problems with the US government. Tesla, a native Yugoslavian who emigrated to the United States, was one of the many scientific minds to be ridiculed for his inventions. His coil could produce up to 10 million volts of artificial lightning. In fact, Tesla's untimely suicide in a cheap hotel room was considered questionable, especially when his private papers relating to his special coil disappeared.

Cobra Mist and Cold Witness

The Cobra Mist, Over the Horizon radar theory has been promoted as a popular cause of the Rendlesham Forest incident, especially by ufologist Jenny Randles. However, in 1993 Dale Goudie, the information director of Computer UFO Network (CUFON), and his colleague Jim Klotz managed to acquire documentation on this project, which seems to prove that Cobra Mist could not have been responsible for the 1980 incident. CUFON were prompted to file for the Freedom of Information documents on Cobra Mist after reading *From Out of the Blue* (1991), an American-published update on *Skycrash*, authored by Jenny Randles. Goudie was not aware of the Orfordness secret installation mentioned in Randles' book, or the Cobra Mist project, and being a paper-trail investigator was curious to acquire information on the subject.

Goudie discovered that the Cobra Mist, Over the Horizon radar project at Orfordness, England, was operational from 1967 and terminated on 30 June 1973. The documents revealed that it was installed to detect and track aircraft, detect missile and earth satellite vehicle launchings and fulfil critical intelligence requirements. The project, which was a disaster from the very beginning, was a joint United States/United Kingdom effort negotiated as a result of the US/UK Agreement between the two countries.

One file that interested me was a letter sent to Goudie from Maxwell Air Force Base. This particular file linked the 81st Tactical Fighter Wing with Project Cobra Mist, and of course it was this very wing that was involved in the Rendlesham Forest incident. In response to Goudie's request, it appears that Maxwell AFB had retrieved the information he required from the actual history of the 81st Tactical Fighter Wing: Attachment (1) History of the 81st Tactical Fighter Wing, volume one, dated 29/30 April – June 1973.

Another declassified file, which stated 'National Security Information unauthorized disclosure subject to criminal sanctions', proves that the UK Ministry of Defence were working with the USAF on the Cobra Mist programme. The name on the document was James E. Miller, Colonel, USAF, Commander. This close liaison is interesting considering both the Ministry of Defence and the United States Air Force appeared divorced from each other when questioned about the Rendlesham Forest incident. I wondered if Colonel Miller had ever served at RAF Bentwaters and tried several times to retrieve his Air Force biography, but it was not listed with the USAF, which I found very odd. However, I did learn that he had been promoted to brigadier general.

The Advanced Research Projects Agency wrote a report that best details the history of Project Cobra Mist. The paper, entitled 'The Enigma of the AN/FPS-95 OTH Radar', was the combined research efforts of E. N. Fowle, E. L. Key, R. I. Millar and R. H. Sear. The document states that the OTH Radar, built to overlook air and missile activity in Eastern Europe and the western areas of the USSR, was the most powerful and sophisticated radar of its day. The programme management for the project was assigned to the Electronic Systems Division of the Air Force Systems Command at Hanscom AFB, Massachusetts. And support was to be furnished by the Naval Research Laboratory, with the contract to build the radar awarded to the Radio Corporation of America. The MITRE Corporation also began working on the project, with the USAF acting as a technical advisory committee to assist in the technical direction of the programme. The project was called the AN/FPS-95 with the code name Cobra Mist. In the United Kingdom it was classified at the security level of 'secret', and on its completion it was intended to be used jointly by the RAF and the USAF.

What I found most interesting from reading these documents, however, was the reason why the project was terminated. The system was plagued by excessive noise of an undetermined origin that prevented it from meeting its operational performance requirements. The appearance of mysterious 'clutter-related' noise affected the project at all times of the day, in all seasons, in all beams and all radio frequencies and in both polarizations, so it was not an isolated phenomenon. The greatest variations in the noise levels were found to occur between adjacent land and sea areas. But the research team concluded that the results of their land and sea experiments were not compatible with a meteor explanation of clutter-related noise and attempts were made to relate the noise to the 'meteor belt', which is located about one hundred kilometres above the earth, but this cause was also rejected. So serious were the problems that the control of operations at the site was shifted from the USAF and given to a civilian scientific director who had been recruited from the Stanford Research Institute. But they made no progress either, and in the absence of any convincing conventional explanation it was speculated that the noise could have been generated deliberately. Because there was a Cold War it was reasonable to suspect that countermeasures could have been put into operation due to the fact that Cobra Mist was engaged in surveillance of the then Soviet Union and Soviet Bloc countries. But the theory of covert jamming was eventually dismissed because it was not the conventional type and, if this were the case, it would have seriously violated international agreements. The research team determined that the strange legacy of the Cobra Mist 'clutter-related' noise was, in fact, anomalous and thus was never identified. It is worth recalling the weird noise phenomenon that followed in the aftermath of the freak weather conditions at Orfordness. Could this be the same noise that affected the Cobra Mist project? Eventually, a joint UK/USA scientific assessment committee was formed to analyse the situation. The committee offered ten recommendations that were briefed to the secretary of the USAF and the Ministry of Defence. The result of these briefings was to terminate the operations at Orfordness and the Ministry of Defence publicly announced the decision in London on 29 June 1973. The project had occupied the efforts of hundreds of people for an interval of several years and had cost the United States government between one hundred and one hundred and fifty million dollars.

I have to disagree with Jenny Randles, who wrote in *UFO Crash*

Landing, Friend or Foe that Cobra Mist was officially terminated at Orfordness in June 1983 and that another project called Cold Witness took its place during the eighties. Jenny links the closure with the release of Colonel Halt's memorandum. Apart from the fact that the project terminated in 1973, ten years earlier, I find it very unlikely that further projects would have been put into operation at Ofordness considering the failure and financial loss of Cobra Mist. The locals remember the dismantling of the enormous structures that consisted of numerous 60-metre-high masts, which looked rather like a giant spider's web inside a saucer-shaped area measuring 705 acres when seen from an aerial view. There certainly appeared to be no covert activity on the Island during 1980, and this is confirmed by local historian Gordon Kinsey in his book *Orfordness, Secret Site*. When the project was terminated, the local press reported the concern of the villagers. The parish council had coined a nice revenue by renting parts of the area to the Ministry of Defence and the forty locals who were employed at the site were instantly made redundant, resulting in an angry mob of technicians invading the building on 6 July 1973. Two of the men locked themselves inside the complex demanding their rights and anxiously seeking redundancy payments. Their employers, the Radio Corporation of America, finally settled by offering the men six weeks' redundancy pay.

Questions about a renewed RAF presence and the site being used as a bomb dump were later put to the then prospective parliamentary Conservative candidate for the area, John Gummer. The explanations given were that the bombs had been stockpiled for disposal in suitable weather, and the RAF were only there to collect railway sleepers from the former tracking station to use at other sites. Although they were supposed to have been cleared years ago, there were still numerous unexploded bombs beneath the marshes of Orfordness. This was because the area had been used on and off as a major bombing range for almost fifty years. By 1977 over 5,000 bombs had been discovered, many of them still unexploded. But due to obstructions, such as poor weather conditions and marshy terrain, only half of the area had been cleared. The work was scheduled to be completed by 1982. The only other station to move into the Orfordness research building was the BBC World Service, two years after the Cobra Mist project closed down in 1973, and much of the area is now in the hands of the National Trust. Due to the afore-mentioned and the lack of constructive evidence to prove otherwise, I can only conclude that Cobra Mist, or the project known as Cold Witness, did not cause the Rendlesham Forest incident. If such a project as Cold Witness ever existed it was unlikely to be operating from Orfordness in 1980. If anything, Cobra Mist itself was a victim of strange phenomena.

Before closing this chapter I discovered, thanks to researcher Nicholas Redfern, that the Ministry of Defence has now declassified several files on Cobra Mist and these are available at the Public Records Office. Nicholas pointed out that the late Ralph Noyes's name was mentioned in these documents, which caught my atten-tion. Noyes was a former Ministry of Defence official who retired in the grade of under secretary of state in 1977. He was well known to ufologists, having once worked at what is commonly known as the UFO desk at the Ministry of Defence and for his novel about an incident that closely resembled the Rendlesham Forest incident. The subject is obviously an attraction to the Ministry men, prompting Nick Pope to write a fictional account of the incident in his latest science-fiction books, *Operation Thunder Child* and *Operation Lightning Strike*, which he claims are based on fact.

Meteors and Meteorites

The RAF and USAF are very adept at explaining away UFO sightings by claiming they must be meteors or comets, and this may apply in some cases. Nevertheless, I am not convinced that the Rendlesham Forest incident comes into this category, although I am inclined to believe there may be a link with these objects. When a comet comes too close to the sun, its surface material melts and vaporizes into particles of dust and ice which will float endlessly in space. But if the path of the comet and the orbit of earth intersect, the particles produce what is known as a meteor shower. As earth passes through the debris of the comet, the particles enter our upper atmosphere and become superheated, thus turning into meteors. As long as the particles remain in space they are referred to as meteoroids, but if they survive the trip through earth's atmosphere and hit the ground they become meteorites.

Barry Greenwood sent me a copy of his April 1999 newsletter entitled 'UFO Historical Revue', which features interesting material on meteors. Barry is what I would call a 'healthy sceptic', and I tend to respect his opinions which are based on dedicated research. I was intrigued to read that during the 1947 blitz of flying-saucer reports, the planet was being blasted by a meteor shower which lasted throughout that duration. Barry refers to a report in *Science News Letter*, dated 23 August 1947. Dr A. C. B. Lovell, the then director of the University of Manchester's radar research programme, told the British Astronomical Association that 'pips' from a meteor shower were detected as early as May 1947 and continued through to August – a period of three months. This would have placed the famous Roswell incident bang in the centre of that time frame. Although Barry does not seem to support the theory that the 1947 alleged crashed UFOs were alien spaceships, he does offer an explanation to believers, suggesting that the saucers could have been hit by the meteor showers. What an excellent theory! Considering that the debris would have been moving at incredible speeds of approximately 2,650 mph, it is very possible that anything in their path would be hit. Barry's research on the subject caused me to look again at the early reports of 25 December, when people all over England were seeing unusual objects in the sky, this even extended to Europe where similar sightings were being reported. One astronomer claims he saw a comet, the first of its kind in fifteen years, and Eastern Radar claimed the sightings were a meteor. There is an argument that if these UFOs are so intelligent, how can they crash or get into trouble? I think it is safe to assume that no matter how advanced technology is, it would take some effort to survive a powerful meteor shower if you happened to get in its way. Therefore it is a possibility that the object which crashed through the treetops and landed in Rendlesham Forest on the night of 25 December was in fact damaged by a meteor shower. However, if that was the case then why did the events continue for at least another two nights?

Maybe our own earthly experiments with certain 'waves' are causing problems for the visitors. For seventy years there was an enormous amount of experimental work achieved at Orfordness and Bawdsey. Could it be that these experiments have penetrated another time or dimension? Goodness knows what havoc could be caused by beaming electromagnetic waves through space. There is no doubt that one of the UFOs came crashing through the trees, and this was noted by Penniston and Burroughs when they investigated the site the next day and found broken branches from the tree tops. It is also recorded on Halt's audio tape when his patrol investigated the landing site two days later: 'Looking directly overhead, one can see an opening in the trees, plus some freshly broken pine branches on the ground underneath. Looks like some of them came off about fifteen feet up . . .' Indeed, why would the object stay on the ground so long, apparently just sitting there? Were they repairing their craft due to an accident, and did we cause that accident? When the American astronauts went to the moon, they were, after all, alien visitors taking samples and exploring the lunar surface. If they had experienced problems with their craft, they would surely have had to deal with them on site. One of the Russian cosmonauts even had to make repairs in space whilst dangling from a wire. So why is it taboo to accept that a crew were possibly repairing their damaged craft? Are we really so conceited as to believe that we are the only intelligent life in the vast universe?

A CASE FOR THE UFO

When it comes to UFOs there are so many theories to consider, and if these objects are not from another planet then what are they and where do they come from? Are they travellers from our own distant future? Are they from a parallel universe? Are they advanced terrestrial aircraft or weapon systems developed by our own governments? Or could the UFOs be fabrications created by elementals capable of carrying out physical scenarios in order to deceive us mortals? Let us examine the more down-to-earth theories and those that might require some lateral thinking and a little open-mindedness.

Britain and America's early attempt at copying the disc-shaped craft (flying saucer) certainly proved unsuccessful, but America's Stealth technology has produced magnificent aircraft, albeit still a long way from the advanced silent objects that continue to intrude on our airspace. According to latest reports, America's new Aurora, although highly advanced, is still just an aircraft with limitations. It may be capable of performing flights at top speeds, but can it perform any of the amazing manoeuvres executed by the as yet unidentified flying triangles? These include accelerating from a dead stop to hypersonic speed in the blink of an eye, stopping suddenly during hypersonic speed, or flipping sideways and disappearing into what appears to be another dimension. Apart from an occasional mild humming sound all this is achieved without any noise.

The April 1999 *Preview, Journal of the Defence Procurement Agency* featured an interesting double-page spread on Britain's Future Offensive Air System. It appears that Britain is engaged in developing revolutionary concepts in collaboration with her

European neighbours. A new stealth concept, featuring manned and unmanned robot combat air vehicles, which are expected to be operational in less than eighteen years, are impressive indeed. Artists' drawings showing 'angel fish'-type craft look like something from our future, but can they perform the tasks of the UFOs?

A few years ago I came across a 1956 declassified report entitled *Electrogravitics Systems, an Examination of Electrostatic Motion, Dynamic Counterbary and Barycentric Control.* The paper was prepared by Aviation Studies (International) Ltd, based in Knightsbridge, London. It was intended for the Wright Aeronautical Laboratories, Wright Patterson Air Force Base, Dayton, Ohio. This fascinating report dealt with research being carried out on electrogravitics, and much of the work was involved in an attempt to produce saucer-shaped flying machines. As well as several government research establishments, it is interesting to note that most of America's major industries had taken an interest in this field of research. They included Clarke Electronics, General Electric, Bell, Convair, Lear, Sperry-Rand, Curtis-Wright, Lockheed, Boeing and North American. At the same time, Britain, France, Canada and Sweden were working on Townsend Brown's electrogravitics studies and early German papers on wave physics. Contrary to the belief that the Germans were ahead on this programme, the paper states: 'Curiously enough the Germans during the war paid no attention to electrogravitics. This is one line of advance they did not pioneer in any way and it was basically a US creation.' On the electrogravitic propulsion system, the report mentions 'Project Winterhaven', and points out that the Pentagon were ready to sponsor a range of devices to help further their industry's knowledge. One wonders what these devices might have been.

In recent years there has been speculation that the United States has been involved in the back engineering of captured alien technology. The late Colonel Philip J. Corso came out of the closet in 1997, claiming that as chief of the US army's Foreign Technology Division, based at the Pentagon, he had been involved in stewarding alien artefacts in a reverse engineering project for the

US government. These objects, allegedly retrieved from the famous Roswell UFO crash of 1947, were said to consist of a visor-type headpiece, tiny clear filament flexible glasslike wires, thin copper wires and wafer-thin circuits. Corso was tasked with the job of discreetly seeding them to American industries, such as IBM, Hughes Aircraft, Bell Laboratories and Dow Corning. He published his findings in his 1997 controversial book *The Day After Roswell*, in which he claims the alien artefacts led to today's technology: namely, integrated circuit chips, lasers, fibre optics and super-tenacity fibres. Following his publication, a US company called the American Computer Corporation claimed they had discovered old files from the late 1940s relating to alien technology, and subsequently began their own research. It begs the question, could the US government have passed on alien technology to research establishments in the hope that it would assist them in building a flying saucer? Indeed, is Stealth technology a result of that research?

By the early 1950s the flying saucer had became a popular sight in American skies, and it must have been of great concern to the US government when, in 1952, several of these objects were seen to hover over the White House. One witness to these events, who has asked not to be identified, recalls the 1952 flap like it was yesterday.

On a warm July evening in 1952 Second Lieutenant James Anderson (pseudonym) was in the control tower at Bolling Air Force Base when suddenly the radar operators became very excited. The reason for the commotion was that several hard radar targets, moving at incredibly fast speeds, had shown up on their radar screens. According to Anderson, everyone was 'shocked' because they thought it was a new Soviet weapon. Fighter planes were instantly scrambled and personnel in the tower were ordered to vacate immediately. When Anderson and his colleagues exited the control tower, they noticed that a crowd of Air Force personnel and civilian maintenance workers had gathered on the flightline to watch the spectacle. 'It was a fantastic sight,' recalls Anderson. 'They accomplished some incredible manoeuvres, which even by today's technology would not be possible to achieve.' Nobody had a clue what they were witnessing, and Anderson recalls the planes were chasing their own tails, never able to catch up with the objects. 'Every time they got close, the UFOs would wink out of sight and reappear elsewhere. Obviously this was technology way beyond ours and we heard no noise,' he explained.

I was not surprised to hear that there was no acceptable Air Force explanation to describe what thousands of Americans had witnessed that night. One can only imagine what was going on in the president's mind as the UFOs hovered tantalizingly over the White House. Anderson and his colleagues were later debriefed by their superiors and ordered not to discuss the incident under penalty of the Uniform Code of Military Justice (UCMJ). This meant that if they talked, they risked being court-martialled. The UCMJ, which goes back to 1947, is the code of law that the US military operate under and is their basis for all legal actions. I understand it is very effective, especially when targeted towards career officers. Having been grilled, the military witnesses were told that if anyone should enquire about the incident: 'Tell them it was the Northern Lights, Venus, Mars, weather balloons, temperature inversion, stars, reflections of city lights [although there was no cloud cover that night] or a myriad of other earthly things.' Anything, it seemed, except a UFO! It is almost fifty years since the incident occurred, and Anderson has long since retired from the Air Force, yet he is still very nervous about the threat he received that July night. 'I would appreciate anonymity, please. Our government agencies have a very long reach and very short tempers. I am now retired and on a pension and am somewhat paranoid about this particular issue.'

An interesting little snippet from the Aviation Studies (International) Ltd file quotes the aviation report for 28 January 1955:

Back in 1948 and 49, the public in the US had a surprisingly clear idea of what a flying saucer should, or could not, do. There has never been any realistic explanation of what propulsion agency could make it do those things, but its ability to move within its own gravitation field was presupposed from its manoeuvrability. Yet all this was at least two years before electro-static energy was shown to produce propulsion. It is curious that the public were so ahead of the empiricists on this occasion.

Science and technology have come a long way since then; but have they managed to back engineer one of these amazing flying machines? I mailed the Aviation Studies report to nuclear physicist Stanton T. Friedman, who thought it was fascinating for its day, and although pointing out that a number of achievements have since been made, he admits he has not seen much progress in harnessing gravity.

I had already been told by a former Bentwaters officer that the stealth F-117 was secretly deployed at RAF Bentwaters in the early 1980s, and this had been confirmed by a high-ranking officer, but it may not have been there in 1980. According to *Pilot*, volume 20, number 4, April 1986, the stealth F-19 had made approximately thirty secret visits to RAF Mildenhall during the 1980s. The leading question has always been: Could the witnesses in Rendlesham Forest have mistaken the UFOs for one of their own advanced aircraft that they were unfamiliar with?

Harry Thompson, the RAF security policeman who witnessed the Watton incident, recalls that he and his co-witness were dispatched to the United States six months afterwards. Thompson was assigned to 'Red Flag', a NATO Air Force bomber meet at Mirama, New Mexico. While at the base he saw hidden in a heavily guarded hangar what could have been described as a UFO. Thompson only had sight of the craft for a couple of minutes, but when his curiosity got the better of him, he was told it was a test-bed model for a stealth fighter. Although he was not involved in the Rendlesham Forest incident, he considers the UFO story may have been a disguise to hide a problem with the landing of a stealth-type craft. He explained his theory:

What better way to put the Russians off the track – it was the high point of the Cold War after all – than by hoaxing a UFO incident. Supposing we Brits only got involved because we might have picked up on radar something that was not meant to be picked up at all! That might explain why I was told to forget the matter and why the log books went missing, especially if the USAF took them. As an afterthought, both my partner on that night and I were posted out of the country within six months: that was strange as we had both only been at Watton for three months of what normally was a two-year tour.

However, Lieutenant Buran, the officer on duty at Bentwaters Central Security Control during 25 December 1980, and the very person who sent Penniston's patrol out to investigate, informed me:

The F-117, to my knowledge, was not operational at the time of this incident. I'm fairly sure that had any stealth or secret aircraft been deployed to BW/WB, the security forces would have known. I have had some experience with protecting classified/unique aircraft, and for all of my career the protection of priority assets (aircraft and weapons) was my bread and butter. No stealth in this incident.

Speculation that the Americans would attempt to bring down a Soviet satellite on British territory is yet another explanation for the UFO. Alan Akeroyd is not usually interested in UFOs but the Rendlesham Forest case intrigued him because it occurred not far from where he lived at the time. Akeroyd, a former modern history student at St Edmund Hall, Oxford University, is currently working as an archivist, but one of his interests is 'satellite recoveries' and he thought this would be an obvious approach to solving the Rendlesham UFO problem.

According to Akeroyd the Soviet Union launched numerous satellites in 1980, but there were only two known to be in orbit at the time of the incident. Cosmos 1227 was launched on Tuesday 16 December 1980 and re-entered on Sunday 28 December where it landed in Kazakhstan. Cosmos 749 is the one most associated with the incident because its upper-stage booster went off into orbit on its own, decaying on 25 December 1980, the night of the first reported sighting. However, it has been established that there was no satellite re-entry, but merely a piece of free-falling charred upper-stage rocket.

Akeroyd explains that Big Bird was an American cylinder satellite with a large Cassegrain telescope and two cameras. Big Bird 16 was launched on Wednesday 16 June 1980 and de-orbited on 6 March 1981. Because it carried sixteen recoverable film capsules (these are large expensive pieces of equipment) it was speculated that one of these capsules was dropped in Rendlesham Forest on 27/28 December 1980 and picked up by the 67th Aerospace Rescue and Recovery Squadron. It is always possible that one of the film capsules strayed and ended up on the doorstep of the ARRS, who were conveniently based at RAF Woodbridge. But if that was the case, would it have prompted a USAF lieutenant colonel to write a memorandum to the Ministry of Defence, titled 'Unidentified Lights', thus bringing undue attention to the incident. Of course, that theory does not account for the radar reports and at least three nights of visible sightings either.

In October 1987, two months after Steve Roberts told her that the UFO story was a hoax, Brenda Butler received a telephone call from an American woman who claimed to be the wife of a member of the ARRS at RAF Woodbridge. The woman, who only gave her name as Karen, told Brenda that she had some information about the Rendlesham Forest incident but would not discuss it on the telephone for fear that their call might be monitored. Brenda agreed to meet Karen provided she could bring along her friend, UFO enthusiast Del Newman. Karen agreed. Brenda was then instructed to drive to the appointed meeting place where she was to park the car, then get out and walk around it three times and return to the driver's seat. After several minutes a female figure surfaced from behind a concrete pillar and called out Brenda's name. The woman, described as being in her late twenties to early thirties, scrambled into the back seat of the car where she lay down and covered herself with a blanket. Brenda told me that Karen was shaking and constantly asked if they were being followed. Karen was taken to

Del's home, a couple of miles from the Woodbridge base, where the researchers recorded an interview with her. Brenda supplied me with a twenty-four-page transcript of the interview and her added notes. Karen was adamant that the incident did not involve a UFO, and mentioned this several times throughout the interview. She claimed it concerned the capture of a Soviet spy plane and two of its crew. Apparently, on 26 December 1980, her husband and a friend, who were part of an ARRS operation, picked up a canister in the North Sea which was alleged to be part of a satellite that had been dropped from a Tupolev TU-142 (Bear). I was aware that the Tupolev was a long-range Soviet maritime patrol aircraft installed with electronic intelligence and anti-shipping missile guidance. British radar stations often picked up the Tupolev on their radar, and according to my sources, it was a regular visitor to the Suffolk coastline, where many a time the RAF had been alerted to intercept it.

Karen told Brenda that the Americans had stolen the aircraft and nobody would ever find out what really happened because it was a 'big cover-up and it had to stay that way'. Her friend had received a call from Germany at 03.00 hrs on the morning of 27 December, and to prove her case Karen produced photocopies from his files which showed travel arrangements and photographs of a cylinder being lifted from the sea. She added that there were more files in her friend's office which included reports that an object was lifted from Rendlesham Forest and taken to the Woodbridge base, then loaded on to a C-5 aircraft and transported to Germany. She also believed that the Soviet aircraft was being hidden on the Woodbridge base and claimed that it had remained there for three months until it was transported to two airfields in the US, one being Kirkland, then finally returned to RAF Woodbridge. But I found it hard to believe that the Americans had stolen a Soviet plane and were blatantly flying it to different airbases. I then began to question Karen's motives for contacting Brenda.

The transcript produced some cryptic clues. Karen made several comments, explaining her anger at the USAF for kidnapping the Soviet aircraft and that she thought the British should know about the cover-up. I thought this was very strange because if the story were true it was surely not something that should have concerned Karen, who after all was the wife of a member of the elite ARRS. She reminded Brenda that if the information came out it could cause a war between the West and the Soviet Union. Why then would Karen want to leak such secret information to a ufologist? For someone who was so nervous, I also found it difficult to understand how she could have had the courage to break into her friend's office and photocopy his files, and she even talks about drugging him and stealing files from his home. This is all too dramatic and I wondered if this was just another attempt at leaking disinformation. Karen produced photographs of a cylinder being picked up from the sea, but these could have been taken during an exercise because the ARRS did use these objects for these purposes. The aircraft hidden in the hangar could have been the new stealth aircraft which was sometimes deployed at the Bentwaters base. Interestingly, one of my Air Force sources had previously mentioned that there was an old French aircraft kept at Bentwaters. In 1979 he was working as a flight chief and doing his rounds on the alert parking area when he noticed an old Super Sabre. There were no markings on the aircraft so he climbed on to the wing and looked into the cockpit, where he discovered everything was written in French. The craft remained at the base for several months and every now and again pieces of it would go missing. What were the Americans doing with an old French aircraft housed on one of their installations?

I asked General Gordon Williams to comment on the alleged theft of a Soviet aircraft, but he could find no words to explain how ridiculous the story was, suggesting that it was more likely to have been an exercise. When I asked him about the French aircraft, he said he knew nothing about it. If Karen was genuine, it is possible that she was confusing the facts. She admitted that she was not privy to her husband's work – that he shredded his orders immediately after reading them. She may have picked up snippets of information and pieced together a story that was essentially based on an exercise. But if such an exercise was taking place over the North Sea on the night of 26 December I wanted to know if it had some relevance to the Rendlesham Forest incident.

Brenda's files produced more information which caught my eye. According to her reports, local fishermen were approached by two men who instructed them not to fish in the waters between Bawdsey and Orfordness during 25–30 December. The fishermen were told that experiments would be taking place and they might be exposed to radiation. Apparently, the two men had paid them cash for their loss of earnings which was far more than they would have earned by fishing. A local ferryman told Brenda about strange craft and green lights he had often seen which would go under the sea near Orfordness and through tunnels which were situated along the coastline. Another source told Brenda that HMS *Norfolk* was in the area during Christmas week, with the purpose of keeping other vessels away from the coastline. If we accept this information as factual then it could mean that the British government were involved in experimental work, or they were using this as a cover for something more sinister. Or could it be that their experiments accidentally damaged one of the UFOs, which caused it to crash through the forest and land off course? If the latter were more to the point, then the government would not have anticipated the Rendlesham Forest incident ever taking place. This might be why there has been so much confusion in this case – because there were two separate events taking place that week. It is most unusual for UFOs to stay around for such long periods of time, and even more unusual that they returned on consecutive nights. But if some type of magnetic experiment damaged their systems then they might have been unable to leave the area. Maybe Adrian Bustinza was right after all; maybe somebody or something in the craft did require help from the electronics division.

It is now safe to say that the majority of people are open-minded enough to accept that we may not be the only intelligent life in the universe. Some individuals are convinced we are being visited by other civilizations; others follow the theory that many of these visitors may actually stem from another dimension or time, our future maybe, and are not necessarily from another planet. Although there are still reports of flying saucers, and any number of other shapes and sizes, the majority of contemporary reports specifically refer to triangular-shaped objects. The Rendlesham Forest UFOs were even capable of shape-shifting, or so it seems. Indeed, the witnesses to these events are still seeking answers to what they encountered that Christmas week. Needless to say, none of them is convinced that the objects were anything they were familiar with, or that they were American or British craft.

Based on Jim Penniston's intricate drawings of the triangular craft, which he and John Burroughs both witnessed, I began searching for something that might resemble it. Penniston's drawings offer excellent descriptions of a triangular craft viewed from all angles, and there is no doubt that this is a solid object of some kind. Looking at the top view one sees a definite triangular shape and in the centre there appears to be a smaller triangle with a centre to it also. Could this be the winking eye that Colonel Charles Halt refers to in his audio tape recording? On some old buildings, especially in eastern Europe, one can see engravings of triangular shapes with an eye in the centre. Almost all these triangles or pyramids feature shafts of light emitting from them. Looking at the side view of Penniston's drawing (see Appendix III) we can distinguish what appear to be two triangles, one resting on top of the other but at different angles. The lower one pointing up like a pyramid and the upper section resting on top like a sunken apex. The actual way the craft is structured is better seen from Penniston's side description. What does this tell us?

I met Sir John Whitmore several years ago and have found him to be a serious and intelligent person. John stems from true British aristocracy, a Sandhurst subaltern who loved to travel the world before settling down with his American wife in England. We first met when I contacted him about an old book I had found in a dusty second-hand shop. The out-of-print publication, entitled *Preparations for Landing on Planet Earth*, caught my attention because it centred around some well-known figures of the day and I wanted to know what was their interest in UFOs. John was deeply involved in the research for the book, but one of the central figures was the late Dr Andrija Puharich, a rather eccentric electronics engineer and a brilliant inventor who is probably best remembered for his discovery of spoon-bender Uri Geller.

For more than thirty years John Whitmore has been involved with a handful of people who claim to communicate with an extra-terrestrial group called the Nine. This group, channelled by psychic Phyllis Schlemmer, are alleged to exist in a higher dimension located within a cold zone, and are known in some circles as the Elohim. I have always been suspicious of any form of channelling, but nevertheless was intrigued by the vast amount of knowledgeable information gathered by this particular group. These people obviously took their research very seriously and had structured an $8 \times 8 \times 12$ Faraday cage that was intended to eliminate most uninvited interference during their channelling sessions.

Approximately one year after my initial meeting with John, I learned that he and his small group were working on another book, entitled *The Only Planet of Choice*. This was essentially an intriguing compilation of messages from the Nine that had been channelled for the last two decades. It was from this material that I found a reference to a triangular UFO that seemed to fit the description of Jim Penniston's drawings. More than any other witness, Penniston has desperately sought an explanation for the object that for the last twenty years has turned his dreams into nightmares. The Nine's description of an extraterrestrial triangular craft was that it functions on two polarities which exactly overlap and overlay, each charging the other 'as is above – so below', two triangles joined together like a six-pointed star. The craft is powered by creating a magnetic field, then discharging the magnetic. Basically, instead of functioning with the magnetic, which would attract all things inward, it is a release of the magnetic, which causes the propulsion to be reversed. The Nine's interpretation of a six-pointed star was also an interesting challenge. By dissecting Penniston's drawing and recapturing the parts as if looking at it from above (which he was unable to do, as he would have needed to be airborne), one can see that it clearly fits the description of a six-pointed star. This made me think, have we been ignorant of the real purpose of this symbology? After all, is not the symbol of two triangles overlapping each other supposed to be the balance of two energies?

Theosophist Madame Blavatsky wrote in *The Secret Doctrine* that Pythagoras viewed the symbol formed of two crossed triangles as the creation. The Egyptians claimed it was a union of fire and water, the Essenes saw it as the seal of Solomon, the Jews recognized it as the shield of David, and the Hindus saw it as the sign of Vishnu. It is no wonder that Blavatsky argued 'there must be something in it'. The use of this ancient symbol is so widespread that there must surely be an answer to its real origin and yet no one has ever been truly able to claim the credit for it. Blavatksy reveals that there is a 'Tantra' work in the British Museum which would bring a terrible curse down upon the head of anyone who divulges to the profane the real secret of the symbol. Could this just have been another threat to keep us from learning the truth? Could the secret of the crossed-over triangles really be the foundation of an advanced propulsion system invented by ancient astronauts? It is certainly an interesting theory.

In 1997 Air Marshal Sir Peter Horsley, former commander in chief of Strike Command and equerry to HRH Prince Philip, shocked the British establishment when he exposed his meeting with an alien back in 1954. Horsley's story was published in his auto-biography, *Sounds from Another Room: Memories of Planes, Princes and the Paranormal.* The alien visitor, who he only ever met once in a Chelsea apartment in London, related fascinating stories about extraterrestrials, but what intrigued me more was the description of the spacecraft that the visitor described to Horsley. He was told that although some of the vehicles were manned, most of them were robot-controlled space probes sent out to monitor our planet and collect information. Could this be what Jim Penniston was referring to when he told me that there seemed to be a robotic presence? When I visited the Science Museum in London and saw one of the Apollo capsules with its landing legs and silver body, I considered how it could resemble an antique version of Penniston's object. I discussed this with him and, although a space capsule was not what he had in mind, he nevertheless agreed that it could have been some type of probe but considered it was far too advanced to be anything that NASA had created.

If governments are in possession of advanced technology then they are keeping it a highly classified secret. In 1992 Ray Boeche was approached by two men claiming to be researchers with the US Department of Defense. They had heard of his earlier research in the Rendlesham Forest case in 1985 and although they only mentioned the incident once during their entire meeting, they offered him a great deal of information on their current research. One wonders why they waited so long. Boeche was not totally convinced as to their motives, however, and pointed out that they could have easily been disinformers because their presentation seemed too 'scripted'.

The government researchers told him that in 1960 the Soviet leader Khrushchev delivered a speech in which he stated, 'We have a new weapon just within the portfolio of our scientists which is so powerful that if unrestrainedly used, it could wipe out all life on earth.' Then, in 1975 Brezhnev had referred to a novel weapons system 'more terrible than anything the world has ever known'. In 1978 Lieutenant Colonel Tom Beardon stated, in what would eventually be known as the Excalibur Briefing, that Brezhnev and Khrushchev were probably referring to 'extinguishing electrical currents flowing in circuits by means of virtual state electron negation patterns modulated in electromagnetic carriers'. This weapon could disable the nervous system in various degrees and could even cause death. The researchers further explained that the Soviets had experimented with numerous psychotronic phenomena, including a weapon capable of exploding nuclear devices in several locations by using paranormal means. Are we to accept the information offered to Ray Boeche, that the Soviets were carrying out these kinds of experiments?

It has been suggested that there was some type of Soviet agenda involved in the Rendlesham Forest incident: even Colonel

Halt brought this up but declined to add to his brief comment. Defence correspondent Chuck de Caro presented an interesting documentary featuring 'electromagic weapons and mind control'. Dr James Fraser, who had researched electromagnetic effects for the USAF, told de Caro that radio-frequency weapons could be the wildcard in the arms race. But physicist Robert Bass, also involved in US weapons research, pointed out that the Americans were lagging behind the Soviets in this field of research by about five years. Bass felt that Soviet research involved a high-powered microwave similar to a focused ultra-high intensity radar beam. De Caro discovered that a number of American experts were of the opinion that the Tesla coil, invented in 1899, was the basis of the new generation of Soviet weapons. It is worth noting that in 1980 scientist Robert Golta was conducting experiments for the USAF using a replica Tesla coil. One of his aims was to produce a phenomenon known as ball lightning, which has often been linked to UFO sightings. Lieutenant Colonel Tom Beardon told de Caro that he believed the Soviets had perfected Tesla's ideas and were developing radio-frequency weapons on a scale unimagined by the USA. He described an incident involving the Soviets where possible discharges of radio-frequency weapons were being tested. It occurred during the reign of Mohammad Reza Pahlavi, the Shah of Iran, when the US was on more friendly relations with that country. Aircraft flying over the Soviet Union had spotted small glowing spherical balls of light that suddenly expanded to a very large size. Beardon suggested these were discharges from a radio-frequency weapon that used intersecting energy beams called scalars. This energy could then be extracted from a distant point, creating a cold explosion weapon. Could the Rendlesham balls of light, which John Burroughs said came out from the UFO, be linked to a similar type of experiment? Certainly these balls of light had been seen in the area many years before the 1980 incident.

According to Ray Boeche's visitors, the Americans were studying Fourier's transforms and David Bohm's contemporary research which involved quantum theory. They explained that holography and Fourier transforms are a way of separating an image from its object, then viewing the image at a distance. In essence, they claim the world is a hologram composed of interference patterns which can be altered by disruptive static frequencies. They believe the human brain is part of this hologram and as such it is capable of performing its own Fourier transforms. However, they concluded that the human brain is unreliable, whereas a psychotronic device, much like a computer, would be able to exert an exact effect on animate and inanimate objects. If the Americans were attempting to electronically recognize frequency interference patterns in space with the aim of transforming the desired Fourier components into holographic images of a kind, could this have been what was seen in Rendlesham Forest? Was the UFO some kind of hologram? This is obviously what the researchers wanted Ray Boeche to believe. They informed him that every avenue was being explored and that the 'Bentwaters experiment', the projection of a three-dimensional object which interacted with its environment, was created and controlled by individuals involved in this field of research.

According to the researchers, the idea was to operate a psycho-tronic device by performing Fourier transforms on background radiation, which would be more reliable when used with a laser. The airborne laser would be capable of observing everything from electrons moving in silicon chips to the depths of the oceans. Such a device would be able to capture the interference patterns and com-puterize the imaging. The receiver could decode the components of entire buildings, landscapes and individuals. Interestingly, Colonel Halt's patrol recorded background radiation. Halt has always insisted that during the incident a pencil-thin beam hit the ground just a few feet away from where he was positioned. Supposing this really was an experiment, and the beam was a laser, but then what would be the purpose of creating such a bizarre scenario on the perimeter of a NATO installation? Why would the Americans carry out such a test on foreign soil?

In 1997 *The Mail on Sunday* featured an article entitled 'An Army of Ghosts to Spook the Foe'. The newspaper's Washington correspondent reported that the Pentagon were perfecting a laser which would project holographic decoys of troops and tanks in order to trick the enemy into thinking it was a real force. The project known as Ghost Gun could also be used to create virtual doubles of the opponent's leaders. The research for this technological breakthrough was being carried out at the Adelphi Laboratory in Maryland, USA. One spokesman was quoted as saying, 'Holographic images will soon be used to make a force seem larger than it is, distract enemy fire and keep enemy troops out of unsecured territory.' At the time of the article the laboratory claimed they had only been working on the project for two years and the only reason it became public knowledge was due to the need for Congress to approve new funding for the research.

A year later, the August 1998 American issue of *UFO Magazine* featured a denial by Army spokesman Dave Davidson, who said the Ghost Gun holographic projector, as reported, had been overstated. 'The holograms being worked on are very small right now. We're a long way from projecting 3-D images that can be viewed from all sides,' he said. This statement was very interesting, because some witnesses have remarked of the Rendlesham UFO as being transparent or invisible when viewed from a different angle. Is this why the residents of the farmhouses could not see the object, because from their point of vision, it was invisible? When asked about UFOs, Davidson was quoted as saying, 'We don't deal with that.'

The hologram might be an excellent theory were it not for the fact that Jim Penniston claims he had physical contact with the object. I also have a collection of photographs taken of the landing site which show three indentations. Penniston also claims to have a photograph of the landing site, which he managed to get from the AFOSI after constantly bothering them for some proof of what happened. However, I do not believe we should dismiss the hologram theory as impossible. Just because we have not invented anything that is able to manifest itself into a psychical mass, does not mean a more advanced civilization has not achieved it.

Researcher Jacques Vallee, who seems to have based his theory on Larry Warren's testimony and from reading *Skycrash*, suggests the UFO was a device or a collection of devices designed for psychological warfare. However, it is difficult to believe that the incident was a test carried out by the Americans, or even the British, simply because it occurred on the perimeter of a sensitive military installation which deployed nuclear weapons. Coupled with this is the fact that on the first night, only three men were sent out to investigate. Hardly worth going to all that trouble to test it on a handful of military personnel.

Guy Lyon wrote an interesting feature for *Mysteries of Mind, Space and Time, The Unexplained*, volume 18, entitled 'Worlds Within Worlds', which attracted my attention. He refers to Reverend Edwin Abbott's publication, *Flatland, a Romance of Many Dimensions*, which tells the story of boring life in Flatland. One day an inhabitant (a square) has a paranormal experience when it receives a visit from a circle in upper space. What it was actually seeing was a three-dimensional body, but it was only aware of its cross section as it penetrated Flatland. Lyon describes the cross section as a disc that grows from a point to the full diameter of the sphere then shrinks again as the sphere passes on. This sounds very much like the description on Colonel Halt's audio recording of the event when he describes the object: '. . . it's sorta a hollow centre right, a dark centre . . . it's like an eye winking at you . . . we got two strange objects . . . half moon shape . . . the half moons have now turned into full circles as though there is an eclipse or something there for a minute or two.' The visitor to Flatland peeled off the square and took it on a trip to the third dimension, but when the square returned nobody would believe its story and the poor thing ended up being imprisoned for being a menace to society. Lyon makes a very profound statement when he asks, 'How would it feel to be a Flatlander?' How indeed? It seemed the square had no conception of anything outside the realm of its own world. Although it could slide around backwards, forwards and sideways, it could not move up or down. Lyon contemplates the games we could play on Flatlanders. By hanging objects of various shapes and sizes above them and moving a light to and fro, it would create frightening shadows, resulting in horrid creatures appearing and suddenly disappearing. But as Lyon points out, unless they had witnessed it, who would believe the phenomenon? Are we like a Flatland to those who reside in other dimensions? After all, we have no knowledge of what those dimensions are like because we reside in our own three-dimensional world.

For years scientists have tirelessly debated that UFOs cannot be real because it is impossible for them to travel the distance from their planets to ours, and this may have brought about the now popular belief that UFOs are travellers from our future. Another interesting article in *Mysteries of Mind, Space and Time, The Unexplained*, volume 24, comes from researcher Joan Forman, who refers to several common factors which have been discovered through her investigation into 'time slips'. She points to a noticeable absence of sound during these encounters and the presence of a silvery light. There is also a sensation of being in two time zones at once and the feeling of being a part of the experience. Forman also describes how the experiencers have a sense of disorientation and detachment as well as a tingling sensation and nausea. The Rendlesham Forest witnesses described all of the aforementioned. Is it possible that they walked into a time warp? We learn that Cabansag, Burroughs and Penniston experienced forty-five minutes of missing time, and Burroughs claimed that everything seemed different during the encounter, including his surroundings. Forman makes reference to certain waves that have the power to carry pictures and sounds through time. She points out that radio waves, infrared and ultra-violet rays, X-rays and gamma rays are all electromagnetic. I remembered that Betty Garfield had made a strong point that we don't know enough about electricity and maybe the visitors use this to penetrate our space. Then I was reminded of RAF Bawdsey's term for UFOs, which, according to local historian Gordon Kinsey, were called X-Rays. Are the UFOs using electromagnetic waves to visit us and, if so, did Bawdsey know what they were?

In this modern age, with technology advancing at such a rate, it is practical to accept that superior civilizations would be able to time travel. This theory is more favourable than assuming the visitors travel millions of miles from other planets. Their manoeuvres seem to imply that they have this capability and I have the sense that there is something 'alive' about these objects. The fact that they can change shape the way they do is also intriguing. Master Sergeant Bobby Ball thought they were doing a grid search, but what if they are using an electromagnetic power grid to travel our skies. There is even speculation that they travel beneath our seas in a similar fashion. What is even more puzzling is how they appear to split into three units forming a triangle or even five units forming a quincunx. Maybe the object Penniston and Burroughs saw was one of these units which had broken away from the central craft. If they are time travelling that might account for why they arrived at the exact same place and same time on consecutive nights. Were they trying to arrive at the same destination on the same day at the same time but, due to our time, did they arrive a day later on each trip, or did they accidentally get stuck in our time?

The fact that the UFOs returned for at least three consecutive nights at the same place, around the same time, has always been extremely puzzling in this case, and this was also addressed by John Burroughs. In the yellowing pages of a thirty-year-old book, *Flying Saucers from Outer Space*, written by Donald E. Keyhoe, I discovered a similar incident had occurred in 1949 over Albuquerque. The incident was found to have been omitted from the USAF files. For four consecutive nights, at exactly the same place and the same time, a strange reddish light was sighted, followed by green balls of light and a UFO that hovered to below 200 feet above a military installation and suddenly exploded in a red spray of light.

But what do these visitors want and why are they visiting us? There are countless theories offered but, unfortunately, unless we have constructive proof of their intentions we can only speculate. Since the 1970s there have been hundreds, maybe thousands of reports of mutilated cattle. These animals have had organs removed with precision cuts that are said to be impossible with our known technology. Much more frightening are the hundreds of reports of human abductions. These people claim they have been taken to some type of spaceship and experimented on. Apparently, the aliens are taking samples of sperm and ovaries in an attempt to cross-breed with humans. I have always had problems trying to understand the human abduction enigma, probably the same as someone might have trying to accept that UFOs are visiting this planet. Being a down-to-earth Capricorn, I was once told that I would not believe in pixies even if one sat on the end of my nose. Well, that is probably true, but I do not believe these UFOs are made on this earth, at least not in our time.

We cannot be sure there was an alien crew but the fact that a craft of unknown origin landed in Rendlesham Forest should no longer be in dispute. It happened! I have presented enough proof for this that even the most sceptical of sceptics cannot argue. Indeed, sceptics will need to have some intelligent answers (not theories) that prove beyond a shadow of doubt, and which take into account the whole incident, not just a fraction as they have chosen to do in the past, to argue against these facts. The proof of at least one landing is obvious enough. Although Lieutenant Colonel Halt's memorandum does not refer to a landing when explaining the actual incident, he later points out: 'The next day, three depressions 1½" deep and 7" in diameter were found where the object had been sighted on the ground.' Reliable witnesses Penniston and Burroughs are adamant the UFO landed. The next day numerous high-ranking officers investigated the landing site, which was measured and tested for radiation. The USAF contacted the Suffolk Constabulary to report that 'a place had been found where a craft of some sort could have landed'. A British police officer was sent to investigate, and although he refused to believe a UFO caused the indentations, he nevertheless did not deny there were marks on the ground. The USAF would not waste valuable police time if they did not consider it important. Witnesses have testified that a research team were flown in to investigate and the area was burned and trees were taken away.

Whether the UFOs visited three nights or four nights is not the argument, what is important is that an incident involving UFOs did happen and Britain and the United States of America tried to cover it up. Some ufologists believe the reason the governments are not disclosing this information is because they are using parts of these downed spaceships and back engineering them in the hope that they might be able to create their own highly advanced military aircraft and weapons systems. An interesting thought! But it is my theory that we should be concentrating on what drives these machines. Who are these visitors and are they hostile or friendly?

MORE STRANGE ENCOUNTERS

Although by far the most momentous, the 1980 incident is not the only one to have occurred in the area surrounding Rendlesham Forest. Throughout my investigations I was to discover that local residents and personnel from the Suffolk military installations had witnessed strange objects in the sky in and around Woodbridge as early as 1947, and possibly even before that time.

Researcher Nicholas Redfern managed to uncover a file from the Public Records Office which revealed an interesting incident concerning RAF Bentwaters. The file consisted of a letter from Canadian Ronald Anstee, who wrote to the Ministry of Defence requesting information about an incident which one of his relatives was witness to. It occurred on a summer's day in 1947 when numerous base personnel from RAF Bentwaters witnessed a huge fifty-foot circular UFO in the vicinity of Rendlesham Forest. Following the incident, senior officers were flown into the bases to investigate. Anstee received no information from the Ministry of Defence regarding this encounter; in fact all they did was send him a one-sentence note acknowledging his letter. The most interesting part of this find is that Anstee mentions the UFO was somehow connected with a new type of radar system that had recently been installed in the area. If this is the case, and the radar experiments were responsible for the UFO sightings, then this may be an important clue, and we can assume the Americans were not responsible for the 1980 Rendlesham Forest incident. It was not until 1952 that the USAF leased RAF Bentwaters, before that the RAF used it.

Andrew Sheepshanks, who was brought up in the area, told me

that when he was a child he heard a story that not long after World War Two an incident had occurred at RAF Woodbridge where a UFO was sighted and two aircraft were sent to intercept it. He claims that at least one aircraft and its pilot disappeared never to be seen again.

The most famous of the East Anglian UFO reports concerns the 1956 Lakenheath/Bentwaters incident. According to a USAF report filed by Captain L. Holt on 31 August 1956, the object was tracked by Airman Second Class John Vaccare of the USAF at RAF Bentwaters. Vaccare was assigned to the Ground Controlled Approach (GCA) radar (type AN/MPN11A) when he picked up the signal of an object flying in at 40–50 mph in less than 30 seconds. Within a few minutes Vaccare was picking up twelve to fifteen unidentified targets and immediately reported the incident to his superior, Technical Sergeant L. Whenry. The ground personnel were puzzled as they watched the objects converge into what appeared to be one very large object several times the size of the largest bomber aircraft at that time, which was a B-36. At 22.00 hrs RAF Bentwaters tracked another object. Then at 22.55 hrs Bentwaters tracked yet another target, which was also observed as a bright white light by someone in the control tower. At the same time the pilot of a US C-47 military transport plane reported that 'a bright light streaked under my aircraft travelling east to west at terrific speed'. Sometime later the USAF at both Bentwaters and Lakenheath reported a stationary object, which then began travelling at a speed of 400–600 mph, making several abrupt changes of direction without having to slow down. Captain Holt's official report states that at approximately 23.30 hrs the RAF launched a Venom jet from RAF Waterbeach:

> Pilot advised he had a bright white light in sight and would investigate. At 13 miles west he reported loss of target and white light. Lakenheath [radar] vectored him to a target 10 miles east of Lakenheath and pilot advised [that] target was locking on. Pilot then reported he had lost target on his radar. Lakenheath GCA reports that as the Venom passed the target on radar, the target began a tail chase of the friendly fighter. Radar requested pilot

acknowledge this chase. Pilot acknowledged and stated he would try to circle and get behind the target. Pilot advised he was unable to 'shake' the target off his tail and requested assistance. One additional Venom was scrambled from RAF station. Original pilot stated: 'Clearest target I have seen on radar.'

The following conversation between the two pilots was heard by the Lakenheath watch supervisor. According to Bernard Thouanel, who has been an aerospace journalist and photographer for more than twenty years and has taken an interest in this particular case, the names of the RAF pilots are John Brady and Yvan Logan. Thus Pilot 1 would be Brady and Pilot 2 Logan.

PILOT 2: Did you see anything?

PILOT 1: I saw something, but I'll be damned if I know what it was.

PILOT 2: What happened?

PILOT 1: He or it got behind me and I did everything I could to get behind him and I couldn't. It's the damnedest thing I've ever seen.

In his excellent book *Bawdsey, Birth of a Beam*, Gordon Kinsey tells of an incident that happened near Woodbridge on 9 June 1961. RAF Bentwaters were alerted when one of the airmen reported seeing an aircraft come down in the area. The incident sparked off one of the biggest searches by military and civilian personnel for many years, but the mystery craft was never found or so it was reported. Apparently, it caused quite a stir among the Bawdsey radar operators who confirmed they had no radar tracking of the object. I asked Gordon if the incident had been reported in the local press, but he doubted it.

F. W. Sone was a security policeman stationed at RAF Bentwaters from 1971 until 1979. On two separate occasions he witnessed a UFO incident at the base. The first occurred in 1973 whilst he was working a midnight shift in the fighter alert area. Says Sone:

This area had F-4 Phantoms that were loaded with nukes ready to take off at a moment's notice. The area was situated near the end of the main runway. At about 3 a.m. I noticed what appeared to be a large landing light hovering over the runway . . . A few minutes later I saw the base fire/rescue trucks respond to the end of the runway with their emergency lights on . . . They turned their spotlights on the hovering light. The light appeared to be about a hundred feet in diameter and was not moving . . . There was no sound . . . That is when I realized it wasn't a plane landing . . . After about five minutes the light suddenly disappeared as if someone had pulled a switch on it.

According to the witness, nothing was ever said about the incident. Sone witnessed a similar encounter in 1974 whilst on duty in the nuclear weapons storage area on Bentwaters. The object appeared twice, and the base responded by sending two F-4 fighter planes to intercept it. As the aircraft approached the object it became smaller and suddenly disappeared only to reappear in another place. This continued for thirty minutes while it seemed to play games with the pilots. Sone mentioned that there were about twenty witnesses to this sighting because it occurred during shift change, but as was to be expected, nothing was ever discussed between personnel.

1978 saw a spate of UFO sightings over the Suffolk and Essex skies. Among the witnesses was Edward Birchall from Felixstowe who was driving home when he spotted an unusual object with far too many lights to be a regular aircraft. The coloured lights of the craft were intensely bright as they beamed down to the ground. RAF Bentwaters were consulted but a spokesman for the base said there were no helicopters up at the time. Stephen Otto and Isobel Taylor sighted a UFO in Great Bentley, which featured flashing coloured lights on its underbelly. This object appeared to be stationary and was low in the sky until it suddenly disappeared from sight.

Lori Rehfeldt was one of the few female Law Enforcement personnel stationed at the Suffolk bases. Her tour was from May 1978 until December 1980, leaving just prior to the big events. Most of the time Lori would work the gates, which entailed checking the passes of those entering the base, but sometimes she would drive a patrol car through the Woodbridge installation. It was here, one night in February 1980, that Lori would encounter a UFO.

> Airman First Class Duffield and I were on patrol with police 4, it was about 3.00 a.m. We were telling stories, trying to keep awake, when we saw a strange light moving in the sky. It didn't make any noise and it really scared us. It appeared to break into three smaller balls that moved up and down, left to right like an Etch-a-Sketch board. I immediately reported it to the police control on Bentwaters and described what we had seen. We were told to report it to the air tower at Woodbridge. On arriving at the tower, we found the controller asleep. We woke him up and told him what we had seen, and he explained it could have been an aircraft from another base. We didn't think so, but by now I was listening to the radio and their attitude was that 'Rehfeldt's seeing UFOs'. I didn't need the grief so I dropped the whole issue.

On 19 November 1979 a tragedy occurred over Norfolk when an RAF helicopter pilot lost his life. The 67th ARRS patrols from RAF Bentwaters were alerted but were unable to save the pilot when the helicopter lifeline he was clinging to suddenly snapped. Around the same time two A-10 tank busters from RAF Bentwaters had a mid-air collision that turned into a fireball over Norfolk. Again, the 67th ARRS were dispatched in their Jolly Green Giants and recovered two bodies. Following the A-10 disaster there were reports of other near misses involving the same aircraft, this resulted in checks being carried out on seventy of the A-10s deployed at RAF Bentwaters and Woodbridge. A commander from the Suffolk base told journalists that the A-10s involved in the accident were only carrying practice bombs. However, some people claim UFOs were responsible for the accidents but there is no evidence to suggest this.

One of the weirdest stories I have come across concerns a man who believes he witnessed the Rendlesham Forest incident through what can only be described as an out-of-body experience. This story was passed to me by Nick Pope, but the person asked that his name be kept in strictest confidence for fear of ridicule, so I am giving him the identity of James. In the early hours of the morning in the spring of 1979 James was suddenly awoken from sleep by a presence in his dark bedroom. He described it as a powerful figure, although he could not see anything but an outline. James had no idea why, but he felt compelled to ask the figure the morbid question 'When will I die?' He was told that the person in the room would die on Sunday 28 December. In the morning James checked the calendar for the year and saw that 28 December was not on a Sunday, but there was a Sunday 28 October. It was not until that date had passed that he felt secure and was able to put the experience behind him.

Meanwhile, he had left home but had returned to visit his parents over the Christmas holidays, 1980. His father had taken to sleeping in James's former bedroom so as not to disturb his wife because he was on night call with his job and was often called out in the middle of the night. So during his visit James slept in the adjacent spare room, which was separated by a partition wall from the main bedroom where his father now slept. Sometime during the night of 27 December he awoke to the sound of thumping noises that seemed to be coming from the partition. A short time later he found that he was unable to move, as if paralysed, and then suddenly he felt very lightweight and began to float over his bed. All the while he sensed there was someone behind him but he could not turn around. Then a voice said, 'I've got something to show you which I think you will find interesting.'

The next moment he was moving at incredible high speed through the air and realized it was bright daylight – or appeared to be. The presence was still behind him, as if guiding him, and as he slowed down he could see that he was floating about 200 feet above a pine forest. Below was a forest track and a clearing containing some short bushes. In the middle of the clearing was a silvery-white object that looked like an upside-down ice-cream cone, but was much wider. It was approximately 15–20 feet in diameter and 10–15 feet in height. Standing on a rim of the object were two non-human figures dressed in silvery-white suits. James was under the impression that they were technicians. Floating in mid-air a few yards away was another figure that he thought was the leader or the supervisor of the group. Crouching among the bushes a short distance away was a human figure in military uniform. The man appeared to be holding a torch but did not seem to have noticed the object in front of him. The next moment James was moving again and suddenly found himself back in his room to the sound of his mother shouting that his father had died. He had died of a heart attack on the morning of Sunday 28 December in his bedroom, just like the voice had predicted. It was not until the late 1990s that James began to connect the strange experience to the Rendlesham Forest incident. It was then that he decided to visit the area, only this time in his physical body. Apparently, he recognized a clearing in the forest that he said was what he had seen in his out-of-body experience, the very same one where the UFO had been sitting.

Lindy 'Cookie' Vaughn also recalls unusual sightings while on duty at the Suffolk bases during 1980/81. She worked in supply, but on occasion drove a delivery truck carrying food packs to on-duty security guards. Cookie reported the first sighting to her superiors, but after being ridiculed by her supervisor for being an overreactive female she never did it again.

> I can tell you that what I saw was not a lighthouse or any aircraft of US or Russian origin. I'm sure someone was watching us. I saw several silent crafts and each time I saw them they would seem to separate into maybe three to five other smaller crafts, and I do mean silent. Not only would I not hear it but I would not hear the normal sounds of birds and animals until it was gone. I had the strongest impression that the locals also saw these craft on a regular basis and just accepted it. For me it was always a feeling of awe, not fright. I didn't feel danger just anticipation. The one incident [December] is only a fraction, a bit of time out of a long history in that part of the world.

Steve La Plume told me about two sightings that occurred just two weeks after the December incidents. Steve, who was with B

Flight, was on the midnight shift between 16 and 17 January 1981 when he and Senior Airman Wendel Palmer encountered two UFOs. On this particular night the airmen were patrolling the east gate when Palmer turned to Steve and said, 'I guess this is where they saw that UFO a few weeks back.' Steve was leaning on the roof of the cruiser discussing the incident when something caught his eye. An object was darting across the sky at a very fast speed; it appeared to go up and down changing altitude at a difference of a few thousand feet within seconds. Palmer decided to check with the control tower but was told there were only two aircraft up at the time and neither fitted the description of their sighting. Steve was annoyed when Palmer called Central Security Control and reported that 'La Plume just saw a UFO', without mentioning that he too had seen the object. Within minutes the phone in the east-gate booth rang and it was Lieutenant Bruce Englund, who wanted to know what they had seen. The object, which was still in the sky, appeared to be about fifteen miles away. Englund ordered the men to stay at their post until he arrived. Steve recalls what took place that night:

> Within twenty minutes I had more brass and people at my post than I had ever seen. There was the deputy base commander, Charles Halt, and an officer's wife and teenage boy. They had cameras and I remember his wife saying something like 'Oh boy, I hope we get to see one'. Lieutenant Englund showed up and told me not to be nervous but Colonel Williams was on his way and he had just made general. I was nervous.

By the time the group had arrived the UFO had disappeared, but Steve La Plume was in awe when he saw high-ranking officers leave their cars behind and pile into an Air Force station wagon and a jeep and take off for Rendlesham Forest. Lieutenant Englund had left the two men at the east gate with a night-vision scope and an order to contact him if they saw the object again. Approximately an hour later, the group, which still included Wing Commander Gordon Williams, returned to the east gate, then departed for Bentwaters. La

Plume and Palmer were instructed to man the gate for the rest of their shift and keep Lieutenant Englund posted if the object was spotted again. Half an hour after the group had left, the UFO returned, only this time it came in much closer and seemed to move at a much slower pace. La Plume describes the encounter:

> It had green, red and blue lights emitting from its underside. I concentrated on the blue. The lights enveloped me as the craft went over. From my line of sight it was about a hundred yards long and kind of cigar shaped. I did not feel afraid. The next thing I remember is that it was right over my head – there is a gap in time from when it was over me to when I saw it back in the southern sky and departing. This has always kind of bugged me. I asked Palmer if he wanted to report it and he said he didn't. We made an agreement and never told anyone about this part of the event.

The next morning La Plume remembers being ridiculed by fellow airmen and was reminded of the harassment the guys involved in the December incident had received. He was not officially debriefed, but missed his bus by having to report to his shift commander about the earlier incident. However, something very strange occurred soon afterwards: he felt he was being watched and followed by two strange men.

> They were both in civilian clothes, one looked foreign, maybe German. I wondered what they were doing on base, but was sure they had been following me around after my sighting. I was in the Airmens' club when I spotted them again, this time I approached them hoping to start a conversation so I could learn who they were. As I approached them they both got up and left through the back door. I followed them and saw them get into a black Lincoln town car. I was surprised when you mentioned that Larry had fallen into a Lincoln, it's not the usual car you see every day in England. He didn't tell me it was a Lincoln and I never mentioned this to Larry.

I was unable to locate Wendel Palmer, who according to Lieutenant Colonel Malcolm Zickler is now serving with the AFOSI

at Andrews AFB, USA. However, when I spoke to Colonel Halt
about this specific incident, he confirmed that he and Gordon
Williams were with the party that night, but Williams has neither
confirmed nor denied that he was there. I have been in contact with
Steve La Plume since April 1998 and we have gone over his
encounter several times and rather than speculate on his lack of
memory, he has preferred to state only that which he positively
recalls. I therefore trust his testimony.

At approximately 01.30 hrs in early January 1981 Airman Tony
Brisciano was at Bentwaters when he was instructed to drive to the
Woodbridge motor pool to service a lox cart. He was told there
would be someone there to meet him, but when he arrived there was
no one in sight. Brisciano called at a nearby building, looking for the
contact, and was told that someone had been looking for him an
hour previously. Brisciano was totally confused; he had driven
straight over to the motor pool and knew that it had not taken an
hour to get there. He called Bentwaters and they managed to trace
the individual who he was supposed to meet. 'Where the hell have
you been?' he shouted as he approached the airman. Brisciano
looked at his watch and realized it was after 03.00 hrs. This incident
of missing time has bothered him for the last twenty years and he is
still trying to find an answer to what happened to him that morning.

When Anthony Johnson arrived at Bentwaters in 1982 he had
heard rumours about the UFO sightings but dismissed them as
nonsense. For the most part, he assumed they were pranks played on
new recruits. He recalls that some personnel would go UFO hunting
in Rendlesham Forest after a few beers at the local pub and admitted
that he was involved in one of these visits himself, but assured me
that nothing unusual ever occurred. However, I was surprised to
hear that Johnson had experienced an unusual encounter at the
Bentwaters base. The incident occurred in 1983, during his mid-
shift duty, when he witnessed an encounter that still warrants an
answer to this day.

It was approximately 03.00 hrs when Airman First Class
Johnson arrived at the Operations building on Bentwaters, which

was near the flightline and the closest to the Woodbridge base. The fog was so thick that morning that he could hardly see in front of his truck. Johnson instructed his partner to collect some schedules whilst he waited in the vehicle. He cannot recall how long he had been waiting but he suddenly noticed the inside of the truck was illuminated green. He looked out the window and saw a giant green sphere hovering approximately 100-200 yards above and then, just as his partner returned, the sphere moved off speedily and silently. Johnson immediately contacted the Bentwaters tower to see if they had anything in the air. The airman on duty told him: 'If you mean big, green and fast, it didn't register on the radar and it's not one of ours.'

The next day, Johnson, his partner and the airman from the tower were instructed to report to the base commander's office, where they were debriefed by two men dressed in civilian suits. Only one of the men spoke, and Johnson recalls that he was very stoic but not threatening. He did not introduce himself but the airmen assumed they were military men (probably AFOSI agents) because they interviewed the witnesses in the base commander's office. The man recommended that they did not discuss the incident as they were part of the military and it would not be in the best interest of the Air Force's image overseas to be starting rumours. When the debriefing terminated Johnson asked what the object could be. In a monotone voice the man stated that without all the facts he could not say.

Johnson explained that he was still trying to understand what the object was:

> I realize it was foggy that morning, and it is difficult to estimate what it could have been, but there was absolutely no sound, that is what really stuck in my mind. Anyway, the following morning Jim contacted the Ipswich paper and I remember they had a record of a merchant ship sighting it as well. Now for years this bugged me, the not knowing, then one day while I was in college I stumbled across something that made perfect sense. It appears that in areas that are prone to high levels of fog there is a

phenomenon that takes place when lightning strikes in concentrated areas of fog, causing electrons to form a spherical shape
and glow with a luminescent green hue. I was a member of the
fuels group on Bentwaters and needed to know about the threat
of lightning due to the safety of our trucks, but I do not remember
receiving any such warning. So while there seems to be a perfectly
logical explanation, there does seem to be some missing pieces to
this puzzle. The reason I told you this is because I believe not all
things can be explained by science, and I must explain that I try
to look for the scientific explanation first. But I still wonder why
this thing stayed in the one spot for so long. Why did it move off
in what appeared to be a planned flight path? Most importantly,
why was it seen in the North Sea seconds after it vanished from
our sight?

Michael Lindemann, editor of *CNI News*, learnt of an unusual
incident involving a member of the security police stationed at RAF
Bentwaters in 1984. Michael did not publish the airman's identity,
but the witness to this strange event contacted other researchers
under the name of Randy. The correspondent was an E-4 sergeant at
the time, involved in high-security investigations and nuclear
weapons, in fact he claimed to have had a much higher clearance
than regular security police personnel. What frustrated Randy was
that when he left Bentwaters none of his records followed him,
and when he confronted his immediate supervisor and asked why
this was so he was told, 'What happens at Bentwaters stays at
Bentwaters.'

Randy explained that on RAF Bentwaters there was a secure area
around the flightline which many people had access to. Inside this
area was another secure area containing the munitions dump –
again, certain people had access, but not many. Inside this area was
another weapons area that only a few people had access to. This
section was heavily guarded and personnel were searched and had to
travel around in pairs. Randy pointed out that access to the bunkers
in this area required an elaborate key and password sequence but one
particular bunker was different.

Inside this special bunker was a vault with two combinations, and because of high-security regulations no one person had access to more than one combination. He pointed out that one guard would have the combination and the other the key and vice versa. Randy claimed that this was the most secure area he had ever come across in the Air Force. To open the vault it required four guards, verifying passwords, combinations and carrying keys. On this particular day Randy was chosen as a key carrier and he, along with three other armed guards, had been instructed to accompany an American civilian who needed access to the vault.

Having opened the vault, Randy was surprised to see a roughly made wooden shelf holding two old wooden crates. The civilian opened one of the crates, which was sealed with lead, and inside was a green styrofoam container in two halves. Inside the container was a solid dull corrosion-free rod measuring a quarter of an inch in diameter and bent in about three places along its length. If straightened out it would have measured about a foot long. After taking a total of four hours to prepare for the opening of the vault, it took only about one minute for the civilian to look at the rod before it was resealed and returned intact to the crate.

Randy became very curious and started asking questions about the rod and why it needed so much security. One officer he knew personally told Randy 'under his breath' that it was proof, but would not expand on his odd reply and when questioned at a later date he denied having commented. The only other responses from people who were just speculating was that it had something to do with the UFOs that supposedly visited the base. He was not aware of any UFO sightings at the time, but he later experienced his own encounter at RAF Bentwaters.

When I asked Jim Penniston if anything had been left behind at the landing site, he replied, 'John and I, thank goodness.'

The sightings continued throughout the 1980s, with reports coming in more than ever before. On 18 February 1988 Peter Robbins and Larry Warren had a strange encounter with what they believe were UFOs. This occurred as they were visiting the area researching for their book *Left at East Gate*. Peter had taken along an audio tape recorder and recorded the entire event. It all began at 21.30 hrs when the two men saw a light over Rendlesham Forest and decided to investigate. To their amazement they could see something hanging in the sky like a pendulum. The object was moving back and forth and as it became bigger it changed its shape from an ellipse to a circle within a matter of minutes. As they trekked through the forest in pursuit of the object it was still changing shape and colour, and at one stage it appeared to be actually hovering near the ground. When they approached, they could see different coloured lights and heard screams, like a woman's scream (probably animals). There were now weird balls of light flying through the trees and pulsating lights that appeared to be moving in different directions The lights were still flying around when Larry and Peter decided to leave the forest, and it is clear from the transcript that something very strange happened that night. It was obviously quite an experience for Peter, who had visited the area to research Larry Warren's case and had no idea he was going to experience his own encounter in Rendlesham Forest and end up making a similar tape recording to Colonel Halt's.

Inspector Mike Topliss of the Martlesham Heath Constabulary shared his UFO experience with me. In November 1993 he was a sector commander at Leiston, which is the nearest town to the Sizewell nuclear power station. It was approximately 22.15 hrs when he was driving home along the 1119 route. It is a winding road and the surrounding countryside is very rural, there are no hedgerows and one can see over the open fields. Mike was driving about 40 mph behind another vehicle when he noticed two bright white lights in his rear-view mirror. He assumed they were car headlights and became concerned when they suddenly gained speed (to about 70 mph) because it was such a winding road and even at 40 mph it was a difficult drive. It was only when the lights were about 50 yards behind him that he realized they were unusual balls of light, which seemed to be throwing light off in all directions. Suddenly they slowed down to his speed and he could hear a hissing noise. Mike admits he became a little nervous because they appeared to be tail chasing him. Then they seemed to change direction and became visible in his right-hand mirror. At this moment he jammed on his breaks and stopped the car, thinking there was a problem and that the driver had lost control. But there was nothing in sight. The driver in front had also pulled over and both witnesses discussed the encounter wondering where the lights had disappeared to. Obviously they did not overtake the drivers. Mike described them as balls of light but other than that he has no explanation for what they were. He is still amazed he did not take any details from the other driver. 'I was just in awe and never thought about it, which I normally would have done,' he explained.

In 1994 it looked like Suffolk and Essex were being invaded when over a hundred UFOs were witnessed by the locals. Angie Christie told reporters she saw a huge, silent, low-flying object with pulsating lights and two smaller objects that suddenly appeared from behind. The objects were still visible when she ran into the house to fetch her husband who was a former chief technical advisor with the RAF. The couple watched the spectacle for almost two and a half hours, and with twenty-three years RAF experience behind him Wallace Christie was still baffled. This mass of UFOs was seen all over the area and amateur astronomer Tom Wilkinson thought they could not be of this planet. David Goddard was fishing off the pier when he spotted three objects coming near Woodbridge that were travelling at about 200 mph. As they got closer all three stopped together, then one suddenly speeded off followed by the other two.

One evening in 1996 Ipswich couple Tony and Maureen Boreham were returning home from visiting relatives near Rendlesham Forest when they sighted a huge spaceship. The sighting happened between Woodbridge and the village of Eyke. According to Maureen, the craft reminded her of a giant fairground Ferris wheel due to its size and the mass of bright orange lights.

Not only is the area plagued by unusual sightings of UFOs, but USAF personnel report weird apparitions having occurred on the twin installations. Americans are known to have a fascination with strange phenomena, but nothing, it seems, had prepared them for the ghostly visitors that were said to haunt Bentwaters and Woodbridge. Personnel recall being terrified by these weird and unholy sights but, because of the fear of ridicule, seldom were these events reported. It is little wonder then that most of the sightings of unexplained flying objects never made it into the log books. It is certainly true that the installations had a history of paranormal events, and some say that the UFO sightings were a part of that phenomenon.

James D. Hudnall was a security guard at RAF Bentwaters during the mid-1970s and he remembers his time at the bases like it was yesterday. He recalls how spooky it was during night duty being surrounded by the thick forest. James obliged by sharing the following two stories with me. The first was an incident that happened to his colleague Andy. Both airmen were qualified to guard the high-security areas, which included the weapons storage area on the Bentwaters installation. It was in this particular area that the first incident took place.

According to James, the nuclear weapons were stored in underground bunkers, which were designated a very high security area. All around were twelve-foot double fences with razor wire and motion detectors, and an armed patrol would drive around the compound. From the tall security tower the whole area could be viewed through standard military binoculars, and the security guards in the tower also had special sensor maps that would alert them if a disturbance caused a trip in a fence alarm or in the compound itself. You can only imagine what would have happened then, were intruders to trespass near the area, but I am told this is exactly what happened. It was a wintry foggy night and Andy had been on duty for some time when he spotted three figures heading towards the tower, *inside* the compound. It was difficult to make out their forms due to the weather conditions, but he knew they should not be there. He immediately got on his radio to alert the patrol car, and as the jeep entered the area and the headlights shone on the figures they simply disappeared into thin air. A search of the area was made but nothing was found and the patrol continued on its rounds. Sometime later that night Andy heard footsteps climbing up the metal steps leading to the tower, and according to James when anyone climbs those steps it makes the tower vibrate like nothing else he knows. By now Andy was getting worried because he was not expecting any visitors, so he opened the trapdoor and shone his torchlight down below but nothing seemed to be there. After closing the trapdoor he returned to the tower window to resume his watch, but within no time he again heard footsteps, only this time they were louder and getting closer and closer. He went for his gun and stood ready, waiting for whatever it was that was haunting him. At that moment the trapdoor swung wide open but there was absolutely nothing there, it then slammed shut, seemingly of its own accord. For the rest of the watch Andy stayed firmly on alert, but the incident remained a mystery that was never to be solved. Apparently, Andy did not report this second incident due to the fact that there was nothing to be seen and he probably thought he would be ridiculed.

The following incident also took place on the Bentwaters site, in a section known as the Quick Response Area. James explained that in the case of an emergency or in the event of war this is where the aircraft carrying nuclear weapons would have been fuelled ready for take-off to fly to Europe. Like the weapons storage area, this section also had very high security. Not only were there manned towers, a security patrol, double fences with razor wire and sensor alarms, but there was a guard for each of the planes. To protect them from the elements, the guards would sit in a telephone booth-sized gate shack and watch over their appointed aircraft. The only way into either of these areas was through a very secure double gate which was manned by security guards and a supervisor. The Quick Response Area was a huge compound that housed aircraft in hardened structures, each structure being widely spaced. Down the centre of this area ran the runway. One night whilst a security guard was sitting in his shack he heard a tapping on the roof. At first he thought it was starting to rain, but he couldn't see any rain on the windows. The tapping got louder and he stepped out to see what was causing the noise but there was nothing in sight. After a while the tapping turned into a thumping noise, and again the guard left the shack to check it out, only this time he took his rifle with him. To his amazement on the top of the gate shack was the figure of a man who appeared to be grinning as he stomped on the roof. The guard cocked his rifle and ordered the man not to move, whilst at the same time he got on his radio and called for assistance. On hearing the patrol car approach he made one quick turn to make sure it was them, but when he looked back to the figure on the roof it was gone. The man had simply disappeared.

A security policeman on duty at the east-end flightline apparently slammed his vehicle into a figure who darted out in front of him. Once over the shock he realized the figure had vanished into thin air, leaving two sooty handprints on the hood of the vehicle. There were several reports of a burning man who would sit on the hood of a jeep laughing his head off. He would then disappear in a flash but there would always be a burn mark on the jeep.

One elusive figure appeared on the base shuttle bus that travelled between the Woodbridge and Bentwaters sites. One day the driver picked up a lone passenger near the flightline at Woodbridge. The man was wearing a World War Two-style flying jacket, not an unusual sight as it was fashionable attire at the time. The driver thought the man was strange, as was the fact he didn't speak a word during the ride. He was the only passenger on the bus, and when it arrived at Melton roundabout the driver glanced back and discovered he was alone – the passenger had disappeared. Considering the Woodbridge flightline had been the emergency landing site for crashed World War Two aircraft, it is no wonder the place is haunted by the ghosts of airmen past.

The most famous phantom of all was that of East End Charlie, thought to be the ghost of a German Luftwaffe pilot shot down in World War Two. He was well known to the American airmen, especially during the early 1950s, although not many claimed to have seen him in recent times. East End Charlie's regular haunt was on the Woodbridge flightline where he would taunt the pilots as they came in to land. He could be seen to laugh and wave his arms about but when the security patrol arrived he would simply vanish into thin air. Woodbridge farmer Bill Kemball related an interesting story to me. During World War Two two German aircraft had crashed in the Rendlesham area, one right on Bill's family property. No one had survived the first crash, but years later in the early 1950s a forestry worker discovered the skeleton of a German pilot, complete with tattered uniform and the remains of a parachute. It seems the young pilot had jumped from his falling plane and ended up caught in an 80-foot pine tree in the thick of the forest. One wonders if, being severely injured, he died a slow and agonizing death or was strangled by his own parachute. Could the ghost of East End Charlie be this poor unfortunate airman? Fortunately for one German pilot there was a happier ending. After being shot down, the only survivor to the second crash had landed with a mere broken collarbone. Having fallen a few miles from Butley, he managed to walk to the village shop where he gave himself up. In 1997 he returned with his son to be welcomed by the friendly locals and walk the same route he had taken when he landed near Rendlesham Forest back in World War Two. Bill Kemball was only a young boy during the war but many years later when farming the land he had found parts of the wreck of the German aircraft. The wreck was photographed and pictures of it can still be seen today on the walls of the Butley Arms. Bill remembers seeing the father and son on his property and asking them what they were doing, only to discover that this was the pilot of the wreck he had dug up in his field. The old pilot was very grateful when Bill gave him a piece of the aircraft to take home with him.

For the men and women who guarded the east gate, there were more than a few scary moments. Late one night a guard reported some activity going on in Rendlesham Forest and a patrol was sent out to investigate. On seeing several hooded figures chanting, they fled back to base to report that there were devil worshippers out in the forest. They were told to leave them alone, because they were not on US property, but to keep an eye on them. More than once the Druids had scared the hell out of new recruits.

East Anglia is probably one of the strangest areas in Britain, with Lowestoft and Butley village known to have been the home of witches. There are reports of phantom creatures, such as black panthers, roaming the countryside, and Sir Arthur Conan Doyle was said to have been inspired by the ghostly fiery-eyed hellhound known as Old Shuck for his masterpiece *The Hound of the Baskervilles*. It is a pity Sherlock Holmes was not around in 1980, he might have been just the person to solve the Rendlesham Forest mystery.

WHATEVER HAPPENED TO RAF WOODBRIDGE AND BENTWATERS?

RAF Bentwaters and Woodbridge officially closed in 1993. To give some idea of the enormity of the Suffolk installations at the time of their disposal, Bentwaters alone measured more than 1,000 acres and consisted of two million square feet of technical buildings. There were more than seventy-two hardened aircraft shelters and associated runways and sixty-eight married quarters. Modern amenities included a community centre, theatre, health centre and shopping facilities. It also had its own private utilities. Together with its sister base, Bentwaters was home to 13,500 military and civilian personnel and their families. It comes as no surprise then that it was of great concern to the British government when, on 26 August 1992, the USAF officially announced their intention to withdraw from the twin bases. The completion date was set for 30 September 1993. The Ministry of Defence were now left with the problem of disposing of these surplus military sites, a difficult task considering their size and location. Of course it was to be expected, due to the end of the Cold War Britain had already taken steps to reduce the size of her armed forces, so it was inevitable that her allies would do the same. There was also concern over the effect their withdrawal would have on the local community, which for the last four decades had benefited from the US dollar.

RAF Bentwaters was officially placed on the market in June 1994, and one of the first interested buyers was the Maharishi Foundation, who proposed to establish an educational facility with a related science and business park. The site would have been known as the University of Natural Law, and would have been equipped for up to 4,000 students. Its intention was that their transcendental meditation and yogic flying techniques would reduce the country's crime rate, improve health and boost educational attainment. However, the Maharishi Foundation soon dropped out of the buyers' market. The official reason for their change of mind remains confidential, but rumours were rife that they had decided against purchasing the site because of the pollution it contained. It is certainly true that soon after the Americans departed several radiation tests were conducted on the installation. Even though the Ministry of Defence gave constant reassurances that there was no potential risk to health, in May 1998 a survey team searching for depleted contaminants discovered radiological contamination. The sections of concern were mostly the weapons storage area, waste dumps and maintenance areas. But after careful evaluation it was indicated that there was no requirement for remediation.

In 1995 the Chris Parker Group of Companies became an interested buyer and applied for planning permission to construct a leisure complex. The Suffolk Coastal District Council, apparently for environmental reasons, rejected their application, but the group did not give up easily. They took their appeal to the Ministry of Defence, offering to buy the site for a substantial sum. Their bid was again rejected and, finally, after several more applicants were turned down, an announcement was made that the contract would go to Bentwaters Investments Ltd. The date of the announcement – Friday 13th December 1996. The so-called unlucky date lived up to its reputation and there were many legal wrangles before the deal was finally completed on 16 May 1997. Ironically, the sale fetched a much lower price than that offered by previous bidders, causing angry protests from the competition. Thus, the future of Bentwaters was thrown into turmoil yet again. After many more disputes with the local community, the new owners launched the Anglia International Airpark. It seemed that Bentwaters would keep its runway after all, albeit that the aircraft flying in and out would be a far cry from the days of military hardware. But in August 1999 more complications arose when the local community voted against any flying in the area. The owners now had a real problem on their hands and within weeks the local press reported that Bentwaters was up for sale again. At the time of writing this there are rumours that the Ministry of Defence are interested in buying the site back and turning it into a British army base. The Woodbridge installation continues to remain in the hands of the Ministry of Defence and although it is no longer an RAF base and not active, the British army use it for helicopter training, as do the police force and the SAS.

According to Bentwaters security chief Vernon Drane, one of the prospective buyers was so fascinated by rumours of underground tunnels on the base that he visited on several occasions searching for them, but much to his disappointment he found nothing. Drane told me that on behalf of the client, the Ministry of Defence were asked to produce blueprints for the facilities. It appeared that none of the documents in Drane's possession showed any sign of them. After several requests the Ministry of Defence agreed to look into it but the blueprints never did materialize. Drane told me that the Ministry of Defence had sealed the underground facilities before the site was placed on the market.

SUMMARY

The Rendlesham Forest mystery is unique because it involves the defence departments of two great nations: the United Kingdom and the United States of America, each working in unison to keep the cover-up under control. This is a joint operation that has been going on for years, but now most people believe it is time for the cover-up to end and the truth to be known. Baroness Thatcher once told me, in relation to the UFO phenomenon, 'You can't tell the people,' but I believe the people have a right to know. We are now in the twenty-first century and with new technology in communications available to the masses, it is becoming increasingly more difficult for this cover-up to continue. When the Rendlesham Forest incident occurred twenty years ago in rural Suffolk, it took three years for it to become public knowledge. If it happened today it could take three days. What will our defence departments tell the people then? Isn't it time we were prepared?

Former US military personnel argue that it is a crime to use the armed forces in confrontations with UFOs because they are not trained to deal with it. Civilian pilots might suffer ridicule when reporting UFO sightings, but military personnel are not even allowed to discuss it among themselves. To make certain they do not talk, US military witnesses reporting a close encounter are interrogated, intimidated, harassed, threatened with prison sentences and, in extreme cases, drugged and hypnotized. Those who pose a risk are usually transferred on temporary duties to other airbases around the world. Alone at the new location and not knowing who to trust, they suppress their fears and try to carry on with their lives as best they can. If they talk they risk ruining their military career. If they are lucky they will serve their time without having to suffer these indignities. The British armed forces have a more subtle way of dealing with the situation: they use the Official Secrets Act.

The Rendlesham Forest incident has left its mental scars on those who were caught up in its web, and twenty years later those scars have not healed. There are still nightmares and self-doubts about what they encountered that December week in 1980, and they are still searching for answers. For these unfortunate witnesses Christmas will always be a reminder of those bizarre events.

Both the United Kingdom and the United States of America are world leaders in defence, but can we compete with the uninvited visitors? We are great nations, we have great military power and dedicated men and women who are trained to protect us from the enemy, but unless these people know who the enemy is how can they be expected to defend us? These visitors might not be hostile, but their technology is far more advanced than ours and that has to be of defence significance. I hope that some time in the near future one of our leaders will bravely stand up and announce the truth about the Rendlesham Forest incident and about the UFO phenomena in general.

The following transcript is of a tape recording that was made by Lieutenant Colonel Halt during his investigation in Rendlesham Forest in December 1980. There are background radio conversations throughout the recording: most feature radio transmissions between Sergeant Bustinza and Central Security Control. Due to these messages being in the background, however, more often than not they are overpowered by Colonel Halt's voice talking into his pocket recorder, so only those that are clear are translated here. My own comments are in brackets.

LT COL HALT: [Officer in charge] 150 feet or more from the initial, I should say suspected impact point. Having a little difficulty, we can't get the light-all to work. There seems to be some kind of mechanical problem. Let's send back and get another light-all. Meantime, we're gonna take some readings from the Geiger counter and, er, chase around the area a little bit waiting for another light-all to come out again.

SGT BUSTINZA: [on a radio in the background, obviously trying to organize more light-alls] . . . to security control . . . that's mark . . . 155 . . . number . . .

LT COL HALT: OK, we're now approaching an area within about twenty-five to thirty feet. What kind of readings are we getting . . . er.

BREAK IN TAPE

SGT NEVILLES: [Geiger operator] Just minor clicks.

LT COL HALT: Minor clicks.

BREAK IN TAPE

VOICE-OVER: [these voice-overs are recorded over the initial recording and are not related to the incident. It is the voice of Colonel Conrad, the base commander] Do you think it's going to be a nice day today?

VOICE-OVER: Yeah, I think so.

LT COL HALT: What are the impressions?

SGT NEVILLES: Just one, but . . .

LT COL HALT: Is that all the bigger they are?

SGT NEVILLES: Well, there's one more well defined over here.

SGT BUSTINZA: [on a radio] . . . Sergeant Bustinza to security control . . .

LT COL HALT: We're still getting clicks.

SGT BUSTINZA: . . . Sergeant Bustinza. Well, we're outta gas . . . We're at east gate . . . east gate, over.

LT COL HALT: Can you read that on the scale?

SGT NEVILLES: [examining the area with a Geiger counter] Yes sir. We're now on a five-tenths scale and we're reading about . . . er . . . third, fourth . . .

LT COL HALT: OK, we're still comfortably safe here?

SGT BUSTINZA: [on a radio] You don't have a light-all or [?] . . . or anything . . . duty security. Can you hear me? . . . Sergeant . . . a light-all, with gas, please.

LT ENGLUND: [the on-duty flight chief] We're still getting minor readings . . . We're getting a good indentation.

SGT BUSTINZA [on radio] . . . security D to security.

SGT NEVILLES: This one's dead.

LT ENGLUND: Let's go to the third one over here.

SGT NEVILLES: Sort of, whatever it is.

SGT BUSTINZA: [on radio] . . . Sergeant Bustinza . . . security . . .

SGT NEVILLES: Yes, now getting some residual.

LT COL HALT: How can you read that? The meter's definitely giving off pulse.

LT ENGLUND: About the centre.

LT COL HALT: Yes, I was gonna say, let's go to the centre of the area next, see what kind of reading we get out there. Keep reading the clicks. I can't hear the clicks. Guess you all . . . is that about centre, Bruce [asking Lt Bruce Englund]?

LT ENGLUND: Yes.

LT COL HALT: OK, let's go to the centre.

SGT NEVILLES: Yes, I'm getting more . . .

LT COL HALT: That's about the best deflection of the needle I've seen yet. OK, can you do an estimation? We're on a point-five scale. We're getting . . . having trouble reading the scale.

LT ENGLUND: At, er, approximately 01.25 hours.

BREAK IN TAPE

NOISE OVER: Deep cough.

SGT NEVILLES: We're getting rad at, er, a half a [sounds like milliroentgens].

UNKNOWN VOICE: Chuck [this is Colonel Halt's name, Charles known as Chuck].

BREAK IN TAPE

NOISE OVER: Loud gong noise [not connected with the forest recording].

LT COL HALT: . . . best point, I haven't seen it go any higher.

LT ENGLUND: Well, it's still flying around.

LT COL HALT: OK, we'll go out toward the . . .

LT ENGLUND: Now it's picking up . . .

LT COL HALT: This out toward the indentation where we first got the strongest reading. It's similar to what we got in the centre.

SGT NEVILLES: Right near the pod. It's right near the centre.

LT ENGLUND: This looks like an area here across where there could be a blast. It's in the centre.

LT ENGLUND: It jumped up towards seven . . .

LT COL HALT: What?

LT ENGLUND: It just jumped towards seven-tenths there.

LT COL HALT: Seven-tenths, right there in the centre?

LT ENGLUND: Ah, Ah.

LT COL HALT: We found a small blast, what looks like a blasted or scruffed up area here. We're getting very positive readings. Let's see, is that near the centre?

LT ENGLUND: Yes, it is.

SGT NEVILLES: Well, we assume it is . . .

LT ENGLUND: This is right in the centre . . . dead centre . . .

SGT NEVILLES: picking up more as you go along the whole area there now . . .

LT COL HALT: Up to seven-tenths . . .

SGT BUSTINZA: [on radio, still struggling with the transmissions] . . . fifty-five, this is our last call . . .

LT COL HALT: . . . or seven units. It's going on the point-five scale.

BREAK IN TAPE

LT COL HALT: OK, why don't we do this, why don't we make a sweep now I've got my gloves on now. Let's make a sweep out around the whole area, about ten foot out, and make a perimeter run around it, starting right back here at the corner, back at the same first corner where we came in. Let's go right back here . . . now I'm gonna have to depend upon you counting the clicks.

LT ENGLUND: Right.

LT COL HALT: OK, get the light-all on it.

LT ENGLUND: Let's sweep around it.

SGT NEVILLES: It was flying.

BREAK IN TAPE

LT COL HALT: Put it on the ground every once in a while.

BACKGROUND: We have lights nearby . . .

LT ENGLUND: This looks like an abrasion on the tree . . .

LT COL HALT: OK, we'll catch that on the way back, let's go around.

LT ENGLUND: We're getting interest right over here. It looks like it's an abrasion pointing into the centre . . .

LT COL HALT: It is.

LT ENGLUND: . . . of the landing area.

LT COL HALT: It may be old though. There's some sap marks or something like that. Let's go on back around.

UNKNOWN VOICE: Er . . .

BREAK IN TAPE

SGT NEVILLES: It also gives some extension on it.

LT COL HALT: Hey, this is an awkward thing to use, isn't it?

SGT NEVILLES: Normally, you see, I carry it on my . . . on my ears but this one broke.

LT COL HALT: Are we getting any further? I'm gonna shut this recorder off until we find something.

SGT NEVILLES: Picking up.

LT COL HALT: Picking up . . . What are we up to? We're up to two/three units deflection. You're getting in close to the pod?

SGT NEVILLES: Picking up something . . . picking up.

LT COL HALT: OK. It's still not going above three to four units.

SGT NEVILLES: Picking up more though, more frequent.

LT COL HALT: Yes, you're staying – you're staying steady up around two to three to four units now.

SGT BUSTINZA: [still struggling with the radio] 155.

LT ENGLUND: Each one of these trees is facing at a blast – what we assume is a landing site – all have abrasion facing in the same direction towards the centre. The same . . .

LT COL HALT: Let's go around a circle here. Turn back down here.

MSGT BALL: Try the other tree.

SGT NEVILLES: Picking up something . . . a . . .

LT COL HALT: Let me see that. You know I've got a funny . . . You're worried about the abrasion. I've never seen a tree that's, er . . .

MSGT BALL: That's a small sap mark.

LT COL HALT: I've never seen a pine tree that's been damaged react that fast [interference, voices all talking together].

SGT NEVILLES: You got a bottle to put that in?

LT COL HALT: You got a sample bottle?

LT ENGLUND: Yes put out the . . . that's for the soil sample . . . [interference]

SGT NEVILLES: Yes sir.

VOICES: [excited]

LT COL HALT: From now on let's [gap] let's . . .

LT ENGLUND: You'll notice they're all at the same . . .

LT COL HALT: Let's, let's, let's identify that as point number one.

That stake there. So you all know where it is if we have to sketch it. You got that Sergeant Nevilles?

SGT NEVILLES: Yes sir. Closest to the Woodbridge . . .

LT COL HALT: Closest to the Woodbridge base.

SGT NEVILLES: Be point one?

LT COL HALT: Be point one. Let's go clockwise from there.

SGT NEVILLES: Point two?

LT ENGLUND: Go ahead . . .

LT COL HALT: Point two. So this tree is between two and point three.

MSGT BALL: Burroughs and two other personnel requesting . . . riding on a jeep, that, er, your location [airman John Burroughs arrives with a patrol].

LT COL HALT: Tell them negative at this time. We'll tell them when they can come out here. We don't want them out here right now.

BREAK IN TAPE

LT COL HALT: OK, the sample, you gonna want this sample number one? Have 'em cut it off, include some of that sap and all . . . is between indentation two and three on a pine tree about, er . . . about five feet away . . . about three and half feet off the ground.

SGT NEVILLES: . . . I'll just put it in there for now, I've got some more . . .

LT COL HALT: There's a round abrasion on the tree about three and a half, four inches diameter. It looks like it might be old but, er, strange, there's a crystalline . . . pine sap that's come that fast.

SGT FRAIL: [seems in the distance] . . . Sergeant Frail . . .

LT COL HALT: You say there are other trees that are damaged in a similar fashion?

LT ENGLUND: . . . centre of the landing site . . . [interference]

LT COL HALT: OK, why don't you take a picture of that and remember your picture. Hey, I hope you're writing this down. It's gonna be on the tape.

SGT NEVILLES: You got a tape measure with you?

LT COL HALT: This is your picture, the first picture will be at the first tree, the one between, er . . . mark two and three. Meantime, I'm gonna look at a couple of those trees over here.

BREAK IN TAPE

UNKNOWN VOICE: We are getting some . . .

BREAK IN TAPE

LT COL HALT: We are getting readings on the tree. You're taking samples from on the side facing the suspected landing site?

LT ENGLUND: Four clicks max.

LT COL HALT: Up to four. Interesting. That's right where you're taking the sample now.

LT ENGLUND: Four.

LT COL HALT: That's the strongest point on the tree?

SGT NEVILLES: Yes sir, and if you come to the back, there's no clicks whatsoever.

LT COL HALT: No clicks at all in the back.

SGT NEVILLES: Maybe one or two.

LT COL HALT: It's all on the side facing the . . . interesting.

LT COL HALT: Looks like it f . . . twisted as it got . . . as it sat down on it, looks like something twisted it from side to side.

LT ENGLUND: Ah, Ah.

LT COL HALT: Very strange. We're at the same tree we took a sample of with this, what do you call it . . . the starscope.

LT ENGLUND: Ah, ah, stargazer.

LT COL HALT: Getting a definite heat reflection off the tree, about three to four feet off the ground?

LT ENGLUND: Yes . . . the same side in . . .

LT COL HALT: The same place where the . . . is.

LT ENGLUND: . . . we're getting heat directly behind us. I think we got the same thing off to your right.

LT COL HALT: There are three trees in the area immediately adjacent to the site within ten feet of the suspected landing site; we're picking up heat reflection off the trees.

LT ENGLUND: Shine the light on that, Bob [Sgt Bob Ball].

LT COL HALT: What's that again?

LT ENGLUND: Well, shine the light on again, Bob.

LT COL HALT: Why, you having trouble finding it? . . . turn the light on.

LT COL HALT: . . . then, when you want 'em, you'll notice the white—

[suddenly there is a very strange humming sound and the men are silent]

LT COL HALT: Hey . . . [long silent gap apart from humming noise]

LT COL HALT: You're right there's a white streak on the tree.

LT ENGLUND: Indicates, er . . .

LT COL HALT: Let's turn around and look at this tree over here now. Just a second. Watch, because you're right in front of the tree. I can see it. OK, give me a little side light so I can find the tree. OK, ahh . . .

SGT BUSTINZA: [still on the radio] Alpha two security . . .

LT COL HALT: I've lost the tree.

LT COL HALT: OK, stop! Stop! Light off. Hey, this is eerie.

MSGT BALL: Why don't you do the pods spots . . .

LT COL HALT: This is strange! Hey, does anyone wanna look at the spots on the ground? Whoops! Watch you don't step . . .

BACKGROUND: Five beeps from a vehicle arriving on the scene.

LT COL HALT: . . . you're walking all over them. OK, let's step back and don't walk all over 'em. Come back here – somebody and put a beam on 'em. You're gonna have to be back about ten, fifteen feet. You see it . . .

LT ENGLUND: OK, fine . . .

LT COL HALT: OK, lights off.

BREAK IN TAPE

VOICE-OVER: [Colonel Conrad] He took this long to document . . .

LT COL HALT: What do you think about the spot?

[Radio interference in background]

LT COL HALT: Yeah.

BREAK IN TAPE

LT COL HALT: . . . ready at the first spot? OK, that's what we'll call spot number three. Let's go in the back corner and get spot number one. Spot number one. Here's spot number one right there, spot number one right there. Do you need some light? There it is right here . . . You focused?

SGT NEVILLES: Focused.

LT COL HALT: OK . . . looking at spot number one through the starlight scope.

LT ENGLUND: Picking up a slight increase in light as I go over it.

LT COL HALT: Slight increase in light in spot number one. Let's go look at spot number two. Spot number two's right over here. Right here, see it?

LT ENGLUND: . . . Slight increase.

LT COL HALT: OK, get focused on it. Tell me when. OK, lights on. Let's see what we get on it.

LT ENGLUND: Slight increase.

LT COL HALT: Just a slight increase?

LT ENGLUND: Try the centre.

LT COL HALT: The centre spot, not really centre, slightly off centre. It's right there.

LT ENGLUND: Right here.

LT COL HALT: OK, we're gonna get your reading on it right there.

LT ENGLUND: OK.

LT COL HALT: Tell me when you're ready.

LT ENGLUND: Ready.

LT COL HALT: OK, lights on. It's the centre spot we're looking at now: almost the centre.

LT ENGLUND: Getting a slight increase.

LT COL HALT: Slight increase there. This is slightly off centre toward the, er . . . one – two side. It's, er . . . some type of abrasion or something in the ground where the pine needles are pushed back where we get a high radioact . . . er, high reading about a detection of, er, two to three, maybe four, depending on the point of it.

LT ENGLUND: Someone wanna check it?

BREAK IN TAPE

SGT NEVILLES: Yes.

LT COL HALT: Are you sure there's a positive after-effect?

SGT NEVILLES: Yes, there is, definitely. That's on the centre spot, there is an after-effect.

LT ENGLUND: What does that mean?

SGT NEVILLES: It means that when the lights are turned off, once we all focused in, allowed time for the eyes to adjust, we are getting an indication of heat source coming out of that centre spot . . . as, er . . . Which will show up on the . . .

LT COL HALT: Heat or some form of energy, it's hardly heat at this stage of the game.

SGT NEVILLES: But it is still heat . . .

BREAK IN TAPE

LT COL HALT: Looking directly overhead, one can see an opening in the trees, plus some freshly broken pine branches on the ground underneath. Looks like some of them came off about fifteen to twenty feet up. Some small branches about inch or less in diameter.

BREAK IN TAPE

LT COL HALT: 01.48. We're hearing some strange sounds out of the farmer's . . .

SGT NEVILLES: Twenty-eight . . . seven . . .

LT COL HALT: . . . barnyard animals. They're very, very active and making an awful lot of noise.

SGT NEVILLES: . . . definite pigmentation . . .

LT COL HALT: You saw a light? Slow down. Where, where?

SGT NEVILLES: Right on this position here. Straight ahead in between the trees . . . [Adrian Bustinza pointed out that someone saw a light going through the trees]

LT ENGLUND: There it is again . . . beginning of the gap . . . right there.

SGT NEVILLES: It throw the hell off my flashlight there.

LT COL HALT: Hey, I see it too. What is it?

SGT NEVILLES: We don't know, sir.

LT COL HALT: OK, it's a strange small red light, looks to be out maybe a quarter – half mile, maybe further out. I'm gonna switch off for a . . .

BREAK IN TAPE

LT COL HALT: The light is gone now. It was approximately 120 degrees from the site.

SGT NEVILLES: It's back again.

LT COL HALT: Is it back again?

SGT NEVILLES: Yes sir.

LT COL HALT: Well, douse flashlights then. Let's go back to the edge of the clearing then, so we can get a better look at it. See if you can get the starscope on it. The light's still there and all the barnyard animals have gotten quiet now. We're heading about 110 to 120 degrees from the site, out through the clearing now. Still getting a reading on the meter about two clicks. Needles jumped three to four clicks getting stronger. [Bustinza said that when he returned with the light-all the patrol were in a clearing on the edge of the forest.]

SGT NEVILLES: Now it's stopped. Now it's coming up. Hold on, here we go. Now it's coming up about approximately four foot off the ground. The compass has 110 degrees.

BREAK IN TAPE

LT COL HALT: Right, I just turned the meter off. Better say that again, about four feet off the ground, about 110 degrees, getting the reading of about four clicks.

SGT NEVILLES: Yes sir . . . [he coughs] Excuse me. Now it's died.

LT COL HALT: I . . . I think it's something here on the ground. I think it's something . . . very large.

SGT NEVILLES: . . . a tree right over . . .

BREAK IN TAPE

LT COL HALT: We just bumped into the first light that we've seen. We're about 150 to 200 yards from the site. Everything else is just deathly calm. There's no doubt about it, there's some kind of strange flashing red light ahead.

SGT NEVILLES: Yeah, it's yellow.

LT COL HALT: I saw a yellow tinge in it too. Weird. It appears to be making a little bit this way?

SGT NEVILLES: Yes sir.

LT COL HALT: It's brighter than it has been . . . It's coming this way. It's definitely coming this way.

MSGT BALL: Pieces are shooting off.

LT COL HALT: Pieces of it are shooting off.

MSGT BALL: at about 11 o'clock . . . [referring to its position]

LT COL HALT: There's no doubt about it; this is weird.

MSGT BALL: Look to the left.

SGT NEVILLES: There's two lights. One light to the right and one light to the left.

LT COL HALT: Keep your flashlight off. There's something very, very strange. Check the headset out, see if it gets any stronger. Give us . . .

SGT NEVILLES: OK, I have an indication that this is a vague reading too.

LT COL HALT: A vague reading?

SGT NEVILLES: The cable has been removed.

LT COL HALT: OK . . . pieces are falling off it again.

MSGT BALL: It just moved to the right . . . went off to the right.

LT COL HALT: Yeah . . . strange. Auh.

LT ENGLUND: Went off to the right.

LT COL HALT: Strange. Ahhh. One again left. Let's approach the edge of the woods at that point. Can we do without lights? Let's do it carefully, come on . . . OK, we're looking at the thing, we're probably about two to three hundred yards away. It looks like an eye winking at you, it's still moving from side to side and when we put the starscope on it, it's sorta a hollow centre, right, a dark centre, it's . . .

LT ENGLUND: It's like a pupil . . .

LT COL HALT: It's like the pupil of an eye looking at you, winking . . . and the flash is so bright to the starscope, that, er . . . it almost burns your eye.

BREAK IN TAPE

LT COL HALT: We've passed the farmer's house and are crossing the next field and we now have multiple sightings of up to five lights with a similar shape and all, but they seem steady rather than pulsating a glow with a red flash. We've just crossed the creek . . .

LT ENGLUND: Here we go . . .

LT COL HALT: What kinda readings are we getting now? We're getting three good clicks on the meter and we're seeing strange lights in the sky.

BREAK IN TAPE

LT COL HALT: 2.44: we're at the far side of the farmer's, the second farmer's field and made sighting again about 110 degrees. This looks clear out to the coast. It's right on the horizon. Moves about a bit and flashes from time to time. Still steady and red in colour. Also, after negative readings in the field, we're picking up slight readings four to five clicks now on the meter.

BREAK IN TAPE

LT COL HALT: 3.05: we see strange, er, strobe-like flashes to the, er . . . almost sporadic, but there's definitely something there, some kind of phenomena. 3.05: at about, er . . . 10 degrees horizon, er, directly north, we got two strange objects, er, half-moon shape, dancing about with coloured lights on them, but, er, it has to be about 5 to 10 miles out, maybe less. The half-moons have now turned into full circles as though there was an eclipse or something there for a minute or two.

BREAK IN TAPE

LT COL HALT: 3.15: now we've got an object about ten degrees directly south . . .

SGT NEVILLES: There's one to the left.

LT COL HALT: Ten degrees off the horizon, and the ones to the north are moving, one's moving away from us.

SGT NEVILLES: It's moving out fast.

LT COL HALT: They're moving out fast.

MSGT BALL: There's one on the right heading away too.

LT COL HALT: Yeah, they're both heading north. Hey, here he comes from the south; he's coming in toward us now.

MSGT BALL: Shit.

LT COL HALT: Now we're observing what appears to be a beam coming down to the ground [excited shouting in the background].

MSGT BALL: Look at the colours . . . shit.

LT COL HALT: This is unreal.

BREAK IN TAPE

LT COL HALT: 3.30: and the objects are still in the sky, although the one to the south looks like it's losing a little bit of altitude. We're turning around and heading back toward the base. The object to the sou . . . the object to the south is still beaming down lights to the ground.

BREAK IN TAPE

LT COL HALT: Zero four hundred hours, one object still hovering over the Woodbridge base at about 5 to 10 degrees off the horizon. Still moving, erratic and similar lights beaming down as earlier.

End of transcript

APPENDIX II

THE SHIFTS

Break	Swing 15.00-23.00	Mid (Midnight) 23.00–7.00
B	D	C Tuesday 23/24
B	D	C Wednesday 24/25
B	D	C Thursday 25/26
C	B	D Friday 26/27
C	B	D Saturday 27/28
C	B	D Sunday 28/29
D	C	B Monday 29/30
D	C	B Tuesday 30/31
D	C	B Wednesday 31/1

Shift Roster for the Security Police and Law Enforcement Squadrons

Both the Security Police and Law Enforcement Squadrons worked around four duty shift rosters. These were called 'Flights' and were categorized A, B, C and D. The A Flight was always a day shift, but members from other Flights were sometimes posted on A Flight and still retained their original Flight identity. Flight B, C and D usually rotated from 15.00–23.00 and from 23.00–07.00. The afternoon shift was called the 'swing' and the midnight shift the 'mids'. During changeover, alerts and exercises, shifts would overlap, and the A Flight would often participate in night exercises. The structure of the shifts is so complex to the uninformed that they have hindered no end the research on this case. It was for this reason that I decided to familiarize myself with the shift rosters.

Although they are qualified in security and law enforcement, the witnesses have had difficulty trying to remember the exact dates they were involved. There are several dates given by various witnesses: 25th, 26th, 27th, 28th and 29th. The confusion has arisen because the incident occurred during shift changes and because it ran into the early hours of the morning. To make it easier to understand I have grouped the nights together 25/26, 26/27, 27/28, 28/29. So a midnight shift starting at 23.00 on the 25th would finish at 07.00 on the 26th (25/26). Based on their flight details and their recollection of events, I have tried to determine what nights they were on duty, not an easy task by any means because during the Christmas holiday period some (mostly senior) staff would work twelve-hour shifts for two days, then take a break.

During the incident personnel from all four flights were on duty and exercises were conveniently being carried out. There were also numerous personnel on standby who were apparently called back from their break on what was termed a Red Alert. Edward Drury, a former major with the Combat Support Group, explained the schedule for that week:

> Christmas schedules were in operation, which meant that for two weeks over the holiday period members from all flights were on duty, sometimes for a period of twelve hours at a time. The idea was to get as many of the kids off for the holidays, as much as possible.

According to Drury, Red Alerts were only put into operation if there was a threatening incident.

APPENDIX III

LETTERS, STATEMENTS AND DRAWINGS

DEPARTMENT OF THE AIR FORCE
HEADQUARTERS 81ST COMBAT SUPPORT GROUP (USAFE)
APO NEW YORK 09755

REPLY TO
TTN OF: CD

13 Jan 81

SUBJECT: Unexplained Lights

TO: RAF/CC

1. Early in the morning of 27 Dec 80 (approximately 0300L), two USAF security police patrolmen saw unusual lights outside the back gate at RAF Woodbridge. Thinking an aircraft might have crashed or been forced down, they called for permission to go outside the gate to investigate. The on-duty flight chief responded and allowed three patrolmen to proceed on foot. The individuals reported seeing a strange glowing object in the forest. The object was described as being metalic in appearance and triangular in shape, approximately two to three meters across the base and approximately two meters high. It illuminated the entire forest with a white light. The object itself had a pulsing red light on top and a bank(s) of blue lights underneath. The object was hovering or on legs. As the patrolmen approached the object, it maneuvered through the trees and disappeared. At this time the animals on a nearby farm went into a frenzy. The object was briefly sighted approximately an hour later near the back gate.

2. The next day, three depressions 1 1/2" deep and 7" in diameter were found where the object had been sighted on the ground. The following night (29 Dec 80) the area was checked for radiation. Beta/gamma readings of 0.1 milliroentgens were recorded with peak readings in the three depressions and near the center of the triangle formed by the depressions. A nearby tree had moderate (.05-.07) readings on the side of the tree toward the depressions.

3. Later in the night a red sun-like light was seen through the trees. It moved about and pulsed. At one point it appeared to throw off glowing particles and then broke into five separate white objects and then disappeared. Immediately thereafter, three star-like objects were noticed in the sky, two objects to the north and one to the south, all of which were about 10° off the horizon. The objects moved rapidly in sharp angular movements and displayed red, green and blue lights. The objects to the north appeared to be elliptical through an 8-12 power lens. They then turned to full circles. The objects to the north remained in the sky for an hour or more. The object to the south was visible for two or three hours and beamed down a stream of light from time to time. Numerous individuals, including the undersigned, witnessed the activities in paragraphs 2 and 3.

CHARLES I. HALT, Lt Col, USAF
Deputy Base Commander

Lieutenant Colonel Halt's memorandum to the Ministry of Defence

on the night of 25-26 Dec at around
0300 while on patrol down at east
gate myself & my partner saw lights
comming from the woods due east of
the gate. The lights were red & blue
the red one above the blue one & they
were flashing on & off. Because I we never
saw anything like that comming from the
woods before we decided to drive down &
see what it was. We went down east gate
Road & took a right at the stop sign & drove
down about 10 to 20 yards to where there is
a road that goes into the forest at the
road I could see a white light shining onto
the trees & I could still see the red
& blue lights. we decided we better
go call it in so we went back up
towards east gate. I was watching
the lights & the white light started
comming down the road that lead
into the forest. we got to the gate
& called it in. The whole time I
could see the lights & the white light
was almost at the edge of the road & the
blue & red lights were still out in the
woods. a security unit was sent down
to the gate & when they got there they
could see it to. We asked permission
to go & see what it was & they told
us we could. We took the truck
down the road that lead into the
forest. as we went down the east gate
Road & the road that lead into the
forest the lights were moving back &
they appeared to stop in a clearing

Handwritten statement by John Burroughs (January 1981)

bunch of tress. We stoped our truck where the road stoped & went on foot. We crossed a small open field that lead into the trees where the lights were comming from & as we were comming into the trees there were strange noises, like a women was screaming also the woods lit up & you could hear the farm animals making alot of noise & there was alot of movement in the woods. all three of us but the ground & whatever it was started moving back towards the open field, after a min or 2 we got up & moved into the trees & the lights moved out into the open field. We got up to a fence that seperated the trees from the open field & you could see the lights down by a farmers house. We climbed over the fence & started moving towards the red & blue lights & they just disappeared once we reached the farmers house we could see a beacon going around so we went towards it. We followed it for about 2 miles before we could it was comming from a lyght house. We had just crossed a creek & were told to come back when we saw a blue light to our left in the trees. It was only there for a min & it just streaked away. After that we didnot see anything so we returned to the truck.

Page 2 of Burroughs' statement

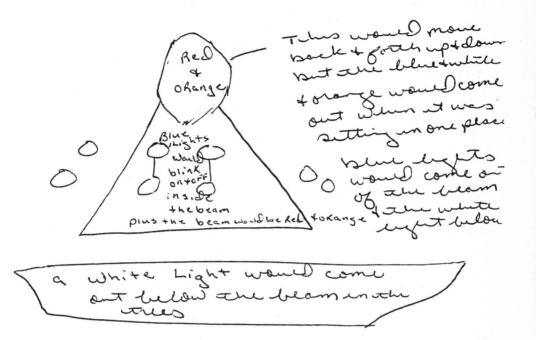

This would move
back & forth up+down
but the blue+white
+ orange would come
out when it was
setting in one place

Red
&
Orange

blue lights
would come out
of the beam
of the white
light below

Blue
Lights
would
blink
on+off
inside
the beam
plus the beam would be Red +orange

a white Light would come
out below the beam in the
trees

AlC John Burroughs
8MSPS   SPOL CFOt

BURROWS IS A STRAIGHT
FORWARD+ HONEST COP. HE
DOES HAVE THE ABILITY TO TAKE
AN INCIDENT + TURN IT INTO A
DISASTER. (HE COMES ON TOO
STRONG). THERE'S NO DOUBT IN
MY MIND HIS STATEMENT IS
ACCURATE. HE REALLY BECAME
OBSESSED WITH THIS. NOW HE'S
WORRIED THAT THIS MIGHT
AFFECT HIS CAREER.

Page 3 of Burroughs' statement depicting drawing of UFO

STATEMENT

Received dispatch from CSC to rendzvous with Police 4 AIC Burroughs, and Police 5 SSgt Caff⸱⸱
at east gate Woodbridge. Upon arriving at east gate directly to the east about 1 ½ miler ⸱
a large wooded area. A large yellow glowing light was emitting above the trees.(refer diag⸱⸱
In the center of the lighted area directly in the center ground leval, there was a red ligh⸱
blinking on and off 5 to 10 sec intervals. And a blue light that was being for the mosl par
steady. After receiving permission from CSC, we proceeded off base pass east gate, down on
logging road. Left vehicle proceeded on foot . Bomroughs and I were approx. 15-20 maters n
and proceeding on a true east direction. from the logging road. The area in front of us was
lighting up a 30 meter area. When we got with in a 50 meter distance. The object was produc⸱
ted and blue light. The blue light was steady and projecting under the object. It was ligh⸱
up the area directly under XXextending a meter or two out. At this point of positive iden⸱
fication I relayed to CSC, SSgt Coffey. Postitive siting of object...l..color of lights and
that it was defidently mechaniclal in nature. This is the closes point that I was near tho ⸱
at any point. We then proceeded after it. It moved in a zig-zagging manner back through the
then lost site of it. On the way back we encounterd a blue streaking light to left lasting ⸱⸱
a few seconds. Aftsi a 45 min wal k arrived at our vehicle.

> SGT PENNISTON HAS A
> LOT TO CONTRIBUTE. HE
> PROMISED ME A PLASTER
> CAST + PHOTOS BUT NEVER
> DELIVERED. I THINK HE'S
> HOLDING OUT TO "SELL" A
> STORY. HE IS, HOWEVER,
> A VERY COMPETENT INDIVIDUAL
> AND CAN BE TRUSTED. I'M
> CONVINCED HIS STORY IS AS
> HE SAYS. HE WAS SO SHOOK
> HE HAD TO HAVE A WEEK OFF
> TO RECOVER.

Jim Penniston's alleged statement (January 1981)

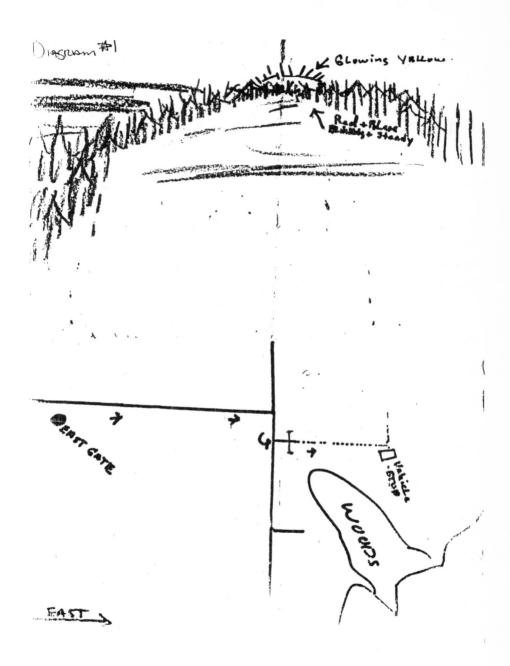

*Jim Penniston's drawings of UFO and directions to landing site
(January 1981)*

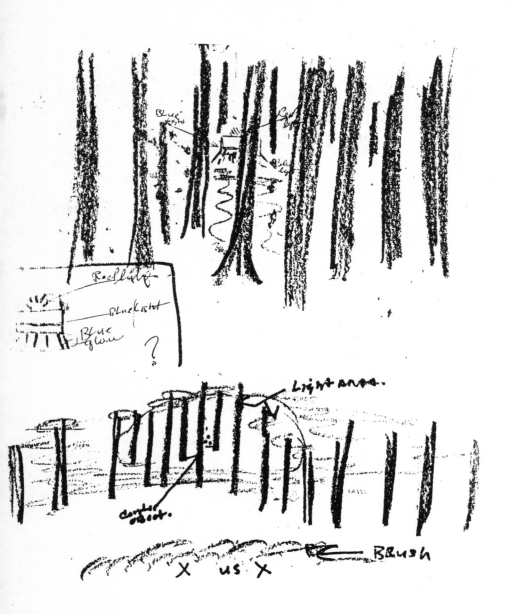

Jim Penniston's 3 drawings of the UFO (January 1981)

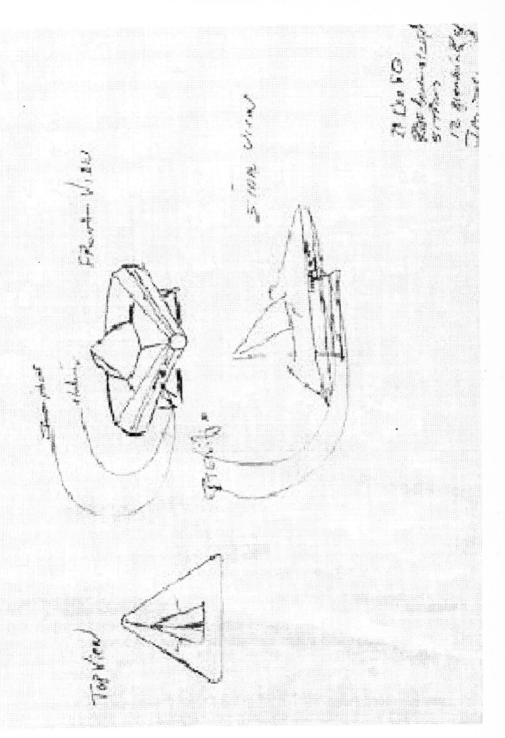

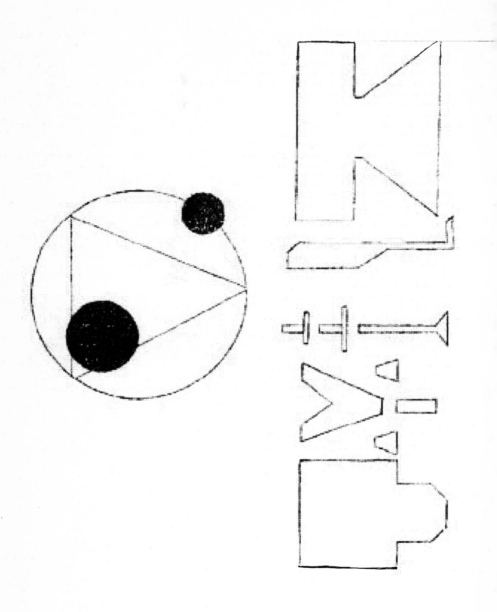

*Jim Penniston's drawing of the symbols he saw on the UFO, which he
copied from the original rough sketches in his notebook*

On 26 Dec 80, SSgt Penningston and I were on Security #6 at Woodbridge Base. I was the member. We were patroling Delta NAPA when we received a call over the radio. It stated that Police #4 had seen some strange lights out past the East Gate and we were to respond. SSgt Penningston and I left Delta NAPA, heading for the East Gate code two. When we got there SSgt Steffens and A]C Burroughs were on patrol. They told us they had seen some funny lights out in the woods. We notified CSC and we asked permission to investigate further. They gave us the go-ahead. We left our weapons with SSgt Steffens who remained at the gate,, Thus the three of us went out to investigate. We stopped the Security Police vehicle about]00 meters from the gate. Due to the terrain we had to on by foot. We kept in constant contact with CSC. While we walked, each one of us would see the lights. Blue, red, white, and yellow. The beckon light turned out to be the yellow light. We would see them periodically, but not in a specific pattern. As we approached, the lights would seem to be at the edge of the forrest. We were about]00 meters from the edge of the forrest when I saw a quick movement, it look visible for a moment . It look like it spun XXXXX left a quarter of a turn, then it was gone. I'x advised SSgt Penningston and AlC Borroughs. We advised CSC and proceeded in extreme caution. When we got about 75-50 meters, MSgt Chandler/Flight Chief, was on the scene. CSC was not reading our transmissions very well,, so we used MSgt Chandler as a go-between. He remained back at our vehicle. As we entered the forrest, the blue and red lights were not visible anymore. Only the beacon light, was still blinking. We figured the lights were coming from past the forrest, since nothing was visible when we past through the woody forrest. We would see a glowing near the beacon light, but as we got closer we found it to be a lit up farm house. After we had passed throught the forrest, we thought it had to be an aircra accident. So did CSC as well. But we ran and walked a good 2 miles past our vehicle, until we got to a vantage point where we could determine that what we were chasing was x only a beacon light off in the distance. Our route through the forrest and field was a direct one,x straight towards the light. We informed CSC thàt the light beacon was farther than we thought,, so CSC terminated our investigation. AlC Burroughs and I took a road, while SSgt Penningston walked straight back from where we came. AlC Borroughs saw the light again, this time it was coming from the left of us , as we were walking back to our patrol vehicle. We got in contact with SSgt Penningston and we took a walk threw where we saw the lights. Nothing. Finally, we made it back to our vehicle, after making contact ;with the PC's and informing them of what we saw. After that we met MSgt Chandler and we went in service again after termination of the sighting.

Edward N. Cabansag (signature)
EDWARD N. CABANSAG, Al0, USAF
81st Security Police Sq.

I'M CONVINCED THIS IS
A "CLEANED UP" VERSION
OF WHAT HAPPENED. I TALCED
WITH AMN CABANSAG + CAN
SAY HE WAS SHOOK UP TO
THE POINT HE DIDN'T WANT
TO TALK. FROM TALKING WITH
CHUCK DE MARCO (C+N) I CAN
SAY HE STILL WORRIES TODAY.
HE MIGHT TALK IF APPROACHED
RIGHT   4

Edward Cabansag's alleged statement (26 December 1980)

STATEMENT OF WITNESS

Bldg 679, RAF Bentwaters
_____ *(Place)*

2 Jan 1981   *(Place)*
_____
                (Date)

I, _____ Fred A. Buran _____, hereby state that
                                              has identified himself to me
as _____ USAF.
        (Special Agent AFOSI, Security Police, Other--Specify)

I do hereby voluntarily and of my own free will make the following statement without having been subjected to any coercion, unlawful influence or unlawful inducement. The following statement is general in nature and may be inaccurate in some instances due to the time lapse involved and the fact that I was not taking notes at the time of the occurrence. At approximately 0300 hrs, 26 December 1980, I was on duty at bldg 679, Central Security Control, when I was notified that A1C Burroughs had sighted some strange lights in the wooded area east of the runway at RAF Woodbridge.

Shortly after this initial report A1C Burroughs was joined by SSgt Penniston and his rider, AMN Cabansag. SSgt Penniston also reported the strange lights. I directed SSgt Coffey, the on duty Security Controller, to attempt to ascertain from SSgt Penniston whether or not the lights could be marker lights of some kind, to which SSgt Penniston said that he had never seen lights of this color or nature in the area before. He described them as red, blue, white, and orange.

SSgt Penniston requested permission to investigate. After he had been joined by the Security Flight Chief, MSgt Chandler, and turned his weapon over to him, I directed them to go ahead. SSgt Penniston had previously informed me that the lights appeared to be no further than 100 yds from the road east of the runway.

I monitored their progress (Penniston, Burroughs, and Cabansag) as they entered the wooded area. They appeared to get very close to the lights, and at one point SSgt Penniston stated that it was a definite mechanical object. Due to the colors they had reported I alerted them to the fact that they may have been approaching a light aircraft crash scene. I directed SSgt Coffey to check with the tower to see if they could throw some light on the subject. They could not help.

SSgt Penniston reported getting near the "object" and then all of a sudden said they had gone past it and were looking at a marker beacon that was in the same general direction as the other lights. I asked him, through SSgt Coffey, if he could have been mistaken, to which Penniston replied that had I seen the other lights I would know the difference. SSgt Penniston seemed somewhat agitated at this point.

They continued to look further, to no avail. At approximately 0354 hrs, I terminated the investigation and ordered all units back to their normal duties.

I directed SSgt Penniston to take notes of the incident when he came in that morning. After talking with him face to face concerning the incident, I am convinced that he saw something out of the realm of explanation for him at that time. I would like to state at this time that SSgt Penniston is a totally reliable and mature individual. He was not overly excited, nor do I think he is subject to overreaction or misinterpretation of circumstances. Later that morning, after conversing with CPT Mike Verano, the day shift commander, I discovered that there had been several other sightings. Any further developments I have no direct knowledge of.

AF FORM 1169   PREVIOUS EDITION WILL BE USED   Page 1 of 2 Pages

Fred Buran's official statement (2 January 1981)

CONTINUATION SHEET FOR AF FORM 1168 and 1169.

NOT USED

FRED BURAN IS A
GOOD & RELIABLE PERSON.
HE MIGHT TALK IF HIS
NAME WERE PROTECTED

I further state that I have read this entire statement, initialed all pages and corrections, and signed this
statement, and that it is correct and true as written.

_____
(Signature)

WITNESSES:

81 SECURITY POLICE SQUADRON
_____
(Address)

_____
(Signature)

Subscribed and sworn to before me, a person authorized
by law to administer oaths, this

_____
(Address)

_____ day of _____ 19 ____

_____
(Signature)

at _____

_____
(Address)

_____
(Signature of Person Administering Oath.)

_____
(Type Name, Grade & Title of Person Administering Oath.)

AF FORM 1170   ☆ U.S. GOVERNMENT PRINTING OFFICE: 1977-241-130/1323   PAGE 2 OF 2 PAGES

Page 2 of Buran's statement

STATEMENT OF WITNESS

2 January 1981 (Place) (Date)

I, _J. D. CHANDLER, msgt. USAF_, hereby state that ~~has identified himself to me~~ USAF.

as _____
(Special Agent AFOSI, Security Police, Other--Specify)

I do hereby voluntarily and of my own free will make the following statement without having been subjected to any coercion, unlawful influence or unlawful inducement.

At approximately 0300 hrs, 26 December 1980 while conducting security checks on RAF Bentwaters, I monitored a radio transmission from A1C Burroughs, Law Enforcement patrol on RAF Woodbridge, stating that he was observing strange lights in the wooded area just beyond the access road, leading from the east gate at RAF Woodbridge. Sgt Penniston, Security Supervisor, was contacted and directed to contact Burroughs at the east gate. Upon arrival, Sgt Penniston immediately notified SSO that he was observing these lights and requested to make a close observation. After several minutes, Penniston requested my presence. I departed RAF Bentwaters through Butley gate for RAF Woodbridge. When I arrived, Sgt Penniston, A1C Burroughs, and Amn Jalensky had entered the wooded area just beyond the clearing at the access road. We set up a radio relay between Sgt Penniston, myself, and SSO. On one occasion Penniston relayed that he was close enough to the object to determine that it was definitely a mechanical object. He stated that he was within approximately 50 meters. He also stated that their was lots of noises in the area which seemed to be animals running around. Each time Penniston gave me the indication that he was about to reach the area where the lights were, he would give an extended estimated location. He eventually arrived at a "beacon light", however, he stated that this was not the light or lights he had originally observed. He was instructed to return. While enroute out of the area he reported seeing lights again almost in direct pass where they had passed earlier. Shortly after this, they reported that the lights were no longer visible. Sgt Penniston returned to RAF Woodbridge. After talking to the three of them, I was sure that they had observed something unusual. At no time did I observe anything from the time I arrived at RAF Woodbridge.

AF FORM 1169   PREVIOUS EDITION WILL BE USED   Page 1 of____ Pages

J. D. Chandler's official statement (2 January 1981)

CONTINUATION SHEET FOR AF FORM 1168 and 1169.

I further state that I have read this entire statement, initialed all pages and corrections, and signed this statement, and that it is correct and true as written.

B.J. Chandler
(Signature)

WITNESSES:

81 Security Police SQ
(Address)

_____
(Signature)

Subscribed and sworn to before me, a person authorized by law to administer oaths, this

_____
(Address)

_____ day of _____ 19 ____

_____
(Signature)

at _____

_____
(Address)

_____
(Signature of Person Administering Oath.)

_____
(Type Name, Grade & Title of Person Administering Oath.)

AF FORM 1170

PAGE ___ OF ___ PAGES

Page 2 of Chandler's statement

RAF LIAISON OFFICE
Royal Air Force Bentwaters Woodbridge Suffolk IP12 2RQ

Telephone Woodbridge 3737 ext ~~2333~~ 2257

MOD (**D**S8a)

Your reference

Our reference BENT/019/76/
                               AIR

Date *15* January 1981

UNIDENTIFIED FLYING OBJECTS (UF**O**'s)

I attach a copy of a report I have received from
the Deputy Base Commander at RAF Bentwaters concerning some mysterious sightings in the Rendlesham forest near RAF Woodbridge. The report is
forwarded for your information and action as considered necessary.

D H MORELAND
Squadron Leader
RAF Commander

Copy to:

SRAFLO, RAF Mildenhall

*Squadron Leader Donald Moreland's letter to the Ministry of Defence
regarding Lieutenant Colonel Halt's memorandum*

From: P A CROWTHER

MINISTRY OF DEFENCE
Headquarters
Ministry of Defence Police
Wethersfield, Braintree, Essex, CM7 4AZ
Direct Dial Telephone 01371 85 4289
Fax 01371 854025

Ms G Bruni
PO Box 697
Chelsea
London
SW3 2BL

Agency Secretary & Director
of Finance & Administration

D/MDP/ 36/2/7(262/99)

17th August 1999

Dear Ms Bruni

Thank you for your letter dated 22nd July 1999, requesting information about an incident in Rendlesham Forest in 1980.

With regard to your request, we have been unable to find any reference to the incident in files held by our Operations and CID departments. However it is worth noting that files of this age are not normally held centrally - they are either destroyed or archived. Several of the more senior officers of the Force have however been contacted with regard to the presence of an MDP detachment at Woodbridge in 1980. It would appear that RAF Woodbridge did not sustain its own detachment; rather it was the subject of infrequent visits by MDP officers stationed elsewhere in Suffolk. There is no recollection of the reporting of such an incident.

The Ministry of Defence Police Agency, like all Government Departments and Agencies, is bound by the Code of Practice on Access to Government Information. This means that we are committed to providing you with the information you require, as long as it is not exempt under the Code. If you wish to make a complaint that your request for information has not been properly dealt with, you should appeal to: Ministry of Defence, OMD14, Room 617, Northumberland House, Northumberland Avenue, London WC2N 5BP.

Yours sincerely,

Letter to the author from the Ministry of Defence Police

SUFFOLK CONSTABULARY
━━ COMMUNITY FIRST ━━

FORCE HEADQUARTERS, MARTLESHAM HEATH, IPSWICH IP5 7QS
Tel: Ipswich (01473) 613500 Telex: 98120 Fax: 474274
All official correspondence should be addressed to the Chief Constable

P J Scott-Lee Esq. QPM
Chief Constable

Your Ref:

Our Ref: 28 July 1999

Dear Ms Bruni,

INCIDENT IN RENDLESHAM FOREST - DECEMBER 1980

I refer to your letter of 22 July 1999 in relation to a series of unusual events which allegedly occurred outside the perimeter of RAF Woodbridge, Suffolk, during the last week of December 1980.

A great deal of interest has understandably been generated in respect of this story, not least because of the apparent number and standing of witnesses. However, over the intervening years, various reports of the incident(s) seem to have taken on a life of their own to the extent that the 'sighting' details and corroborative evidence have been substantially embellished. This contrasts sharply with the views of the local police who attended at the time and did not perceive this occurrence as being anything unusual considering the festive significance of the date and expected high spirits.

Such a perception lends support to the lack of police documentary evidence and one needs to understand the minimalistic nature of rural policing in order to appreciate the answers which I will attempt to give to your questions.

(1)   Both Pc King and Pc Brophy have retired from the force but, being a long standing friend of the former, I have spoken to him recently and at great length in response to other similar journalistic enquiries. He does not recall making any official report and there is no evidence that one was made.

(2)   Dave King has confirmed that he and Pc Brophy were in the Law Enforcement Office at RAF Bentwaters when they were diverted to a 'higher priority' task at Otley post office. As rural night-duty officers they would have sole responsibility for policing a huge territorial area (approx 400 square miles) and would certainly have treated a post office burglary as more important than a recurrence of an earlier incident which was seen as somewhat frivolous.

(3)   Pc Brian Cresswell's (also now retired) visit to the alleged landing site would not have generated more than a standard incident log unless he was convinced that something worth reporting had occurred. Pc King had discussed the matter with him and it appeared that all three officers were equally unimpressed with the nights events.

(4)   Civilian police officers were not employed in guarding the area surrounding the alleged landing site(s) or to deter access as there was no evidence to indicate that anything of immediate concern to the police had occurred.

continued ....

Georgina Bruni
PO Box 697
Chelsea
London SW3 2BL

Awarded for excellence

Letter to the author from the Suffolk Constabulary

(5)   There is no documentary evidence that police officers were involved in similar incidents on 27-31 December that year and Pc King cannot recall any further requests for police attendance.

(6)   Special Branch officers should have been aware of the incident(s) through having sight of the Incident Log(s) but would not have shown an interest unless there was evidence of a potential threat to national security. No such threat was evident.

I have tried to be as objective as possible with the answers provided and, like yourself, would undoubtedly be pleased to see a local incident such as this substantiated as an authentic 'UFO' experience. Pc King holds similar views to myself and returned to the forest site in daylight in case he had missed some evidence in the darkness. There was nothing to be seen and he remains unconvinced that the occurrence was genuine. The immediate area was swept by powerful light beams from a landing beacon at RAF Bentwaters and the Orfordness lighthouse. I know from personal experience that at night, in certain weather and cloud conditions, these beams were very pronounced and certainly caused strange visual effects.

If you have any other query in respect of this subject I will be pleased to discuss the issues further. My direct dial telephone number is 01473 613709.

Yours sincerely,

Mike Topliss
Inspector - Operations (Planning)

Page 2 of the letter from the Suffolk Constabulary

From: **Miss G F South, Secretariat(Air Staff)2a, Room 8245**
MINISTRY OF DEFENCE
Main Building, Whitehall, London, SW1A 2HB

	Telephone	(Direct dial)	0171 218 2140
		(Switchboard)	0171 218 9000
		(Fax)	0171 218 2680

Ms G Bruni
PO Box 697,
Chelsea,
London.
SW3 2BL

Your Reference

Our Reference
D/Sec(AS)/64/3
Date
23 July 1999

Dear Ms Bruni,

Thank you for your letter of 29 June regarding the alleged incident at Rendlesham Forest.

When the Ministry of Defence was informed of the events which are alleged to have occurred at Rendlesham Forest/RAF Woodbridge in December 1980, all available substantiated evidence was looked at in the usual manner by those within the MOD/RAF with responsibility for air defence matters. I believe the Directorate of Air Defence would have looked into the case but this branch no longer exists. The judgement was that there was no indication that a breach of the United Kingdom's air defences had occurred on the nights in question. As there was no evidence to substantiate an event of defence concern no further investigation into the matter was necessary. Although a number of allegations have subsequently been made about these reported events, nothing has emerged over the last 19 years which has given us reason to believe that the original assessment made by this Department was incorrect.

Yours sincerely,

Gaynor South.

Letter to the author from the Ministry of Defence

Admiral of the Fleet The Lord Hill-Norton GCB

The Lord Gilbert
House of Lords
Westminster
London SW1A

                                    22 September, 1997

I have just received your reply (I presume that the illegible
squiggle is your signature) to my Question for Written Answer
of 31 July, about Colonel Halt's report on an incident at RAF
Woodbridge, in 1981.

You have not answered my question, which was " .... Did
the MOD reply to the Memo from Lt Col Halt .....", so I shall
have to put it down again in a different form. The answer
must be, simply, Yes or No. I need the formal reply for the
dossier which is being prepared.

You may wish to know that his Memo, which has been in the
public domain for 15 years, covers a great deal more than
"lights in the sky". Five books have been written about the
incident, of which the latest published two months ago, is
"Left at East Gate" by one Larry Warren, who was one of the
enlisted men sent to investigate the violation of British Air
Space.

Letter to Lord Gilbert from Lord Hill-Norton

MINISTRY OF DEFENCE
WHITEHALL LONDON SW1A 2HB

Telephone 071-21 86621 (Direct Dialling)
          071-21 89000 (Switchboard)

Minister of State
for Defence Procurement

From: **THE RT HON DR THE LORD GILBERT**

D/Min(DP)/JWG/MP/3842/97/M   *16* October 1997

Dear Lord Hill-Norton.

Thank you for your letter of 22 September concerning the alleged events at Rendlesham Forest of December 1980.

From Departmental records available from that period we have found no evidence to suggest that this Department contacted Lieutenant Colonel Charles Halt following receipt of his memo of January 1981 recording "Unexplained Lights" in the area in December 1980. Some 16 years after the event we can only conclude, therefore, that it was not considered necessary to make further enquiries in the light of the lack of any evidence to suggest that the UK's Air Defence Region had been compromised by unauthorized foreign military activity.

It was then, and is still the case, that MOD does not routinely contact witnesses who submit reports of "unexplained" aerial sightings. Follow-up action is only deemed necessary if there is corroborating evidence to suggest an unauthorized incursion of the UK Air Defence Region or other evidence of a matter of defence concern.

I hope this clarifies the position.

Admiral of the Fleet The Lord Hill-Norton GCB

dppsMb39/pe/3842hillno/an/cs

Recycled Paper

MOD letter from Lord Gilbert to Lord Hill-Norton

Admiral of the Fleet The Lord Hill-Norton GCB

The Lord Gilbert
Minister of State
Ministry of Defence
Whitehall
London SW1A 2HB

22 October, 1997

Thank you for your letter of 16 October (it took five days to get here!) about my Question and Colonel Halt's Memo. It was good of you to take the trouble to reply.

I do not want to go on and on, but because you are new to this particular matter I would like to put you more fully in the picture. Your officials, and those (perhaps the same individuals) of the previous Administration, have sought to pretend that Col. Halt's report was only about "unexplained lights in the sky", but as I said in my letter of 22 September it was about a good deal more than that.

So that there is no possibility of further misunderstanding I attach a copy of the Memo in full, and I beg you to read it yourself. From this you will see that he reported that an unidentified object breached UK Air Space and landed in close proximity to the US/RAF Air Base. He gives considerable detail about what happened at the time, and subsequently; together with physical evidence of an intrusion.

My position both privately and publicly expressed over the last dozen years or more, is that there are only two possibilities, either:

a.   An intrusion into our Air Space and a landing by unidentified craft took place at Rendlesham, as described.

or

b.   The Deputy Commander of an operational, nuclear armed, US Air Force Base in England, and a large number of his enlisted men, were either hallucinating or lying.

Continued:

Letter to Lord Gilbert from Lord Hill-Norton

- 2 -

Either of these simply must be "of interest to the Ministry of Defence", which has been repeatedly denied , in precisely those terms. They, or words very like them, are used again in your letter and I believe, in the light of the above, you would not feel inclined to sign your name to them again.

I could give you a great deal more evidence in similar vein, not only about this incident but about many others, but on this occasion I will spare you. I ought, however, in all fairness let you know that the routine denials by the Ministry - usually the ubiquitous Ms Phillips - will very soon become extremely damaging to its general credibility in this field.

Page 2 of Lord Hill-Norton's letter

SUFFOLK CONSTABULARY

**FORCE HEADQUARTERS, MARTLESHAM HEATH,
IPSWICH IP5 7QS Tel. Ipswich (0473) 624848 Telex: 98120**

All official correspondence should be addressed to the Chief Constable

Your Ref.

Our Ref. 25(3)3/83 DJ/SRP   23 November 1983

Dear Sir

SIGHTING OF UNUSUAL LIGHTS IN THE SKY AT WOODBRIDGE ON 26 DECEMBER 80

With reference to your letter dated 3 November 83 which related to the above
mentioned incident.

Police knowledge of this matter is limited to a telephone report of the
alleged incident timed at 4.11 am on 26 December and received from a person
at RAF Bentwaters together with the two subsequent visits to the location by
police officers.

The first visit followed immediately the reported incident and the two
officers who attended made a search of the area with a negative result. A
note on the log indicates that Air Traffic Control at West Drayton were
contacted and that there was no known knowledge of aircraft in that area to
coincide with the time of the sighting. Mention is also made on the log of
reports received of aerial phenomena over Southern England during that
night. The only lights visible to the officers visiting the incident were
those from Orford Light House.

A further report was received at 10.30 am on 26 December 80 from a staff
member at RAF Bentwaters indicating that a place had been found where a
craft of some sort could have landed. An officer attended and the area
involved did bear three marks of an indeterminate pattern. The marks were
apparently of no depth and the officer attending thought they could have
been made by an animal.

It is considered little more would be gained by you making direct contact
with the officers involved as the above information constitutes the sum of
their knowledge in relation to this matter. It is hoped the information
supplied will be of assistance to you in formulating your intended account
of the circumstances. .

Yours faithfully

Chief Constable

Letter to Ian Ridpath from the Suffolk Constabulary

Steve Roberts' drawing

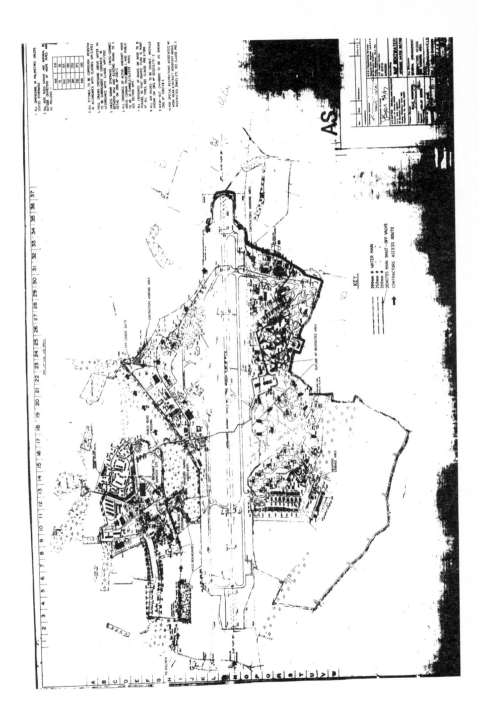

Map of Bentwaters Air Force Base

BIBLIOGRAPHY

Bennet, Mary (ed.), *The Only Planet of Choice*, Gateway Books, Bath, 1994.

Blanford, James, *The Puzzle Palace: A Report on America's Most Secret Agency*, Penguin Books, London, 1983.

Blavatsky, Madame, *The Secret Doctrine*, Theosophical Publishing, New York, 1897.

Bowen, E. G., *Radar Days*, Adam Hilger, Bristol, 1987

Brown, Hanbury, Minnett, Harry C., and White, Frederick W. G., *Edward George Bowen 1911–1991*, Australian Academy of Science Archives Project, c. 1990.

Butler, Brenda, Street, Dot, and Randles, Jenny, *Skycrash*, Neville Spearman, Suffolk, 1984.

Corso, Colonel Philip J., and Birnes, William J., *The Day After Roswell*, Simon and Schuster, New York, 1997.

Fawcett, Larry, and Greenwood, Barry, *Clear Intent* (re-titled *The UFO Cover-up*), Simon and Schuster, New York, 1992

Forman, Joan, and Lyon, Guy, *Mysteries of Mind, Space and Time*, volumes 18 and 24, H. Stuttman Inc, Connecticut, 1992.

Good, Timothy, *Above Top Secret, The Worldwide UFO Cover-up*, Sidgwick and Jackson, London, 1987.

Holroyd, Stuart, *Briefing for the Landing on Planet Earth*, W. H. Allen, London, 1977.

Hopkins, Budd, *Missing Time*, Ballantine, New York, 1981.

Horsley, Sir Peter, *Sounds from Another Room, Memories of Planes, Princes and the Paranormal*, Leo Cooper, London 1997.

Keyhoe, Donald E., *Flying Saucers from Outer Space*, Hutchinson, London, 1954.

Kinsey, Gordon, *Ordfordness, Secret Site*, Terence Dalton Ltd, Suffolk, 1981.

— *Bawdsey, Birth of a Beam*, Terence Dalton Ltd, Suffolk, 1981.

Lammer, Dr Helmut, and Lammer, Marion, *MILABS*, Illuminet Press, Atlanta, Ga, 1999.

Marks, John, *The Search for the Manchurian Candidate*, Times Books, New York, 1979.

Pope, Nick, *Open Skies, Closed Minds*, Simon and Schuster, London, 1996.

— *Operation Thunder Child*, Simon and Schuster, London, 1999.

— *Operation Lightning Strike*, Simon and Schuster, London, 2000.

Project MKULTRA, The CIA's Program of Research in Behavior Science, Washington Government Printing Press, 1977.

Randles, Jenny, *UFO Crash Landing, Friend or Foe?*, Blandford, London, 1998.

— *From Out of the Blue*, Berkley Publishing Co, New York, 1991.

Redfern, Nicholas, *A Covert Agenda*, Simon and Schuster, London, 1997.

Sherman, Dan, *Above Black*, One Team Publishing, Tualatin, Or, 1997.

Warren, Larry, and Robbins, Peter, *Left at East Gate*, Marlowe and Company, New York, 1997, www.leftateastgate.com.

Webb, Gary, *Dark Alliance*, Seven Stories Press, New York, 1998.

INDEX